HITLER'S
LAST COURIER

HITLER'S
LAST COURIER

A Life in Transition

Armin D. Lehmann

To order additional copies of this book, contact:
Xlibris Corporation
1-888-7-XLIBRIS
www.Xlibris.com
Orders@Xlibris.com

CONTENTS

PREFACE

"There is only victory or annihilation. Know no bounds in your love of your people; equally know no bounds in your hatred of the enemy. It is your duty to watch when others tire, to stand when others weaken. Your greatest honor is your unshakeable fidelity to Adolf Hitler."

It was with words such as these that the *Reich* Youth Leader, Artur Axmann, exhorted the ten-year-olds being sworn into the Hitler Youth in Berlin on the eve of Hitler's last birthday. Looking on was the author, then sixteen years old and one of nine Hitler Youths already awarded the Iron Cross for bravery in action against the enemy, and selected for presentation to the *Fuehrer* the next day as examples of what German youth could accomplish in devotion to the cause.

Armin Lehmann's account of his life up to the end of the Second World War provides an interesting insight into the influences on his upbringing and education that led to this state of affairs, where Axmann could form and direct his teenage combat teams in the *Fuehrer's* name, bypassing the military chain of command, which was against employing them, and for which he was to be rewarded with the Golden Cross of the German Order by a grateful Hitler.

Axmann then selects Lehmann to be one of his runners delivering his messages and orders to "stand fast to the last man" to the various Hitler Youth units deployed around the city. When Axmann moves his headquarters to the vicinity of Hitler's command bunker, Lehmann goes too, knocking out a Soviet tank on the way and earning a second award for bravery together with a second wound badge, before becoming a runner on the hazardous link between the bunker itself and a radio station across the street. Thus we have a welcome new witness to some of the final events in the *Fuehrerbunker* and to some of the personalities involved. In all, this book is a valuable contribution to contemporary history, particularly at a time when today's German youth are displaying an increasing interest in what hitherto has been "forbidden territory" in their country's history.

Tony Le Tissier
Author of the *Battle of Berlin 1945*

FOREWORD

After reading the manuscript before it was published and became this book, I felt compelled to comment on the time and people it covers.

I have known Armin D. Lehmann since 1961 and have always been impressed by his sensitiveness for historical events. He is a thoughtful judge for what happened in the middle of this century and a strong believer and advocate for human rights.

As one who left his native Austria for religious reasons in 1938, but yet had observed the development of Nazism, I can fully understand a person like Armin, who in his early years was taught to believe that Hitler and his henchmen would create a super-race which would become the supreme power in our world. He learned from his relatives, teachers, friends and the regulated media, radio and press, that being German was good. The rest of the world was inferior.

We must give full credit to Armin that he not only defrocked the ideas and lies of Nazism for himself, but managed to create a clear picture of what this movement was able to do to destroy the laws and teachings of many great Western leaders, as well as redirect all human achievement of the last two thousand years. It would be very important for young people throughout the world to read this book and thereby learn what can happen if one accepts certain theories without properly analyzing them and using the capability with which all human beings are blessed, to think and judge.

Congratulations to Armin D. Lehmann for having written this courageous book. It helps us to understand those who were cornered and who had no way of learning the truth.

Francis H. Goranin
Past President, ASTA
American Society of Travel Agents
Chicago, February 1999

AUTHOR'S INTRODUCTION AND DEDICATION

I was four years old when Adolf Hitler, on January 30, 1933, became *Reich* Chancellor of a coalition cabinet in Germany. Later, this historic date became known as *Machtergreifung*, the day of seizing might.

Absolute power, as history has taught us, often reverts to primal chaos. In Hitler's case it went beyond, into an inferno of scorched earth and massacred life in mammoth numbers, too immense to fully comprehend.

It all started with promises for a better life. My grandfather, for example, an old guard party member and an early follower of Hitler, was convinced that a fast economic recovery would come about. It did. He was also sure that Germany would be avenged for the Treaty of Versailles. It was.

My father believed in Hitler as well, joining the movement as millions did. He not only became a member of the National Socialist Worker's Party, he turned into a fanatic disciple of what he looked upon as the tenets of a new order needed to restore Germany to the glory it deserved.

I grew up in the woods, sheltered from the outside world. As a young boy, I witnessed, with a great sense of excitement, the first rally and torchlight procession of storm-trooper units.

At the age of ten, I became a *Pimpf*, Cub Scout, in the *Deutsche Jungvolk*, the junior section of the Hitler Youth. I advanced in rank to lead, within two years, my own *Jungzug*, a 30-member unit. I became an enthusiastic youth leader.

At the age of 14, for the first time, I touched a non-Aryan

person. She was a stranger who wore two identification marks, the Star of David, signifying that she was Jewish, and a yellow band with three black dots, indicating that she was blind. Over her right eye she wore a black patch, just like the one worn by my paternal grandmother, whom she also resembled in height, stature and appearance. I helped her across the street and, for doing so, was beaten up.

I had been taught that Germans were members of a superior race, destined to dominate over the inferior and weak. The prominence of the Aryan race was the accepted view. Jews were regarded as parasites.

Why didn't I realize at the time that to belong to one race or another shouldn't be a privilege or a curse?

After the war, I saw the documentaries about the holocaust. By then, having read about Hitler's abominable "Final Solution," I surmised that sometime after my encounter with this blind woman, she had probably been rounded up and mass-transported to one of the extermination concentration camps and murdered.

But before I came to this dreadful realization, I thought that it was my duty to defend my Fatherland, and I fought with death-defying determination, nearly to the bitter end. An end that I experienced in the *Fuehrerbunker*, as I had been chosen to join a delegation of highly decorated members of Hitler's last-ditch home defense force, led by Artur Axmann, leader of the Hitler Youth. Regardless of perspective, it was an historical event.

Years later, I was fortunate enough to travel the world—to meet people of all races, on all populated continents. I met and worked with many outstanding human beings of different racial and cultural backgrounds. Several of the most sensitive, creative, and trustworthy men and women I became acquainted with were Jewish. Among the most caring people I know are people of a variety of races and heritages.

I wrote this book in a quest for answers, truthful answers. Honesty bestows amelioration.

Mass destruction of human life occurred during my lifetime:

Stalin's and Hitler's reigns of terror; Mao's cultural Revolution; the slaughter of Bengalis in Pakistan; the bloodshed on the Khmer Rouge killing fields; the Rwanda catastrophe; the Mozambique and Somalia civil wars; the slaying of Communists and Chinese in Indonesia; in the Balkans, the Bosnian "ethnic cleansing" and Kosovo.

For me these occurrences reflect not merely cold statistical numbers. Because of my past, I relate to the cruelties and to the suffering. I am touched by the pain.

Although the Nuremberg Tribunal would remove from within me the feeling of guilt for what I had not done, I have been unable to root out the memories of the events that had taken place.

Throughout my life, I have had nightmares. For me the past remains a painful present. New atrocities, wherever they take place, only reinforce this. It has not held true that, if I distanced myself far enough and lived an exemplary life, I would eventually forget. I have not yet.

But I have changed course.

I now question the competence and righteousness of many in leadership positions. I uphold my convictions and principles, no matter what others think. For more than 40 years now, having never been hungry or without shelter, I treasure nothing more than my personal liberty.

I was born into the subjection of glory and terror. I will die as a free man.

Why am I still experiencing nightmares, dreams arousing feelings of inescapable horror? Why am I not able to let go of the demons of a past, of what I experienced during the first 17 years of my life?

I can only hope that, before I die, the mounting heaps of skeletons in my dreams will leave me, as well as the execution squads, the lamppost gallows, the violations of women—even young girls, still children—the agonies of countless victims. There was the Holocaust and, to my mind, the slaughter at war's end was another one. More followed. When will we see the end?

I have lived a most rewarding life.

Without a doubt, my life was not *common*.

In the German language, we find the term *Massenmensch* (mass man). It designates any ordinary man or woman, the prototype of a human being in a mass society looked upon as a follower, someone easily manipulated.

The book you are about to read was written by one who became an *Einzelgaenger* (individualist), who functions from within and draws from the knowledge of a huge support group.

My father saw himself as a leader, a member of a dominant group, empowered by an ideology to rule. But he was not an individualist—he followed orders without his conscience's approval. In fairness to my father, his character was formed, to a great extent, by his own past. As a result, he was dogmatic and authoritarian.

My mother, on the other hand, wasn't a *Massenmensch*. As a young girl, she was very restricted in her thinking. Later on, after going through a process of liberation, she reflected on her life as a girl and as a young woman: "Service to others was my purpose in life—first to my parents, then to my husband, and, of course, to my children."

She was intelligent, made every possible attempt to keep her mind active, read as much as she could, and, as she put it, "avoided small talk and engaged in meaningful conversations."

She admitted that she "adored Hitler" until she came to recognize that he had been an *Unmensch* (an inhumane being). But it was only after the war that she came to realize this.

From then on my parents grew apart. My father rationalized and remained determined to defend the past and his old ideals.

My mother, deeply shocked over what had happened, became vehemently opposed to the ideology of the past. She grew increasingly independent, and found more and more opportunities for her humaneness to unfold. She practiced her beliefs.

She explained at a time when she managed a *Teestube* (tea room) in Hamburg: "If you give from your heart, you feel good and don't yearn for rewards or gratitude."

My mother was truly a *Mensch*, a caring human being.

I have never reached my mother's capacity for caring. My limited ability to serve others unselfishly is an ongoing tribute to her.

I have had a sizeable support group and received help, not just from relatives and friends, but also from strangers, all interested in my project, who were all eager to assist.

My late brother Friedrich Wulf, who went to Auschwitz before the extent of the mass killings was questioned, made one comment I have never forgot.

"Mir ist dort der Kopf geplatzt!" (There, my head exploded!).

What had happened there, he could not comprehend. His untimely death (he died of a sudden, first heart attack; I have been fortunate enough to survive five) occurred shortly after I had started with my research.

This book, then, is a basket, woven of many reeds of recollections, perceptions, visions and dreams where I have attempted to draw legacies of a horrifying past into valuable lessons for the future.

It takes many reeds to create a basket to be filled with contributions for progress.

I hope that after my life is over, my wife Kim, the children and children's children will carry the basket and keep it filled.

Unlike my brother Wulf, my other siblings are, of this writing, still alive. All answered reams of pages filled with questions to help me with refreshing my memory or with putting incidental events in appropriate time frames.

My cousin, Thomas Lehmann, his wife Hannelore, and Jens Lemcke, son of my cousin, Eckhard Lemcke, emerged as research assistants par excellence. Jens, especially, was able to establish invaluable connections and dig up essential source materials for verifications of happenings as well as when and where they took place. My aunt, Helga Lehmann, who sent me old books from the library of my late uncle, Dr. med. Hans Lehmann, also has my gratitude.

After the war, I met and corresponded with many former class-

mates as well as other fellow students. Some contributed signifi-
cantly: the late Werner Schubel, the late Klaus Schauermann[1],
Martin Scholtz (who is also preparing the German translation),
Dieter Kara (who also became a U.S. citizen and experienced a
transformation similar to mine), Wolfgang Huebner, Klaus Ulrich
Koch and Walther Troeger.

I have to thank all those who assisted me with historical research: Dr. Michael Buddrus, Dr. Hubert Becker, Oliver Schmidt,
the late Artur Axmann, Egon Bruno, Arnim Christgen, Kurt
Ruppelt, Wolfgang Buwert, Ida Schapiro, Guenter Kaufmann,
Juergen Mueller, Rolf Hermann, Reiner & Gudrun Janick, the
late Prof. Dr. Dr. Schenck, Dieter Rosenbaum, Alfred Nordhaus,
Doris Liskey and many more I have been in contact with, including Horst Gleiss, whose monumental work, *Breslauer Apokalypse
1945,* is one of the most comprehensive private document collections assembled after the war.

Last, but not least, I am indebted for hands-on performance,
editorial assistance, writing, typing and retyping to Evelyn
Reichman and Judith Taylor. The latter helped me with cutting
the original draft from 180,000 words to 140,000 and better organizing its contents.

All names of persons that were participants in the historical
events are authentic. The names of my fallen and missing comrades are those that I remember, although in some cases I am unsure of the correct spelling. I included them anyway, to honor
their memories. Those private individuals that I was able to contact were asked for permission to use their real names. Some decided to remain anonymous and, thus, were given pseudonyms.
Those I was unable to find, and whose approval might have been
doubtful, are identified with nicknames or initials. Every person
mentioned is real; there are no fictional characters in this book.

This is a firsthand account of personal experiences. Source is
my memory, aided by notes taken between 1945 and now. Not all
of my notes survived. A train robber, many moves, a divorce, a
major earthquake, and a flood took their toll.

Supporting sources, I identify in the text. When supplemental information was given, I provided references. A wide range of reference materials was used to ascertain locations and times, to verify events and people's involvement. Books by individual authors are listed in "Recommended Relevant Reading."

Aside from those already named, I owe thanks to every writer who wrote a book I read, and I read many thousands in my lifetime.

I owe thanks to the many playwrights and scriptwriters whose plays and motion pictures I saw, to the many composers whose music I enjoyed, to the many artists whose creations I viewed, to the many performers whose attainments I have cherished.

I owe thanks to some of my teachers and to several mentors.

I owe thanks to many physicians.

I owe thanks to my friends, past and present, including many former classmates and my comrades-in-arms of 1945, and to all members of our ever-growing family, cousins and their children included, near and far. All have a special place in my heart.

For as long as I live, I will be grateful to my late mother, a loving and caring person who practiced being human in a humanitarian way.

As already expressed in the preface of my book *Travel and Tourism*, my SITA World Travel colleagues around the globe formed the nucleus of a United Nations and, without exception each of them opened up cultural boundaries and enriched my life. For as long as this organization functioned as a whole, it provided all of us with a feeling of true brotherhood and with a premise for world citizenship. SITA's founder, Jack Dengler, listened to what I had to say in this book. He was blind when he died in 1998.

I feel fortunate to be where I am, and with whom I share the remainder of my life, and to whom I dedicate this book: my beloved Kim.

Armin Dieter Lehmann
Yaquina John Point
Waldport, Oregon

ABBREVIATIONS
USED IN BOOK

Brdgf.	*Brigadefuehrer*	Brigadier-General
FHQ	*Fuehrerhauptquartier*	(Chief) Headquarters
Flak	*Fliegerabwehr Kanone*	Anti-aircraft Cannons
Gestapo	*Geheime Staats Polizei*	Secret State Police
Hptm.	*Hauptmann*	Captain
HJ	*Hitlerjugend*	Hitler Youth
Krad	*Kraftrad*	Motorcycle
Lt.	*Leutnant*	Second Lieutenant
NSDAP	*Nationalsozialistische*	National Socialist
	Deutsche Arbeiter Partei	German Labor Party
Oblt.	*Oberleutnant*	First Lieutenant
Obstf	*Obersturmfuehrer*	First Lieutenant (SS)
Rjfr.	*Reichsjugendfuehrer*	*Reich* Youth Leader
Sani	*Sanitaeter*	First Aid Man (Medic)
SS	*Schutzstaffel*	Security Service
	Allgemeine SS	(Non-combat SS)
LSAH	*SS-Leibstandarte*	Adolf Hitler's
	Adolf Hitler'	Bodyguard Regiment(SS)
Uffz.	*Unteroffizier*	Corporal
Vlkstm.	*Volkssturmmann*	Militia Man
		(Home Defense)
Waffen-SS	*SS im Wehrdienst*	Military-*SS*
	(Elite Einheiten)	(Elite Units)

CHAPTER 1

Early Memories

I cried.

I don't remember why I cried, only that I cried. My father demanded that I shut up. I didn't. He stopped the car, got out, opened the door on my mother's side, tore me out of her arms, and put me down on the sidewalk. Then, he got back in the car and drove off.

The automobile disappeared. I kept sobbing, gasping for air and remained, panic-stricken, where he had put me down.

It seemed forever, although it might have been only a minute or two, until he had driven around the block and picked me up again.

"Now you know what happens to boys who cry!" he ranted. I was three years old.

I tried to stop but couldn't. I kept on weeping. My mother held me closer and closer, trying to muffle my sobs.

Now his anger turned toward her. "If you can't make him stop crying, I'll take you both back home!" and that's what he did. He slammed the car door and drove off alone.

By now, my mother was in tears, too. "You must mind your father or you make him very angry," she whispered. Then she gave me a bath, and, finally, clean again and comforted by her, I was able to stop crying.

In 1945, I remembered this incident. Then a 16-year-old, my feeling was similar to what I had felt as a three-year-old: a feeling of helplessness, as if destined to drown in a woeful slough of despair.

CHAPTER 2

The Gypsies

A year later, in 1932, my parents wanted to leave the city, and we moved into the upstairs quarters of a manor-house, called *Schloss Deschkau*, in the country north of Goerlitz. When I asked my mother forty years later how they had found residence for us in a *Schloss* (castle), she wasn't sure anymore. She thought the owner of the estate was a general and diplomat, and he and his family were stationed in Turkey during the year we lived there.

A brick wall with a huge wooden gate surrounded the front and back yards. During the day, this gate was kept open.

One afternoon, a small gypsy caravan entered the yard. My grandfather came running out of the house. He raised his voice to tell the gypsies to leave immediately, while grabbing me and taking me back into the house.

"Gypsies steal children," he admonished me, making sure the door was bolted and all of the windows were closed.

At that time, I already had heard stories about gypsies, how they wandered, gathering around campfires at night, playing their violins soulfully, singing, dancing and creating magic of sorts. Now that I had actually seen some, I felt drawn to these strange people. They couldn't have gone too far, I thought. Bursting with anticipation, I sneaked out of the back door, ran after them, and soon caught up.

The women wore gold bangles and other glittering jewelry and had braided black hair, large dark eyes and shiny, sun-tanned skin.

Wild fantasies flooded through my 4-year-old mind as I trotted alongside their last cart.

Suddenly someone grabbed me from behind. It was my father. He dragged me home and punished me severely with a leather dog whip. My grandfather tried to stop him. They got into a fierce argument. It ended with my father telling his father in a rage, "I am the master in this house!" This was the only time in my life I witnessed a quarrel between my father and his father.

The spanking had been in vain, however. Soon thereafter, I wandered off again.

As my mother recalled, she had gone shopping at the weekend market in the town where her parents lived. While she chose produce, I strayed. As soon as she noticed I was gone, she panicked and hurried to her parents' house to call the police. But there I was. I had found my way through the crowd back to my grandparents. My mother, overjoyed to see me, hugged me and hugged me.

I had expected punishment.

CHAPTER 3

Waldgut Horka

During the next four years (1932-36), we lived in a forest called Waldgut Horka. When I returned during the war for a visit, the name had been changed to Waldgut Wehrkirch, because the word *Horka* was of Slavic origin.

Horka or *Wehrkirch* designated the location. *Waldgut* means "forest estate." The "estate" consisted of two houses, two barns, a couple of chicken coops, and doghouses.

For a short time, when I was six or seven, I had a tame deer for a pet. It began like a fairy tale, only to turn into a horror story.

One day late in the afternoon, I heard close by the gentle ring of a bell. I went to the window to look outside and saw the deer, a buck with antlers. A small bell dangled on a golden-looking collar around his neck.

At first, I wondered if I was dreaming. Never had I seen a live deer so close, right in our yard, and never one with a collar and a gilded one at that. I slowly opened the window. The deer looked up, unruffled. I went outside. It did not run away. I reached out and petted it.

Even our dogs didn't chase the deer away. It all seemed so strange.

My parents cautioned me that we would have to give the deer up as soon as its rightful owner was located.

Time went on and no one claimed it. I loved the deer. I was determined to never give it up.

Unanticipated by me, the mating season came, and one morning my deer was gone. I looked everywhere and couldn't find it. That night I could hardly sleep.

The next afternoon, a strange woman, a berry-picker, came to our house and asked to see my parents. They were not home and our maid had the day off. My grandfather was taking his afternoon nap. The stranger told me that a poacher had killed a deer. I wanted to see the deer and asked the woman to take me to it.

At the site of the freshly killed buck, I went into shock. He had wire slits around his neck. His antlers had been cut off. I was convinced it was "my" deer, that it had been strangled, and that the poacher, who apparently had killed for the trophy, had also removed the gilded collar and bell.

At night, when my parents returned, my grandfather told them what had happened. I was in bed, still sleepless. I got up and showed my father, by flashlight, the way to the killed deer. He determined that the deer had been caught in a trap that the poacher had removed afterward.

I couldn't help the tears that filled my eyes. Father insisted it was not the tame deer and there was nothing to cry about. Grabbing two legs each, my father and I carried the deer, dragging it at times, to the house.

The next day it was hanging on a butcher's hook in our cellar, cut open with the intestines removed. The head without the antlers was a gory sight.

A couple of days later, I was required to watch my father skin my deer and then cut it up.

Not long thereafter, he taught me how to skin hare and deer. I was queasy and almost threw up. He called me a weakling.

He decided I was now old enough to perform the manly function of killing one of our chickens by chopping off its head. I dreaded it.

The day came. The ax used for chopping wood was too heavy, so I was given a meat cleaver small enough for me to handle.

I botched my first kill. With barely enough strength to hold the wings tight with my left hand, while putting the chicken's head on the chopping block to cut it off, I became so scared I closed my eyes at the moment of decapitation. Strong muscle spasms jolted the wings with such a jerk I let go of the chicken. It flew against my body without a head, spewing blood all over me then dropped to the ground.

Horrified, I ran away. My father scolded me for my awkwardness and belittled me for acting like a girl.

This "lesson in manliness" took place during the first year after Hitler had become Germany's *Fuehrer* (leader).

CHAPTER 4

Rudi

It took me forty-five minutes to reach Niesky, the small town where the nearest school was located. In those days, we had no school buses, and no public transportation to and from the Waldgut. It took me half an hour to walk through the woods alone.

On my first day of school, Mother took me to my classroom and, as is customary in Germany, had bought me a *Zuckertuete*, a large cone filled with candy. Most kids had one of similar size except for one boy. His cone was huge, almost as big as he was. My mother noted it, too, but then, in a sudden outburst, she said sadly, "Oh my god, the poor one, he has a humpback."

I asked, "Why is he crippled?" My mother just shrugged, "Fate."

His name was Rudi. While our mothers conversed, we boys hardly spoke. I felt ill at ease standing next to him while he looked away. Just before class started, his mother had put him in the first row, right in front of the teacher's desk.

At first Rudi did not become my friend. Quite the opposite. After only a few days in school, two other classmates and I began to make fun of him. We ended up ganging up against him.

He had no friends, and it didn't take long until we, during a break, started a scuffle, not expecting him to fight back. But he did—and furiously. Even though no one came to his help, it took all three of us to overpower him. As soon as he noticed the turmoil, our teacher came out and stopped the fight. We looked like little roughnecks, all scratched up and bruised. My nose was bleeding, and blood was all over my shirt.

As if I had been the ringleader, the teacher grabbed me with one arm, Rudi with the other, and took us inside. The other two boys followed.

Afraid of the penalty ahead, my heart sank. I expected severe scolding and a flogging, which, in those years, was the typical punishment in Germany, at home, and in school.

The teacher did not whip us. He told the three of us to bend over and gave his bamboo-spanking rod to Rudi.

"Each one deserves twelve on the behind!" he told the hunchback.

"I can't do it! They would get me again," Rudi replied, handing the rod back to the teacher who then gave us a stern talking-to. I felt abashed and never forgot what he said.

"It's God's doing he is a hunchback and if you hurt him, then sometime, somehow, God will get back at you."

Silence. The teacher looked at me.

"How would you feel if you were he?"

I couldn't think. I couldn't talk.

My nosebleed had stopped, the teacher asked me to wash my face and go home. Apparently he didn't want me in class with my bloody shirt.

Troubled inside and looking soiled, I avoided coming near people and felt relieved when I reached the woods.

How would I feel if I were he?

In my mind I heard the teacher's question over and over again.

How would I feel?

How do hunchbacks feel?

How could I know?

I kicked stones. I even kicked a tree stump so hard my toe hurt.

I knew my father was away, so I went straight home. The dogs barked; my mother came out of the house and hurried toward me to find out why I had come home early. She noticed my shirt.

"What happened?"

I told her that my nose bled, that I was in a fight. When she learned it was about Rudi, she became angry.

She scolded me and then said: "The poor boy."

She rode off on her bicycle to see Rudi's mother.

On her way home, when crossing a small wooden bridge, she hit a slick spot and lost control of her bicycle. She fell, suffered a deep cut over her left eye and had to return to Niesky to see the doctor. The cut required several stitches, and she arrived home with a bandage over her eye.

When my father heard what had happened, he became annoyed at both of us. He told my mother, "As long as there are boys, there will be fights." He felt it unbecoming that she went to see Rudi's mother to apologize. Me, he scolded severely for taking part in a fight of three against one. He called me a coward and ordered me to bed early.

Neither my mother nor I had mentioned to my father that Rudi was a hunchback. I didn't dare to do or say anything but to follow my father's orders. Dejected and despondent, the teacher's question began to ring in my head again.

How would I feel if I were he?

How, indeed?

Now calmed down and able to think, I realized that if I were he, I would feel pain, would suffer, and would fight back as he had done.

CHAPTER 5

Inner Voices

From as far back as I can remember I have always had to deal with very powerful thoughts within me. Often thoughts and counter thoughts, currents and cross currents of the mind.

There are people, and I know this to be true, who are sensitive to inner voices. I have experienced, from time to time, the emergence of thoughts as if clearly spoken inside my head.

In later years, this voice would often give me directions—would provide me with the guidance of an inner teacher.

An early example of this occurred when we lived in Waldgut Horka.

The access to our house branched off the forest road that connected the town of Niesky with a timberland clearing. Developed as an industrial site, there was a loam pit, with a firing kiln in operation. The bricks were transported on a small-gauge tramway to the railroad station. Aside from the lorry and a few workers going to and from work on bicycles, there was hardly ever any traffic on this roadway.

Thus, we were all surprised when one Saturday a stranger on a motorcycle drove up to our house asking for directions to get to the brickworks. While my mother described how to get there, I, intrigued by the motorcycle, offered to show him where it was and to ride with him.

The stranger invited me to sit behind him. Then revving his motor as if we were on a racetrack, he took off like a madman. I had no idea then what decisive parts motorcycles would play in many a life or death situation the future held in store for me.

What a sensation! It was a rough ride but, momentarily, I experienced a feeling of great exhilaration. Our house was already out of sight when, clutching the handle of my seat behind the driver, I recalled the grisly story of a murder that had taken place some time ago at the brickyard. I suddenly realized we were heading to the site of the slaying.

My parents and my grandfather had never mentioned it, but Kaethe, our live-in maid, had told me all about it. In school, too, it had been a topic of discussion. A woman, after having been beaten, had been strangled. The murderer was still at large.

Abruptly, I was overcome with fear that the stranger on whose motorcycle I was riding could be the murderer and I might become his next victim. Should I jump off the speeding bike and run into the woods to hide?

Through the wild pounding of my heart, I suddenly heard the voice from inside tell me: "He is not the murderer!" I yelled to tell him where the turnoff was, we arrived at the brickyard, and he thanked me. He even gave me a few *Groschen* (10-pfennig coins) to reward me for having been helpful.

I was mystified by what I had perceived as my inner voice. How could the voice have come about? I thought of it as a twin brother, who existed only in my head.

The first one I questioned about the voice was Kaethe. "Nonsense," she replied and laughed, "You just imagined it."

Then I asked my grandfather if voices were inside of us. "Only in dreams," he replied.

I knew I had not been dreaming while riding on the motorcycle. When I turned to my mother with my dilemma, she seemed understanding. "Sometimes, God talks to us directly through a voice he puts inside of us."

"Does God really talk?"

"He always does, but we seldom hear."

Noticing the amazement on my face, she added, "It could also have been your guardian angel."

***

Both of my parents had been brought up as Lutherans, but then in their youth they lost interest in church. They had joined a movement called *Wandervoegel* (birds of passage), originally a hiking companionship, which grew into a powerful, romantic youth movement. Long before the Hitler salute had become commonplace in Germany, the members of this movement greeted each other with *"Heil!"* meaning, "Hail," a shout of welcome.

The branch of the movement my parents belonged to was called *Adler und Falken* (Eagles and Falcons). They wandered and hiked, at first within Germany but later to other parts of Europe, mostly where German settlements could be found.

My parents, thus, became very concerned with the fate of the Germans who had settled in other countries. They were among the many young Germans during the 1920's who made it their mission to contact ethnic Germans outside the Fatherland to renew cultural ties and to practice nationalism. Such German settlements could be found, not only in territories that had formerly belonged to Germany, but also in Russia, Poland, and the Baltic and Balkan countries because of migrations of many centuries ago.

My parents, according to my mother, took special interest in German settlements in southeastern Europe. Before I was born, they had visited the Saxons and Swabians of Rumania. Their settlements in Transylvania and in the Banat dated back to the twelfth century. These early German settlers had followed an invitation extended by a Hungarian king, Geza II, who had promised them the right of self-government under the Gold Freedom Charter. These Germans became well-to-do farmers and craftsmen. This alienated the native Rumanians who were less well off. It created tensions and animosities.

But no incidents were experienced when the group my parents were part of visited there in 1926. One of the disappointments, according to my mother, was the fact the local leaders of the German farmers were mostly village priests and pastors and not heads of youth movements or political organizations. Although these ethnic Germans had clung to their language, culture, and customs, their devotion to the Fatherland and sense of nationalism was not as pronounced as had been anticipated. My parents, nevertheless, had made some friends among the young people there and talked frequently about their memorable trip to Siebenbuergen (seven boroughs). Later, many of these ethnic Germans supported Hitler's efforts to strengthen their Germandom as a matter of pride and commitment to their heritage. It seemed a noble cause.

My parents, with their *Wandervoegel* activities, revived folk dancing, staged song festivals and outdoor theater performances, lit bonfires, and celebrated the summer and winter solstices. Having drifted away from the church and organized religion, my father decided to officially leave the church before I was born. I wasn't baptized. Neither were any of my sisters and brothers.[2]

CHAPTER 6

Snakes

My treating Rudi without malice had become important to my
mother. What motivated her? She had what I can only describe as
a "non-violent consciousness." She lived by it throughout her life.

Soon after the fight in school my mother and I went to Rudi's
house for coffee and cake. Rudi's father arrived later in the afternoon in uniform, returning from a political activity. He was an
SA[3] man.

I remember both of Rudi's parents were tall and slim. His
mother's hair was long and tousled compared to my mother's,
who wore her hair pulled back in a knot. His father seemed to be
a cheerful man, but loud and rough, a boisterous paladin-type, in
temperament just the opposite of his crippled son who, although
physically strong, came across as timid and reclusive.

While the adults talked, Rudi took me to his room. When I
heard all kinds of strange noises and looked around, I noticed a
jumble of cages. Rudi's room was like a mini-zoo. There were ca-
naries, tropical fish, white mice, and a gold hamster. Amazingly,
he also had a glass terrarium with snakes in it. Live snakes! He took
one out to show me, and this, in my eyes, made him an instant
hero.

I was frightened of snakes, mainly because of Kaethe, our maid,
who feared and constantly warned me of poisonous vipers. When I
saw Rudi take a snake out of his terrarium and hand it over to me,
I was terrified for a moment, but I realized right away that if he
could handle it, I could handle it too. It had to be harmless. In

fact, I reasoned, to hold a wiggling, squirmy snake would not be as upsetting as having to chop off a chicken's head. Nevertheless, I dropped Rudi's snake. He was able to handle snakes. I was not. Not yet.

***

Snakes played a weighty role in the early years of my life. I remember that my grandfather had one on his desk in a jar filled with liquid. The dead snake had almost turned white. More apprehensive than curious, I never tried to open the jar. It was probably sealed with paraffin anyway.

At Waldgut Horka the two most common types were *Kreuzottern* and *Blindschleichen*.

Kreuzottern (cross otters) are common vipers and poisonous. *Blindschleichen* (blindworms) are limbless lizards with small eyes and are harmless.

Kaethe made me aware of all the risks associated with living where there were poisonous serpents. Once, returning from picking wild mushrooms, she noticed a garden snake curled up on the side of the road that led back to our house. Kaethe picked up a big stone, carefully approached the unsuspecting serpent, dropped the rock on it and killed it. She practiced killing harmless ones; she still ran away from the poisonous ones.

Some time later, I was walking home with my grandfather when we saw several snakes out on the road, basking in the sun, not moving. These were poisonous ones. To my surprise, my grandfather, who had a walking stick, put it under the first one and threw it off the road. Two or three other snakes, alarmed, slithered away.

One did not move. He picked it up with his hand, using a tight grip behind the snake's head. He showed me the fangs that contained the deadly poison. Then he threw this snake away too.

My grandfather had not killed the poisonous snake. I was in awe and afraid at the same time. He noticed my amazement and promised me that when I grew older, he would teach me how to safely pick up poisonous snakes.

Meanwhile, he told me that whenever I encountered snakes, I should bypass them and be careful not to frighten them. He also told me that whenever I went into the woods, I should wear thick socks and high boots.

Kaethe had attempted to make a snake-killer out of me and caused me to have nightmares. But after I had seen Rudi handle pet snakes, and, after my grandfather had shown me how to remove venomous snakes with a stick and told me how to dress so as to not get poisoned (even if I should get bitten), these frightful dreams receded.

There was no need to slay. Both the snakes and I could go on living.

I wanted to be able to hold Rudi's pet snake without dropping it. I decided I should practice by picking up blindworms. The first one I spotted was too fast for me. It slithered away before I was able to grab it.

Days later, after several unsuccessful attempts, I finally caught hold of one, but just for seconds. It felt so slick and wiggled so wildly I was afraid and let go of it. But I kept on trying and in a week or so I was finally able to hold on to one.

Once, at Rudi's house, we talked about what we wanted to be when grown up. We were seven years old. Rudi had no second thoughts. He wanted to become a veterinarian.

His parents, although they had bought and shared in caring for his many pets, resisted this idea. I still remember how vehemently Rudi's father objected.

"For you it will be best to remain in elementary school and then to learn a befitting trade."

Why would his father, a blue-collar worker, have opposed his aim for a higher education? What was wrong with wanting to become an animal doctor?

Didn't most parents who belonged to the worker's class want a better life for their children, especially since one of the constantly propagated aims of the National Socialists was to eliminate class barriers?

In retrospect, it seems ominous, indeed, that his parents had wanted him to only complete elementary school instead of going on to high school. They might have known already that those considered unfit, the handicapped and mentally retarded, would be excluded from opportunities to advance. Or, perhaps even worse, they might be institutionalized.

Unknown to us children, the "Law to Protect Hereditary Health" of 1935 had just gone into effect, and Rudi's father, an *SA* man, might indeed have known about it and concluded his son had a better chance of survival as a manual laborer.

On the other hand, one of the regime's most prominent leaders, Joseph Goebbels, was known to have a clubfoot. A misshapen spine wasn't a crippling hereditary disease either, just more noticeable. The thoughts of Rudi's father remain unknown.

When we were young, we didn't press our fathers for answers to questions they thought we shouldn't concern ourselves with. It was expected of us to obey or accept what we were told.

In my case, the situation was reversed. I had just been allocated my own little patch in our big garden behind the house. My grandfather had given me different seeds and bulbs and taught me how to insert them in the soil to make sure they would sprout.

He also had reminded me to water them regularly, and it seemed like a miracle to me when the little plants appeared and kept growing and growing. I spent time at my patch gazing at the shape of these various seedlings. I was so fascinated by what was happening on my small piece of ground that, at that time in my life, I wanted to become a gardener. To make a living growing flowers and vegetables would have required a term of apprenticeship in a garden, farm, or nursery and not a college education.

I knew, of course, my father's plans were that I become a *Forstmeister*—a forester with a university degree. His plans and my desires, nevertheless, would change in a few years as I grew older and political trends increasingly influenced our lives.

Meanwhile, I visited Rudi and his pets frequently and every time, unhesitatingly, with sureness and a firm grip, he would hand a snake to me. Not shying away from it anymore, I could hold on to it now.

I ended up feeling comfortable with Rudi's snakes. I suggested he bring one to school sometime to show it in class, but he never did.

My mother, to whom I related my experiences and new fascination with these limbless reptiles, remained concerned about the danger of poisonous snakes. She made sure I would follow my grandfather's instructions, and saw to it I always wore thick socks and high leather boots when gathering wild mushrooms or picking berries in the woods. She also insisted I always take a dog with me.

We had two retrievers and an Irish setter. Once, I had taken all three along when I encountered a *Kreuzotter* hissing at me. The dogs barked at it viciously and chased it away.

In looking back and in trying to recapture some of the feelings I had as a boy, I can only say that quite often I was fearful and brave at the same time, as would be the case ten years later when I was thrown into battle. Fear can be destructive. It can also trigger courage, as a defensive action.

CHAPTER 7

Kaethe

Dreams created many encounters within my imaginary world, from
early childhood up to the very present. Many were beautiful, but
there were also frequent, spine-chilling, repulsive, even horrendous and frightening apparitions.

Many, many times throughout my entire life, intense nightmares, at their peak, would tear me out of my sleep.

I clearly remember one dream that bewildered and startled
me. It remained with me in frightful details. I dreamt I was pinned
down on my back, fighting off a monster, a dragon. Snakes crawled
up on the beast. I got away from under it and ran away as fast as I
could. I reached a road, layered with fallen leaves. Through the
blood-drenched foliage slithered more snakes. Leaving this road, I
turned into a dense passage of thickset trees. Suddenly everything
turned dark, and all I saw were the glowing eyes of the monster
chasing after me. I screamed as hard as I could and woke up.

The following day my neck hurt. I had a headache as well.
Kaethe wanted to know what was the matter with me. I told her I
had been hit by a monster in my sleep.

She laughed, and then she asked, "You didn't pray last night,
did you?"

What had prayer to do with my horrible dream, I wanted to
know.

"It's one of God's punishments for boys who don't pray."

"But you don't pray either!"

"Oh, yes, I do."

I did not believe her. As far as I knew, Kaethe wasn't religious and she did not go to church. Or was she religious but didn't go to church because my parents didn't? At that time it was the trend not to go to church. The National Socialists had created their own god, one who was not worshipped in church. Perhaps she had gone to church when she was a child and was still praying secretly?

"If you lie, will God punish you then too?"

I was not prepared for how this question incensed her.

"I don't lie, do you understand?" She slapped my face and left the room and slammed the door.

***

Often over weekends my parents were gone, and we children—my sister Anje, the baby Ute, and I—were at home with our grandfather and with Kaethe.

On Sundays, she slept in. I was normally up first and would take the dogs into the woods on a walk. Meanwhile, my grandfather would get up ahead of Kaethe and prepare breakfast—not the usual hot grits or oatmeal—no, he boiled eggs, sliced bread, and served cold-cuts, as well as butter and marmalade. He called it a fork-breakfast. He would also fix hot chocolate, my favorite. As a rule, we had finished by the time Kaethe came down.

At midday, she would make apple pancakes for all of us, another favorite of mine. On Sunday afternoons, the adults would go to their rooms and take naps, and we children had to do the same, but I seldom slept. Usually, I daydreamed, looked at picture books or, later on, read stories. As far as I can think back, I always had books piled up next to my bed.

When my parents or at least my mother, were home over the weekend, Kaethe would get her day off on Sundays. As I remember, she liked to go to the movies and often saw two shows—one in the afternoon and one in the evening. On the following day, she couldn't wait to tell my mother all about the films she had seen.

I longed to see movies, too, and Kaethe picked up on it, but when she suggested taking my sister and me to a children's film, my mother didn't allow it. She knew my father wouldn't approve of it. In later years, I would make up for it and would go to the movies at every possible opportunity.

I remember how ill tempered Kaethe could become. As I look back, I think of her with mixed feelings. I remember she was tall, well proportioned, and her hair was dark blond. She had steely blue eyes, and her lips were thin and pallid.

Kaethe obviously enjoyed giving me orders and telling my sister and me how to behave. She probably thought, as my father did, that I was weak physically. I recall, for example, that when I had to bring firewood into the house, she would belittle me because she thought I wasn't carrying enough. My arms were short and I loaded the wood up to my chin.

There always seemed to be a discrepancy between her demands and my ability to meet them.

However, there was also a shrinking side of her that would emerge when both of my parents and my grandfather were gone and she was alone with us children. Then, Kaethe would sleep in my father and mother's bedroom and had me sleep next to her. She had sworn me to secrecy never to tell anyone. I never did.

Whenever the dogs barked or there was a disturbing noise inside or outside the house, she woke me up and made me investigate what was going on, while she would practically hide under the covers.

When I came back and reassured her there was nothing, she always seemed to doubt me. "Go out once more, just to be certain!" she would demand.

Usually, it was just the wind, or the dogs barking at some stray animal, a mouse in the house, or, outside, a rabbit or chicken had gotten out of the coop. At times, it might even have been a fox. It was just part of living in the woods.

During the day, she was in control and bossed me around. At night, however, she was frightened and her fears put me in charge.

Once, when she heard a noise, she had me go through all

rooms to make sure nobody had entered and roamed through the house. My grandfather's room was locked and he had taken the key with him. Thus, I could not open the door. All through the night, she remained afraid somebody could be in there. It must have been at the time that someone was killed and a murderer remained at large.

She also feared thunderstorms and lightning. The noise of thunder or the possibility lightning could strike seemed to terrorize her, and I couldn't be of much help except to talk to her. She couldn't go to sleep and kept on talking all night to keep me from sleeping. When I fell asleep, nevertheless, she would shake me awake again.

To me, thunderstorms were exciting. I felt safe inside the house because we had lightning rods on the roof. My grandfather had explained that if struck, the lightning bolts would be channeled into the ground by the metal posts on the roof. Thunder, no matter how it sounded, was just a big, explosive noise like fireworks and nothing to be afraid of.

I had been taught that boys conquer fear. Not until I was an armed young adult did I realize that fear, in many a life situation, is a survival device.

CHAPTER 8

The Woods

In school, a couple of classmates asked me if I knew anything about another murder that had been committed. Again, a woman had been killed—this time on a desolate county road. I had heard about it from Kaethe. She called it a *Teufelstat* (a devil's deed). Apparently, it had been another rape killing, the second one committed not very far from where we lived. At that time, I didn't know anything about sex crimes. A murder was a murder. Rudi mentioned the victim was a farm girl. He had also heard she had been beaten and strangled, on a Saturday night, after she had been to a dance. The road where she had been found was not the road that led to the farm where she worked.

The following week, in school, some of my classmates remarked that they would be afraid to go home on a lonely road as I had to. I could become the murderer's next victim. Rudi offered to walk home with me. I was about to accept his offer when we realized that after we reached our house, he would have to walk back alone. So, this wasn't a solution.

I got the idea that if there were a murderer waiting for me, he would be hiding close to the road. I decided to avoid the road and to enter the forest from a paddock and then criss-cross through the woods to get home. It was not as easy as I had thought it would be. Although I knew the woods quite well, I got lost. In the early evening, when I finally arrived, only my grandfather and my sisters were home. My mother and Kaethe had left to search for me. When they returned and I explained, there was no punishment.

Soon thereafter, the murderer was captured.

I walked on the road again, but intermittently, fright re-emerged and I avoided the road and walked home, straight through the woods where I felt more secure.

One other time I got lost in the forest. It must have been on the Sunday following my birthday. As a present, I had received a knapsack. I arose early in the morning before anyone in the house was awake. In the pantry, I filled my knapsack with bread, ham, and apples. I got Sonja, our lean, reddish-brown Irish setter, put her leash on, and off we went on a hike. As far as I can remember, I did not have a specific goal, just a longing for new discoveries.

I wanted to put my gift to use and picnic somewhere with the dog. On a clearing, around midday, we did. Everything I had taken, I ate and I shared some of my provisions with Sonja. I hadn't taken anything to drink and now went looking for a little stream to find water. I had become very thirsty. We didn't find the brook I knew was somewhere around, only a small pond of standing water. It tasted muddy. My spirits took a dive. Now, I realized that the search for water had distorted my sense of direction. I sat down again, contemplating my predicament.

I decided to take the dog off the leash and told her "Let's go home!" First she looked at me and waited. Then I clapped my hands and told her once more, "Let's go!" It worked. She sniffed her way back and I followed.

We returned late, of course. This time my father was home, and I ended up being punished; not for having taken off or for having gotten lost and returning home late, but because I had raided the pantry and taken with me, without permission, his *Raeucherschinken*, a special brand of expensive smoked ham.

The blows hurt, but it was not the most severe beating I ever received from him. This would come at another place, almost a year later.

CHAPTER 9

My Family

Suddenly, our life in the forest came to an end. At first I didn't realize it, because it started with another visit to my grandparents, my mother's parents, in Goerlitz. I always enjoyed being with them, especially with my grandmother, whom I called *Grossmuttel*, an affectionate expression meaning "endeared great mother" or "endeared grandmother."

As far back as I can remember, whenever I visited there, my grandmother would tell me Bible stories, teach me prayers, and on Sundays, we both would attend services. My grandfather stayed at home.

I clearly remember the first time she took me to church. I felt ill at ease among so many people, but I enjoyed hearing the singing and the end of each prayer when all in unison said "Amen." It sounded just like my name!

For a time, praying became important to me, and soon I made up my own prayers. They became longer and longer as my creativeness unfolded and my belief grew that I was talking directly to God. My young mind soon felt overwhelmed and tempted. Just before Christmas, I would ask God for more and more favors. Instead of writing to Santa Claus, I prayed to God at length, wishing for things. My praying had become selfish and intemperate.

One night, after my grandmother had tucked me in and listened to me commune with God, she shook her head and grasped my folded hands. Perturbed about my immoderate wishing spree, she silenced me before I could finish. In her gentle manner, she explained that God is so busy performing great miracles. No one, not I, not anyone, should ask Him to do little things for us. "For that, He has no time," she maintained. "He lets us grow so that, later on, we ourselves can fulfill our yearnings." She concluded I should ask only for His blessing but not for favors upon favors, as this might annoy Him.

My grandmother's solemn scolding made an everlasting impression on me. I certainly did not want to anger God. I ceased praying altogether—until late in the war, and then I prayed silently.

It was also this grandmother who I overheard once, in a conversation with my father, remarking that: "Jews are human beings too."

I did not grasp what the conversation was all about. I had never met a Jewish person. When I asked my grandmother, after my father had left, what the argument had been all about, she would only say, "I can't talk about it." It was not until the *Kristallnacht*,[4] several years later that I became aware of the fate of Jews in Germany and what this argument might have been about.

While visiting my maternal grandparents, my parents were packing. I wanted to know why we had to move again. We, with the exception of Kaethe, had loved living in Waldgut Horka. We had a whole house to live in and always had enough to eat. We children grew up relatively secure, sheltered by nature. My father's prime hobby was hunting, and there he had leased the right to hunt.

Although no one mentioned it, I sensed it was because of *Opa*, my paternal grandfather moving away. In later years, my mother confirmed that without my grandfather sharing expenses, my parents could not afford to live in Waldgut Horka. My father was, at that time, a car salesman and driving instructor. He had decided to move closer to his place of work in Weisswasser.

Two years after I was born, he, in silent partnership with his father, had acquired a Mercedes Benz dealership in Goerlitz. In less than a year, he was insolvent. What had caused him to lose this business?

"It was undercapitalized, times were bad, and he lacked experience," my mother told me when I asked her about it after the war. My father, nevertheless, maintained until he died and without ever explaining how, that he had been betrayed by a Jew, the one who became the subsequent owner. I have a clear memory of witnessing an argument between my father and my maternal grandmother when, once again, the loss of the business was talked about. All my grandmother said was, "the Jew was the more experienced businessman."

Her remark made my father furious. He raised his voice. It struck like thunder. He felt insulted, and my grandmother apologized to him. My mother, who was also present, felt ashamed (she told me many years later) of how my father had treated her mother, "as if she had transgressed and insulted him."

Ever since he had lost his business, my father worked for other dealerships. At that time, cars were not delivered by the manufacturer. They had to be picked up at the factory, often by the salesman who had sold them. That's why my father was seldom at home; he seemed to be constantly on the road. Since his income fluctuated and was not sufficient to keep us in Waldgut Horka, we had moved to a two-story house in a small village called Krauschwitz, not far from the river Neisse, today's border between Germany and Poland.

When the move was completed, my mother picked me up at my grandparents. She prepared me for the change and reassured me, saying: "We still have the dogs!"

But *Opa* Lehmann was gone and I missed him.

I have so many memories of him. He was a true teacher although not by profession. Often, he lectured me, but in a pleasant way. He never seemed annoyed by any question I had and always responded with an understandable explanation. In my mind, he kindled a lasting desire for knowledge.

In his room, he had a dead snake on display, preserved in a glass jar filled with *Spiritus* (alcohol). He explained to me—this was before I went to school and met Rudi—that snakes move by means of body muscles alone and that twice a year they shed their skin. He also told me what their fangs are all about, and how the venom would pass through their hollow teeth. He made sure I saw snakes as just another of God's creatures and not as symbols of enmity and deceit.

He, as did my father, believed in Darwin's concept of evolution and in survival of the fittest. But he must have loved most animals, big and small, strong and weak. Once he found a wild duck with an injured wing. He took the feathered invalid to a veterinarian in Niesky and had the bird treated until it could fly again.

In later years, whenever *Opa* Lehmann visited us, he used the railroads. I was always fascinated by the station and the people getting on and off the incoming and outgoing trains. Their many destinations galvanized my young mind.

Once when he arrived, I couldn't wait to tell him about a trip I had taken on the railway when, several weeks earlier, I went by myself to visit my maternal grandparents in Goerlitz. In Bautzen, a junction point, I had to change, and I boarded a wrong train. It was destined for Dresden.

Luckily, I had listened to the departure announcement before the train pulled out. I got off while the train was already moving. Then, on another track, found and boarded the right train.

Throughout my childhood, travel by train was always a big event for me. I enjoyed it until the end of World War II, when trips would turn into cramped and hazardous rides. In February 1945, I was to be on a military hospital train once again destined for Dresden. Had it reached its destination and not been detoured, I would have perished.

***

Opa (Georg) Lehmann, was not only an expert on steam engines and locomotives, he also was a railroad buff. Of the many stories about train travel he had told me, none impressed me more and remained as lucid in my memory than the one about his grandfather, Gotthelf Schoenert, a restaurant owner who enjoyed the reputation of being a daredevil. With horse and buggy, ignoring the pleading of his wife, but cheered on by many of his guests, he took off from Kaditz to Fuerth. For him it was an historical occasion.

In Fuerth, he bought passage for a railroad trip to Nuremberg. Upon returning home, the adventurer was received like a hero—not only by his wife, who had been so frightened, but also by his family, friends, neighbors and, most of all, by his steady customers. His ticket, duly framed, was put on display in his restaurant.

My grandfather was born in 1871; his grandfather, my great-great-grandfather, Gotthelf Schoenert, was born in 1800. Railroads started operating in Germany in 1835. Thus my great great-grandfather must have been 35 years old when he took this historic trip.

My grandfather had a railroad scrapbook with pictures, notes, and clippings he had collected over the years. Although the first trains looked like toys, he told me that in the very early days of passenger service, people were afraid of the velocity. Speeds in excess of 15 km/ph (10 mph) were thought of as dangerous, and those who were timid implied that anyone wanting to travel by train must be insane.

The first passengers were actually warned they might have difficulties breathing after the train reached full speed. If they had weak lungs, they might collapse and their blood circulation might go haywire. Those daring, foolhardy maniacs, upon completing their first train rides at full speed, were admonished not to do it again because experiencing such great speeds repeatedly might eventually cause insanity.

Some of the early travelers, after coming home, bragged how dangerous a trip it had been. Fellow passengers had gotten nosebleeds and, a few even bled from their ears and mouths. My grandfather explained to me that unsuspecting people are often misled and that the adventurous types are usually those who greatly exaggerate when telling about their perilous encounters and conquests of the unknown.

***

Another much-talked-about, great-great-grandfather, this one on my mother's side, had three wives and a total of 22 children and stepchildren and over 50 grandchildren. As I recall the story, he had married young and founded a family, without restraint. Every other year a child was born until after the fifth or sixth, his wife died in childbirth. He then married a widow who brought several children into the marriage and had still more children with her. He outlived her, too, married once more, this time to a very young girl, and kept on procreating until he died.

My mother later explained that, in those times, the rate of survival was very low, and only one out of three children born had a chance to become an adult. With 22 children alive, she imagined many more had been born, but did not survive.

My maternal grandmother once told me about her grand-mother who had died in childbirth during a fierce thunderstorm. To protect the newborn baby from the rumbling, roaring sounds, it was wrapped into several layers of linen so tightly he almost died of suffocation. He was already blue when the thunderstorm at long last receded and the wraps around him were finally loosened. I thought that if Kaethe ever had a baby, she might react like this.

My mother was an engaging storyteller.

So was her mother, *Grossmuttel* Lemcke.

However, my paternal grandmother, *Oma* Lehmann, I was made to believe, was a chatterbox, if not a gossip monger, rather than a storyteller. I found out this was only partly true. Because she and my grandfather had been divorced, she did not come to visit during the time he lived with us. On my first visit to her home (I must have been four or five years old), I recall she took me to the theater in Bad Warmbrunn. It was a matinee performance for children, a Christmas play, and on the stage it snowed. This amazed me. I had no idea then that fake snow could be produced to create a winter scene in an enclosed room. I thought the roof above the stage was open and the snow came from heaven and was real.

When we left the theatre and the ground was not white and not even wet, I was baffled and wanted to know what had happened to the snow.

"It didn't snow out here," my grandmother explained. "The stage has its own heaven."

This kept me mystified for some time.

Therefore, whenever I visited *Oma*, I wanted to go to the theater, and she obliged. It became a tradition. She took me to a play whenever I spent time with her, except when I saw her last in January 1945. Then the theater was closed. It had become a shelter for refugees.

In ten years, we saw five or six plays together. After I turned ten, she even took me to Hirschberg, the next big town, to performances for adults. One was not a play but a musical, "*Die Fledermaus*" by Johann Strauss.

I remember her, with her feeble, rasping voice, reciting poetry—not nursery rhymes. I don't recall their contents, just that they cast spells of magic upon me. I wasn't sure if for me as a boy, it was all right to feel touched the way I was, so I kept my feelings to myself.

My parents' concern (my grandfather's probably, too) was that she would "baby me to death."

I don't recall her ever smothering me. She spoiled me, perhaps, just as she spoiled herself, but she didn't come down to a childish level. She tried and succeeded in interesting me in many things that she, herself, was interested in. Not only was I compliant, I was absorbed by her lifestyle.

When I was nine years old, I started participating in a children's hour at the radio station where my father was employed.

Whether or not my paternal grandmother, the often-taunted black sheep of the family who was frequently ridiculed by my father, spawned or just awakened my interests in writing poetry and in play-acting, I am not sure. I am certain, however, she influenced my mental orientation and my love for imagery.

During the six years, between 1933 and 1939, I visited *Oma*

Lehmann only two or three times. It was after the outbreak of the war that my visits increased to one or two every year.

Though she was given to outbursts of anger, I remember most her gentle, sensitive, and exuberant side. She would walk through the *Stadtpark* (city park) with me and with great animation teach me the names of all the flowers we saw. When she was feeling elated, she would recite a verse or a whole poem. Birds singing in the trees, the sound of church bells, the sun setting behind the mountains, a little girl wearing a pretty dress, could all exalt her and give rise to a jubilant expression or an appropriate recitation.

***

The silent one among my grandparents, so it seemed to me, was my maternal grandfather, *Grossvatel* Lemcke. I remember him as a man of few words. He answered my questions with "yes" or "no" or with brief explanations. Among my grandparents, he was the least expressive. I don't think he wrote much either. I recall my grandmother, his wife, once stated: "He has a mathematical mind," to explain why he didn't have a way with words. The only letter I ever saw was one he wrote in great pain after the end of the war. It expressed his sorrow at my grandmother's death and stated how much she had meant to him and how much he missed her. He was, nevertheless, an enterprising man. During his life, he owned several small businesses, among them, at the beginning of the century, a livery stable and a small shipping company, with nine horses and three transport carriages. According to my mother, this business failed when the horse-carriage trade had to give way to the automobile.

He then acquired a cigar shop, which was also his office for selling insurance. I remember this store, with a huge wooden desk, visible through the shop window. From behind this massive piece of oak furniture with a sloping top, filled with stacks of paperwork, he conducted his business. He was the district agent for the German crematory society.

Yet my memories of him are warm, of sitting on his lap listening while my grandmother talked, of walking at his side to his office—my little hand securely clasped by his big one. I saw how other people greeted him with great respect, men lifting their hats.

When we walked together, I would feel shielded and proud being in the presence of such a highly regarded person.

I felt almost as close to him as I felt to my other grandfather with whom I had spent so much more time and who was so much more talkative, instructive and, at times, enlightening.

My grandfathers were both good-natured and well intentioned. Without exception, that was always my experience.

***

My father had a very staid and presumptuous demeanor. As a rule, he seemed unapproachable, and, most of the time, I dreaded just being near him. He could be the most entertaining person when people came to visit us. With me he was always a terse communicator when he would make his point or answer my questions. When I was in the second or third grade, he inquired (I forget what prompted the question) if I had learned in school about the *Koenigsstrafe* (king's punishment) yet. He thought I ought to know that, for good reasons, even kings punished their sons harshly.

Always expected to obey and to meet my father's expectations, I was often deprived of my own initiative. I endured in dread of him. I also began to discover that he would, at times, slant the truth to serve his purpose or to make things appear as he wanted to see them.

This became particularly clear when I first read the story of Alexander the Great and Diogenes. My father, after learning that I had been given a book in which one of the stories glorified Diogenes, did not agree with its content. He explained that Diogenes was really nothing but a screwball-philosopher, whom Alexander the Great encountered by chance. While halting to acknowledge the shabby philosopher, Alexander, with his impressive physique, blocked the sunlight from above. Diogenes complained, which prompted the supreme conqueror to put down the insignificant, insubordinate, unsuccessful seeker with a harsh remark, "The sun is mine to capture!"

As unbelievable as it might seem, my father actually claimed Alexander as a German national hero, a great conqueror who had created the type of empire that served as a model, for it was governed with all powers emanating from the leader. I recall my father wanted me to realize that the King of Macedonia and the *Fuehrer* of Germany shared greatness, and thus, I had to venerate both.

The story in the book, as my mother had read it to me, described the event in an altogether different way:

> *Over 300 years before Christ was born, there lived in Athens a Greek philosopher, Diogenes, who taught ideals connected with a simple life. In fact, he demonstrated his strong beliefs by living in a tub on the side of the road. Alexander the Great, who had heard of him and his teachings, one day, decided to visit him. When he arrived at the tub, he asked the philosopher if there was anything he could do for him. Diogenes looked up to the King of Macedonia and said: "Yes, step out of my sunlight!" Alexander, who to everyone's surprise complied, replied without irritation: "If I were not Alexander, I would be Diogenes."*

My mother, in accord with the story she had read to me, didn't view Diogenes as a crackpot, but as a master of philosophy, one who advocated the simple life, promoted self-sufficiency, and who frowned upon social conventions. Moreover, she added that he was also known to have carried a lantern in bright daylight, symbolizing his search for an honest man.

How ironic it had been that my father would bend the truth about a truth-seeker. I remember asking my mother why his tale differed from the one in the book. She replied that was the way he must have learned it in school.

CHAPTER 10

New Homes

I had always found new places to be savory and fascinating. Not Krauschwitz. Except for my parents and my three younger sisters, I didn't know anyone. My inner voice seemed subdued, and I had dreams during this time expressing feelings of dejection.

Among my new classmates, I felt like an outsider. I didn't make a single friend. One day I brought Sonja to school. I tied her up at the schoolyard fence. She barked without stopping.

The teacher asked if anyone knew to whom the barking dog belonged. I told him she was mine. He asked why I had brought her to school. I stammered, "We both feel lonely here."

The whole class burst into laughter.

I had to leave school and take her home. On the way home, Sonja, instead of pulling as she usually did, trudged with her tail down, very close beside me. We both seemed forlorn.

I missed Rudi. For a short time, he and I corresponded. We mailed each other a few postcards and two or three letters. I remember in the first letter Rudi sent me, he mentioned that he had experienced beatings again, but not on school grounds. Thus, the teacher wasn't aware of the fights and no one else had stopped them. The beatings must have been severe. Did Rudi feel as sad as I did?

Since we had moved, I was without a friend.

***

In less than a year, we moved again.

My father had discovered what advantages could be gained from following political trends. Already a member of the elite SS^5, he had now been admitted to the SD^6, Hitler's intelligence and security service. Soon thereafter, he would start a new career and advance rapidly in a field in which he had no prior training, no background whatsoever.

Of Hoyerswerda, I have an abundance of recollections. I even remember our address there: Am Adler 12. Meanwhile, this part of town has been incorporated as a separate community named Doergenhausen.

My three sisters (Anje, Ute, and Doerte) shared a room, while I had a small one, a room in the attic, all to myself.

The house was located on the outskirts of town and was a big improvement over the one in Krauschwitz where all of us four children had to sleep in a room.

Now I had my own quarters and the girls had theirs. There was, however, one great disadvantage. We had only a small yard, and my father decided it was far too small for three big dogs. He kept Sonja, the Irish setter, while Troll and Treff, the two pointers, were boarded with forester Moldenhauer in the forest of Muskau. They remained there until the end of the war when we learned that they had been shot—a mercy death when the Red Army swept through Silesia and the Moldenhauers had to flee. Troll and Treff were both 14 years old when they were killed.

***

My father's study was called the master's room, but he referred to it as the hunter's room. In it he had a two-door cabinet with glass doors that were locked. One side of this cabinet was a bookcase. On the other side he displayed his weapons: three rifles, two shotguns, and one WWI carbine. The walls were covered with hunting trophies, mostly antlers. On each trophy was neatly recorded in India ink the date of the kill.

For me, the main attraction in his room was the fireplace. One of the few really heartwarming remembrances I have of my father goes back to this room. In front of the open fire, he played his guitar and sang folk songs. I sat there listening to him and watching the glow of the crackling flames. To be permitted in his room was like a special honor bestowed upon one on very rare occasions.

***

I have other fond memories of Hoyerswerda. Aunt Else always brought us children chocolate when she came to visit. She also rewarded us with chocolate when we went to visit her. We children soon referred to her as the "chocolate aunt." She was much older than my father and could have been his aunt. What I did not know then, and only learned later, was Aunt Else's political views differed greatly from those of my father. That explains why her visits became fewer and fewer, and one day we were forbidden to visit her. "She doesn't fit in with us anymore," was the only explanation given. Of course, we children were at a loss to understand it.

She owned a grocery store in town. On my way home from school, I continued to visit her secretly at least once a week, never mentioning it to anyone. Before I arrived home, I consumed the chocolate received from her, usually a big bar.

***

Soon after being settled in Hoyerswerda, my parents were able to hire a live-in maid again. She was good-natured and not as harsh a disciplinarian as Kaethe had been. Her name was Lieselotte, but everyone called her "Lilo" (pronounced leelow). When the need arose, she would talk seriously to us children but not threateningly. Nevertheless, she remains linked in my mind with the most severe bodily punishment I ever endured, the harshest and most painful, aside from wartime injuries when no medical help was at hand.

The school I went to in Hoyerswerda was the *Evangelische Jungenschule* (Evangelical Boy's School). There was one for girls too, which my sister attended. These were the only elementary schools in town. The few Catholics who lived in Hoyerswerda attended the same school and were separated from us only during lessons in religion.

Our neighbor in Hoyerswerda, Egon Werner, was the son of my father's employer, an Opel dealer.

Egon and I were not in the same class since he was two years older than I. We often played together. I remember that he—or his parents—owned a horse and it was then, at the age of 8 or 9 that I added to my love of dogs also one for horses.

Egon has also reminded me of my toy-car that we played with at that time. It was a black Mercedes. Just like Hitler's.

In fact, as I would come to see at the end of April 1945, in the subterranean garage of the *Reich* Chancellery, it was an exact replica of the *Fuehrer's* car.

CHAPTER 11

Squirters and Scratchers

My first teacher had been a short man who wore glasses. Probably only in his late twenties, he already had a receding hairline. He was friendly looking and mild-mannered, and as far as I can remember, he always treated all of his pupils considerately. He obviously made special efforts to be kind and fair to those who were disadvantaged. Rudi was not the only one he had taken under his wing. That was not what was expected of teachers in those times.

One event touched all of our hearts. When a classmate returned to school after his mother had died, our teacher scheduled a field trip the next day and asked us to bring flowers to class. He took us all to the cemetery, where we placed our flowers on the fresh grave of our classmate's mother.

All German teachers were authoritarians at that time. Nevertheless, he concerned himself with teaching more than knowledge, providing us with initial guidance for becoming good human beings. While he opened up the world for us, teaching us how to read and write and how to count, he also looked after us in a way in which we, at that early age, were genuinely motivated to learn. Frequent field trips, which we loved, were the major attractions on which he built his effective reward system.

One of these trips was an excursion into the woods where we had to find and identify wild mushrooms. I found the most and recognized all of them: fly agarics, yellow boletus, chanterelles, and several others. I knew them all. For one day, I was looked upon by my teacher with pride and by my classmates as being smarter than they were. I cherished this feeling, and I still remember it lucidly.

Now in Hoyerswerda, the class atmosphere was quite different from what it had been in Niesky and Krauschwitz. I was in fourth grade, and a lot went on outside the classroom. Before and after school and during breaks, various types of mischief making took place, turning at times into utter rowdyism.

Although they weren't really gangs, as we know gangs today, there were two bands in our class, the *Spritzer* (squirters) and the *Kratzer* (scratchers), conducting juvenile warfare with pesky armaments.

The *Spritzer* had small squirting devices such as droppers, syringes and sprays dispensers. They were filled with soapy water or other irritants to be aimed at faces, with the solution meant to irritate the eyes. While a *Spritzer* would usually attack from the front, a *Kratzer* would get you mostly from behind, because he used dry irritants, among them fuzzy seeds, such as hairy rose-hip kernels, poured down your neck.

I experienced both types of attacks several times. The squirts in the face and the eye irritations were bothersome, but the effects of the *Kratzer* attacks were much more annoying—painful—and lasted much longer. The seeds would creep down the back into the crevice of the behind and, when not removed right away, would cause inflammations.

When one of the *Spritzers* had made a hit, it was proclaimed that one more had been *"gespritzt."* This expression, *gespritzt*, would haunt me in later years, after I had seen a documentary in which medically supervised killing methods in concentrations camps were mentioned. The very same expression was used.

I also remember stone-throwing fights. They usually started with pebbles, causing minor pain when hit. But soon there were some severe injuries too. In the heat of battle, bigger and bigger stones were thrown. One *Spritzer* ended up with a hole in his head, screaming and bleeding profusely. Everyone on both sides ran away, and the victim was left—until picked up by a stranger who administered first aid.

Seeking protection to avoid assaults from both sides, I became a *Kratzer*. I joined the group, which I thought was the stronger one.

Soon there were fistfights too, between members of our two gangs. I remember coming home once, badly beaten up, with a cut above my eye and a bleeding nose. My father inquired with whom I had fought and if I had lost or won the fight. I wasn't sure who had won. We had stopped because of the blood.

Popular in those days were so-called *Mutspiele* (games of courage) of the "I dare you" type. Both the *Spritzer* and the *Kratzer* tried to outdo each other with brazenness.

The bully in our group was looked upon as our leader. He called the shots. His name was Helmut, and he used to say, "*Ich heisse nicht umsonst Helmut.*"[7] (I am called Helmut for good reason; I am brave.) Helmut was the tallest and heaviest in our entire class. He had a need to constantly reassert his dominance by bumping into others in the hallway and in the schoolyard and by starting fights with those who objected to his riding roughshod over them. Although Helmut wasn't the brightest among us, he was, in a way, smart. He was crafty and, at times, outright cunning. Apparently what made him feel good was beating up others and getting away with lies and deceit. I had mixed feelings about him. I did not trust him, but I was very impressed by his physical strength and craftiness, and I have to admit that for a time, I secretly wished to have as much power over others as he had.

***

Instinctively, at the age of nine, I looked for ways not to be daunted, to become stronger and more courageous, to get respect from others and, subconsciously, perhaps to gain more self-confidence as well.

Some of the games of courage Helmut came up with were

illegal, as was the one in which our maid, Lilo, caught me in the act.

Right after school, Helmut had lined us up at a street corner opposite a grocery store. Vegetables and fruits, including a few crates of freshly harvested apples, were openly displayed on the sidewalk.

In brief intervals, Helmut would dispatch us one by one to run by the display boxes and to snatch an apple.

My turn came. I started with speed, crossed the side street, ran by the store, and grabbed one of the apples, when suddenly, I felt as if I had been hit by a bolt. Out of the corner of my eye, I had seen Lilo on her bicycle, riding by on the other side of the street. She had noticed me. She had seen me steal the apple and she blurted out my name.

I didn't wait with the others on the next corner for Helmut but kept on running several blocks until I ran out of breath. And then, instead of going straight home, I hesitated and detoured, realizing I had done something wrong and would be punished.

I wished now more than ever that Kaethe were still with us. She would have stopped, given me a couple of slaps right there on the spot, and then although embarrassing, it would have been all over.

Lilo had not stopped. She had turned and pedaled home ahead of me.

My decision not to walk straight home increased the degree of my punishment as time progressed. In Hoyerswerda, unless he was out of town, my father would come home for *Mittagessen* (dinner, eaten at noon in Germany) and then take a half-hour nap before returning to work. I thought if I didn't arrive home before 2 p.m., by which time my father had usually returned to work, I might not have to face him until he came home in the evening. So I lingered until the church tower clock ding-donged, ringing the higher bell four times and the lower bell two times. Now, it was 2 o'clock; still dragging my feet, I went home.

There was my father, to whom Lilo had reported what she had seen. He had been waiting for me, filled with rising anger.

I took my chance to point out how I had gotten into this situation and explained it had been a game. "A game?" he yelled. "You call stealing a game? What has come over you? You get caught stealing and now you dare to lie on top of it!" His voice broke. He had me over his knee, my pants pulled down. He beat me with the leather whip, lash upon lash. I screamed and when I slid down from his knee, his blows hit my back and my neck. I yelled my head off. He turned me around and slapped my face a couple of times before he finally let go. "In your room and to bed, and nothing to eat until tomorrow!"

I went upstairs and threw myself on my bed. Shortly, my mother came. She wasn't able to hold back tears and wept while I kept moaning in pain.

I still can hear her sobbing, "Oh my God!" Some of my skin had broken and I was bleeding. She put iodine on it. The gnawing, throbbing, burning pain kept coming as if sharp blows continued striking me. I didn't even feel the sting of the iodine.

Mother had pulled up a chair and remained at my bedside. She held my hand and caressed me intermittently until the pain finally lessened, and my breathing returned to normal.

I talked to her, described exactly what had happened and why I had been involved. She listened and nodded her head several times, as if she understood. However, after I had finished—and I remember it as clearly as if it had been yesterday—she said calmly but unwaveringly, "It was theft, nevertheless. The merchant paid for the apple and you did not."

She admonished me never to steal again, not to twist things around, never to make up lies but always to face up to the truth, even if I had done something wrong.

I promised her then and there I would never again lie or steal.

She left and I had a difficult time going to sleep. At first, I tried to figure out how I could leave the *Kratzer* gang without repercussions, because I knew how violently Helmut reacted toward anyone who turned his back on him.

I thought of Rudi. Before we had become friends, it had taken three of us in a fight to bring him down. Was he now as strong as Helmut?

There was no one like Rudi among my new classmates. I missed him. Now more than ever.

My room had a small window. It was a clear night with an almost full moon. I noticed shadows moving, patterns created by the leaves and branches of the tree in front of my dormer.

My memory is clear about what transpired in my head. It came to me that at a sight like this, my grandmother, *Oma* Lehmann, would recite a poem. I did not know one.

Even before entering elementary school, impulses had frequently occupied my little head expressing rhythms, not rhymes; sound patterns, not words.

Now I created a verse inside my head. It just happened.

> *Who has put up*
> *The moon in heaven*
> *To calm me down?*
> *In the shadows of*
> *Leaves and twigs*
> *The wind turns silent*
> *And brings me*
> *Stillness, too.*
> *Who has put up*
> *The moon in heaven*
> *And with enough light*
> *For me to write*
> *My first poem tonight?*
> *I don't know.*

During the night, fearful I might not remember my poem until morning, I crawled out of bed, located my schoolbag, got my notebook and a pencil and, without turning on the lamp, wrote down in faint moonlight this very first poetic attempt. I felt elated and afflicted at the same time.

Moving light patterns, traced by the moon on my wall, connected the pain I still felt with my heart and the anxieties I experienced in my soul. My thoughts eventually became a faraway fortress, a citadel of dreams. The garret below the roof of our modest house expanded into a big hall in a fortified castle. I had just been punished severely and deservedly, yet, after composing my very first poem, I felt a sense of mystifying nobility. With it, I went to sleep, and with it, I woke up the next morning.

***

At breakfast, hardly anyone said a word. I kept my head down. My father ate in chilling silence. He was the first one to leave. My mother followed him to the door. Only Lilo and I were left at the table. Hesitatingly, I looked up and asked her why she had told my father. She looked me straight in the eyes. "I had to," she said.

Following a short moment of silence, she asked, "You don't want to become a thief, do you?"

"No, I am going to be a forester," and after some hesitation, "or a poet," I replied.

"A poet?" she asked in amazement.

Should I show her my first poem, I wondered?

"Did your father change his mind?"

"About what?"

"What will become of you?"

"I know he wants me to become a forester."

"I don't think so," was her surprising reply.

Did Lilo know something I didn't?

As I was to learn, she did.

CHAPTER 12

Our Family Tree

A few days following the beating, a thick registered letter arrived. My father told me he had new plans for my future. Success would depend on how well I could be conditioned mentally and physically. If I had been caught stealing the apple, my chances would have been wiped out already.

He had, without ever mentioning anything to me, found sponsors who applied to have me admitted to a *NAPOLA*, (Acronym: *Nationalpolitische Erziehungsanstalt*—national political training establishment) located in Naumburg an der Saale, near Halle in Saxony. The all-important letter stated that I would be considered and explained the provisions for the admission exam, which would take an entire week. Every applicant had to undergo rigorous physical, mental, and scholastic testing.

A *NAPOLA* was an elite school of the Third *Reich*, modeled after the traditional Prussian officers' academies. The principal aim was to select and train the future leadership of Hitler's new nation.

The *NAPOLAs* were highly regarded by members of the *SS*, the corps in which my father had been promoted so rapidly. In just two years, he had reached officer's status and become an *Untersturmfuehrer* (second lieutenant). Meanwhile, he had also been admitted to the *SD*, the *Sicherheitsdienst*, which was the intelligence branch, "the elite of the elite." This he considered a prime accomplishment and a great honor. To have gained membership in the National Socialists' own intelligence and security unit represented success beyond all expectations. As it turned out, it provided him with a springboard for a meteoric career in a line of work other than selling cars or giving driving instructions.

It could also provide his son with a great educational once-in-a-lifetime chance, and he was absolutely determined I take advantage of this opportunity. That I might fail the entrance exam was, for him, completely out of the question.

To qualify for membership in the *SS* or admittance to a *NAPOLA*, proof was required of a "pure" heritage, in accordance with the regime's new racial doctrine. Racialism[8] had been widely accepted in Germany. It became identified with nationalism. My father, who did not look Nordic at all, produced a family tree, providing proof that both my paternal and maternal bloodlines were pure Aryan.

Overlooked, obviously intentionally, in my father's research was that the Lemcke (maternal) bloodline was not as "pure" as he wanted it reflected in the *Ahnenpass* (genealogical record book). Some evidence of an unwanted interloper had apparently emerged among the ancestors of my maternal grandfather who, by the way, was the most Nordic-looking of all of my grandparents.

One of our ancestors in the 17th century, so the story went, was an Eastern merchant who had established himself in Stettin (now Szezechin). First, he changed his name, made it Italian-sounding, and became Nathan Boccy. He married a wealthy banker's daughter, Sara Bernstein, and they had a son, Samuel Boccy, who attended the best schools. Samuel left Stettin for a smaller provincial town and became a banker, following in the footsteps of his maternal grandfather. A handsome man, a Mediterranean type, he was considered to be the best catch among eligible bachelors in the entire province.

He fell in love with the local minister's daughter, known for her great beauty, good manners, and sunny disposition.

At first the blooming romance between the rich bachelor and the beautiful maiden was openly opposed by the parents on both sides. Samuel, however, could not be deterred; he kept showering her with unceasing attention and precious gifts. Upon having a talk with her father, without his family's consent, he converted to Christianity and changed his name to Boccius. Thus, he succeeded in convincing the Rev. Carl Christoph Schlaaf he was worthy of becoming his daughter's husband.

The marriage between Samuel and Maria Christina supposedly took place without the Boccy family's blessing. Maria's father performed the ceremony in his Christian church, which was shunned by the Boccy family.[9]

The facts of this fairy tale-like event in the Lemcke family history had been long ago well documented by records of the births, marriages, and deaths of the Boccys and Schlaafs. These records were contained in an old genealogical record in the *Ahnenpass*. My father corrected this: Samuel Boccius' father is listed, without a first name, as "Herr Boccy," and in the space for his mother where Bernstein should be, the record simply states "not named."

My maternal grandmother had often mentioned that among her ancestors had been *Wenden* (Wends), Slavic people who, in the 8th and 9th centuries, had migrated from Russia to Saxony and Silesia and kept their own language and customs alive. Her grandmother and mother were known for their Russian-style cooking. Even my mother would, from time-to-time, serve cold and hot borscht.

In my father's background, too, following his father's lineage, there seem to have been Wends among his ancestors. In fact, my father had in his face some distinct Slavic features, pronounced Asiatic cheekbones, and not much of a beard—just some growth above his upper lip and on his lower chin.

Yet in the entries to the *Ahnenpass* my father had produced, I can find no trace of a Wend ancestry on either side, neither my mother's nor his.

The Wends were Slavs, and the National Socialists considered all members of the Slavic race to be inferior. As my father saw it, it would have been a disgrace to our family to have been burdened with some shoddy ancestral bloodlines. He might have been kicked out of the SS and SD, and I would not have been qualified to seek admission to a *NAPOLA*.

After the war, I located some distant relatives with whom we had no previous contact: the Gieses, the Jensens, and the Griebels. One, Dr. Jensen, was *Chefarzt* (chief physician) of a hospital in Altena, Westphalia. His wife mentioned some of the Haller ancestors who had been Huguenots. They had come from France to Erlangen, where they had settled, and some of their descendants had moved to Bamberg and Nuremberg. Coincidentally, my paternal grandparents were married in Nuremberg on June 23, 1896, in a church where Catholic and Protestant services were performed under the same roof.

During the time I grew up, the French were often referred to as our archenemies. My father made no entries of our French ancestors.

The *Ahnenpass* assembled by my father was sufficient to qualify him and our family as pure Aryans in the eyes of the regime—and that was what counted.

***

Grandmother Lemcke's father, Theodor Kosmael, had been a master mason in business for himself, who always had several journeymen and apprentices working for him. As my mother put it, her mother came from a well-situated worker's family.

One of my mother's great-grandfathers, Ernst Wilhelm Kosmael, was a bell founder whose carillons would ring from church towers in Lauban, Goerlitz, and many other towns in Lower Silesia. Another of her ancestors, Benjamin Haym, was a free weaver, an independent entrepreneur engaged in weaving. He was born in 1774, lived 84 years, and must have been quite successful because on his death certificate his profession was listed as factory owner. His factory had been a textile mill.

One set of my grandfather's grandparents also had foreign names. His was George Howder. Most likely he was an Englishman. Her name was Hanna Kaudonka, a common Wend surname, although my father maintained the name was of Baltic origin.

Howder was a merchant. He became a German citizen and changed his name to Georg Holder.

One of the aims during the Third *Reich* was to encourage "*Blut und Boden*" (blood and soil) awareness, and it was during the time we lived in Hoyerswerda that my parents took a trip to the village of Sedlitz to visit the Lehmann *Erbhof* (hereditary farm). According to my mother, the reception had not been very warm until the old farmer, his son, and my father had established that all of them were National Socialists. My father returned with photographs he had taken, of which one was enlarged and framed and put in the hallway of our home.

My grandmother *Oma* Lehmann, née Haller was by far the most illustrious of all my ancestors who were still alive while I was growing up. She, of course, had impressed upon me that her side of the family was the most interesting and distinguished. What made this grandmother's antecedents stand out were their academic achievements and the fame some of them experienced during their lifetimes.

She was born March 24, 1873, Wilhelmina Theresia Ida Haller, the daughter of a physician, *Dr. med.* Joseph Haller and his wife Carolina Agnes Bertha, née Loew, whose brother was Prof. Dr. Oscar Loew. He had studied with Justus von Liebig,[10] before becoming a renowned scientist in his own right. He supposedly spoke six languages fluently and was a sought-after lecturer whose distinguished teaching career included professorships at universities in Germany, Switzerland, Italy, Japan, Brazil, and the United States of America.

Oscar Loew's major lifetime accomplishment, according to my late grandmother, was his research that established the medicinal importance of calcium. His father, Wilhelm Christian Loew, who was 98 years old when he died in 1908, owned a pharmacy in Marktredwitz in Lower Bavaria. There, his son Oscar created easy-to-swallow calcium tablets, emphasizing their importance for maintaining healthy bones, especially for those of advanced age.

Prof. Dr. Oscar Loew, in the year 1932 at the age of 92, wrote a monograph entitled *Hohes Alter und Gesundheit* (Old Age and Good Health), distributed by a publisher in Berlin specializing in medical texts, in which he described his apprenticeship with Justus von Liebig and reflected on his life and high age:

> From my youth on, I was tough and resistant, spared from serious illnesses. In addition to physical education in school, hiking, and mountain climbing, I wasn't involved with any sports. However, up to my 86th year, I would, from time to time, bathe in the cold waters of the ocean.
>
> My way of living followed simple principles. I practiced moderation in every way, including food consumption.
>
> As I grew older, I turned more and more to vegetarian-type meals, although I have been adding a little meat lately to avoid a protein deficiency.
>
> In fact, I discovered the benefits of vegetarian meals by accident. In the years 1873-75, I was a member of three scientific expeditions named "U.S. Geological Surveys West of the 100th Meridian." Our food supply consisted of beans, macaroni, flour, zwieback and dried apples. The only animal product was bacon. Our outfitters in Washington had expected us to hunt, but we found very little game in New Mexico, Arizona, Colorado, Utah, Nevada, and Southern California and hardly had time to hunt. Populated settlements were very scarce too. Thus, we ate mostly vegetarian meals that provided me with such a great feeling of well being that I kept myself on a similar diet from then on.
>
> When it comes to alcoholic beverages, I never drank more than 1/4 liter of beer a day and, when wine was served, I drank just a half glass or less.
>
> I did smoke briefly, when I was a student, but I didn't like it and gave it up soon enough.
>
> I loved to travel and visited many countries, spending long periods of time in the United States, Brazil, and Japan.
>
> Among the arts, I especially love music. I still play the

clarinet, as I have done throughout my life, and I prefer classical music.

Satisfaction and a joy for living I derived throughout my life from my studies and fact-finding work in the fields of chemistry, biology, and physiology. My research, which established the increasing need of calcium for the aging body, has been important and rewarding, benefiting myself.

Although I still feel energetic and productive, I know, of course, that there is no such thing as eternal youth, but senility can be prevented through a healthy lifestyle such as mine.

A street in the Nymphenburg district of Munich, the Dr. Oskar Loew Strasse, was named after him.

Until shortly before his death, my grandmother had corresponded with him; she also had pictures of him and, probably, all of his published writings. Nothing was saved when my grandmother, limited to two suitcases and what she was able to wear, was deported from Bad Warmbrunn after the Poles had taken possession of the Silesian territory east of the Neisse River. It was given to them in return for their Eastern provinces taken by the Russians.

During the Hitler regime, the German nobility was looked upon with suspicion. Many German aristocrats were landowners, especially in Prussia. They had flourished within the Imperial Germany. Although there were notable exceptions, most German aristocrats never fully supported National Socialism. Going with the trends of the time, my father hardly ever spoke of his "blue-blooded" ancestors.

My grandmother, however, from as far back as I can remember, again and again alluded to the fact we were descendants of old aristocracy. She referred to the Gotha Almanach[11] of which she had a copy. I distinctly remember her remarking that Germany's foreign minister then, Joachim von Ribbentrop, whom she referred to as a "champagne salesman," was new nobility. She also said that in the Hapsburg (Austrian/Hungarian) empire it was possible for those seeking nobility status to acquire aristocratic titles if they were willing and able to pay for one. She knew of some families who had used their wealth to acquire such titles.

However, this had not been possible under the Wittelsbach dynasty. Her ancestors of a small, privileged hereditary class had been truly blue-blooded, and she could not understand why both of her sons and her ex-husband thought the Hallers had been progressive when in 1848 they had voluntarily surrendered their aristocratic title.

Both the Haller and the Loew families had illustrious ancestors. One, Ulrich von Burchtorf, had been a princely court stable master of the Thurn and Taxis principality. The von Glass von Woelsauerhammer family were owners of a manorial estate, and the male members of this family were seated as Chamber Lords at the royal court or held cabinet posts.

I remember one of the ancestral oil paintings she possessed— a portrait in a wide gilded frame of a face with well-bred, self-assured facial features, very captivating eyes, and a jaded smile. He had been one of the Chamber Lords.

CHAPTER 13

NAPOLA

The last months we lived in Hoyerswerda, in late summer and early fall of 1937, were filled with exciting, exhausting, and in the end, traumatic events.

To prepare me to fulfill the admission requirements for the *NAPOLA* in Naumburg, my father had taken time out from work to tutor and coach me intensely. He wanted to be sure I would pass enough of the exams during the week of tests to be admitted to this elite political and educational establishment.

I sat at his desk in his master's room, trembling, with butterflies in my stomach.

The mathematical calculations he expected of me were far advanced to what I had learned in school, so he ended up impatiently teaching me how to solve these problems. Apparently I didn't comprehend fast enough, which made him irritable and angry.

By the time I finally had caught on, I was exhausted and hurting, because whenever I lacked concentration and made stupid mistakes, he angrily smacked me on the head or twisted one of my ears.

As well as working on math problems, he had me write several compositions. One I remember was titled "Why I am Proud To Be a German."

I had written that I loved the woods and the land we lived on, which was German, and I was gratified to be an offspring of a German family devoted to the Fatherland.

I can still see him reading it and then tearing up the sheets. He had me do it over again because I had not mentioned that, as a German youth, I had the privilege of growing up under Hitler's great leadership, which assured our nation would soon be the best of all nations on this earth. He also wanted me to include how fortunate I felt to belong, as all Germans did, to the Nordic race, how much I cherished my Aryan purity, and how grateful I was to be a member of the people soon to achieve world dominance. He ended up dictating, word by word, what I was to say, pausing long enough after each sentence to make sure I got it all, verbatim.

After it was all on paper, he demanded I read it over and over again, and I ended up having practically memorized this composition, which in fact he had authored. Wouldn't it be cheating if I claimed to have written it myself? The question crossed my mind, but I didn't dare to ask it.

He also demanded that I recite the lyrics of the German national hymn, *Deutschland, Deutschland, ueber alles, ueber alles in der Welt*[12] (Germany, Germany, over all in all the world) and of the *Horst Wessel*[13] *Lied* (Horst Wessel song). He was appalled I didn't know all of the lyrics of the latter. It should have been taught in first grade, he insisted. None of my teachers had done so. Most children had probably learned these songs from their parents and, if not, knew at least the melodies and then just moved their lips as if they knew the words, as I had been doing.

Incensed, his voice raised, my father recited the lyrics and then made me memorize them:

> *The flag up high, the ranks locked tight together SA marches on with steps, reticent and firm. Our comrades, shot by the Red Front or Reactionaries, in spirit keep marching on in our ranks.*

And then he sang it with me a couple of times—he, loud and bellowing, and I, with my quivering young voice. In one of my memory's deep-down sound chambers, I can still hear the vexed vibrations of us singing together.

The night before my departure to Naumburg was moonless, and a strong autumn wind howled outside my window. I felt shuddering bubbles passing through my stomach as if rubbing against my chest. Was it fear? A deep anxiety I might fail? I hardly slept. The next morning, my mother thought I might be ill. She took my temperature, but I had no fever. My father decided there was no reason she should call the doctor. I had a train to catch, and he took me to the station.

There were last-minute instructions, one by one. With long pauses between.

"Always pay attention!"

"I will."

"Make sure to concentrate on what is asked of you!"

"I will."

"Remember, you are my son and I expect you to succeed."

"Yes."

"It's the chance of a lifetime."

"Yes, I know."

He admonished me to keep in mind that the *Fuehrer* had established the *NAPOLAs*. Without him there would be no opportunity. He told me to keep this in mind and to express it as well.

I promised I would.

The last kilometer or so we both remained silent.

At the station, I took my suitcase. My father had gotten out of the car.

"Goodbye."

"Goodbye."

We shook hands.

Then he reached in his coat pocket and handed me a little case with the name of a jewelry store imprinted.

"Mach's gut!" (Do well!)

He slapped me on the back, turned, went back to his car, and drove off.

I opened the little box. To say I was astounded would be an understatement. I was absolutely stunned.

My father had given me a watch. A brand-new watch. The most precious gift I had ever received during all of my young life, not from my mother, not from any of my grandparents, but from my father; my father who had always seemed disappointed in me. Gratified and perplexed at the same time, I wondered if I had reached a turning point and if my feelings toward my father were about to change.

Riding alone on a train was nothing new to me. I already had taken many trips on my own and had looked forward to every one of them. There were special rewards. In addition to sandwiches, my mother would always add a few hard-boiled eggs and a chocolate bar.

As soon as the train left the station, I opened my suitcase, pulled out the chocolate and ate it all at once.

I had put on my watch and kept looking at it—constantly. Everyone else in the compartment noticed it.

"My father gave it to me," I explained, gratified. It was the very first instance I felt proud to be my father's son.

I had to change trains in Leipzig. From there until the arrival, I studied the instructions on how to get from the railroad station to the *NAPOLA*, located in the buildings of an old cadet school. Since there were two *NAPOLAs* in the Naumburg area, I had to make sure to report to the right one. It was a huge complex with some new buildings just being completed.

***

The *Pruefungswoche* (week of entry examinations) at the *NAPOLA* in Naumburg was hectic. We got up at 5:30 a.m. After jogging and calisthenics, we took cold showers and readied ourselves for morning roll call. Our national flag[14] was hoisted before we were dismissed for breakfast. After cleaning our tables in the mess hall, we were assigned to different classrooms. The time had come to prove ourselves. Nothing for which my father had so diligently prepared me came up. On several occasions, our national hymn and the *Horst Wessel Lied* were sung, but no one ever tested us to see if we knew all of the lyrics correctly.

The math problems were similar to those covered in elementary school and were not as difficult as those my father had prepared me for.

We had to write only one comprehensive composition, and it was not about why I was proud to be a German. The whole week was one of surprises. What we examinees experienced was not school in the common sense. Mostly, we were exposed to *Weltanschauung* (world view), the way things were thought of as ideologically correct by the National Socialist leadership, which, of course, were views originated or approved by Adolf Hitler. The National Socialist revolution, as one instructor explained, had to be fulfilled by us, Germany's future leaders, so all of the *Fuehrer's* visions would be realized for the benefit of the German people. It was not easy to comprehend all of this at the age of nine.

Historical events, racial doctrines, the Darwinian struggle for existence, development of character and stout-heartedness, were among other subjects covered in rapid succession by various instructors, usually followed by verbal quizzes or, in a few cases, written exams.

The lectures were fast-moving and, without exception, presented with great enthusiasm. Despite some intestinal discomfort, I felt uplifted and important. During the entire week, I wasn't criticized once.

Throughout the week, we were exposed to a highly organized, well-thought-out program of persuasion. The strongly held convictions of those who enforced the so-called "new order" were passed on to us, the very young, who were being tested, first, for our ability to comprehend and, second, for our capacity to become committed unconditionally to the cause.

In this environment, we took into our minds what was presented to us, without thinking and without comparing, because all of it was impressive and new to us. We had no knowledge of anything to the contrary. We were never encouraged to question any kind of information or passed-on knowledge. We were given no reasons for doubt, and there was no intimation of any kind that what made up this mixture of exciting instructions, which lifted our spirits to such a great height of elation, often consisted of twisted facts and, at times, of outright lies.

The laws of natural selection, life's perpetual struggle for existence, the survival of the strong and the ingenerate demise of the weak, were illustrated for us analogically as victories and defeats. Victories, it was impressed upon us, were dependent on will power, discipline, and bravery. Self-actualization, derived from purpose, order, and self-esteem, was to be the key to mold elite leaders. Treasured examples of the past were recited and then recounted, again and again.

History—what was presented as history—was by far the foremost academic subject during *Pruefungswoche* at the *NAPOLA*, and it focused on heroic personalities.

The names I remember were those whom the new leaders decided to recognize as heroes. Albert Schlageter, for example, a young *Freikorps* (volunteer unit) officer who, after World War I, had openly opposed and sabotaged the French occupation of the Rhine/Ruhr region. Betrayed by an informer, he was executed, and now he was remembered as one of Germany's immortal heroes. In the main hallway of the *NAPOLA*, there was a picture of him, as there was one of Horst Wessel and also one of Herbert Norkus. Norkus who, at the age of 12 as a *Pimpf* (pre-Hitler Youth Scout), while posting bills in communist-infiltrated Wedding, a district of Berlin, was stabbed to death by communists.

There were others we learned about, the young heroes of Langemarck, who in World War I were thrown into a barrage of merciless fire, attacking the enemy lines again and again, until they fell with the *Deutschland Lied* on their lips. That they had sacrificed their lives while singing *Deutchland, Deutschland ueber alles, ueber alles in der Welt* . . . made them forever heroes, although the battle and eventually the war, were lost.

We also learned how brave a soldier Adolf Hitler had been in

World War I; that as a *Melder* (dispatch runner) he had been awarded the Iron Cross Second and First Class; that he had been blinded by chlorine gas near Ypres and regained his sight in a military hospital. By the time he departed for Munich, the war was lost, the Kaiser had left Germany for exile in Holland, and Hitler felt betrayed, as most German soldiers did.

We were told that Hitler, because of his abilities and determination to save Germany from total ruin, became the leader of the *NSDAP* (National Socialist German Worker's Party). We learned about the members of the old guard, their loyalty and heroic dedication. Following Hitler's failed attempt to seize power, they marched together with Hitler and von Ludendorff[15] by the Felderrnhalle in Munich on November 9, 1923 in an attempt to reverse the situation. Unexpectedly, the police opened fire. The fourteen marchers who lost their lives would forever be remembered as *Helden der Bewegung* (heroes of the movement).

Since assuming power, every year on the anniversary of this historic event, Hitler met in Munich's Buergerbraeukeller (a restaurant in Munich—a beer cellar) with members of his old guard. This was not the only official holiday created by the National Socialists; January 30, day of the *Machtergreifung* (seizure of power) by Hitler, was another one.

***

One of the last and most comprehensive lectures at the *NAPOLA* was devoted to Friedrich der Grosse (Frederick the Great)[16] highlighting his military victories that secured Prussia's leadership of the German states. The instructor read to us the king's speech to his generals before the battle of Leuthen on December 4, 1757, whereby he instilled them with courage to attack an enemy nearly twice as strong and well entrenched on higher ground. At the end of the speech the king proclaimed: "By this hour tomorrow, we shall have defeated the enemy, or we shall not see another again."

"Er war ein Heldenkoenig" (A hero-king he was), our instructor impressed upon us before dismissing us.

We returned to class after the noon break. With my stomach flu gone, I had eaten a hearty lunch, which in Germany compares to dinner. I felt somewhat tired, but my spirits rose immediately when, as I had expected, we were told to write a composition titled: "The Conquests of King Frederick the Great," because I felt very knowledgeable about him. The instructor had not even touched on many of the king's outstanding achievements. My grandfather, *Opa* Lehmann, had always held Frederick the Great in high esteem. He had been the savior of Silesia and, therefore, many a story about this prolific ruler had been passed on to me.

Even my father had, from time to time, referred to Frederick's youth and the *Koenigsstrafe* (king's punishment) he had been subjected to by his father while still a prince.

We were given one hour for this assignment, which seemed to me more than adequate time to write an extensive piece. The few compositions I had written before in grade school had usually been 30 to 45 minute assignments. A whole hour seemed more than ample time.

I was determined to do well. I made short notes on what I wanted to depict and in what order. After I had started with the composition, I wrote boldly.

Although, I wore my proud possession—my new watch—I never looked at it. When the instructor suddenly announced we had five minutes left, I wasn't even close to the ending as projected in my sketchy outline. I had about covered half of what I wanted to write.

Several of my classmates were finished already and stepped forward and turned in their papers. For a moment, I panicked. I raised my hand and asked for additional time. "Five minutes, not one more!" My request was denied. What was I to do now?

I had wanted to evince that I knew much more about Frederick the Great than just his military victories, which had been covered during the morning hours. Aside from his soldierly accomplishments, I took also into account his savoir faire, his many cultural interests and achievements, and especially that he had been an accomplished musician, played the flute, and conducted *Hofkonzerte* (court concerts).

I had also written what my grandfather had told me more than once—that although an absolute ruler—he was the king who had proclaimed that the state exists for the welfare of the individuals.

It had not been beneath him to personally listen to grievances of his subjects and resolve them, always in a fair manner. Moreover, I had elaborated that this king, later known affectionately as *der alte Fritz* (the old Fritz), had coined the phrase *"Jeder soll nach seiner Fasson seelig werden!"* (Everyone should be free to practice what he believes in). It was he who had eliminated torture and who had made all officials responsible for their actions.

I had just finished writing that Frederick the Great had Sans Souci[17] ("Without Cares") built. This his royal palace with the stately residence in which he had made many historical decisions such as doubling the size of the Prussian army, formulating what he expected of his soldiers, and establishing models for military conduct including the high ideals of loyalty, discipline and sacrifice, maintained by the Prussian army ever since.

That's where I was, ready now to recount all of his accomplishments as *Feldherr* (military leader) and all of the battles he had fought and the decisive victories he had won . . . but I had run out of time. All I had left were five minutes (probably four by now) to end my composition.

Remembering my father's admonition to always keep the *Fuehrer* and his accomplishments in mind and his importance to Germany, I decided to end my composition concluding that many of Frederick the Great's qualities were also possessed by our *Fuehrer* and that our nation was blessed for having had such a great king then and for having someone like him now: our great *Fuehrer,* Adolf Hitler.

Time was up and the instructor collected all of the papers.

I had portrayed Frederick the Great with the enthusiasm and pathos of a nine-year-old, who had already written poems and who envisioned a great future as a writer. But I knew, of course, I had turned in an unfinished piece.

After the war, I realized that to compare Hitler with Frederick the Great had been naïve. Although not always victorious, he had nevertheless won deciding battles and, in the end, wars. He had also granted religious freedom to all of his subjects.

The Prussian king had made significant contributions to improve human conditions and not just those of his subjects. Under his reign, the use of torture had been abolished, while Hitler, through the *Gestapo* (secret state police) and *Einsatzgruppen* (special action groups), became one of history's greatest torturers and murderers.

During *Pruefungswoche* at the *NAPOLA,* all quiz and test results remained confidential, and none of our papers were ever returned to us. Even though my last work was somewhat incomplete, I felt very confident that what I had written was expressed well enough for a passing grade. Writing, I was convinced, was my strong suit, even at the age of nine.

At least one-third of our time had been scheduled for activities outside the classroom, in the gym, on track-and-field, or in the indoor swimming pool. I had not learned to swim yet, and all of us who couldn't swim were asked to jump into the deep side of the pool. After sinking to the bottom, we would be rescued by one of the lifeguards.

Needless to say, I was somewhat hesitant to jump into the deep water, but one of the lifeguards whispered in my ear, "Jump if you want to be admitted; I'll get you out right away." This did it. I jumped. I went to the bottom, my mouth and nose full of water; I swallowed, gulped and choked and, lacking air, experienced panic. It seemed a very long time, and I was badly frightened before the lifeguard finally pulled me up. I coughed and coughed and had to go to the bathroom, where I vomited. Afterward, however, I began to feel good; I was proud of myself for having been brave enough to jump. I was convinced I had not only passed the academic and athletic requirements, but the bravery test as well.

***

When I returned home, my father's first question was, "Did you make it?" and I answered confidently, "Yes, I am sure I did."

A few days later, however, my father received a letter advising him I had not met the entrance requirements, signed by Dr. Hellmann, the school's headmaster.

How could that be? I was devastated.

My father called Dr. Hellmann and addressed him as *"Herr Obersturmfuehrer."* This was an *SS* rank comparable to first lieutenant. My father's *SS* rank was then *Untersturmfuehrer* (second lieutenant). He just listened, astonished. Then he uttered, *"Heil Hitler"* and put down the phone, visibly upset.

First he conferred with my mother.

"Our son is a *Waschlappen* (washrag)," I overheard him say sarcastically. "I just learned from Dr. Hellmann there might be a chance in two years to have him qualify for admittance at one of the new Adolf Hitler Schools,[18] but it will take a lot of conditioning!"

Then he recited a list of my shortcomings.

"This might be so," is all I heard her say, while my father reiterated, "The boy is a total disappointment, a flop, an utter failure!"

Crushed, I wanted to know in what subjects or activities I had not succeeded. What he told me was that I lacked mental and physical stamina. I was not tough enough and not sufficiently strong-willed to measure up to the sturdy image of a *NAPOLA's Jungmann* (A *Jungmann* in a *NAPOLA* is a freshman or a cadet). "You are a dream-away flabby tail," he summed up in disgust.

When I was alone with my mother, she told me the main reason I was not admitted was that I appeared to be *zu anfaellig* (too delicate or illness-prone).

I recalled the intestinal discomfort. However, except for the physical examination, I didn't see the doctor and had not missed a single class. There had to be more to it. Whatever the reasons were, none changed the fact that I, once again, ended up being a failure—and this time in a really big way.

One of the results of having failed the *NAPOLA* entrance exam was that my mother had to take me to a chiropodist to prescribe arch supports. I was flat-footed.

This time my father did not punish me physically but made sure that I felt ashamed and humiliated.

He grabbed my arm and pulled off the precious timepiece he had given me. Not a word. Just an expression that showed I was not worthy of this wristwatch.

To condition me, he bought a 5-kg medicine ball. In the yard, he threw the ball at me with such a force it knocked me down. I had to get up and throw the ball back at him. This continued until I was completely exhausted. Then, with a cutting voice, he asked me, "And what is expected of a German boy?" And I had to answer, "To be as fast as a greyhound, as tough as leather, and as hard as Krupp steel!"

For years to come, I hated the medicine ball, but my father continued, whenever he found time, to work me out exhaustingly. Especially on Sundays, when he was home and whenever the weather was suitable, he would insist the whole family walk to the park. I had to carry the heavy ball and then I had to compete with him until I was totally fatigued and not able to throw the ball any more. His final comment would be "softy" or "lightweight." Only years later, after he had joined the armed forces, would this ordeal come finally to an end.

Meanwhile, while still in Hoyerswerda, there were a couple more weeks of school to attend before we moved to the capital city in the late autumn of 1937.

After I had returned from exams-week at the *NAPOLA,* I had been able to distance myself from Helmut and his gang without problems. He must have concluded I wasn't disloyal but had been preoccupied with our forthcoming move to Breslau. Soon I would be gone anyway.

And so it went. We didn't even say goodbye to each other. I did not leave a real friend behind in Hoyerswerda, as I had in Niesky. Although I had not corresponded much with Rudi, we had exchanged some letters and cards, and I did write to him after the Naumburg fiasco but didn't receive a reply and never heard from him again.

CHAPTER 14

Breslau

One morning, a huge moving van arrived. In a day, all of the furniture and all of our belongings were loaded. They had been carefully packed and marked in boxes, cartons, baskets, and suitcases. The next day we moved. My sisters traveled with my parents in a passenger car, while I rode with the movers in the cab of the van. I don't think that we owned a car then, so my father must have borrowed it from Willy Werner, the owner of the *Opel Haus,* his former employer.

While riding through the long stretches of rural countryside, I thought I might miss the woods, and I voiced my concern. But the driver of the moving van assured me the apartment we were moving to was on the outskirts of town, with forests nearby and even a small tributary of the mighty Oder River, called Lohe.

"Nearby, where you will live, there are the Lohe Meadows and the Lohe Woods."

He himself did not live far from there, knew the area well, and seemed to like everything about it. There were also skiing hills, the Hardenberghuegel and Kinderzobten, nearby, as were soccer fields, tennis courts, and a garden restaurant called Gartenschoenheit, a favorite of his and his family. Breslau was his hometown, and he was proud to be a Breslauer.

With so much going on and new ventures to look forward to, I decided I must cease to dwell on the past. What had happened could not be changed, but there would be a fine future even without my attending a *NAPOLA.* My mother had told me the entrance exam for a *Gymnasium*[19] in Breslau would be strictly academic, and I was confident I would pass it, having had good grades in all subjects except handwriting throughout my four elementary-school years.

My thoughts roamed. Being on the road opened new vistas, and moving to a big city was an exciting experience. I was hopeful that ahead of me, a spirited life and a future full of exciting things to do were waiting for me. My father would start a new job, one of great responsibility, as he had stated repeatedly. He might be seeing less of me, and perhaps his attitude toward me might change too. Surely, I would make new friends. I had a *Volksschule* (elementary school) to attend for a few more months before entering a *Gymnasium* or *Oberschule* (high school) as it is called now. It would be at least two years before I could be considered for admission to the Adolf Hitler School my father wanted me to attend.

Why were we moving to Breslau? For as long as my father was alive, he never admitted it, but I thought, and still think, that the only reason for his having been assigned to this new position was because he was a member of the *SS* security service—the *SD,* which was Hitler's own intelligence force. This service was headed by Reinhard Heydrich who in 1939 would also become chief of the Gestapo, the agency responsible for national security. Thus, my father, who had become an *SD* member a year earlier, had in all likelihood been designated as a watchdog to *Intendant* (director) Hans-Otto Fricke, who was in charge of the *Reich* radio station in Breslau with satellite stations in Goerlitz and in Gleiwitz.

Father's version was that a close friend, Fritz G., had known of the opening and urged him to apply, assuring him of a top-notch recommendation. Fritz G., in party circles, was a man of high influence. Maybe he did, indeed, pick my father, but certainly not for his office skills—more likely for his political reliability.

My father not only got the job, but also was soon promoted from secretary to personal assistant. Thereafter, he became chief counselor and assistant program director and finally program director pro-tem, just before voluntarily joining the armed forces in 1943 as war correspondent. Could he have received these four significant promotions in just four years—in a field in which he had no previous training—had it not been for his absolute devotion to National Socialism, its leaders, and its objectives?

My father, no doubt, had exceptional organizational abilities, and according to my mother, after some tension in the beginning, he and his boss, *Intendant* Fricke, came to respect each other. In strictly political matters, my father became his reliable trouble-shooter, especially in dealings with Joseph Goebbels' Propaganda Ministry, which controlled all of Germany's radio stations during the time the National Socialists were in power.

Breslau, (now Wroclaw), at the time we moved there, was the capital of the province of Lower Silesia. The city was situated on both banks of the Oder River. The old town had retained a medieval character, with narrow streets and old churches of both Catholic and Protestant denominations.

The streets of the inner city converge on the market square on which the city hall is located, a splendid Gothic building of the 16th century. In its sovereign hall, the diets of Silesia had formerly been held. In its cellar was a restaurant, which we would visit on occasions, especially when we had out-of-town visitors who were shown around town. Even my father, who had little interest in churches, seemed proud when taking visitors to the church of St. Elizabeth, which housed one of the largest bells in Silesia, a magnificent organ, and a famous portrait of Martin Luther.

CHAPTER 15

New Friends

My parents had rented a second-floor apartment in the southwest outskirts of Breslau in a block of red-bricked apartment houses on Kuerassierstrasse 123. The front yard was dominated by three huge poplar trees. In the backyard were small areas with poles connecting clotheslines where, when it didn't rain, laundry was hung up to dry. It was also the only place for children to play. This courtyard didn't appeal to me at all. Boys in the neighborhood who played soccer did so on an empty lot a block away on the other side of the street.

It was a 20-minute walk to the radio station—my father's place of work and soon to be mine. We followed a small path below the elevated tracks of the railroad surrounding the city. It passed by the *Kinderzobten,* a favored hill for play with a short and not-too-steep toboggan and ski run. It would soon snow, but only my parents had skis.

My newfound enthusiasm faded rapidly. After the excitement of the move had subsided, I was disturbed, confused, and felt like a castaway.

When, after going to bed, I was unable to fall asleep, my thoughts took me back to the woods and to the dogs, which I missed most. First, we had to leave Troll and Treff behind; now Sonja was gone too, and I felt so alone.

I started a diary and, using a flashlight, made entries in the dark. I remember describing a dream where my tears inexorably dried up and turned into cutting crystals. Invisible, self-inflicted wounds, bled with pain. The duration of my forlornness stretched over a couple of weeks only, but to me it seemed time eternal.

The transitions from living in the woods, then in a village, thereafter in a small town, and now in a big city, the passage from nature into an urban sprawl of mass housing, was painful.

I didn't mind not seeing much of my father who was very busy settling into his new job and meeting influential people in party circles and on the cultural scene. However, my mother, who in the past had always had time to listen and take care of most of my emotional needs, seemed not well and on the brink of exhaustion.

In her third or fourth month of pregnancy and suffering from severe morning sickness, she had a new household to set up and little time for us children. Years later, she told me she hadn't received nearly enough for living expenses to make ends meet. Although in his new position my father's salary was more than double what he had averaged in the past as a car salesman and part-time driving instructor, my mother had a difficult time providing for us. He gave her less than half of what he earned to cover rent, utilities, food, clothing, school supplies, and transportation costs. He, on the other hand, spent money lavishly on luxuries, especially hunting parties and his new, expensive hobby—photography.

Even though we children never witnessed any quarrels about finances, my mother later told me they were frequent. My father, at times red-faced with anger, would tell her it was he who earned the money, and therefore it was up to him to decide how much of it should cover the family's household expenses and how much he, himself, was entitled to with no questions to be asked by her.

What upset my mother most was my father's habit of calling her on very short notice to announce he would bring guests home, often for supper. She would then declare she didn't have enough time and money to meet his expectations, whereupon he would get angry and tell her she should put money aside each month for entertaining guests and spend less on us, her children. I remember being sent to the grocery store and butcher shop across the street to buy food and meat and having had to request, "Please add to our tab," meaning we bought on credit, with my mother settling the bill at the beginning of the month.

She had grown up during the Depression and hated debts, but she had no choice. We children might have never received pocket money had it not been for the opportunity to work at the *Reich* radio station Breslau where, apparently, my father was already looked upon as an influential person, even though he had just started to work there.

***

I finished my fourth and final year of elementary education at the Roon[20] School, which was situated on Roon Street, within walking distance from where we lived. The area was considered to be a "blue-collar" section, and, in my class, there were many tough and rowdy boys, even more roughnecks than there had been in my class in Hoyerswerda.

I remember making only one close friend during this time of less than half a year. He was Dieter Heinrich. Soon we would be members of the same *Jungvolk* unit. Two years later, it was he who was selected to enter the Adolf Hitler *Schule* and not I. In 1945, he would be killed, next to me, in our first battle as members of the home defense force.

In fact, in my new surroundings, except for Dieter at school, only three of the new people I became acquainted with made a memorable impression. They were: middle-aged Frau Opitz; old Schuster Stefan; and my neighbor Kurt, almost a young adult.

Frau Opitz, a slender, sinewy woman in her forties, was the superintendent of our apartment complex. She assigned the use of the laundry facilities to the tenants of the building. I don't know if she feared my father or disliked him or both, but she avoided him. She would always ask me if my father was home before coming up to talk to my mother. If he were home, she wouldn't come. I also remember she mentioned, again and again, that her husband's work required great physical strength, that he was tough and couldn't be intimidated. I recall a remark she made about my father. Dressed up in his black *SS* attire, he had complained to her about something. After he was out of sight, but I was still in the hall, she remarked, hitting back at him, "Dashing uniform but no medals."

Had my father heard her remark, hell would have broken loose, but he didn't, and I kept what she said to myself, realizing for the first time that my father's official garb looked pretty bare. Because he never learned how to swim, he didn't even possess the sport achievement badge most uniformed men were wearing proudly. Except for the regular party badge, his rank insignia, and a patch with the letters *SD* on his lower left sleeve, nothing enhanced his uniform. I recalled then that even Rudi's father, who must have been about my father's age, had several decorations he wore on his *SA* uniform.

Most people in Germany had a great reverence for uniforms and medals of any kind, but especially for war decorations. Both Hitler and Mr. Opitz had, in World War I, earned the Iron Cross, First Class, for bravery and the Wound Badge in Black for their battle injuries.

Herr Opitz apparently was a heavy drinker. He would become boisterous, if not violent, when intoxicated, although his wife would downplay these occurrences. Once, two gendarmes had come after midnight to investigate. The next morning, Frau Opitz asked me if it had been my father who had called the police. I didn't know. I hadn't even known about the incident. Her husband, as the *Blockwart,* was the official party informer and, she maintained, no one was entitled to report on him, not even a member of the *SS.* Thereafter, she complained more often and, increasingly, uttered curses.

Eventually, the Opitzes moved away, but not until the war had started, because, before they left, I remember her bragging about the extra rations they received. Aside from her husband, no one else who lived in the apartment complex had been classified as a heavy laborer. Although he was a habitual drinker, it didn't stop the party from promoting him. His promotion to the position of a leader responsible for a town section is why they moved.

***

The second person I remember is *Schuster* Stefan, the cobbler in the neighborhood who repaired all of our shoes and was a different kind of man. A real Hans Sachs[21] type, he had his workplace a block from where we lived. He seemed always eager to talk. Whenever I came to bring or pick up some shoes, he would encourage me to remain awhile and to sit down on one of his low, three-legged footstools. He offered me, and I am sure other children as well, hard candy from a big glass jar he always kept next to his cash box.

As I think back, I realize that even during the first year of the war, he was able to keep his candy jar filled. Business people, as I would learn later, frequently set up bartering arrangements that would supplement the meager ration card allocations.

Hard candies and interesting stories increased my visits to the old cobbler. Both of my grandfathers lived far away now and seldom visited. The old man repairing shoes, whom I found so intelligent, with a resourceful mind and a caring heart, I came to look upon as still another grandfather.

"One has to learn to understand our world," was one of his favorite remarks, leading into whatever he wanted to say, and ever more often, *Schuster* Stefan talked about wondrous things. Some I would puzzle over. For example, he liked to talk about how many animals had much better senses than humans. He taught that dogs could detect smells a human couldn't, that cats had better eyesight, and that in birds the sense of sight was many times as keen as that of man.

The old cobbler seemed particularly fascinated with bats and bees. He explained that bats, the only mammal with power of true flight, flit about in tight swarms without ever colliding by responding to their individual echo signals.

Bees, he thought of as the most amazing insects. He illustrated in great detail how they form colonies with a single queen who, after mating once on her nuptial flight with one of her idle drones, lays an abundance of eggs to assure birth of the hive's next generation. Thousands of worker bees who serve her, build wax cells, gather and store honey, will also defend her and their hive whenever necessary.

Aside from being a cobbler, he was a beekeeper, and thus, he knew all there was to know about honeybees. He explained that bees could see rays of light invisible to us. Bees can see what man cannot.

Schuster Stefan was also fond of heroic legends and mythological tales.

Whenever I had enough time, such as evenings after supper while he was still working, he would relate a whole epic, with me listening with intense fascination, captivated by the heroes or mythical gods in one of his spellbinding narratives. Engaging my mind in sagas of deities and other idols might have been one reason why I became and remained such an ardent reader.

How had *Schuster* Stefan attained so many skills and so much literary knowledge? I remember him mentioning medieval troubadours, as well as master singers, of whom Hans Sachs must have been his favorite. These poets who for the most part were artisans and craftsmen like he was, reflected in their writings a keen awareness of conditions and a blunt honesty of purpose for expressing themselves.

He made me realize everyone is not of the same mold. The simplest person can discover precious inner treasures, as long as he keeps searching. Some are able to compose tunes or write poetry or narrations, others are able to draw pictures or build things that had never been thought of or invented before. Those who appear shallow need only to discover their depths where they can find goodness!

At any age, this storytelling cobbler would have fascinated me, but at nine and during the years that followed, I was probably especially impressed. I watched him intensely, and I listened to him attentively, no matter what subject he touched on.

He also listened and had a knack for comforting me. One memory of him that never faded is that he assured me it was all right for a boy to cry. I had told him how much I missed Sonja, our dog that I wasn't able to see anymore. Tears started running down my cheeks, and I was embarrassed and apologized.

He said, "I understand. It would make me cry too!" He was compassionate and thoughtful.

Over twenty years later, on a brief visit to Dr. Schweitzer's jungle hospital, it suddenly struck me that in physical appearance and facial expressions, there were some similarities between the great humanitarian and the simple cobbler-philosopher who had repaired my family's shoes and to whom, in my youth, I had listened for hours and hours.

***

The other neighbor who never left my memory owned a motor-cycle. Kurt was a young man who lived a block from us on Tulpenweg. I don't recall how we met and why we met. He was at least six years older than I, and he wasn't a high school student, as I would become soon. He was a mechanic and belonged to the motorized unit of the Hitler Youth.

For him, his motorcycle was more than a two-wheeled motorized vehicle; it was a means to the end of power and prestige.

When Kurt took me on rides, I felt elated—just as I had years ago when I rode on the back with a stranger in Waldgut Horka. The wind blew through my hair. It felt as if I had made contact with the driving forces that make life really exciting and exhilarating.

Kurt also played soccer, belonged to a club, participated in official games on Sundays and often worked out on one or two evenings during the week, practicing penalty shots and using me as a goalkeeper. The goal was big, I was small, and most of his shots were well aimed and fast, so I caught few and frequently scraped my knees and elbows. Practice shooting was often followed by motorcycle rides, something I always looked forward to.

Kurt, although he had not received a higher education, seemed very intelligent. Mechanically inclined, he always knew how to fix things. He also had interests other than of a technical nature. Fascinated with symbols and their significance, he believed they lead us on to accomplishments and give us strength. On the wall in his workshop, he had large posters with runic characters and one with rune stones.

Kurt could and would talk for hours about runes, those discovered in England and Germany, and of the vast majority of rune-inscribed monuments discovered on the Scandinavian Peninsula.

I remember Kurt observing that runes could be arranged to form magical associations of mystical significance. He maintained that there were runic ceremonial activities where a state of divination can be reached, giving us powers to see into the future. I wondered, but I did not understand then. The thrill of a motorcycle ride was much more exciting to me than the mystical significance of magical symbols.

Kurt's father was an astonishing man who was a gardener by trade or avocation. Not only did he have a well-kept garden in the backyard of the house, he also owned a large allotment garden, not far from the cemetery. There he grew a great variety of vegetables, even potatoes.

My interest in gardening gave way to playing soccer or riding on a motorcycle with Kurt, although there were still times when I helped Kurt's father, pulling weeds and watering.

As early as spring of 1938, a year and a half before the start of WWII, Kurt's father was convinced war would break out. At that time he started to build additional rabbit hutches. He already raised rabbits and must have had a dozen or so.

"Don't you have enough?" I asked.

His answer I remember as clearly as if he had said it yesterday.

"There will be war and thus we need to have 52 rabbits, one for every Sunday." Half of his little garden was turned into a rabbit-breeding setting, and he remarked that now he had to use part of his garden to grow rabbit fodder. He decided, "No more flowers until the war is over." The war hadn't even started.

CHAPTER 16

Radio Days

I don't remember the first Christmas in Breslau at all, the one in 1937. I believe that we were hardly settled in—Lilo was still with us. My mother surely did the traditional baking of fruitcake and gingerbread cookies. On Christmas Eve, as was the tradition in our family, carp must have been served. The next Christmas, however, I remember because of the gifts I received—skis and ski boots. I spent, regardless of weather conditions, every day of the Christmas vacation on *Kinderzobten*, a hill with a slope for children. Adults who were beginner skiers used it too.

In fact, 1938 had started promisingly. My unanchored feelings diminished. My fragile sense of self-confidence emerged again. I had discovered within walking distance a small forest and a river, the Lohe, which I could escape to, getting out from under my father's shadow for periods of time. His new job made him feel important. He often worked late or had evening functions to attend. Every night he was not home, I could go to bed without having to answer his questions about what I had learned in school and accomplished during the day. I treasured these nights of relief from reproach and criticism.

It must have been the end of January or the beginning of February that one day upon my returning from school, my mother was waiting for me with great expectation and exaltation. She had laid out my best outfit and asked me to dress up. Right after lunch, I was to walk to the radio station where at 4 p.m. a lady by the name of Ria Hans would audition me for a part in a children's program called the "Do Handicrafts Hour."

"If she takes you," my mother explained, "you will earn plenty of pocket money." It wasn't an audition; it was an actual program I had to participate in. A boy who had been a member of the regular cast had dropped out and had to be replaced on very short notice—in fact, on the day of the show. I was the right age and Ria Hans' first choice, probably because of my father having started his new position at the station. If he was pleased, he didn't tell me.

I, on the other hand, enjoyed being a member of this small cast of one girl (I remember her name: Anneliese Grill) and three boys (whose names I don't recall). During my first show, we built a simple birdfeeder. Ria Hans gave the instructions. The four of us had been given a kit with the necessary materials, including glue, nails and a hammer, and we all succeeded with putting the feeder together while asking questions and making comments as we progressed.

It was a live program, and after some initial butterflies in my stomach, I felt at ease. I worked with enthusiasm on my little project and communicated as the show went along. Apparently, I did well and was assured a steady part in this weekly program. My honorarium was two marks per show, of which I was allowed to keep 50 pfennige as pocket money, while 1.50 marks, as decreed by my parents, had to go into my piggy bank and then into a savings account opened for me in the nearby *Sparkasse,* a savings & loan association. Even when my pay per show was raised to three marks, I could keep only 50 pfennige; the balance had to be saved.

I soon advanced from just a craft hour participant to a young radio actor of children's parts, and Ria Hans, who directed most of these radio plays, wanted me to join the *Rundfunkspielschar* (radio performance group, a special unit of the *Jungvolk*). I was all for it and excited about it, but this idea did not appeal to my father. He said no. My mother told me later that he was opposed to his son ever becoming an actor.

He would later permit my two sisters to join this group of artistically inclined youngsters, but I had to be toughened up and belonged in the regular *Jungvolk* where, as he saw it, more rigid service would apply and stricter discipline would be enforced. In two years, he emphasized, he wanted me to be selected as a candidate for the Adolf Hitler School and be in shape mentally and physically to pass the entrance exam.

CHAPTER 17

High School

Easter of 1938 approached, and the time neared for entering high school. In 1937-38, I had gone through the trials and tribulations of three high-school-level entrance examinations. The first one to the *NAPOLA*, I had failed. Based on the report he had received from the *NAPOLA* in Naumburg, my father had surmised that I might not be physically fit and mentally tough enough to be admitted two years hence to an Adolf Hitler School. My father was determined to change this.

Meanwhile, I would have to attend a local high school where the average burghers sent their sons. An entrance examination was given, which I passed, because it was strictly of an academic nature.

The Koenig Wilhelm Gymnasium[22] was located near the Freiburger *Bahnhof* (railroad station), easy for me to reach via streetcar, with only one connection, from line 18 to line 6.

Thus, I was prepared to enter after Easter recess the *Sexta* (first class) at this school.

My father, however, changed his mind and decided I should attend another high school. It was located near the main railway station and regarded as a high school of superior quality. His brother, my Uncle Hans, had attended the school and was now a doctor.

My father, somewhat sarcastically, challenged me: "Let's see if you are at least bright enough to pass the entrance exam to get into the Elisabet Gymnasium."[23]

I dreaded having to pass another entrance exam, perhaps a more difficult one but I had no choice and I passed. It probably was the best school for me—although not in the way my father envisioned. The school's prevailing domain remained one of academic knowledge in a distinctly humanistic tradition.

The faculty, with only three or four exceptions, was not one of political activists. Issues of right and wrong were approached on a moral basis. By National Socialist standards they should have been changed to conform to the new ideology.

This school had an elected body consisting of three students from each class. They constituted a *Schueleraufsicht* (self-policing committee), which was allowed on campus until 1941.

The academics were all men in this all-boys high school.

As a ten-year-old, I thought of most of these distinguished pedagogues as being somewhat old-fashioned, as they were mostly older men and civil servants in a school in existence for over 700 years.

Our class was made up of all kinds of personalities from many walks of life, ranging from the son of a blue-blooded family to one whose father was a small farmer and another one whose father was a blue-collar worker. Most of us, however, came from middle-class families, with fathers who were professionals, teachers, lawyers, etc., or owners of small businesses or civil servants.

I made friends fast. Next to me sat Klaus Schauermann. We would soon seal a pact becoming "blood brothers" supportive of each other for life, and indeed, our friendship has lasted to this day. He died, Oct. 19, 1999, a week after he had come to visit me and read the last chapters of this book.

In many ways we were of contrasting dispositions and talents. Klaus, who had the mind of a mathematician and engineer, was much more practical than I. He also was taller, sturdier built, and physically much stronger. But he was neither intimidating nor confrontational. He had a way of spurring me on, and I usually responded to his challenges while my mind would often march against my father's demands.

In Klaus, I had found a friend who was reasonable.

High school for me was a mixed bag. I did well in my favorite subjects: German, geography, biology, and sports. Although history was also one of my favorite subjects, during the first four years of high school, I had a teacher who demanded we memorize historical timetables, and since I had problems memorizing numbers, I received only a passing grade. *Studienrat* (high school teacher with a Master's degree) Michler was a party member who would, as was the custom, display his party badge on the left lapel of his jacket.

Studienrat Poppe, my first German teacher in high school, was my favorite for one simple reason. He had discovered I wrote poetry and encouraged me to continue. He even told my mother I was gifted.

On the other hand, he had some traits of a zealot. One of them was to "Germanize" all words of foreign origin in our language. For example, when in one of my compositions I used the word *"Portemonnaie"* (money pouch), which was of French origin but commonly in use, he crossed it out and wrote *Geldboerse* in the margin. His handwriting was almost of calligraphic quality.

My former classmate, Martin Scholtz, when we talked about *Studienrat* Poppe at my retirement party, also reminded me he had often treated us like a troop of soldiers. He made us jump up and stand at attention from the second he entered the classroom, and, with our eyes fixed on him, we had to move our heads in the direction he was walking from the door to his teacher's desk. Whenever we had not performed to his satisfaction, he would hit his wooden leg with his walking stick, return to the door, and have us repeat this ritual all over again.

He usually wore a white coat that looked like a hairdresser's smock, which explained his nickname "the barber." Some of my classmates thought he was mildly psychopathic. I didn't. For me he was an idol, because he gave my compositions the highest grades: "very good" (1) or "good" (2).

Besides German, my favorite subjects were physical education (not so much indoor gymnastics, but track and field and ball games), biology, and geography. I disliked mathematics and

English, and neither in art nor in music was I talented enough to be above average—although later in life I gained great appreciation for, and interest in, music and art.

Thus, my marks were always mixed; "very good" and "good" in the courses of study I liked; "satisfactory" and "barely sufficient" in the subjects I didn't care for, which, three years later, would include Latin.

Mathematics, English, and Latin, however, were the subjects my father thought of as being the most important ones. Thus, he was never pleased with my performances, and since his new, very important job didn't leave him time to supervise any of my school assignments, he directed my mother to check my homework daily and whenever necessary, to coach and discipline me and keep drilling me until I did comprehend.

For me, to comprehend and to retain were not identical aspects of learning. Often I would forget what I had understood and absorbed just a short time earlier. When she found this out, she would lose her patience.

"Why do you lack the will to learn?" she asked in desperation.

I had no answer. I didn't know. I wanted to learn. I concentrated on remembering.

Although determined, when studying, to stop thoughts that crossed my mind, I was seldom successful in doing so. The flow of imagination and reflections were, at times, those of a daydreamer, a word-weaver, or visualizer. Often, they were just about the neighborhood boys who were playing soccer already, while I was stuck at home with my homework. Whenever I was not able to finish it before dark and couldn't play, I was angry and disappointed, making attention more difficult.

Still, every subject had to be successfully mastered—every subject but one, and that was religion. The Catholics and Protestants parted and were instructed separately. The few of us who were *gottglaeubig* (God-believing but not attached to a particular faith) had an hour off. *Gottglaeubig* was a term invented by the National Socialists for those who, as my parents had, severed relations with their church. Out of a class of over 40, there were just a few who were *gottglaeubig*, and in the Elisabet Gymnasium, there was no instructor available to keep us occupied during this hour.

We were on our own. I usually ended up in the *Turnhalle*, the domain of Kuddel Wiesner, the school's well-liked sports instructor, and watched whatever class was exercising on the ropes, the vaulting horses, horizontal bars, or parallel bars.

There were also times when with questions of religion on my mind, I just left the school, walked to Teichaecker Park, sat down on a bench and tried to conceptualize in my mind the enigmatic God I believed in. But I remained mystified–and still am.

Then, I realized that my intellect was not as potent as I wanted it to be. I was dispirited by the fact that some of my classmates seemed so much smarter than I. Our *Klassenprimus* (top student in class), a short, frail fellow with a crew cut, once remarked how little time it took him to complete his homework when it had taken me many hours—until late in the evening—to finish mine. I just didn't know what to do to my mind to become more receptive and retentive. If it was lack of concentration, why then didn't I have the ability to concentrate better?

I remember one particular instance when my mother quizzed my English vocabulary from the last lesson. I missed the same word over and over. Again, it upset her and she seemed disheartened.

"Why don't you hold on to it? Is your brain a sieve?"

I felt stricken.

"It's such an easy word," she drilled on. "Why can't you remember it?"

I did not know.

In desperation, I repeated it again and again. But repetition was the solution only for as long as I kept reiterating. Then I lost it again.

I believe the word was "shiver" or "quiver." My mother waited. I drew a blank.

Suddenly, I was overcome by an impulse to hit my mother. Although I was able to resist this rash impetus, I felt terrified and shivered with fright. What kind of demon hid inside me, waiting to break loose?

I had to get away.

I left the room, slammed the door, and ran into the Lohe River woods. Had my father been there and witnessed that I abandoned my homework in such a fit of bad temper, he would have beaten me.

My mother, who until then had always been my refuge, must have perceived some reason for my inner turmoil, because when I left like a runaway, she didn't make any attempt to hold me back.

On the way to the woods, in a state of exasperation, I repeated this one English word over and over again, just this one word.

Could I quit school, go back to the *Volksschule* (elementary school), and upon completion go into apprenticeship to become a gardener or, even better, become a mechanic and perhaps a race-car driver like Bernd Rosemeyer, Rudolf Carraciola, Manfred von Brauchitsch or Hermann Lang—some of my heroes at that time?

When I returned, my father was home. I trembled since my homework needed still to be finished, and I was frightened at having been away. But he was busy and remained in his room. As it turned out, my mother hadn't told him anything.

My exasperation had burned out, and I kept my defeatist thoughts to myself. After supper—still feeling dispirited—I nevertheless finished my assignments.

CHAPTER 18

Hitler Youth

We boys sought excitement. Some of what we experienced had an intoxicating effect. I saw Hitler in person for the first time, and even from a great distance, the effect he had on me was hypnotic, and I shared in the jubilant behavior of all those surrounding me. I still can't describe this emotional wave, the enthusiasm created by those who filled the *Jahrunderthalle* (Century Hall) where Hitler addressed the crowd. There wasn't room for all who wanted to be admitted. Many had lined up outside. I forget how I got inside— it must have been with the radio crew through arrangements my father had made.

This was the time when the majority of the population seemed uplifted and thrilled about Hitler's accomplishments. The economy flourished. Unemployment had been eliminated; there seemed to be work for all.

The network of the new *Autobahnen* (freeways) kept expand- ing, now connecting all major cities, Breslau included. The Volkswagen had been introduced and was to be mass-produced as a low-priced "people's car."

Germany had become a nation of mostly enthusiastic followers. I, not yet a teen-ager, became one of them.

Hitler had himself established firmly as a benevolent dictator with the abilities of a genius, as my father would frequently point out when talking about political events.

I felt nothing of the harshness and cold-bloodedness his to- talitarian regime applied toward those in opposition or to those

oppressed. I didn't know. I had no suspicions. I knew
Konzentrationslager (concentration camps) existed, but I also remember how my mother had once, when the question came up,
explained to me that ordinary offenders were put into a prison.
Dangerous criminals were put into a maximum-security peniten-
tiary and criminals/public offenders/enemies of the state were put
into concentration camps that—so she believed and thus I did,
too—were correctional facilities similar to labor camps. At that
time, detention in a concentration camp was even called protective custody. Those detained, as I remember, were described as
reactionary Communists and other terrorists, opponents of the
Reich who had to be re-educated.

None of my teachers, not even any of my *Jungvolk* leaders, ever
discussed why there were concentration camps and what went on
inside.

In fact, I actually believed inmates in *Kazets,* as Germans called
the concentration camps, upon being converted to the ideology of
National Socialism, regained their freedom. I vaguely remember
some church dignitaries had been released from concentration
camps. Youth-time friends of my parents, Richard and Grete
Suessmuth, who had remained devout Catholics, were once informed by my father that a detained priest known to them had
been released.

It wasn't until 1945 that I was shown documentaries about
the liberation of concentration camps and not until 1948 that,
together with fellow classmates, I visited Dachau. My brother Wulf,
who later visited Auschwitz, thereafter shared with me, in a night
long talk, the horror-filled impressions and insensible perturba-
tions he had returned with and which kept haunting him. But
that was over 20 years later.

At the time my mother explained to me what concentration
camps were all about, the extermination camps had not been established. Unknown to the general public, many *KZ*[24] inmates
were already being murdered in these early camps, as witness upon
witness would testify after the war.

About the same time, shortly after I had become a *Pennaeler*[25] and *Pimpf*,[26] my father took out two volumes from his bookcase and remarked that the time had come for me to read two important books. One was *Mein Kampf (My Struggle)* by Adolf Hitler; the other one was *Der Mythus des 20 Jahrhunderts (The Myth of the Twentieth Century)* by Alfred Rosenberg.

I expected that soon, as was his habit, my father would question me about the contents of these books, so I made attempts at reading them both. After a few pages, I felt as if I had lost the ability to concentrate. I forced myself to read on. In Hitler's book, I must have skipped where he spelled out his political aims in shocking details, since only his narrations about the time he spent in Vienna as a struggling artist and his experiences in the First World War aroused some interest.

That's all I remembered. Obviously, my young mind didn't pick up on how dangerous his nonscientific racial views were, as was his dictatorial *"Fuehrerprinzip"* (leader principle), as history would later demonstrate.

The Rosenberg book seemed completely beyond my range of interest and understanding, and, after thumbing through it several times, it remained unread. I don't recall my father ever questioning me about these books.

I do remember, however, that later on in one of our evenings of indoctrination in a *Jungvolk* camp, both books were discussed. Mainly, it was pointed out to us how important it was to develop strong characters, strength of will, and self-control and that although raised by our parents, we belonged to the nation. We were fortunate to have come under the influence of a great teacher and model: Adolf Hitler. It was impressed upon us that Germany had never had such a great leader.

We were taught that as "Nordic people," we constituted the earth's supreme race, and it was our responsibility to rid ourselves of all bad habits that had been perpetuated by inferior races, and that the Jews and the Communists were out to destroy Germany.

Since, at that time, I didn't know any Jews or Communists

and as far as I know had never come into contact with any, these were non-personal, ideational enemies. A few months later, the infamous Crystal Night made me realize the nice people in a candy store I frequented occasionally were Jewish. They had become victims and afterward had to wear the Star of David.

A family in our neighborhood was said to have been Jew-Christians. They insisted they were Germans and Christians, but had been unable to document their Aryan ancestry. Thus, their son who was my age was not allowed to enter the *Jungvolk*.

I felt sorry for him because he, too, wanted to belong and was just as eager to be admitted as I was at that time. He remained alive, and we met again 10 years later in Bavaria and told each other how we, in so drastically different, but similarly dangerous ways, had been able to survive.

The day of entry into the *Jungvolk* approached—April 20, 1938, Hitler's birthday. I needed a uniform, but my mother had not been given money to buy my uniform. It was a matter of little concern to my father. He said that eventually I would get one. Most of my classmates had theirs already, and I wanted to get at least my summer service outfit: brown shirt, black shorts, the belt with the official buckle, and, most of all, my hiking knife, carried in a metal sheath attached to the waist belt.

As the day grew close, she urged: "Ask your father if you could have it now!"

I dreaded having to ask him, but I did.

It obviously annoyed him. He told me that just now he needed the money for something else and I had to wait.

"Without a uniform, I can't join."

"Yes, you can—in a white shirt!" he replied angrily.

I didn't even own a plain white one.

So everyone else appeared in uniform except me. I appeared in a light ivory shirt, looking like a white sheep in a herd of black ones and sticking out like a sore thumb.

That evening, still in my ivory-colored shirt, I told my father I had been the only one who did not wear a uniform; it didn't change his mind. I would have to wait until he was ready to give my mother the money. It made me sick, and while pondering over my predicament, it suddenly crossed my mind that there was already enough money in my savings account to cover the cost of the uniform. I had to have his permission, of course, and to my amazement, he seemed pleased with this solution and permitted me to use this money. My mother and I not only bought a complete summer uniform but the one needed for winter as well and, of course, the all-important hiking knife that went with it.

My youth squad, a local unit with 48 members, met at the Roon School every Wednesday afternoon and for special events on weekends as well.

In later years, I have often been asked if I joined voluntarily. I did. In Germany it was the only youth movement one could join. Everyone I knew wanted to join and would have joined even if it had not been mandatory.[27]

I would have preferred to be part of the entertainment unit connected with the radio station, but not permitted to do so, I was glad to be a member of a regular unit.

Had I for any reason not wanted to become a member, my father most certainly would have ordered me to join. He saw in the *Jungvolk* the continuation of many of the *Wandervoegel* traditions he had valued so highly.

One of the tenets of the Hitler Youth was that youth is to be led by youth and that we were all committed to a close-knit comradeship. Field games, outings with campfires, and many of the sports activities, I enjoyed most.

But even drills to develop soldierly skills and attitudes, historical indoctrinations, and world-view, as seen by the regime, were absorbed enthusiastically. We didn't know differently, and no one who might have known otherwise ever talked to us.

I truly enjoyed being a *Pimpf,* as I would have enjoyed being a Scout had I grown up in another country. Perhaps even more, I might have liked belonging to a troop of a wandering circus or being a child actor in a repertory or stock company.

In the *Jungvolk*, we were drilled to follow orders and to become unquestionably obedient. But we were also provided with opportunities to advance, to become leaders within this framework of conformity where our orders had to be followed. To have the opportunity to ascend to a position where my commands would be carried out provided me, early on, with a great motivation to become a leader.

CHAPTER 19

Brother

On my tenth birthday, May 23, 1938, my brother Wulf was born. I have vivid recollections of the chain of events that took place on this day.

My sisters were with family friends, and I was home alone with my mother. It had been her washday, and she had felt pain when hanging up the wash on the clothesline, thinking she had strained herself and not realizing these could be beginning labor pains. My brother was not due for another two weeks.

Having been physically active all day must have accelerated her contractions, leading to a much shorter labor than she had experienced when she had given births previously. Now, she expected her fifth child.

When she suddenly realized the birth was imminent, she called the midwife, only to learn she had been called earlier to assist with a birth somewhere else. After this baby was delivered, she would come to our house.

My mother instructed me to fill the two biggest pots we had with water, to put them on the stove to boil, and also to gather towels and a fresh set of bed sheets.

She kept herself covered, clutched a pillow, moaned in pain, muffled her screams. My brother was being born. I could barely understand what she said: "Call the doctor and ask her if she knows of another midwife who could come right away!"

The telephone was on her nightstand. I dialed. There was movement under the sheet, and it turned red with blood. Shaking like an aspen, I talked to the doctor's nurse, who said the doctor would come herself as soon as possible. Now my mother was panting, and I broke out in a cold sweat. Feeling as desperate as I did, I rushed downstairs to look for the doctor; when I couldn't see her, I knocked on *Frau* Opitz's door. No answer. No one was home. I rushed upstairs again.

Just then, the midwife arrived, out of breath, telling me to close the bedroom door and to wait outside.

Shortly thereafter, our doctor arrived too. She made sure my mother was all right, and when she left she asked where my father was. I didn't know—only that my sisters were at the Binners'. She assured me all was well, that I could see my mother now and my baby brother.

"Had he arrived ten years earlier, he could have been your twin brother," mother whispered.

The event turned from one of intense dread to one of sheer wonderment.

When the midwife left, she praised me for having not panicked and for having been of great help. I felt proud, singled out and filled with feelings of attainment and joy. My mother later remarked that she had been more frightened ten years earlier, when I was born in a suburb of Munich. The midwife had arrived after my birth.

CHAPTER 20

Crystal Night

All of Germany's youth at the time were born into, grew up, and were instructed at home, in school, and in the *Jungvolk* to be loyal, honest, considerate, and helpful.

It was nothing short of a mission to be dedicated to *Fuehrer, Volk und Vaterland* (leader, people and Fatherland), fervently accepted as one of immense purpose and supported by a *Volksgemeinschaft* (people's community) in which people cared for each other in terms of *Alle fuer Einen-Einer fuer Alle!* (All for one—one for all).

Called to participate to make my country great, being educated in a renowned high school which still emphasized academic teaching rather than political indoctrination (but operated within the guidelines set forth by the new regime), and being a member of the *Jungvolk*, among my peers, who were all enthusiastic about the designated activities, what was there for a 10-or 11-year-old to question?

Thus when the *Kristallnacht* (Crystal Night, known also as "Night of the Broken Glass") took place, my mind did not react humanely. I should have remembered my first teacher's teaching and asked myself, "If I were Jewish, how would I feel if this had happened to me?" Such thoughts didn't even cross my mind.

I probably had my mind on soccer, or motorcycle rides, or struggles with homework, because on the day prior to the Crystal Night, I was unaware that an enraged 17-year-old, a Polish Jew, Herschel Grynszpan, had shot Ernst vom Rath, a German embassy secretary in Paris. He consequently died on November 9, the night Adolf Hitler and his *alte Kaempfer* (old guard) assembled in Munich to pay tribute to the victims of the Beer-Hall Putch of 1923.

My father was at home that night, and after I had already fallen asleep, he must have received a phone call from his *SD* unit. The telephone was in my parents' bedroom. I didn't hear it ring nor did I hear him leave. But when he returned early the next morning before six o'clock, I awoke and so did my mother, who got up right away because my father demanded she prepare break-fast. Seemingly aroused, he spoke with a loud voice, and I could understand him clearly.

I remember this, as if he had said it today, word by word: "Tonight, for once, we really made it hot for the Jews!"

After the war, he denied ever having made this statement and became very angry when I reminded him and wanted to talk about it. My mother also remembered as distinctly as I did that this was exactly what he had said.

My personal recollections following the *Kristallnacht* are, in fact, of broken glass. At the corner where I changed streetcars on my way to school, a basement shoe store owned by Jews had been one of the targets. Glass from the broken shop windows was still scattered along the sidewalk. The display windows were already covered with boards. I, as did others, looked through the cracks and watched two men, in black caftans with long beards and wear-ing black hats, taking inventory. The younger-looking one was counting; the older one, who might have been his father, wrote down the information.

A few days later, I also walked by the candy shop where I occasionally had bought bonbons or a chocolate. It had either been spared or the plate-glass windows had already been replaced. I saw no damage. But the store was empty. It had been closed.

I also remember driving in a streetcar by the burned-out syna-gogue. The ruins were still smoldering. The entire site of the fire had been roped off. There was no one on the sidewalk.

How many people were ashamed of what had happened? We

will never know. They kept it to themselves. Both of my grandmothers were, as I found out much later.

I was not aware of this but learned just recently that in some of the upper classes of the Elisabet Gymnasium, a few students had ceased coming to school. Not so in the class I attended. We had not a single Jewish classmate.

Over fifty years later, in the anniversary edition commemorating the founding of the Elisabet Gymnasium, Walter Horn, whom I did not know but who had been a student in one of those upper classes, reported that he was forced to leave our school, following the night of the broken glass. Although his family didn't survive the holocaust, he did. After his expulsion from our school, his parents, through connections, were able to send him to a boarding school in England. In his article, he mentioned that some of the older teachers had been protective of the Jews who attended our school. Since 1981, he and his wife, who live in Chalfort St. Giles, England, returned to Germany several times to participate in class reunions.

The Crystal Night was one of the many events that took place in the year 1938. Austria was annexed by Germany. By now the great majority of the German people living inside and outside of the *Reich* had become *Anhaenger* (adherents). My parents, too, were in favor of Hitler expanding the borders of Germany to permit the homecoming of millions of Germans who were separated from the Fatherland when, after World War I, the Versailles Peace Treaty had virtually dismembered our nation. Most of West Prussia had been handed over to Poland, creating the Polish Corridor and disconnecting East Prussia from the German mainland.

Austria, reduced to less than a quarter of its former size, nevertheless, now consisted of the territory whose people spoke German. Most of them desired a union with Germany.

The Germans of the *Sudetenland,*[28] which had become a territory of Czechoslovakia,[29] also desired geographic and political reunification with Germany.

Hitler, who had stated in *Mein Kampf* "the psyche of the

masses is not receptive to anything that is weak," increasingly used strong-armed methods and swept the German people off its feet, especially the young like me. Organized by him, educated and trained by him, ideologically streamlined by him, how could it have been otherwise?

My father, who since his *Wandervogel* days had made it his mission to promote nationalism among *Auslandsdeutsche* (Germans living outside Germany), had nothing but praise for Hitler's actions, and that seemed to be the consensus of the entire population. It's difficult now to describe the emotional wave that swept the country, probably affecting the young most of all.

Many of my vivid memories of 1938 relate to news events documented by the *Deutsche Wochenschau,* the official German newsreel preceding all feature films, and news and speeches that were broadcast over the German radio station. These were controlled by the Propaganda Ministry, headed by Dr. Joseph Goebbels, a genius in his own right and also one with a black soul.

A master of his craft, he transformed news into events affecting the masses, and in retrospect I can only say his censorship was just as effective as his demagogic skills. Nothing entered my mind I could have used for comparisons, and nothing emerged to pull me back from all the elation.

When German troops marched into Austria and the Sudetenland was occupied, both of these actions could have led to war but didn't. Hitler gained more fame and glory. The newsreels highlighted the faces of the local populations. They cheered the arriving troops with great enthusiasm and went into a frenzy upon viewing their *Fuehrer* who, his arm raised saluting them, traveled in an open automobile, an easy target for an armed assassin. There was none.

Once, as I recall clearly, even the audience in the movie theater applauded when Hitler was shown in a black Mercedes, escorted by roaring motorcycles, as he was greeted by a huge hailing crowd. As I remember, extensive footage was shown of a speech he made from the balcony of a public building or a hotel, saying

Germans shall never be divided. The applause in the newsreel and in the movie theater went on and on and on.

My father was convinced of Hitler's invincibility and talked about it at length. At that time, it was one of the few topics I enjoyed talking with him about.

CHAPTER 21

Summer Recess

The winter vacation, 1938-39, I spent skiing in the Riesengebirge, Silesia's dominant mountain range. In spring, I again spent a couple of weeks there at the country home of the Elisabet Gymnasium— a lodge in the mountains at Strickerhaeuser, near Schreiberhau, which had been bequeathed to our high school.

By the time my classmates and I arrived, the old building had been renovated and expanded to accommodate up to 50 students on the upper floors. Downstairs was a sizable classroom, because the time we spent there was not a vacation. In order to accommodate all students for a three-week period, occupation was year-round; one class would leave, another one would arrive, and school had to go on.

Memories I have of this first trip of our *Sexta* are of extensive nature excursions. On clear days, I never failed to be impressed by the magnificent mountain landscape that surrounded us. One particular incident during one of the hikes, I still recall. A fellow classmate sprained his ankle, and my friend Klaus, who must have been in charge of carrying a first-aid kit, knew just what to do. He expertly bandaged his injured joint, whereupon our hurting classmate, with his arms around our shoulders, was able to hobble back to the lodge.

At supper, *Studienrat* Geister, the teacher in charge of our class who had accompanied us, made a short speech, lauding Klaus and me for having been so helpful to the injured. We had shown genuine comradeship, he said.

***

In Germany, summer recess is called *Grosse Ferien* (great vacation). In 1939, I spent it in Bavaria for several weeks at my uncle's, who a year earlier had moved his medical practice to a picturesque resort village, Utting am Ammersee. The Ammersee was a sizeable body of water, and the view from my uncle's house over the lake was spectacular.

I was impressed with the house, which accommodated both his family's living quarters—including a luxurious guest room I had all to myself—as well as his medical offices. It had an x-ray room in the basement with state-of-the-art equipment, something that set him apart from other country doctors. My uncle was obviously a very sought-after physician, since many of his patients, including party dignitaries, came to see him from as far as Munich.

He had an automobile, of course, and made house calls, often twice a day, early in the morning and then again after office hours in the evening. I was allowed to accompany him, enjoying the rides and meeting his patients or their family members who showed a great amount of respect toward my uncle.

His son, my cousin Juergen, who was six years younger than I and only five years old at that time, stayed home with his mother, who spoiled both of us. She often asked what meals we liked and prepared what we wanted. Most of the time, my uncle was too busy to eat with us and was served a snack in the office or late at night after we boys had already gone to bed.

On occasions when we all ate together at the family table, I sometimes lost my appetite when my uncle would describe to my aunt, in gory details, the conditions of patients, accident victims in particular, medical procedures, and other events commonplace to a physician. It made me sick, but I didn't want to show it.

I remember one of his remarks, after a boat on the lake had capsized during a thunderstorm. A young boy had drowned, and after his body had been retrieved from the lake, my uncle had to issue the death certificate and console the parents, whom he knew well.

"Death is merciless," he said, and repeated it once more. Then he asked: "Why didn't they come ashore when the storm approached?" He shook his head, "Once death captures a life, it's gone forever!" I realized for the first time how close death was and was filled with dread.

***

That summer, I was also supposed to visit my grandfather who lived in nearby Seefeld, but "Tante Musch," the woman he lived with, had apparently overruled his invitation.

Instead, my grandfather came and picked me up early one morning, and we went to Munich by bus where he bought me a 35mm camera. Even by today's standards, it was a sophisticated camera with a good lens. Its price was nearly 50 Marks, a huge amount of money at that time. I was astonished, having been given such a valuable gift.

This was the same grandfather, *Opa* Lehmann, who had lived with us in the forest in Waldgut Horka, who had walked with me through the woods countless times, who had taught me most of what I knew about trees and plants, who had instilled in me a love for animals, who had liberated me from my fear of snakes. It was he with whom I shared so many early childhood memories.

Now we were in a big city, not surrounded by trees, but on a busy street amidst rows of huge houses. We went to a park and sat down on a bench. He had me go over the camera's instruction sheet, explained things to me, and then we went through what one might call a practice session.

There are few educational inputs I was given in my youth which I remember as vividly as the basic hands-on instructions in photography received from my grandfather on this memorable morning in Munich.

"The camera sees what the eye sees, nothing more, nothing

less. To properly record what you see, the lens has to be focused and the time of exposure has to be measured in accordance with the sensitivity of the film."

We figured out the correct f-stop setting and shutter speed, and then before putting in the first film, he had me practice shooting. That became my most memorable lesson because he taught me how to "compose" each picture individually.

"With a camera, everybody can become an artist," he impressed upon me. He showed me, for example, how two trees could serve as a natural frame for a statue in the park.

"It's the same when you photograph people," he told me. "The closer you move, the more of a person you will capture. And choose as neutral a background as you can find."

He taught me many other lessons. I was eager, of course, to take pictures of everything we would see, and after I had put my first film into my new camera, we took off.

My grandfather, who at that time was already 67 years old, maintained the pace of a much younger person. In nearly seven hours, he had shown me the *Rathaus* (city hall) the *Frauenkirche* (cathedral), and many of the sites and buildings that had become important to, or had been created by, the National Socialists. My grandfather was an old party member. He proudly wore his golden party badge and took great pleasure in showing me the *Haus der Kunst* (house of art), where artists approved by the regime exhibited their works, and *das Braune Haus* (Brown House), the party headquarters that overlooked the Koenigsplatz. We went to the Odeonsplatz so I could see the *Feldherrnhalle* (hall of generals) where 14 of Hitler's early followers had lost their lives in 1923 when shot at by Munich police. He also showed me the Buergerbraeu Keller, a huge beer hall where the failed Putch had taken place and where, since assuming power, Hitler met annually with his early followers to remember those who had become martyrs of the Third *Reich*.

My grandfather knew where Hitler had lived on *Prinzregentenplatz*, and we walked by there. For a late *Mittagessen* (midday fare), the main meal in Germany, we went to an artists' tavern, which Hitler had supposedly frequented in the olden days. The restaurant must have had an Italian chef. I do remember I had spaghetti, and my grandfather had a dish unknown to me, pasta filled with meat.

Another stop we made was at a military barracks, the home of his unit that had been a railroad regiment. Although he had never been employed by the state-owned German railroad, he had, as a member of a control unit, inspected steam locomotives to see they were maintained to safety standards. He had completed his mandatory military service prior to the end of the 19th century, long before the outbreak of World War I, at which time he was already over 40 years old.

My grandfather was a railroad buff but very military-oriented as well. He had kept in touch with some of his old comrades, and together they had followed the activities of their regiment, attended anniversary meetings, and kept photos. I remember my grandfather had a whole album full of them and seemed filled with pride whenever he showed it to anyone.

Of the political events that took place during the time of my vacation in Bavaria, I remember one. Hitler's foreign minister (Secretary of State) von Ribbentrop had signed a friendship pact[30] with Josef Stalin. Aghast, my grandfather called it an unholy alliance (after the war he used the term "devil's pact"). Hitler, who had been forever denouncing Stalin, had as recently as three months prior to the signing, labeled him as one of Germany's archenemies. My grandfather just couldn't believe it. How could his *Fuehrer* have signed a non-aggression pact with a foe as despicable as Stalin?

"That won't go well!"[31] I heard my grandfather repeat several times. He just couldn't get over it. Shortly thereafter, Hitler's propaganda machine increased his demands for Danzig and the Polish Corridor.[32]

As ironical as it seems now, one of my grandfather's biggest concerns then was that Stalin could not be trusted. That was true, of course, but as we all know now, it was Hitler and not Stalin who broke the 10-year non-aggression treaty, when two years later he launched a surprise attack against the Soviet Union.

***

I returned to Breslau from my vacation in Bavaria with a stack of my own photographs. At first, no one seemed to believe I had taken them. When I explained about Grandfather's giving me instructions, that I had indeed taken them myself, everyone seemed amazed. Even my father who was very much into photography, seemed astonished at how well my Munich pictures had turned out and commented: "That, at least, is something!"

My grandfather's gift and encouragement would, almost 30 years later, turn into a real vocation. In 1968, after my second heart attack, I acquired a fine camera and took a course taught at the Winona School of Professional Photography.

There in class, remembering my grandfather's early instructions, when the subject of composition was covered, I coined the phrase: "The name of the game is a perfect frame!" The instructor liked it and wrote it on the board, and by the time the course ended it had become a slogan among my classmates.

For several years, I participated in shows, contests and traveling exhibits, won ribbons, and many a meaningful prize. When, in 1978, my book *Travel and Tourism* was published by Bobbs-Merrill, the section on World Travel Areas was abundantly illustrated, and almost two-thirds of all the photographs it contained had been taken by me.

In my youth, however, photography remained strictly a hobby and a restricted one at that, since my allowance was needed for other, more important things—like buying my own soccer ball, which I had to keep hidden at Kurt's house.

At home, it was my father who photographed constantly, and by 1938 his bookcase contained 18 sizable albums filled with pictures he had taken. These were usually shown to first-time visitors to our home.

One of these visitors was Alfred Naujocks, a fellow *SD* officer. My father introduced him as an old friend dating back to the *Wandervogel* time. My mother had no memory of him.

However, shortly after the war, my mother recognized him when his picture appeared in a newspaper. He had been in charge of staging an attack against the radio station in Gleiwitz with concentration camp inmates dressed in Polish military uniforms. This incident was meant to prove to the world Poland had started the war and not Germany.

***

Sixteen months after the birth of my brother Friedrich Wulf and the day before the war began, my second brother Ulrich Georg was born, also at our apartment at Kuerassierstrasse 123. This time, however, the midwife arrived on time. Thus, my mother bore her sixth child, the number required to be awarded the mother's medal in silver. The one in bronze she already possessed, was an award my father seemed to be more proud of than she, since he always insisted she wear it on special occasions.

I also remember that a few days prior to my brother Ulrich's birth, it was announced ration cards would be issued, causing my mother to remark: "Now there will be war for sure." To which my father added somewhat laconically, "How fortunate we are, because with the birth of yet another child, we will be issued an additional ration card."

Two days after the happy event, at 5 a.m. on September 1, 1939, Hitler invaded Poland. I woke up in the morning and was told by my mother we were now at war.

I saw motorized troops driving through town on my way to school that day. I waved and some waved back.

CHAPTER 22

The Fall of Poland

At the beginning of the war, Hitler was victorious, according to the news presented to us, with no major setbacks. For the most part, this was true. Although all news was controlled and propaganda shrewdly created, the military bulletins, from what I can determine after having read numerous historical accounts of World War II, reflected the facts. They were partial to the German cause, of course, and contained exaggerations to embellish victories and omissions to minimize defeats.

We had no access to any but the government-controlled press. We were forbidden to listen to foreign broadcasts and threatened with penalties for treason—which included death should we do so. Our sphere of information was a very isolated one.

Not even a teenager yet, not being aware of the insularity and never having lived under different conditions, I did not realize that strict measures to keep us isolated were in force. I accepted as a necessary safeguard the ban on listening to foreign broadcasts. There were times I found BBC "accidentally" while searching for stations with clear signals. I would turn down the volume to the lowest possible point and I, too, would listen to enemy news broadcasts. But this occurred during the last years of the war.

After Hitler had unleashed his *Blitzkrieg*,[33] I was glued to our radio every evening. The news started with the daily report issued by the *OKW*,[34] the German Armed Forces High Command. In addition, there were *Sondermeldungen,* special bulletins important enough to warrant the interruption of the regular program. Fanfares were interjected, followed by the announcements of significant victories, such as the one broadcast on September 4, 1939, proclaiming that German troops had crossed the entire Polish Corridor and set foot on Eastern Prussia. This province, severed from the *Reich* after World War I, had been reunited with the Fatherland. The news elated me. Probably starting at this time, I kept track of all special bulletins and kept notes of victories proclaimed.

On September 6th, our troops had conquered Krakow as well as Bromberg, a city in which Poles, supposedly, had murdered many Germans prior to the outbreak of the war. A victory bulletin, late in the evening of September 8th, proclaimed our forces had advanced into Warsaw, the Polish capital.

Fanfares upon fanfares! Victories upon victories! Jubilance upon jubilance!

At one of my visits with *Schuster* Stefan, now working late with regularity, he brought to my attention how much of a racial melting pot Poland had become during its turbulent history. While hammering fresh heels onto old shoes, he expressed concerns most Germans didn't realize.

Besides the *Volksdeutschen* (ethnic Germans), there were many Poles with a lot of German blood in their veins, he said. The population surrounding the city of Lodz was mostly of German stock although their names sounded Slavic. I forget how he had obtained such knowledge but remember him waiting to hear from some relatives belonging to an ethnic group known as *Weichseldeutsche* (Vistula Germans).

In a subtle way, just as the last battles were being fought, he made me realize that many racial mixtures were to be found within the Polish population, pointing out that—in reverse—many Silesians had Polish family names but were considered pure Germans. There was Polish blood in many Silesians. He named people in the neighborhood whose names I no longer recall. I also thought of Rudi then, my friend in first and second grade. He had a Polish-sounding name, but his father was tall and Nordic looking, as were Rudi's facial features.

Schuster Stefan, who for over a year now had been putting new heels and soles on my father's black boots, knew he was a member of the *SS*. I have a hunch, but no proof, he didn't approve. He might not have liked that I belonged to the *Jungvolk* or the great enthusiasm with which other boys and I followed the rapid military advances or how we belittled the Polish army due to their devastating defeats.

It was then *Schuster* Stefan quizzed me by asking questions about Nikolaus Kopernikus,[35] Marie Sklodowska,[36] Frederic Chopin,[37] and even Marshall Pulaski.[38] Perhaps he wanted me to realize that the derogatory term "Polacks," commonly used to refer to the Polish people, was inappropriate in view of all these notable Poles.

He could also have had in mind that the war with Poland had some aspects of a *Buergerkrieg*, a civil war. In those days, I didn't entertain such thoughts. I believed what I was expected to believe. The Poles were our enemies, they hated and massacred Germans, and they were now, deservedly, being defeated by our brave soldiers.

On October 16th, the news came that German and Russia troops had met at the agreed upon German-Russian *Interessengrenze* (sphere-of-influence border). The war was finished, and the occupation had been concluded. This military bulletin proclaimed itself as the last from the eastern front.

I remember literature in our home about *Wehrbauern* (armed farmers). Apparently an attempt was being made to recruit farmers to settle in the conquered territories. The pamphlet might have had something to do with my father's work at the radio station or might have been related to one of his many *SS* undertakings.

My father referred frequently to *Polnische Wirtschaft*, a metaphor used by Prussians to indicate disorder in Poland—if not outright subhuman conditions. He believed, as did many Germans, that following the *Wehrmacht's* (armed forces) decisive victory, things would be put in order.

My father was among many who emphasized that our *Fuehrer*, having eliminated the Polish Corridor, had removed another of the injustices caused by the Treaty of Versailles. Under its terms, Alsace and Lorraine had been ceded to France, the Saar Territory had been placed under French administration, and Poland had added most of West Prussia. All of Germany's colonies were placed under the rule of the League of Nations. To maintain this status, the Treaty had significantly limited the amount of troops and armaments and had put the extreme burden of reparation payments on Germany. These payments were one cause of the runaway inflation and economic collapse in the late twenties.

Not only to my father, but also to most Germans, revenge seemed so sweet, and it was Hitler who had, one by one, avenged most of the "injustices" of Versailles. That is what we had been taught. This satisfaction for righting past wrongs was shared by us, the young, perhaps with even more enthusiasm than most adults felt.

What about the treaties dictated by Hitler twenty years after the Treaty of Versailles? Following Germany's total victory over Poland, Hitler and Stalin agreed to annex Polish territory,[39] with the Russians gaining nearly 75,000 square miles in the East and the Germans over 70,000 square miles in the West.

Perhaps *Schuster* Stefan had realized that this treaty—signed in Moscow—contained conditions as catastrophic for Poland as those in the Versailles Treaty of 1919 had been for Germany. In his philosophical way, he stressed repeatedly that by replacing one injustice with another, no peaceful solution would be gained. Each revenge would provide a reason to be revenged again.

Meanwhile, Stalin, having gained Polish territory without any participation in the war, looked at Russia's northern border and ordered the Finns to demilitarize the Mannerheim Line,[40] facing Leningrad.[41] He demanded cession of key military bases. This small country, however, had the guts to refuse the demands of its mighty neighbor. It resulted in the winter campaign between the Soviet Union and Finland. The USSR had become an ally of Germany, but most of the German people were pro-Finland. Little was reported about this war that ended in March 1940.

***

It must have been in 1940, during summer vacation, that my uncle—Mother's oldest brother—was assigned as administrator to a large agriculture grange near Radom in the Warthegau.[42] His wife and children were still in Germany. While my sister Anje visited our aunt and cousins in Osterholz, near Bremen, I, a boy, was allowed to visit my uncle in occupied territory. It turned out to be an exciting experience.

One night we were attacked, supposedly by stray Polish soldiers still hiding in the woods. They were not out to kill Germans but in dire need of provision—food to keep them alive. My uncle and I, as well as the caretaker and a live-in maid, had to take refuge in the cellar. Outside, a gun-battle took place between our guards and the attackers. Seeing flashes coming from the guns of the attackers, I aimed my revolver, shooting through the cellar window in front of me.

Shattering the glass, some splinters must have been repelled (how, is still a mystery to me) and hit my face. I didn't feel any cuts from the sharp pieces of glass, but after awhile, I became aware of the blood running down my face. It was the Polish maid who put iodine and bandages on my gashes, and I felt as if I had received my first battle wounds at the age of 12.

My uncle, however, looked at my action with some distress. He scolded me. Through my action, I had revealed to the attackers that we occupied the cellar. I had endangered all of us. It was not up to me but to the guards to protect us in this type of situation.

Yet, I was allowed to keep my revolver for as long as I remained with my uncle. At home, the only weapon I possessed was an air rifle, a gift received from my father on my tenth or eleventh birthday. Through practice, I had become a good marksman. There was a big difference, of course, between shooting an air rifle and an army revolver, a *Mauser*, if I remember correctly. I had not been prepared for the recoil.

Later, after my aunt and the children had joined my uncle, an attack took place at noon. In a surprise attack, Polish partisans disarmed the guards. My uncle and a visiting forester (ranger) fired through the upper windows, while my aunt and the children huddled in a protective corner of the cellar and were spared. The whole family would have perished had not an off-duty guard been able to reach on horseback a nearby military unit. The unit arrived just in time to ward off the partisans before they stormed into the house.

Five years later, as we now know, the Red Army would liberate Poland. The Poles, in exchange for the territory lost to the Soviet Union in 1939, would occupy Silesia advancing all the way to the Neisse River. The German territory added in the West, made up for the region Stalin—with Hitler's blessings—had taken from them in the East in 1939. In the summer of 1940, however, when I was 12 years old, no one foresaw or dared to predict such an outcome of the war.

After Poland, France was defeated and Hitler's victories were seen as magnificent.

CHAPTER 23

My Heroes

At the age of eleven, I was a fairly good skier. I also had my first lessons in dressage horseback riding. Worried the war might be over before I was old enough to serve, I nevertheless, contemplated what branch I wanted to belong to and hoped the war would still be on. Initially, Klaus and I had fantasized of becoming fighter pilots or U-boat commanders. Later, I vacillated between the mountain troops and the cavalry. After reading reports I came to realize the Polish army had been an antiquated one. It consisted mostly of cavalry units. They had been beaten badly by our panzer forces. The future seemed to belong to armored troops. My love for horses would no longer be a good enough reason for wanting to join the cavalry. There might not even be one when I reached draft age.

At the conclusion of the fighting against Poland, special mention was made of the bravery and effectiveness of the mountain troops and their great contribution to the victorious campaign. I considered volunteering to join them. But this had to wait. One had to be 16 years old before volunteer applications for any branch of the armed forces would be officially accepted.

In the years to come, I changed my mind several times. The focus of my wishful anticipations would be altered by newly emerging luminary fighters as they were highlighted in newspaper stories and radio reports.

The heroic accomplishments by U-boat commanders, *Stuka*[43] divers, ace fighter pilots, non-commissioned reconnaissance patrol leaders, and field commanders resulted in a steadily growing number of *Ritterkreuze* (Knight's Crosses of the Iron Cross) being awarded by the *Fuehrer*. Klaus and I wanted to become *Ritterkreuztraeger* (bearers of the Knight's cross) too. At one point, probably before the invasion of Russia, we debated what course to take to accomplish this in the shortest possible time. What crystallized in my mind, more and more, was the wish to emulate one of the famous German fighter aces, Moelders or Galland.

Dive-bombers also became very famous and many a *Stuka*-pilot would be awarded the Knight's Cross. I still remember that during and after the Poland campaign, the German newsreel would show breathtaking *Stuka* attacks. The sharp, high-pitched, whistling sound of the bombers when diving would fill the theater with vibrations so abrasive it seemed we were not watching projections on a screen but were actually there.

The prolific U-boat commanders, Guenther Prien[44] and Otto Kretschmer,[45] achieved great victorious feats on the high seas, while the Luftwaffen aces, Werner Moelders and Adolf Galland, accomplished their feats in fierce aerial combat. These aces downed enemy aircraft in astonishing numbers, following the footsteps of the "Red Baron," World War I flying ace, Manfred Freiherr von Richthofen.

I had started a *Sammelalbum* (scrapbook) filled with newspaper and magazine clippings. It started with a thrilling report describing how Prien, in October of 1939, with his U-47 had penetrated the bight (bay) at Scapa Flow and sank the British battleship, Royal Oak. This was followed by a story about *Kapitaen* Kretschmer who then only 28 years old, commandeered U-99 that hunted down and torpedoed many a freighter en route to Britain. Kretschmer and his crew hit and tore open many British vessels conveying over 300,000 Allied tonnage to the bottom of the sea.

Kretschmer, as I read in a British historical account after the war, was nevertheless recognized as a thoughtful and gallant leader. He would, upon surfacing after his attacks, make special efforts to spot English sailors, and to save their lives—to the extent his small boat could accommodate prisoners. If needed, he would radio SOS rescue requests to friendly or even enemy vessels nearby, so the sailors still afloat might be saved.

The German military bulletins, with regularity, mentioned naval activities and victories, citing occasionally that prisoners were taken. This meant, of course, that enemy survivors had been rescued. What about the British? Would they, too, pick up German sailors from a sinking ship? For several weeks, no reports about Prien's or Kretschmer's U-boat activities had been forthcoming. They did not tell us that for over a month they had been missing. During this time, the German high command kept their disappearance a secret. I still remember how shocked I was when finally a report appeared about the loss of U-47.

It was shortly after Hitler's birthday. Tributes to the *Fuehrer* had been aired over the radio and published in newspapers. They emphasized what a great leader and *Feldherr* (field commander) he was, that soon he would bring the war to a victorious completion. He would finish his magnificent task of creating *Grossdeutschland* (Greater Germany)—which was destined to become the world's most powerful nation.

However, the first report about the loss of U-47 was distressing news. It underscored that the valiant *Kapitaen* Prien and his heroic crew were now being added to the names of all those who had sacrificed their lives for the Fatherland—to be preserved forever in the nation's sacred annals of heroism. Written with great pathos, it assured those already serving in the armed forces and those who would follow, that heroes, upon their deaths, would forever be revered. It galvanized my young soul.

Words such as heroic, fearless, steadfast, unwavering, courageous, valiant, glorious, majestic, noble, distinguished, lustrous were used as abundantly as possible, and increasingly in conjunction with death and dying. Death, even for the very young, was something to be embraced since it would leave behind memories of bravery and glory.

I don't think I nourished a death wish, but I had convinced

myself I had to be willing and prepared to die. My main concern was that I be given the opportunity to prove I was capable of bravery, perhaps even of becoming a hero. If the war lasted long enough, as I hoped it would, I, too, envisioned my name on the honor roll of the heroes who had fought in great battles so valiantly. I was immovably certain of a supreme German victory.

Prien perished in his U-47 when it was sunk on March 17, 1941. It was officially reported at the end of April, more than a month hence.

Kretschmer and his crew, upon being encircled, scuttled their boat and surrendered. This I learned over 20 years later. During the war, we had been conditioned to expect heroes to die heroic deaths and not to be taken prisoners. Brave German soldiers always fought to the bitter end. After their last bullet was shot, they mounted their bayonets and advanced to engage in man-to-man combat.

We learned that death does not diminish one who fights for his country. Such venerated patriotic notions forged our code of honor. As I see it now, the hero Kretschmer, in the eyes of the National Socialists, violated this code.

Lt. Commander Otto Kretschmer and his U-99 mariners were the remarkable team that had perfected the technique of infiltrating convoys and then committed surface attacks to the point that, at one such assault, they had sunk seven ships. These accomplishments were no longer written about as extensively as was written about the fallen commanders, Prien and Schepke. Although the contents of my scrapbook should have given me a clue, I didn't discover the truth of his surrender. A navy buff, a great admirer of Kretschmer, brought this to my attention long after World War II had ended.

The eminent historian Gilbert, mentions in his book *The Second World War*:[46]

> *The Atlantic sinkings greatly threatened Britain's ability to survive. But the counter measures were continuous. Not only was Guenther Prien and his U-47 sunk that month, but three*

> *more U-boats were destroyed. Two of Germany's leading subma-*
> *rine commanders, 'aces' in the destruction of merchant ship-*
> *ping, were also victims of a vigilant British naval response that*
> *March, Captain Joachim Schepke being drowned and Cap-*
> *tain Otto Kretschmer captured.*

Because of the way I was brought up, I subscribed to the *Fuehrer's* demand that German heroes were expected to die, not become prisoners. I never questioned it—or even if it was moral.

Lt. Commander Joachim Schepke, who had participated with Kretschmer in the last, fatal convoy action, had obviously chosen loyalty unto death and might have wanted to make the statement that a true captain never leaves his ship. Or he wanted to please Hitler. Or he died not wanting to become a prisoner.

All we will ever know is that he died a hero's death. He, having surfaced, was reported to have stood on the bridge. His craft was rammed and he was killed. That's how heroes die. Obviously, it had pleased the *Fuehrer.* Prien's and Schepke's tributes in the party-controlled newspapers by far exceeded Kretschmer's. The glory belonged to the fallen.

***

The first *Ritterkreuztraeger* (bearers of the Knight's Cross) of the *Luftwaffe* were two fighter aces—Majors Werner Moelders[47] and Adolf Galland.[48] Moelders was first to down 20 enemy planes. Galland, almost as fast-paced, also accumulated an ever-increasing number of "kills." Both men had previously distinguished themselves as squadron leaders in the Spanish Civil War, on Generalissimo Franco's side.

The number of officers and soldiers from all branches of the Armed Forces was increasing rapidly and so was the number of heroes performing heroic deeds. Hitler added accelerating grades to the Knight's Cross as follows: Knight's Cross with Oak Leaves, Knight's Cross with Oak Leaves and Swords, and Knight's Cross with Oak Leaves, Swords, and Diamonds.

Before the end of the war, Hitler added to the assemblage the Knight's Cross with Golden Oak Leaves, Swords and Diamonds. It was awarded only once, to the Silesian *Stuka* Pilot Col. Hans-Ulrich Rudel, who had become known as the *Panzervernichter* (armor destroyer). He was wounded five times, flew his last missions with a wooden leg, and destroyed a record total of 519 enemy tanks.

For Hermann Goering, who in World War I had received the then highest decoration for valor, the Pour-le-Merite, the *Fuehrer* had created the Grand Cross of the Iron Cross. He awarded it to his *Reichsmarshall* after the Battle of France, just before the effectiveness of the *Luftwaffe* began to dwindle.

One has to realize Hitler was not only a virtuoso, captivating orator but also a shrewd motivator. The more decorations could be earned, the higher the incentives were for the brave officers and soldiers to keep on risking their lives and to outdo themselves with deeds of valor.

We boys were greatly inspired by the many valiant fighters, and my scrapbook, filled with pictures and stories of fearless warriors, became thicker and thicker.

Why would a young boy have questioned Hitler's purpose and goals at that time? Hitler, not only supreme commander by virtue of his position as Head of State, had also assumed the function of Commander-in-Chief of the German Armed Forces. This enabled him to prove to his people he was not only a great *Fuehrer*, but also just as great a strategist.

My feelings, opinions, and judgment were based on how my parents, teachers, and friends reacted to the unfolding events and on what I heard on the radio and read in newspapers and magazines.

CHAPTER 24

The Written Word

My life was not solely occupied with the war. The fascinations of acting had gotten hold of me, and I had discovered the tantalizing impact of feature films. My parents were not in favor of my constant visits to movie theaters. I could, in my own mind, justify wanting to see all of the films shown. I was studying my craft. Moreover, through school and because of my participation in radio plays, I became ever more exposed to written art, especially drama and poetry.

Since I wrote poetry and some short stories, my interest in the written word increased. I pored over literature more and more, mostly at night in bed using a flashlight. After 10 p.m., my room light had to be turned off. I remember reading sometimes until 2:00 a.m. and having to get up four hours later at 6:00 a.m.

Germany's greatest poet was, of course, Johann Wolfgang von Goethe,[49] a universal genius. One of his first dramas, based on the memoirs of Goetz von Berlichingen,[50] became a favorite on the stages of German theaters during the time of the Third *Reich*. His plays *Egmont, Iphigenie of Tauris* and of course *Faust*, his masterpiece of Olympian proportion, were produced continually, even by small theaters of which Germany had (and again has) many.

No dramatist performed in Germany at the time of my youth made as deep and stirring an impression on me as Friedrich von Schiller's[51] *Die Raeuber (The Robbers)*. Schiller, confronted in his youth with the hardships and injustices caused by the use and abuse of power, had written this play in protest.

In it, a vital, high-spirited student, Karl Moor, is disowned by his unyielding father and betrayed by his brother who had plotted against him. Karl's rebellious reaction results in his becoming a leader of a gang of robbers. With enthusiasm, he plotted insurrection. However, due to his upbringing and because of his intellect, Karl comes to realize that, although the laws of the land are corrupt, to oppose them with violence and anarchy would defeat his aim to improve conditions. Thus, his reasoning power prevails and he gives himself up to justice. The play is a scathing indictment of a society that drove someone, fundamentally noble in character, to crime before he realized wrongdoing does not restore right conditions.

What a play to have seen at a young age when ideas of idealism filled one's mind! And how uplifting it was. It mirrored despicable conditions of the past, similar to those that—as we had been taught—Hitler had changed.

Later, I saw a film about Schiller with Horst Caspar in the leading role. His captivating portrayal of the great poet and playwright brought Schiller, his life and his work, even closer to my heart. My parents' library contained the biography, *The Life of Schiller*, which I read (I don't recall the name of the author). I read it before I saw the film. I was fascinated by the way Schiller's life unfolded and by the hardships he had to endure.

The poet's father had been a captain, an army physician in the services of Karl Eugene, Duke of Wuerttemberg. The Duke—who found the captain's son to be very bright—ordered young Schiller to be entered as a cadet in his *Kadettenanstalt* (military school). Instead of his chosen subject, theology, Schiller was mandated by the reigning ruler to undergo early military training.

The strict, soldierly discipline of the school intensified in him a spirit of rebellion that nurtured first on Rousseau[52] and consequently on the emerging *Sturm und Drang*[53] poets.

Schiller finished *The Robbers* before he graduated. Upon commencement, Schiller became a regimental physician in one of the

Duke's military units garrisoned in Stuttgart. From his meager pay, he saved enough to self-publish his play.

It was first performed in the National Theater of Mannheim. To attend opening night, Schiller had to secretly steal away from his post in Stuttgart. The performance was successful beyond imagination, and Schiller went on to become one of Germany's great poets.

What fascinated me at the time (and perhaps in a sense gave me hope) was that even a great poet and dramatist such as Schiller had found no encouragement in his youth to become a writer.

I had written "*Ode to Schiller*" shortly after I had seen *Die Raeuber*. A year or so later, I wrote "Ode to Gerhart Hauptmann"[54] upon seeing his play *The Weavers*. It also dramatized an uprising of the spirit. A strike of workers in Silesia's textile industry ended up being squelched by military force. This drama projected human misery and the misfortunes of the less privileged.

Such conditions were no longer prevalent in Germany because of Hitler, who had brought about drastic social changes. There were no more uprisings of weavers or any other groups of workers during the Third *Reich*. The Communists, we were told, were being detained in concentration camps because their subversive activities had undermined the productivity of the *Reich*'s workforce. That these inmates were treated inhumanely was never mentioned, nor ever imagined by me.

***

I must have questioned if the Communists would be released as a result of the Friendship Pact signed between Germany and the Soviet Union, because I remember my mother saying: "We don't want Communists in Germany, even German Communists are dangerous."

Since I had not known any Communists or where they had lived, I was not cognizant of their fate or whether any of them were released and came home. My mother pointed out that German

Communists received their orders from Moscow and that Communist parents taught their children there was no God. My grandfather was not the only one in our family who did not understand the Hitler-Stalin pact. Neither did my mother.

I did not know until after the war that one of my uncles had a girlfriend who was a Communist, The book *Das Kapital* by Karl Marx[55] was talked about but was not available for reading. Neither were there books by or about Friedrich Engels or Vladmir Lenin in my father's library. The only political books were those about National Socialism.

The poets and writers that impressed my young mind were those works that had the blessing of the regime. I had heard at one time and another about the book burning of May 10, 1933, which had turned into ashes so many literary works. Since they were no longer available, I had no access to them. Despite my natural sense of curiosity, it was not until after the war I would devour many of them.

The literature I read during the Third *Reich* ranged from the classics to writers who celebrated the struggle and "back-to-the-soil" movement—such as Loens, Dahn, Miegel, Hamsun, Trenker, Wiechert, Zoeberlein, Juenger, and Dwinger, among others. I also read Karl May, who wrote about North-American Indians without ever having visited the United States, Canada, or Mexico.

Erich Maria Remarque was not even known to me then. I didn't read his book, *All Quiet On the Western Front*, until 1946, when more and more of the once-forbidden books were published again in occupied Germany. It was one of the books burned when I was only five years old. It described war realistically, not heroically.

Pacifist novels were considered unsuitable for German youth to read, as were many other important works by such authors as Albert Einstein, Thomas Mann, Sigmund Freud, Romain Rolland, Arnold Zweig, Lion Feuchtwanger, Heinrich Heine, to name just a few. Not until 1946-47 were there opportunities for me to get acquainted with the works of these important authors.

CHAPTER 25

1940

1939 and 1940 had been years of ongoing, spectacular German victories. But for me personally, 1940 was also a year of disappointments. Sudden, severe abdominal pain caused me to collapse on the street, and I was taken to a hospital where an emergency appendectomy had to be performed. I was out of school for almost four weeks and missed out on two major roles in radio plays already in rehearsal at that time.

My neighborhood friend Kurt, who owned the motorcycle and who had been the keeper of the soccer ball that I had secretly acquired, joined the *Wehrmacht*. (I don't remember ever taking the ball home. It must have remained in Kurt's garage).

This was also the year my father expected me to become an Adolf Hitler *Schueler* (student of an Adolf Hitler School). In the *Jungvolk* I had already become one of the youngest *Jungzugfuehrer* (leader of 30 to 40) in our *Faehnlein* (unit of more than 100).[56] Moreover, having just reached the qualifying age of 12, I had completed in rapid succession all of the requirements for obtaining the *DJ-Leistungsabzeichen*, the *Jungvolk* proficiency badge. This was duly recorded in my *DJ-Leistungsbuch*, the qualification booklet in which all of the necessary achievements had been noted.

Still, I wasn't even selected to be given the entrance examination for the Adolf Hitler School. My father's conditioning had been in vain. My friend, Dieter Heinrich, was among those selected, who ended up fulfilling the examination requirements. I was, once again, a failure. I remained *"ein schwacher Kerl"* (a feeble fellow).

As such, I was taken with the accomplishments of Germany's heroes, which emerged in rapidly increasing numbers.

On the battlefields, wherever our forces fought, they won. That was the ongoing news. If there were minor setbacks somewhere, immediate counterattacks took place. Defeats on land were never mentioned. Were there none? When losses of aircraft and navy vessels were announced, they were usually compared with those suffered by the enemy. Ours appeared to be few, theirs sizeable.

***

The dying on the battlefield was reflected in *Todesanzeigen* (death announcements) that appeared in newspapers. In Germany, it was—and as far as I know it still is—the custom to place in the newspaper, upon someone's death, a display ad. This ad, often with a cross on top, named the deceased, his or her standing in society, and listed honors, medals, and awards received. Often, expressions of love and appreciation followed, before the names of the surviving relatives were listed.

The wording of these death-notices became more patriotic, with phrases being used such as: "fallen for *Fuehrer*, people and the Fatherland." Others might say: "fallen for Adolf Hitler and our eternal Germany."

Of course the dead soldiers were buried far away, on or near the battlefields where they had died. In local cemeteries, memorial plaques were erected whereupon the names of the fallen were inscribed.

Everyone who died on the battlefield was declared a *Held* (hero) and the official *Heldentod* (hero's death) notices were hand-delivered—at least at the beginning of the war. It was frequently the case in our immediate neighborhood. They were usually delivered by an officer and expressed Hitler's sympathy—as if he kept track of individual casualties.

I attended one memorial service in an evangelical church for a soldier from our neighborhood who had lost his life in Poland. The pastor glorified him as a great military hero. However, the family, through a comrade of his, learned he had been killed behind the lines.

Soldiers who died, no matter how, deserved to be ennobled. Looked upon as heroes, their next of kin were assured of their immortality. Death at the beginning of the war was treated with great dignity.

Not so at the end of the trouncing, when soldiers and civilians ended up in cauldrons of slaughter. Death, first looked upon as the highest, most sacred offering, had become commonplace. By then, my comrades who fell were left with no crosses and no helmets above their final resting places.

If graves were dug, they were left unmarked.

***

An annual book, *Die Wehrmacht* (The Armed Forces) was published by the government. One, titled *The Freedom Fight of the Great-German People*, emphasized how Germany regained its freedom. Another one, *For Europe's Freedom*, drove home the message that our soldiers were not only fighting for Germany, but for all of Europe—a new Europe!

What we had been told was that the first twelve months of the war had been devoted to disengaging Germany from the chains of the Treaty of Versailles, while the second year of the war was being fought to free Europe from British Imperialism and, after the invasion of Russia, from the threat of Bolshevism.

Before Hitler invaded Russia, he had exchanged Lithuania for the Lublin area and the territory up to the line of the Bug River. This trade surprised even my father. He rationalized that it must have been a "political necessity." With his fanatic idealism, he never showed the slightest doubt about the rightness of any of the *Fuehrer's* decisions.

***

Danzig and West Prussia again belonged to Germany. A newly formed province called *Warthegau* also became part of the *Reich*. The rest of Poland was placed under the callous rule of a German Governor. He was Hans Frank,[57] a law professor who, in his early thirties, had been appointed president of the Academy of German Law.

His declaration that love of the *Fuehrer* had become a concept in German law was quoted in textbooks. Frank not only embraced the new ideology fully, he also saw to it that our young minds, throughout the nation, were effectively indoctrinated.

Later, during the proceedings at Nuremberg, I became aware that the same Hans Frank, who wanted us to love Hitler, had exerted from his palace in Krakau (now spelled Kraków) a master-race rule that was savage and barbarous. He viewed conquered Poland as a German colony and Poles as nothing but slaves. By his own admission,[58] over ten thousand of them were sent to forced labor camps.

Poles in western Poland were expelled from their houses and from the land they owned. The entire region was resettled by ethnic Germans—many from the Baltic States.

***

Such was the propaganda following the occupation of Denmark and Norway. Hitler had outwitted Churchill and had beaten the British to the punch. Denmark, with no choice but to agree to the occupation, remained friendly, we were made to believe. In Norway, we were told, many Norwegians were as "German-friendly" as the Danes. The King and the government, however, sided with the British and some Norwegian units put up bitter struggles, especially around Narvik.

Mountain troops were engaged in hostilities and I followed with avid interest the German victories there. Another Great War hero would emerge, Eduard Dietl,[59] leader of the German mountain troops.

Hitler had Vidkun Quisling installed as the new head of the Norwegian government and hailed him as a great, foresighted leader. Quisling shared Hitler's vision of a powerful United Europe.

Today, the name Quisling is a commonly used synonym for betrayal.

Many Danish and Norwegian young men believed in Hitler's ideal of a great United Europe dominated by the Nordic race. They volunteered and fought in units especially established for them on Germany's side as members of the *Waffen-SS*.[60]

At the end of the war, I personally encountered not only Danes and Norwegians but also French members of the *Waffen-SS* defending Hitler in his last command post, the Berlin Bunker.

In May of 1940, Hitler gave notice to the Belgium and Dutch governments that he wanted to protect them. Yes, protect them. That's how we were guided to think. France, of course, had declared war but as yet, remained in a defensive position. Now, two German army groups crossed the borders of Luxembourg, Belgium and the Netherlands and continued across the rivers Meuse and Somme to the Channel coast. This time, Germany's troops, having returned to the fields of Flanders, could not be stopped. Holland fell in five days. As was the case during the Polish Campaign, one *Sondermeldung* (special victory bulletin) would follow the next. I still kept track of them and my list grew and grew.

***

On my birthday (May 23, 1940), Dunkirk was mentioned for the first time. On its coast, a British destroyer had been sunk. The British and French had decided to reinforce the Belgians and were trapped. Five days later the Belgian king capitulated. The French and British kept on fighting—but not for long. I remember the enormous number of British ships reported as having been sunk at Dunkirk, at the end of May and in the beginning of June. We, at home, had no indication the British had been able to evacuate the majority of their expedition forces, leaving only their heavy weapons behind. The German troops conquered Dunkirk on the 4th of June.

Later that same day, a special bulletin proclaimed that the "Fortress Dunkirk," after heavy fighting, had been taken. Forty thousand enemy soldiers had surrendered, among them three generals.

On June 6th, it was reported the number of POWs had increased to 58,000. On June 8th, a further increase of prisoners, to 88,000, was officially announced.

Then, no more mention of Dunkirk and not even an estimate of how many members of the British expedition force might have been able to get away and back to their homeland.

Once again, it was not until after the war that I found out in detail what had happened. The British sea borne operation was successful in evacuating a large number of the encircled British and French troops. This indicated that the Germans fell short of "finishing" the war on the Western front. Hitler, I learned, had ordered his tanks to stop. It wasn't a humanitarian gesture by a victorious leader to save lives. No, Goering[61] had convinced the *Fuehrer* that the *Luftwaffe* could finish the job and avert any large-scale evacuation.

Casualties inflicted were great, but the rescue mission succeeded. Britain's Vice-Admiral Ramsay had successfully organized a fleet of small craft that included a sizable flotilla of French fishing boats.

The *Luftwaffe* did sink six British and three French destroyers, along with 56 other ships and over 150 small craft. The Royal Air Force lost over 100 aircraft. But before, during, and after the German air attacks, nearly 340,000 Allied soldiers had been able to cross the channel and reach the coast of England.

What I remember specifically about this time was a victory bulletin that had nothing to do with the Western Front. It announced that *Generalleutnant* Eduard Dietl's mountain troops had achieved final victory in Narvik, Norway. I looked it up. The date was June 10th. The British forces had been driven out and the remaining Norwegian troops had capitulated. I cheered for the *Gebirgsjaeger*, the mountain soldiers.

HM

CHAPTER 26

Many Fronts

To the complete surprise of many people in Germany, and for sure of everyone in our family, on June 22, 1941, Hitler invaded Russia.

I did not know then that Soviet forces had occupied Northern Bukovina and Bessarabia in Rumania. I do remember the Russian takeover of the Baltic countries. My uncle had been affected by the fate of those German families from Estonia, Latvia and Lithuania. These families had arrived in the province annexed from Poland and were settled there. The branches of the government responsible to coordinate and prepare for the resettlement had messed up. The new settlers had arrived ahead of schedule. Conditions were miserable. Some, according to my uncle, ended up feeling sorry for the Poles and became disgusted with the Germans that had been put in charge. These beer-belly party officials were nicknamed "gold-pheasants" because of their lustrous uniforms and because they did not live up to the expected efficiency of Prussian officialdom.

Prior to the unexpected Russian invasion, and one week after the swastika flag had been hoisted atop the Eiffel Tower, Hitler and his staff arrived at the rail car in the forest of Compiegne where, 22 years earlier, Germany's WWI defeat had been sealed. His goal was to take revenge and to reverse the situation.

The newsreel of this event must have been held over, because I saw it several times. And, every time, a feeling of great triumph rushed through me. I shared in the joy of this great victory. It filled me with pride.

With a new French government formed by Marshal Petain[62] willing to cease fighting, the signing of the Armistice had taken place in the same railroad car used by the Allies after World War I.

The German press, and especially the newsreel, reported the event of this great historic victory exhaustively as a momentous triumph in German history. Most of the credit was given to Hitler. He was declared to be the greatest general of all time, and with my limited knowledge of history, I had no reason for questioning such judgment.

The waves of acclaim and accolades were momentous. The fact Mussolini had entered the war on Germany's side seemed just another progressive development. It had been expected for some time because of the heralded friendship between the *Fuehrer* and *Il Duce.*

Only later, when Italy got into trouble in Greece and needed German help, did I sense that Italian and German forces performed differently. Then, although not in our home, some derogatory remarks and jokes began to circulate that "spaghetti soldiers had no backbone," that most of them, in fact, were more concerned with staying alive. Many German soldiers, when fighting next to Italian units, were concerned about their faintheartedness in battle. Since soldiers from the front confirmed this, there may have been some truth to it.

My father, I remember clearly, had anticipated that an invasion of the British Isles would follow soon and England would be defeated just as swiftly as France was. In fact, he claimed to have been involved in some aspects of the planning. The code name for the operation was "Sea Lion."

It never materialized. The invasion of the British Isles was postponed. And postponed again. And in the end, never took place.

Why my father would have had access to secret military information while still a civilian, he never revealed.

After the war, he mentioned only that one of the initial objectives would have been to take over and, if necessary, rebuild the BBC[63] facilities.

My father had a sparse knowledge of Latin, spoke some French, but hardly any English. Had Hitler invaded the British Isles, my father's assignment could not have involved broadcasts aimed for the British. I wanted to know what his designation could have been, but he never elaborated. With him, what had been secret remained secret.

In 1941, after the war reached the Balkans, not only young men of German heritage but from various national backgrounds, even Moslems, became volunteers in such *Waffen-SS* (military *SS* units) as the divisions of *Prinz Eugen, Skanderbeg, Kama*, and others (See Appendix B). According to testimony given years later at the Nuremburg Trials, these military *SS* units (before they were reduced by heavy losses or annihilated) included roughly 300,000 *Volksdeutsche* (ethnic Germans) and 200,000 *Auslaender* (foreigners). All met the rigid qualification requirements of these elite units.

The war on the Balkan proceeded rapidly. Following the events was like a geography lesson of the various countries involved.

Italy invaded Albania so that they could attack Greece. Greek forces, however, counterattacked bravely and were successful in driving the Italian forces back into Albania. This must have alarmed Hitler, who put pressure on all of the Balkan states to strengthen Germany's presence. Permanent access to the oil fields located in southeast Europe was vital to keep his war machine fueled. This was discussed openly. Everyone who expressed an opinion in my presence approved of the *Fuehrer's* aim to capture all of the available oil fields in the Balkan and in the Soviet Union. "Wheels need to be turned for victory" was one of the slogans displayed on posters, accelerating the war effort. To turn wheels required fuel.

***

In the fall of 1941, Rumania and Slovakia joined the Axis alliance (the Tripartite Pact of Germany, Italy and Japan). Rumania's General Antonescu,[64] after he had established a dictatorship, became a familiar figure in German propaganda.

Initially, Bulgaria had refused to join the Axis alliance but, later, was pressured into it. Yugoslavia joined at first but then denounced its decision. Angry, Hitler reacted with a successful offensive and conquered the country within one week.

Thereupon, Hitler awarded Yugoslavian provinces to Hungary and Bulgaria for having supported his invasion and his campaign against Greece. The invasion of Greece started on the 6th of April 1941. My only recollection about the fighting in Greece involves an officer who spoke to our *Jungzug* unit in 1941 and mentioned that he had fought against Commonwealth soldiers from as far as Australia and New Zealand. It made a great impression on me. This distinguished troop leader, on leave after he had been severely wounded, made it a point to impress upon us that the British had a knack for finding others to fight for them.

Hitler recruited volunteers from many countries in occupied Europe. He attracted those who were eager to join. They fought with commitment for the ideals Hitler stood for. They believed these ideals would, in the end, benefit them and their families and create a united Europe. They felt that they were privileged to have been given the opportunity to die for such a great cause.

During this time, I read a book about Lt. Col. Paul von Lettow-Vorbeck[65] who, in WWI, had commandeered the triumphant colonial forces of German East African Colonial Forces. Ironically, his soldiers had not only been from another country, but had been black soldiers—yes, native Africans. And they had been victorious.

But we were in WW II now. On the Balkan with Hitler's blessings, a Croation republic was formed in 1942 led by a Roman Catholic, Ante Pavelic.[66] Under his rule, over half a million people were murdered, most of them Orthodox Serbs. They had been given a choice between rebaptism and death.

Many Jews were killed as well. Few, if any, of the Germans at home were aware that such brutal acts were committed by us or by our newly appointed leaders there.

As revealed recently, Pavelik had, during his rule, awarded Kurt Waldheim, later to become Secretary General of the United Nations

(1972-1981), with a medal in recognition of his accomplishments. Over 2,000 partisans had been killed and thousands of peasants had been rounded up and shot or forced into slave labor. Waldheim, of course, denied responsibility for any of these atrocities. He would later become the revered President (1986-1992) of his country. Surprisingly, he was a first-generation Austrian. His father, a Czech, had immigrated and Germanized his Slavic name from Waclawik to Waldheim.

***

In 1942, German troops were occupying Yugoslavia and dispatching paratroopers into Greece to bail out Mussolini's tottering troops. They were also coming to the aid of Italy in the Western Desert, preventing the Italian army from being forced out of Libya by the Allied forces. This would have endangered the German troops that, since the victory over France, occupied Tunisia.

The *Deutsche Afrika Korps* (German Africa Corps) made headlines and a new hero emerged—Field Marshal Rommel. I would follow his initial victories very closely because an uncle of mine, my mother's youngest brother Joachim, served under him. Both my uncle and I became great admirers of Field Marshal Rommel. I listened to the news and read, in awe, the glowing reports written about him and his heroic men. The British called Rommel the "Desert Fox." I did not hear this expression until after the war.

My uncle, who had been a professional *Reichsarbeitsdienstfuehrer* (RAD), a *Reich* Labor Service leader, served under Rommel as a supply sergeant. It was he who told me that the soldiers often feared their commander as much as they revered him and they considered him very brave. He was always up front and, several times, he narrowly escaped capture by the British. The pace and surprise elements of his maneuvers became legendary.

When he received the Knight's Cross of the Iron Cross, Rommel, according to my uncle, dedicated this decoration to all members of his troops. He expressed his thanks in a declaration, stating that their achievements would forever provide them with proud memories.

Eventually forced to yield to an army far superior in strength, Rommel extricated his army. He waited for replacements for lost manpower, weapons, and ammunition. His faith in Hitler began to crumble when the *Fuehrer* refused to authorize this strategic withdrawal, nor did he provide the needed arms and manpower. This ruled out a victorious completion of the desert war.

Rommel returned from Africa but did not survive the war. Although not instrumental in the attempt to assassinate Hitler, he, after realizing that Germany could not win this war, had been willing to seek peace and to assume a leadership role, had the plot been successful.

Hitler was informed that one of the conspirators, Lt. Col. Caesar von Hofacker, under torture, had blurted out Rommel's name. Still, Hitler decided against having his popular Field Marshal executed on the spot. He realized that Rommel had become a "folk hero." He decided to give him the choice of facing a public trial by the "People's Court," or of committing suicide—with his death to be ascribed to his war injuries.

For the benefit of his family and, probably, for all the men who had served under him, Rommel chose the latter. Hitler, in turn, awarded him a state funeral.

My uncle, after the war, related to me the fate of his former commander. He never mentioned, however, that prior to leading the Africa Corps in 1939, Rommel had been commander of Hitler's special field headquarters. During the war against Poland, he had been at his *Fuehrer's* side constantly. Rommel, who had been awarded the *Pour-le-Merite* in World War I, wanted to see action again. By then one of Hitler's favored generals, he was given command of an armored division. He distinguished himself as a tactician in France, before he became commander of the Africa Corps.

Based on entries in his own diaries, as preserved in the *Rommel Papers* (Collins, 1953), Rommel admired Hitler greatly up to the very time when he felt finally betrayed.

Even before the war had ended, my uncle, at his last visit to his parents in Goerlitz, stated that the *Fuehrer* had left the Africa *Korps* in the lurch. He held his Field Commander in higher regard than his Commander-in-Chief. And I remember that it was my grandmother who warned him not to express his feelings publicly since an informer could turn him in. My uncle could have been condemned to death for making such mutinous remarks.

CHAPTER 27

Jungvolk Camp

At the beginning of the unexpected invasion of Russia, there was at first a news blackout so that the Soviet leadership wouldn't know how far the German troops had advanced.

There was also a *Heimatfront* (home front).

We had gotten used to *Verdunkelung* (blackout), which was enforced from dusk to dawn. Motorcar headlights were covered with black paint except for very narrow slits at the center. During night hours, traffic was slow. To walk was difficult at times.

We boys of the *Jungvolk* made contributions. At street crossings, we painted the curbs white so that they could be seen better in the dark. We also helped with outfitting air raid shelters and practiced putting gas masks on and off.

In Breslau, however, sirens only wailed for tests a couple of times and no actual air raids took place until the very end of the war. Our city was not located within flying range of the British or American bombers, and the Soviet Air Force didn't wage their first bombing attack until three years later at the end of October 1944. It was minor compared to the massive raids by the Allies on many German cities.

In that October 1944 bombing of Breslau, I remember that my mother and I left the air raid shelter to see if something was going on. We saw so-called "Christmas trees" (light flares) and heard some distant flak fire, but saw none of the planes or explosions from the few bombs they had dropped.

By the start of the Russian Campaign, we also became used to food rationing. There were several cards for different products. My mother, of course, kept all of the cards issued to our family, except sometimes she would hand over to me a *Reichsbrotkarte (Reich* bread card) with 50 gram[67] stamps on it so that, when very hungry, I could buy myself rolls or even sweet-rolls in a bakery. On my way to school or the *Jungvolk* service or on errands, I often would become very hungry. A typical brown-bag lunch taken to school usually consisted of a couple of slices of rye bread with a thin spread of lard or just marmalade on it. No wonder it didn't satisfy for very long.

Ration cards in Germany would become, as the war went on, even more valuable than money.

My mother could be strict too! Once I lost my precious, orange-colored bread card. I had to wait until the new ones were issued before she gave me a ration card again.

"Hunger will teach you a lesson not to be so careless with your ration card!" She was right. It never happened again. Throughout my life, I have handled money and objects of value with great care, even though at the end of the war our family had lost nearly everything. I wore torn clothes taken off dead soldiers. It did not change my attitude to look after what I possessed, no matter how small or what little value it had.

We were not only issued ration cards that entitled us to buy food, but *Reichskleiderkarten*—clothing cards, as well.

Seldom did we children wear ready-made apparel in our family—with a few exceptions such as uniforms for *Jungvolk* and *Jungmaedel.*[68] My mother mostly bought materials and had a seamstress make our clothing, getting more out of the allocations than if she had bought at Wertheims, the large department store. The seamstress made jackets, pants and shirts for me and dresses, skirts and blouses for my sisters. Since I was the oldest, there were no hand-me-downs for me. With my three sisters, the second inherited from the first and the third from the second. My brother, ten years younger than I, was still too young to wear anything I had outgrown.

Shoes were always bought one size too large. I would often wear two pairs of socks—something my grandfather had recommended from as far back as when we lived in the woods.

Big shoes didn't bother me, but I remember distinctly that most of what the seamstress had sewn for us did not fit at first. It was too loose and not as becoming as we wished it to be. The standard reply to any lamentations was always "soon you will grow into it." And we did—although, my favorite outfit to wear in those days was my *Jungvolk* uniform. It fit.

***

Two lasting memories I have are of events that took place in a *Jungvolk* camp. I am no longer able to pinpoint the exact time, but it must have been during autumn recess of 1940 or '41 (the previous year, we were sent to farmers to help harvest potatoes).

Somewhere, east of Breslau, we arrived at a designated site and pitched our tents before it turned dark. We built a campfire, sat in front of it on the ground, and sang songs. Not the type of songs we used to sing when marching, but mostly folk songs, some quite old.

Of the songs of the *Bewegung* (movement), our own Baldur von Schirach, former *Reich* Youth Leader, wrote three. One was *"Vorwaerts! Vorwaerts!"* (Move on! Move on!). The second was *"Stellt Euch um die Standarte Rund"* (Assemble all Around the Banner). The third one was *"Unsere Fahne flatter uns voran"* (Our Flag Leads Us On)*, which became the banner song of the Hitler Youth. Von Schirach had written the lyrics while contemporary musicians, Borgmann and Blumensaat, had composed the melodies.

Many of the then contemporary songs were written by a lyricist/composer, Hans Baumann. I recall his songbook called *Hans Trommel der Rebellen (Drums of the Rebels).*

Songs had a unifying effect, whatever they expressed.

The two specific events that happened during this camping trip were both marked by personal accomplishments. Twice, I came off with flying colors.

The first one was a *Stockdegen* (cane-sword) tournament. My friend, Dieter Heinrich, had owned a pair of cane-swords, and for almost two years before he went to the Adolf Hitler School in Wartha, we frequently dueled at his home. He usually outscored me. I had not practiced recently (since Dieter left Breslau) and I was concerned I might be rusty. It turned out, however, I was in great form.

My opponent was from another *Jungvolk Unit* and on each side our comrades rooted for us. My supporters yelled themselves hoarse.

"Armin!—Armin!—Armin!" I heard them roar. This caused me to really concentrate and to focus on winning. And I won! Klaus Schauermann wasn't at this camp either since he belonged to another *Faehnlein,* the one located in the inner city. Without these two rivals present, I ended up being unbeatable.

Horseback riding and fencing were among the noble sports of the elite and cane-sword dueling was, of course, a preparation for young boys that would later lead to swordsmanship. How proud I was of this victory.

The second event at this particular camp—it has stayed in my mind so vividly—was a beginner-type survival exercise that, as was later determined, shouldn't even have taken place.

After we had completed our morning run and washed up with cold water, we had breakfast. Thereafter, we had to fill our backpacks and were given an emergency food pack called *eiserne Ration* (iron ration or K ration).

First we marched on the road and then halted. What now?

A *Gelaendeuebung* (terrain exercise) was to follow.

We were taken on a three or four kilometer off-road hike. Our unit leader zigzagged with us through the woods until we reached a small stream, rippling between the tall pine trees. The many turns were intentional—meant to confuse us. It worked. Even those among us who claimed to have good direction sense were at odds as to which direction our camp was located.

The stream was our resting and turnaround point. There we took off our backpacks, filled our *Feldflaschen* (water bottles, hooked on to our belts) with fresh water and as there were no toilet facilities, disappeared behind trees.

Some of the boys' feet hurt already, a few had blisters and received bandages. Our leaders all had first aid kits in their well-organized backpacks.

My feet were in good shape as I wore shoes that were well broken in. *Schuster* Stefan had just put new soles and heels on them. As the shoes were big enough, I had put on two pair of woolen socks, as my grandfather had taught me. They provided extra cushioning and lessened the chance of rubbing off skin. To this day, I buy hiking shoes big enough for me to wear very thick woolen socks.

Refreshed but hungry, we were broken up into separate *Jungenschaften*, platoon-size units. Now, the challenge was to find, in these separate units, our way back to the camp and not to touch the *eiserne Ration* we had with us, but instead, to find food in the forest. The young leaders of these small groups—of which I was one—were given each a compass and a topographic map that indicated where we were and where our tents were located.

One of the older leaders was assigned to each group to observe—but not to assist—unless we got totally lost and did not make it back to the camp by dusk.

What a challenge! Woods everywhere. An environment I felt versed in. To mind came the hike I had taken with my dog on my eighth birthday using the new gift of a knapsack. This time I didn't have a dog to show me how to return, but I had a map and a compass and was able to determine the direction we would follow.

We were sent off in ten to fifteen minute intervals, and I had volunteered to leave last with my little troop. This provided us with valuable preparatory time. Without having had lunch, we were hungry, of course, but determined not to touch our *eiserne Ration*.

My ability to identify mushrooms and knowing which ones were edible and which ones were poisonous paid off again—just as it had years ago, when in grade school, our class went into the

woods on a field trip. I had been able to identify all the mushrooms we found. The same mushrooms that grew in the woods
west of Breslau grew in the woods east of Breslau. I knew them all.

I separated the "good" ones from the "bad" again, with absolute
certainty.

No one had seen any berry bushes, but we had passed some
clearings with patches of grass. It was safe to eat but not very pal-
atable. But wouldn't we find sorrels there and an abundance of
dandelions? I knew they tasted very bitter except for the very young
leaves, so we had to be selective.

After half an hour of gathering mushrooms (we found mostly
yellow boletus), sorrel and dandelion leaves, we built a fire and
roasted the mushrooms on sticks and with it ate the greens we had
found.

Everything went according to plan. Although our wilderness
nourishment was not very satisfying, it enabled us to save our
emergency rations, and it instilled in us a sense of confidence.

After our improvised survival fare, we unhesitatingly made our
way straight to the road that led back to the camp. We were the
first to arrive, just before a downpour. Our comrades in the other
groups had run into each other and, united, arrived at least a quarter
of an hour later, all together.

On our way, we had never seen any of the groups that had left
ahead of us, so they must have veered early and taken a wrong
direction until they got back on course. They were delayed and, at
the end, were caught in a sudden rain shower. Returning soaking
wet, some of them were visibly disgruntled. I do not recall exactly
what was said, but those few boys who were openly discontented
were given to understand they did not measure up to our leader's
expectations.

After we returned home, a few boys came down with colds
and some of the parents complained. It was determined our
Faehnleinfuehrer, the responsible leader for the backpack hike, had
indeed violated the directives for camp activities and had no authority to conduct this type of survival training with boys our age.

My parents, however, were not among those who found fault, which pleased me. I had enjoyed the challenge. Above all, I savored how my little group had emerged as the winning team. It had given me a boost of confidence and a sense of achievement.

It is difficult to say if I realized then how my feelings of insecurity and inadequacy could be overcome more easily when I was away from home. The Hitler Youth tenet that youth must be led by youth applied to the *Jungvolk* too, and—I am certain—had a beneficial effect on my ability to cope with the trials of growing up.

I cherished every opportunity to prove myself among my peers. Receiving their approval lifted my spirits. In marksmanship, as a performer in radio plays, and, later with my writing and photography, I attained some recognition. Now, I had been successful at a cane sword tournament and had finished ahead of all others in the path finding showdown.

The camp leader, who had to face a disciplinary board, was found guilty of several violations, including that he had taken us on this exercise without rain gear. My father secured a written statement from the radio station's meteorologist for the day of our exercise—no rain had been in the forecast. Did it help my *Faehnleinfuehrer*? If there was punishment, I am sure it wasn't a monetary fine.

That wasn't the way things worked in those days. The camp leader was probably reprimanded for the infractions and sent for instructions to the *Akademie fuer Jugendfuehrung* (Academy for Youth Leadership) to study the directives contained in the Hitler Youth manuals. This, however, is merely an assumption of mine. I am only sure this leader, whom I liked, was not removed.

A year later, he was promoted, and shortly thereafter he changed uniforms and became a soldier, having to advance through boot camp. Later, he lost his life on the battlefield. That I still remember him is a tribute to the challenge he had provided me.

CHAPTER 28

The Power of Belief

Winter had arrived and shortly before Christmas (it must have been 1941 or 1942), I almost perished in a snowstorm. I had to get our Christmas goose from a farm near the old Polish border. The train I had scheduled to take, I missed. While playing soccer, I had lost track of time. My father was very angry about this and made me take the later train, which arrived around midnight. No one was at the station to meet me. Worse than that, the weather had turned bad.

I ended up in a blizzard with snowdrifts partially hiding the roads. Shortly before 2:00 a.m., I finally reached the farm—utterly exhausted and wet from the snow that had penetrated my clothing. Had I given in to my desire to rest just a little while on my way, I might have fallen asleep and frozen to death.

Until this day I remember the faint far-away light I visioned or envisioned while fighting the elements on that stormy night. The question crossed my mind then whether my father would feel guilty if I froze to death.

I talked to myself. I spoke aloud, giving myself orders, directions to follow, told myself not to rest, not to fall asleep.

The weather was so bad not even the dog had barked when I arrived. The farmer's wife actually wrapped me in a horse blanket.

Later on in battle, I would draw on some of my boyhood experiences and, with added *Soldatenglueck* (soldier's luck), manage to survive against overwhelming odds.

In situations of danger, I have often been able to marshal my resources to get out of whatever peril I faced. I had (and still have) good instincts. When I was 12 or 13 years old, there was a lot of talk about the power of an "iron will." Hitler supposedly achieved things with an iron will, and he set examples for us to follow.

Willensstaerke (willpower), the ability to control one's actions and emotions, and *Glaubensstaerke* (faith force), the capacity to determine one's fate through strength derived from beliefs, were monumental pylons of the mental conditioning aimed at Germany's youth during the Third *Reich*.

I can only speak for myself, but I believed unconditionally in Germany and its mission to emerge as a leader among the nations of this world. I believed in Hitler and his calling to lead our nation to its greatest achievements ever.

As I would come to realize later in my life, belief is the most powerful directing force in human behavior and those able to create beliefs hold in their hands much of humankind's fate. Hitler was such a leader and not the only one to misdirect this power.

My father believed in a strong Prussian upbringing, harsh, authoritative, and unforgiving. In the *Jungvolk*, we had to obey and be disciplined, but we were also rewarded for achievements.

I never slugged or muscled myself to the top. A desire grew in me to advance intellectually, thereby taking control. I was then (and still am) more of a "thinker" than a "talker." Physically, I was more of a "defender" than an "attacker." This dated back to my first-grade teacher who broke up the fight where we beat up Rudi.

My teacher's message convinced me that it was my duty to defend my comrades, classmates, or friends that needed help. I was twice as old now—but I hadn't forgotten. Perhaps I didn't want to forget. Maybe it served me as a psychological escape hatch. It kept me from starting fights. When I had to defend myself, I often became angry. I realize now that I feared anger—my own included.

Often, my will power seemed to fail me. When it came to drawing, for example, I was determined to become a good drafts-man. But, for lack of talent, I failed. At that time though, I attributed this failure to a lack of determination. More will power was needed and I was not able to generate it.

To express myself in words was an altogether different situation. It did not require anything I did not possess. Except for practice to gain perfection, no will power had to be generated. All I had to do was channel the flow that existed.

My love for language must have gone back to my very early childhood. My mother told me that, before I could read, I would take a big book as a prop, open it up and put it on the rim of the balcony and make short speeches. I would raise my voice and repeat some phrases over and over again, trying to imitate the oratory style of those who had spoken to us over the radio, Hitler and Goebbels most of all. Declarations such as "I will be your leader!" or "Follow me, follow me!" or even *"Sieg Heil, Sieg Heil!"* I had no audience. Mostly, I spoke to the trees.

When in school, whenever I could, I addressed my class. I enjoyed the opportunity. In the *Jungvolk,* as a *Jungzugfuehrer* (group leader) I was able to give orders and even make speeches.

My father had always insisted we must control our minds, and he was not the only one to do so. Discipline was one virtue by which we were judged, at home, in school and in the *Jungvolk.* Not until my first heart attack did I ever relax enough to let go of the compulsion to keep my mind governed with the next task at hand and the goals ahead of me.

I had military heroes then, men of fierce willpower—Galland, Moelders, Prien, Schepke, Dietl, Rommel, and others, such as Schiller, Goethe, Rilke. After the war, more would follow such as the great spiritual leaders and peace activists: Gandhi, Schweitzer and Pauling. Without them I would have become a different person—at least, in some respects. I was fortunate. Had I been just a few years older, I could have been labeled a war criminal, just by following orders. Just by being loyal.

As a boy, I looked up to my heroes and down on people who were declared to be enemies or not worthy, those who supposedly caused the misfortunes in this world. I had been convinced to hate our enemies whoever and wherever they were. It was, however, a detached, dispassionate hate, an impersonal hate. I never harbored hostile feelings toward people I knew. My own father, subconsciously, might have been the only exception. On Christmas day, we all seemed happy. For dinner, my mother served the goose I had returned with. We feasted while on the front, east of us many of our soldiers were killed, more even froze, lost limbs, and were crippled for life.

In WW II, I had to hate those we fought against, without comprehending what hate really was and how devastating it could become. Of course, those who fought against us hated too. As is well known now, many on both sides had sadistic and bloodthirsty impulses.

I came to realize that Hitler's hate backfired. At the very end, it went so far that he would bear malice toward his own people. Hitler demonstrated what hate can lead to—cruelties, mass murder, ravages, and total destruction.

***

Jungvolk activities were not limited to sports, camping, terrain exercises, marching, or singing. They also included instructions, youth films, vacation programs, and later, special assignments. Schooling and motion picture showings often covered German history and NSDAP party history.

The topics I remember most covered shining leaders of national significance, such as Armin the Cherusker, Henry the Fowler, Frederick the Great, Bismarck the Iron Chancellor, and Hitler, of course. It also featured many other heroes of the movement, among them Herbert Norkus, prominent among members of the *Jungvolk* and the Hitler Youth because he had become the martyr of the movement. An account of how he lived and died was told to us repeatedly by different leaders at various occasions.

As the story went, he was the son of a storm trooper who lived in Wedding, known as the "red" district of Berlin, because its inhabitants were predominantly Communists.

Norkus and fellow Hitler Youths had been posting announcements of a scheduled party rally titled "Swastika or Red Star?" Spotted by an informant, they soon were assaulted by a troop of Communists. While the boys scattered, one of the Communists caught Herbert Norkus and attacked him with a knife. The injured boy staggered to a house. There he was refused help. The owner slammed the door shut. The stabber struck the wounded boy again and again and mutilated his face.

The outcome, as reported to us, was ghastly and tragic. Herbert Norkus had succumbed cruelly. The twelve-year-old had sacrificed his life for his *Fuehrer* and it was impressed upon us that he had sustained a hero's death! In our memories, he should forever remain as the shining example of one who had bravely relinquished his young life for the great cause.

We, the living, were declared the standard-bearers of Herbert Norkus' legacy. (At that time, he was believed to be the youngest of Hitler's followers who had sacrificed his life.) We were indebted to Herbert Norkus and all the others who, in struggles for Hitler, had lost their lives, since we were the ones that benefited from their ultimate sacrifices.

All this affected me and the boys and girls of our generation. We "belonged" and there was a fallen hero to look up to. Having been designated "standard-bearers" not only sounded important, but we were made to understand it carried responsibilities. The movement had assumed power—control over all people—and we were destined to carry on. Few, if any, of us imagined that this commitment would lead us prematurely to the battlefields of this war that had started so victoriously and would become so atrocious.

There was a song that contained the words "For Hitler we march, past night and death, carrying the flag, promising freedom and bread . . ."[69] that typically concluded the Herbert Norkus remembrances.

The last portrayal of Herbert Norkus, his life and sacrifice, I remember clearly. It was not an anniversary tribute but a lecture during a training course given at the Youth Leader School[70] in Braunschweig late in 1944 while German losses were amounting already to gargantuan numbers. The emphasis again was that a heroic death for the Fatherland is the ultimate fulfillment of life.

CHAPTER 29

Aryan Purity and Politics

I recall many movement-related lectures.

Presentations on race were few. Specifically, I can recall only one. The text was written by a professor from Breslau (possibly Dr. Martin Stammler), who once appeared in person to read from his writings. Moreover, the name of the publisher of his writings was Lehmann.[71] Although no relation to my immediate family, I recall that I asked my mother if there was a chance that they would publish my poems. She didn't think that they even published poetry and then remarked that my poetry wasn't mature enough for publication. This, of course, was not what I wanted to hear. It prompted her to send some of my poems to a woman's magazine she subscribed to, which contained a small section for children. They did publish one of my poems on the children's page that I found disillusioning. It came across as a poem for children, written by a child.

I also recall that the text on race contained a chart of heads showing racial characteristics. Every one in the group had to step forward, face the group, then turn to show his profile. After some discussion, it was determined what race each of us belonged to. When it was my turn, it was decided that I didn't look Nordic but *faelisch*, which surprised me, because our family had no known Westphalian ancestors whatsoever.

I, of course, had hoped that I would be judged a Nordic type. There was some discussion and it was pointed out that my hair was not blond enough, my eyes were not blue, my forehead not high enough. Although I was very slim then, my legs were short (compared to my torso), and I did not have a "Viking figure" but a rather stocky one.

I must have been visibly disappointed because our leader pointed out that such distinguished Germans as President Hindenburg[72] and Chancellor Bismarck[73] exemplified those who belonged to this very racial group. The comparison threw me off even more, because I did not see any resemblance and couldn't imagine that, when grown up, I would look even remotely like Hindenburg or Bismarck. And I was right. When I look at me in the mirror now, to whom do I bear a likeness? Perhaps "The Sower"[74] by Oskar Martin Amorbach.

Since our *Jungvolk* unit consisted of various racial types, our leader made it a point to stress that everyone's accomplishments will serve the nation, but that those who are inferior and unfit stand in the way of progress and attainment. That's why they were being removed.

Obviously there were no "inferiors" in our group. But I could not help but be concerned about Rudi, my very first friend. Would he be considered a misfit because of his protrusive spine? In Breslau at least two Hitler Youth units existed whose members had impaired vision or were even blind and those whose hearing was impaired. But what about those who were deformed?

I did not know. I didn't even know if Rudi was still in Niesky and if he had been accepted in the *Jungvolk* or not. Here, in Breslau, I had not noticed anyone with a bodily defect or mental deficiency who wore a uniform. The church seemed to take care of all those who were deformed or retarded. I had noticed that, at such religious care centers, the girls wore all the same dresses and the boys wore identical suits. School garb—not uniforms.

***

Not only was the press controlled during the Third *Reich*, the motion picture industry was just as censored. Dr. Josef Goebbels,

Hitler's Propaganda Minister and Minister of People's Enlightenment (yes, there was such an office!), took a special interest in the
production of films as well as in the actors and actresses selected
for leading roles. It became common knowledge (even my father
knew it and talked about it openly) that several actresses owed
their successful careers to this man who decided to what and what
not the German mind should be exposed.

A mix of escapist fare, heroic and patriotic topics and, of course
anti-Semitic propaganda films were produced for the German public
and some specifically for Germany's youth. I still remember my
grandfather, who rarely went to the movies, talk about a film "The
Log of U-35." It must have impressed him as much then as my
wife and I were galvanized, just recently, when we saw a World
War II U-boat film, *"Das Boot"* (The Boat).

The first full-length feature film I remember seeing, was
"Hitlerjunge Quex" (Hitler Youth Quex), the story of a 15-year-old
printer's apprentice whose parents were both Communists. Against
their wishes, he joined the Hitler Youth. I don't recall where I saw
this film—perhaps it was during examination week at the *NAPOLA*
in Naumburg.

I saw it shortly after the stolen apple incident in Hoyerswerda.
My heart stopped when the movie opened with a scene depicting
a boy stealing an apple. He did not, however, get away with it but
was caught by the merchant who punished the boy.

In the film, the bystanders were incensed by what they saw
and the incident accelerated into a mob scene, with the shop-
keeper suffering losses and damages and with a window being
smashed. Broken glass. An omen then for what had happened later
during Crystal Night?

Obviously, the Communist youths were portrayed as the bad
guys and the Hitler Youth members as the good ones. Quex, the
martyr, after he lost his mother who committed suicide, had
experienced a fate similar to that of Herbert Norkus.

There were differences, however, between the *Hitlerjunge Quex*
film version and the real life story of Herbert Norkus. In the film,

when the boy was murdered, his face was not cut. Norkus' father was a storm trooper; Quex's father was a Communist.

When I was watching the *Hitlerjunge Quex* film, I heard for the first time the expression "Nazi." In our home, in school, or among acquaintances we had never heard it used. "Nazis!" That's what the National-Socialists were called. To me it sounded like a curse.

I had no idea that everywhere else in the world the National Socialists were already being called "Nazis," with an accursed and woeful connotation. Today, of course, the word conveys a malediction of horrendous proportions.

The dominating character in this film was Quex's father, played by Heinrich George. He would later be awarded the designation *Staatsschauspieler* (state-recognized actor)—the highest honor attainable for members of the acting profession in Germany under Hitler's reign.

In this film, he acted the part of a working-class communist— and did it very convincingly. Ten years later, George would also play the leading role in the Third *Reich's* last film. I would see this movie the night after my arrival in the nation's capital, as a member of a group of honored guests. The film, called *Kolberg,* was a last, massive attempt to strengthen public morale and to mobilize everyone's fighting spirit.

It featured the story of the Baltic town's heroic resistance during the Napoleonic siege (1806-07). Heinrich George portrayed Nettelbeck, the city's mayor. I also remember the beginning of this film very vividly since the first scenes were filmed in Breslau. They were filmed there to recall the historical year of 1813 when Prussian Field Marshall Gneisenau persuaded the king to create a *Volksarmee*—similar to what became the *Volksturm* at the end of World War II of which I became a member.

When I was still a *Hoerspieler* (child radio actor), I met Heinrich George, who struck me as being even more monumental in person than on the screen. He and I were to do a radio play together. This gigantic man held with his left hand a script from which he read his lines into the microphone and rested his right hand on my slight shoulder, leaning on it heavily.

On first take, I missed the few lines assigned to me. On second try, all went well.

Even though my part consisted only of a few sentences, I was in awe and proud of myself for having worked with this performer. He radiated strength so intense that one could feel it.

Consequently, I would see all of the films he played in.

Heinrich George died in 1946 in the Sachsenhausen Concentration Camp, located in the Russian occupation zone. It seems ironic that George, whose first role that I had seen him portray was as a Communist, would die in a Communist concentration camp (concentration camps were not invented by the Germans. The British in the Boer War of 1899 used them and Stalin continued concentration camps after World War II.)

***

My father, who looked upon my frequent visits to movie houses disapprovingly, nevertheless, made sure that I saw the film *Der alte und der junge Koenig* (The Old King and the Young King). It featured the events that lead to the *Koenigsstrafe* (king's punishment), one of his favorite topics. In fact, since my early childhood, he had recounted this story frequently, always emphasizing that the king's harsh punishment eventually benefited not only the prince (who later became Frederic the Great) but also the whole German nation.

The young prince and his friend Katte had attempted unsuccessfully to flee from the Royal Prussian Court. Upon their capture, the crown prince was jailed and forced to watch, from the cell window, the bloody execution of his trusted and depended-upon friend.

Obviously, Hitler or Goebbels (or both) knew the profound impact motion pictures had on the masses and wanted such influence utilized for mind conditioning. Goebbels had established a *Reichskulturkammer (Reich* Chamber of Culture), a specific section governing all aspect of, and jurisdiction over, Germany's entire film industry. This included the *Wochenschau* (weekly newsreel). Goebbels—and he let it be known—personally oversaw its productions.

He was a noncombatant, evaluating footage from the front and deciding what would impress and move the German public to ever-increasing commitments toward the war effort. Of course, the German servicemen featured, whether belonging to the army, navy, air force, or *Waffen-SS*, were always brave and chivalrous. Those maimed or dismembered were never in sight close-up, for us to see war's cruelties, the horrendous inflections causing death, the many images of nightmarish savagery. On the screen, the true face of war was kept concealed.

(The same was the case in Great Britain and in the United States, until the Vietnam War. I learned, however, that Stalin made sure that the Russian people during World War II saw the graphic details and the atrocities alleged to have been committed by Germans and even by Ukrainians that had joined the invaders).

For me, the image of Norkus' bloodied face had already been implanted. It would come to haunt me when one of the fallen comrades I caught sight of after my first battle, horrified me beyond any image of death. I had seen many a maimed animal in my childhood—such as the deer's head with the antlers cut out and the headless chicken I had been unable to hold when killed, spattering blood all over me.

The shock, however, when I would see headless corpses, a perished comrade with a horrendously mangled head, a distorted bloody eye sockets-smashed countenance, made me nearly faint at times. It often would cause vomiting.

In less than a year, I would be overwhelmed by war's images. It seemed as if they ravaged the fabric of my soul tearing it into blood-soaked shreds. The heroic visions of my early youth would change, but the concept that death would be required to preserve the life of the nation remained. It contributed to an aspiring poet's emotional fervor.

***

I became a fervent moviegoer during the five years from 1940 through 1944. I probably saw over 200 feature films including the morbific *Jud Suess* (Jew Suess).

In hindsight, it was a diabolical masterpiece of mind-bending indoctrination. Right at the beginning, it was proclaimed that the film's contents were based on historical facts![75]

Historical facts?

This is what I was able to determine the historical facts to be:

> Karl Alexander, hereditary Duke of Wuerttemberg, had embraced the Roman Catholic faith while a successful general in the Austrian army. In 1733, he became ruler of Wuerttemberg[76] at a time when the duchy was impoverished, following the French invasion. The Duke, determined to restore prosperity and to establish a formidable guard unit, named Joseph Suess Oppenheimer his Finance Director. This Director became unpopular because of the taxes he had to impose in order to satisfy the Duke's increasing demands. This culminated in efforts to abolish both the council and the constitution. Upon the Duke's sudden death, Oppenheimer was put on trial by the new regent, Karl-Rudolf, and sentenced to death.

Two feature films are now available as videos from International Historic Films, Inc., in Chicago.

One was produced in 1934 in Great Britain and adapted from the historical novel by Feuchtwanger.[77] The other one is the German (Third *Reich*) version produced in 1940 and directed by Veit Harlan that made no reference to Feuchtwanger, himself a Jew.

Listed as writers of the film script are Veit Harlan, Wolfgang Eberhard Moeller and Ludwig Metzger. Their plot centered on a Councilor's daughter who hastily marries to stop the Jew's advances. But it was all in vain; her husband is tortured while she ends up being raped. She drowns herself. The Jew is tried and condemned to death.

As a boy, I couldn't help but feel enraged over the dramatized events and sorrowful about the woman and her tragic fate. The story, as portrayed in the British film, contains no rape—only an attempted one, undertaken not by Jew Suess, but by the Duke who was attracted by the Jew's beautiful daughter Naomi. She, too, commits suicide and Joseph Suess Oppenheimer accuses the Duke of having killed her—only to be hanged himself upon the Duke's sudden death.

Another film, *Der ewige Jude (The Eternal Jew)* was also shown. However, after seeing *Jud Suess,* I had no desire to see a second anti-Semitic film—not because I was opposed to them—I just didn't want to watch another film that had such an effect on me. I had felt enraged as well as dispirited—enraged over the fate of the woman, dispirited that, as a solution, she chose death. Some unresolved questions remained in my mind. It was only after the war that I searched for answers and became horrified at what I would discover.

CHAPTER 30

Dr. Goebbels

Dr. Goebbels, a cynical Jew baiter, wanted us to believe that personal relationships with Jews amounted to dishonorable behavior. We were taught if such a relationship existed with a member of the opposite sex and resulted in intercourse, then it desecrated the blood and corrupted the partners morally.[78] Goebbels publicly went along with this imputation, but he must have known that such a concept lacked any scientific basis.

My father seemed to have inside knowledge of Dr. Goebbel's personal life, perhaps because Goebbels had a close relationship with Karl Hanke, the party leader of Lower Silesia. Goebbels was said to have had affairs with movie stars, especially Lida Baarova. Hanke, who, from 1933 to 1941 had been Dr. Goebbels' assistant, fell in love with the Propaganda Minister's wife, Magda.

Obviously, my father never talked with me about these rumors, but I overheard bits and pieces of such stories when we had visitors. Sometimes, the door was not completely closed, and I was all ears. Also, whenever my father was bragging, his voice became louder and, I am sure, he did not realize that I was occasionally within listening range.

The Goebbels family had been members of Hitler's social circle and were frequent guests at his alpine residence. At the end, they joined him in his bunker and died shortly after him by staging a ghastly murder and suicide plot. He would sacrifice the lives of his own innocent children.

Ironically, Dr. Goebbels, the relentless Jew-baiter and strong advocate of racial pureness, preached (and wrote) about the virtues of tall, blond and blue-eyed Aryans, although he was of small stature, with dark hair and was crippled as well. He was once an eager student of the Jesuits and not even of pure German ancestry. French blood flowed through his veins. My father, perhaps because of his unconfirmed Huguenot ancestors, had some slight resemblance to Dr. Goebbels.

Huguenots were actually not a racial but a religious group, Calvinist Protestants. However, being of French stock made them, by Nazi standards, less desirable than Germans with Aryan features. Goebbels was the author of the "Ten Commandments" for party members. In the early years of the war, they were passed on to us boys as guidelines for us and generations to follow.

Written for the early National Socialists, by now referred to as *alte Kaempfer* (the old guard), we boys of the *Jungvolk* were told to look upon ourselves as the *Junge Kaempfer* (the young guard). *Kaempfer* actually means "fighter." Fighting for Hitler meant guarding him and his ideas.

In one of the few letters I wrote to my grandfather, *Opa* Lehmann, who was an *alter Kaempfer;* I mentioned that I felt proud to follow in his footsteps. After the war, he returned this letter to me and I tore it up.

Before I left Germany after the war, I destroyed whatever could have remained a link. Understandable, from a psychological standpoint. It was nevertheless, a shortsighted reaction, since now, over fifty years later, such remnants could have provided me with some valuable keys to unlock the past that I am now endeavoring to put on record.

Goebbels' commandments, preserved in the literature of Nazism, demanded that:
- We love our Fatherland above all—more through action than through words;
- We look upon Germany's adversaries as our personal enemies and hate them whole-heartedly;
- We view every fellow-German as a comrade, regardless of his social standing.

New laws were put in place and were upheld by strict enforcement.

Those not protected by the laws would suffer and countless would die. But that was not apparent to the privileged young of the nation—the youth bearing Hitler's name.

I remember vaguely that one of Goebbels' commandments demanded that we strike with our fists those who abuse Germany. It sounded intriguing, but at the time we became acquainted with this commandment, no known rogues reviling the Fatherland were around. No one was left for us to beat up. They had been removed from public life.

Instead, rivals in competitions were established. We had to wrestle and we were given boxing gloves. We had to hit each other in a sportsmanlike fashion, to become tough and tougher. We fought as comrades and remained friends.

Once, when we discussed Goebbels' commandments, one of the boys my age referred to Jews as *Judenschweine* (Jewish pigs) in a hateful manner. A malediction I would soon hear again.

This curse called down upon strangers sounded so hateful and now, in retrospect, I wonder why I didn't feel outraged.

I had no intense aversions against anyone. I probably hated my father more than any Jew. Him I knew. Him I feared. I didn't feel threatened by anyone I did not know. I knew no Jews. When I subconsciously in dreams wished my father to die, I must have longed for freedom from fear.

***

As far as I can think back, persons who influenced my thinking when I was a boy expressed pride over what Germans had accomplished. People who viewed German music, literature, science, and technological accomplishments as superior to all others. Writers, musicians and painters, with whose work I became familiar, undoubtedly followed the desired guidelines, especially regarding racial policies.

Hitler's *Rassenpolitik*—to purify the race and then to multiply—

was accepted unquestionably by us who were young and didn't know better. What we saw and read was reinforced constantly.

A law was passed that everyone belonging to the *SS* had to obtain permission to marry. My father and mother were married before. My mother received the *Mutterkreuz* (Cross of Motherhood) in bronze after her fourth child and in silver after her sixth child.

No one ever mentioned to me that, in occupied territory, so-called racially undesirable people, especially Jews, were *ausgerottet* (exterminated), systematically and barbarously. Nor did I ever suspect or have reason to imagine that German soldiers or policemen were ordered to act as executioners of innocent people.

Earlier, when I had visited my uncle in Poland, most of the Poles there were farmhands and overseers. I remember manual laborers were harassed and yelled at by supervisors, but no infliction of bodily harm much less of any killing. My uncle, while I was present, once told a foreman to lower his voice.

After the war with Russia began, another incident occurred at the farm. The watch-commander assigned to the estate suspected that the maid was secretly in contact with the local partisans. He wanted her turned over to the Gestapo. But my aunt stood up for her. My uncle, through high-level connections, was able to save her life.

After the war, in Hamburg, I met a survivor of a police unit whose assignment it was to execute Jews in Poland. He told me, in strictest confidence, that this battalion[79] was not a fighting unit but an execution squad. By then, I had seen the concentration camp documentary and had followed the Nuremberg Trials. I could no longer doubt that these mass executions had taken place.

CHAPTER 31

Going to the Movies

If films let one escape, then I escaped with ever increasing frequency. Many of the movies I saw made indelible impressions on me. I already mentioned how much the film *Schiller* moved me. Several film biographies affected me almost as profoundly.

Famous people were always fascinating subjects and—whatever their fate—a source of great interest. Emil Jannings portrayed Robert Koch, the German physician who discovered organisms of infectious diseases and who was awarded the Nobel Prize in Medicine after inventing a test for tuberculosis.

In 1941 I saw Paul Hartmann's portrayal of Bismarck, the Iron Chancellor, sometime after June 4th. I remember this because Kaiser Wilhelm II, exiled since 1918 in the Netherlands, was dead already. It was he who had Bismarck dismissed in 1890, then intensified armament and encouraged Austria's Balkan policy that led to the outbreak of the First World War.

Schuster Stefan had reviewed this with me. He feared the Kaiser might be killed when Hitler invaded Holland, just as the Bolsheviks had murdered the former Russian Czar.

Hitler, who had fought in World War I under the Kaiser and for the Kaiser, never had such plans. As it turned out, the monarch, grandson of Queen Victoria of England, died of natural causes at the age of 82 in Doorn, during the German occupation.

One or two years later, after an extended illness, I had a tutor, an old, retired high school teacher. As I would discover, he remained *kaiser-treu* (loyal to the emperor). Although not openly, he most probably opposed Hitler and the new Nazi rulers. He stressed repeatedly that the Kaiser did not renounce power voluntarily. He was forced by none other than President Woodrow Wilson to resign from power completely, to abdicate.

It happened in the past; it did not concern me. The same seemed true with the developments that had brought, once again, the United States as a participant in a European war. In 1941 I was 13 years old. I had no concept of how huge America was, how abundantly rich she was in industrial facilities, goods, manpower, and gifted leaders. I knew nothing of the people's resolve to protect democracy, not just as a form of government, but as a way of life. The U.S. had all of the resources and ideological foundations that, in reality, win wars.

In my young, constricted mind, I believed that the war would be won, above all, with unwavering determination, great will power, death-defying bravery, and loyalty to the *Fuehrer.*

I saw my tutor shake his head occasionally. Now I know why. Had he explained his amazement about my naivete, he might have risked his life. After all, I was the son of an *SD* officer, a fact that was known to him.

***

Many films produced during the Third *Reich*—some in a very subtle way—depicted Hitler's ideology, even when featuring non-Germans, such as Rembrandt, the great Dutch painter, portrayed by Ewald Balser as the great genius of Germanic art. Rembrandt was an artist with great determination. When he faced the onslaught of enemies and creditors, he displayed admirable strength and an unflagging sense of purpose.

I also remember seeing the anti-British film, *Ohm Krueger,* with Emil Jannings portraying Paul Krueger who led the fight against British aggression in South Africa. I also saw *Carl Peters* with Hans Albers in the role of the German colonist in East Africa.

Friedemann Bach, played by Gustaf Gruendgens, a noted actor and director, brought to the screen the trials and tribulations of Johann Sebastian Bach's oldest son. Its message was of a talent neglected because of excessive indulgence in sensual pleasures.

Diesel, featuring Rudolf Diesel, the inventor of the crude-oil engine, was played by Willy Birgel. This was another memorable film. So was *Andreas Schlueter* featuring the famous architect and sculptor portrayed by Heinrich George. Paul Hartmann portrayed Dietrich von Roedern in *The Affair Roedern* and it made a lasting impression on me. Roedern built fortresses for Frederick the Great and was thrown in jail for treason. He was sent to the front in the Seven Year War, where he ended up fighting for Prussia.

The Immortal Heart was a dramatized biography of Peter Henlein, the 16th century German clockmaker who invented the spring-driven watch before he was, accidentally, struck and killed by a bullet he had invented!

Dive Bombers is the story of a pilot who, after experiencing depressions, is uplifted by Richard Wagner's music and regains his will to fight. Enthusiastically, he resumes his deadly missions.

These films were meant to exalt our minds. They did, in my case, or these films wouldn't have remained embedded so deeply in my memory.

There were three films that would become, for different reasons, my favorites of all the films I saw—until the war's end.

One, *The Postmaster,* was based on a story by the Russian dramatist, Pushkin.[80] The great Heinrich George played the role of the postmaster. The beautiful Hilde Krahl portrayed the daughter, Dunja; Captain Minskij was played by the debonair Siegfried Breuer.

Dunja succumbs to the worldly charm of the cavalry officer who never marries her but agrees to stage a mock wedding when her father comes to visit them. The old man is fooled, but a younger officer who had wanted to marry her feels deceived and breaks up with her. The postmaster returns from St. Petersburg happily, thinking all is well with his daughter. The despondent Dunja takes her life. She had made sure, however, that the death notice names her as the Captain's wife.

This film was produced after the German-Soviet Friendship Pact had been signed and was shown before Hitler attacked Russia. It had an intriguing plot with memorable dialogues, masterful acting, and catchy music.

Secretly, I wished to become able to write as artfully as Pushkin. I searched for everything he had written. All I could find was another of his stories, *The Captain's Daughter*, which I found just as captivating. Although the great Russian writers were not banned by the Nationalist-Socialists, their books were not contained in the extensive library we had at home. Only after the war would I be deeply absorbed by Russian literature. Leo Tolstoy became another one of my Russian idols.

The second film, *Riding for Germany*, had strong nationalistic undertones, but this was not the reason for my great enthusiasm. The film was about a beautiful horse and a gifted equestrian who secured, against all odds, a victory at a major tournament in Switzerland. It was the first for Germany after the end of the First World War. Horses and horseback riding were one of my great passions during my formative years. I identified with the hero of this film, which was somewhat prophetic. He overcame, at the end of World War I, a short-term paralysis from the waist down—just as I would at the end of World War II.

The third movie is the reason that, since boyhood, I have felt so strongly attracted to the sea. *The Girl from Fanoe* was about a triangular love story that unfolded on an island located off the west coast of Denmark, south of Esbjerg. The leading actress was Brigitte Horney. She played major roles in two films that related to the sea. In one, *Love, Death and the Devil*, she sang, with a hoarse yet sensual voice, a haunting song in which she expressed that life has to be taken in stride, that life and the sea are alike, both swayed by high tides and low tides.

I saw *Das Maedchen von Fanoe* shortly after its release. Both films were banned to youth under 18. I had to dress up—cushion my jacket and lift my shoulders—to appear old enough to gain admission. I did this several times for I would view this film at least four times, if not five. Brigitte Horney portrays an island girl who falls in love with a fisherman. Soon she discovers that he is married already and father of a child. In her initial reaction, she turns her affection toward his friend and fellow-fisherman but is unable to suppress her passion for the one who is married. Both men are in love with her. They decide on a duel at sea but, on the way, their boat capsizes. Having to battle the sea, they no longer oppose each other but, instead, reaffirm their friendship.

When they return to shore alive, the island girl, who had feared for both, realizes that she loves the fisherman who isn't married even more and vows to become his faithful companion for life.

Horney's acting style was intense and her husky voice seemed to entice me, perhaps because it had so much sex appeal. Needless to say, Brigitte Horney became my favorite actress during my early teen-age years. I made every effort to view all films that featured her.

That she was much older and married did not prevent me from writing poems for her, with great admiration and bold dedications. On the walls of my room, between pictures of war heroes (only one was a woman, the pilot, Hanna Reitsch), I put up several pictures of this actress with her dark eyes, high cheekbones, and black hair. It was not the charm of a Nordic-type woman that, for the first time, cast the mystic spell of a seductive female over me, but one who resembled a gypsy.

***

During the seven years from 1937 to the end of 1944, we were shown many so-called *Kulturfilme* (cultural films). They emphasized the realistic aspects of life, which, based on nature's laws, could be very cruel. We became acquainted with violence in the animal kingdom. In dramatic sequences, we were shown how predators hunt down and kill their prey with commentaries referring to Darwin's concept that only the fittest survive.

We had to become the fittest. Species establish territories.

Strong males fight off weaker rivals, reach their prime, and establish sexual primacy. These were often represented in a way that showed cruelty as strength and strength as necessary for survival.

Admiration for hardhearted strength was instilled. There was never a discussion, never any encouragement to view what was shown with a critical eye. It was constantly stressed that we had natural and historical enemies to defeat. Fighting was a noble undertaking.

CHAPTER 32

Leaving Home

I had many friends in the *Jungvolk,* in school, and in the neighborhood. Klaus Schauermann and I sat together in class. Frequently after school, we went together to the restaurant[81] his parents owned where his mother always served us something to eat. Another friend, Werner Schubel, was even more into sports than I was, and often we practiced track and field together. I believe it was he who began calling me Nurmi, after the Finnish track star Paavo Nurmi, a famous runner in the twenties.

Another bright and athletic classmate of ours was Walther Troeger.[82] He didn't live far from us, and we both went to school via the streetcar on line 18. As the war progressed, with more manpower needed, most of the male streetcar conductors were replaced by females. When they were very pretty, we boys attempted to impress by scaring them. We would jump up and down from the moving tram, which, of course, was not allowed.

For a period of time, Walther and I dared each other as to how many times we would jump down from the moving car. We would keep our hands on the handle, with our feet on the street, take at least three steps—jumps—before pulling ourselves back up into the car again.

Walther beat me a couple of times, and once a conductress had the motorman stop the tram to eject us. We both had passes so we didn't lose our fare but had to walk to the next stop and wait. We were probably late for school that day and received a reprimand.

I received warnings occasionally, not only for tardiness, but also for lack of homework and once or twice for mischievous behavior. Stink bombs found their way into our classroom on a few occasions emitting such evil smells that, even with all windows and doors opened widely, instructions were delayed 15 to 30 minutes. I also remember winter snowball fights in front of the school and summer shenanigans such as squirting pedestrians from the upper windows of the school.

***

In 1941 our Elisabet Gymnasium building became a military hospital and we had to move to another high school and share their facilities, rotating morning and afternoon schedules.

After we had been transferred from our own school on Arletiusstrasse to the Zwinger Gymnasium on Sonnenstrasse, I, for the first and only time during the Nazi era, came in personal contact with a Jewish person. Occasionally, I had observed this blind or near-blind woman with a seeing-eye dog crossing a street to the Sonnenplatz.

She was an old lady who reminded me of my own grandmother. My grandmother had lost only one eye and wore a black patch over it. She could still see well with the other eye. The old lady was led by a beautiful German shepherd dog and was apparently blind in both eyes.

I first saw her in 1941, before it was mandatory for Jews to wear a yellow star. Perhaps it was the dog that triggered my attention, but I noted that she wore a yellow armlet with three big dots, indicating that she was blind.

On the last occasion that I saw this sightless woman, I also saw the yellow star. I believe this was in late October or early November 1941 or 1942, most likely on a Wednesday because I do remember that I wore my *Jungvolk* uniform.

This time, she was without her dog and seemed insecure, almost lost, traversing with her cane to where she wanted to go.

When she had to cross the street, I went to assist her and asked: "Where is your dog?" I still remember clearly her reply because she used the German word *eingezogen* that means "drafted."[83] She explained that the army had claimed her loyal companion, on whom she depended so much. Seeing Eye dogs were needed for soldiers who had lost their sight. She also mentioned that she hoped to get another through the Association for the Blind, an older seeing-eye dog no longer suitable for service in the military.

She shed tears and asked, "Can I cross now?" With our arms linked, I guided her across the street.

A stranger—probably two or three years older than I, jumped off his bicycle and punched me in the face. He shouted: "Don't give help to the Jew-pig!" I tried to fight back.

A small crowd had assembled, although the old woman wisely disappeared, and the cyclist, apparently with my blood on his shirt, took off. It was most likely my nose that had been bleeding. Although I was wearing my hiking knife, the official blade sidearm of the *Jungvolk*, it had been strictly a fistfight and, as I recall, I was the only one bleeding

After the war, I discussed the incident with an interrogator, Captain Rosen. I told him that the question flashed through my head at the time as to whether I was doing something I shouldn't. It shows how indoctrinated I was—that I should even have questioned my action. Captain Rosen asked how anyone could have called an old, fragile, helpless lady, who probably was totally blind, a "Jew-pig."

I was at a loss for words. I thought back and realized that, lacking critical intelligence, I had become used to the expressions of the time. I grew up with *groben* (uncouth), degrading Nazi expressions. They had become part of the common language.

***

I did not mention the episode with the blind old woman to my father until after the war during a heated argument about how the

Jews had been liquidated. By this time I had fought in battles, had been wounded four times, and was 18 or 19 years old. He still treated me as if I wasn't full-grown and I was not mature enough to understand.

"Had you had to suffer under the Jews as we did, then you would understand why it had come to this. For their fate the Jews have to blame themselves!" he shouted.

I was shocked and speechless. At the time I assisted the blind woman, I knew that concentration camps existed. Their purpose, I believed, was to detain all those who needed to be re-educated to become productive and supportive members of the so-called *Volksgemeinschaft* (people's community).

Even when alone at home and secretly listening to the BBC, there was never any indication that concentration camps were sites of planned exterminations. We know now that the Allies knew.

***

During my youth, I was ill quite often—several times very seriously. My mother told me after the war that the main reason I had not been admitted to the *NAPOLA* was not that they had judged me of weak character and a sissy, but that my body appeared to be fragile and illness-prone. They also mentioned that I seemed inclined to fantasize. My thinking was not disciplined enough.

I had made several additional attempts to get father's permission to change from the regular *Jungvolk* (where I was a leader already) to the *Rundfunkspielschar* (radio performance unit). These attempts failed. He insisted that I keep serving in the regular *Jungvolk* unit and keep pursuing leadership development. He felt there was not enough emphasis on soldier-like behavior in the entertainment group. Choral and instrumental presentations were often produced jointly with the *Jungmaedel* (young girl) unit attached to the radio station of which both my oldest sisters were members.

Cultural activities and entertainment functions would take time away from being conditioned physically.

My father, as an *SS/SD* member, obviously had some influence. In 1937, in Hoyerswerda, I was considered for admittance to the *NAPOLA* in Naumburg. However, although risen in rank, my father had no power or influence that would get me entered into the selection process to qualify for admission in the Adolf Hitler School (AHS). The two types of schools, although both were established to secure future leadership for the National Socialist system, had been placed under different jurisdictions.

There even seemed to be a rivalry between the *NAPOLA*'s founder Rust[84] and the AHS founders, Ley[85] and von Schirach.[86]

The *NAPOLA*'s were based on the foundations of the old Prussian academies to promote a high sense of duty and soldierly traditions. They were meant to provide training for candidates of the National-Socialist *Ordensburgen* (literally: castles of order). These were political cadet academies for training the Nazi elite. The AHS actually had an anti-academic bias (in the traditional sense) and stressed discipline even more than the *NAPOLAS*.

My father, after obtaining literature that explained the requirements and the selection process, had outlined a strict program for me. Aside from the medicine ball workouts, I had to learn how to swim since this was one of the conditions to meet the requirements for the *DJ-Leistungsabzeichen* (achievement badge).

I earned this badge, months before the beginning of the selection process. Would I be recommended by my Hitler Youth Province Leader and our Party District Leader? With my father's *SS* membership having no bearing on who was selected, he, nevertheless, made sure that the *HJ* and party leaders knew of his desire to have his son qualify for the AHS.

But then I became ill. It happened several weeks before the selection process. With very high fever and great difficulties breathing, I was admitted to the quarantine station of the University Hospital. I had diphtheria. While hospitalized, I was additionally infected with Scarlet Fever and had to remain another six weeks. But this wasn't the end of it either. Painful symptoms of articular rheumatism followed.

Another health problem came to light. I have always had occurrences of stabbing pain in the chest, mostly at sporting events. These symptoms were finally diagnosed as angina pectoris. I received some medications and was ordered to curtail my athletic activities—until I "grew out of it." This was just at a time when I had distinguished myself with some notable victories as a middle-distance runner.

I had to withdraw from sports, and now I could no longer be considered as a candidate for the Adolf Hitler School.

Because of this chain of illnesses, I had missed over seven months of school. Repeating the school year was out of the question as far as my father was concerned. I ended up back in class (where I was lost most of the time) half-days and with a private tutor the other half.

The tutor was a former high school teacher who had remained loyal to the emperor. I now wish that I had paid more attention to what he thought and believed in, because he concerned himself intensely with eastern philosophy. He had a library filled with books I had never heard of. I don't recall specific titles but some were about Hinduism and Buddhism.

Between the mandatory lessons to bring me up to the level of my classmates, he would interject his thoughts on many a subject other than those contained in my textbooks.

He even touched on religion and would make statements like: "There is no need to involve the human mind in God's problems." He tried to plant thoughts into my young head, which could have led to revelations. But, at that time, I was not receptive and must have disappointed him in not drawing the conclusions he might have hoped for. A generation gap definitely existed.

Probably in his late sixties, if not in his early seventies, he didn't openly attack Hitler's leadership, but he did make observations such as that war interrupts life's natural processes. Here again, he condemned war. But the former Kaiser had not been known as a peace-loving person either. Was it only Hitler's war he condemned?

What my tutor did accomplish was to introduce me to some

basic meditation techniques. My ability to concentrate was greatly improved. With his help, I advanced from the *Untertertia* level 4th year in high school) to *Obertertia* level (5th year in high school). I did not, however, join with my classmates in their quasi-military duties. They became anti-aircraft battery crews,[87] auxiliary air force members—flak gunners. Because of my health problems, I was ordered to undergo training to become a leader of boys in a school that had been evacuated.[88] The camp leader was in charge of free-time activities.

***

Several kaleidoscopic memory fragments about Stalingrad remained with me. I remember Kurt's father (the gardener who raised rabbits in his backyard) telling me with pride *"Der Junge ist in Stalingrad"* ("The boy is in Stalingrad"). This must have been sometime in the fall of 1942, before this city on the Volga became a turning point, with strategic and operational failures following to the war's bitter end.

At the time I ran into Kurt's father and he mentioned his son's whereabouts, the offensive seemed still in progress and the battlegrounds far, far away.

Another recollection I have is that of *Schuster* Stefan (perhaps in a scoffing, if not outright cynical way), mentioning that Stalin already had a city named after him. We discussed whether a German city would become Hitlerstadt, with me speculating that Munich might be his choice. The cobbler laughed and said the *Muenchner* (citizen of Munich) would never agree to a name change under any circumstances and if forced on them, it would cause a revolution. I knew Munich but none of its inhabitants. Both my uncle and grandfather who lived in Bavaria were "Prussians."

Schuster Stefan also alluded to rumors that circulated after the victory over France. These rumors were that Berlin would be transformed into a city more majestic and more beautiful than Paris and would be renamed *Germania*. He remarked that this might appeal to everyone but the Berliners themselves. I never heard anything more about plans for this *Germania* metropolis until after the war when it was mentioned in Albert Speer's memoirs.

This might have been the last time that I saw *Schuster* Stefan. We parted with his thoughts that if any city would become Hitlerstadt, it would not be one in Germany but the city of Linz in Austria. Stalingrad, as it turned out, added luster to Stalin's name. There, Hitler's Sixth Army perished, but not without adding eternal honor to the history of the German army according to the *Fuehrer*. He proclaimed this immortality for those who valued sacrificial death above life when things were hopeless.

I never saw Kurt's father again and don't know what happened to Kurt. Stalingrad, now Volgograd, might have become his final resting place, as it did for more than 250,000 other human beings. A graveyard of over a quarter million people signified mass-scale slaughter. More than 20 years later, I would learn from a survivor, once a Hitler Youth leader, how cruel the suffering had been.

Today, most Germans—and many people in this world—know about *Die weisse Rose* (The White Rose), a short-lived (1942/43) resistance group at the University of Munich. Among their leaders were Hans and Sophie Scholl, a medical student and his sister who studied biology. One of the University's professors, Dr. Kurt Huber, who taught history and psychology and in his spare time collected and researched folk songs, was the oppositionist's guiding spirit.

At the time I was hospitalized, the White Rose was uncovered and reported about in the German press. I overheard two nurses, an older one, the floor head nurse and a younger one, probably still a student nurse, arguing about the severity of this treachery and the method with which the culprits were put to death.

The head-nurse voiced her aversion to decapitation. She called it an unnecessary cruelty. I was surprised to learn that under National Socialist rule, people were still put to death by guillotine. The younger nurse countered her superior fervently. This astonished me even more. Why would a young girl feel this way? She argued vehemently that traitors deserved to die in such a way to deter others from rebelling.

"Our brave soldiers are sacrificing their lives. What has come over these perfidious students to try to stab them in the back? That's high treason!"

Her voice broke with emotion.

I had mixed feelings. "Betrayal is betrayal," I thought, and I knew it was punishable by death—especially in times of war. I also realized that the sentence had to discourage others from civil disorder and from weakening the home front. I thought then that these students and their Swiss-born professor must have been part of a conspiracy organized by our enemies.

To have joined secretly with others for such an evil purpose, could not—to my way of thinking then—have originated from within our own country.

But decapitation? It made me shudder.

I wasn't aware of all the facts. The nurses probably weren't either. They were made known to me only after the war. Hans and Sophie had both been members of the Hitler Youth (she of the *BDM,* the girl's affiliate). They even had advanced to leadership positions before they became disillusioned. Hans had fought as a soldier on the Eastern Front and experienced the beginning of the battle of Stalingrad.

The discussion between the two nurses sounded like a dispute over moral depravity. The young one, probably 19 or 20 years old, was outraged. With her voice raised, she claimed that it was Hitler, who had given us freedom, was restoring Germany to greatness. It was our duty to bolster the *Fuehrer's* efforts and to support our soldiers who fought for the glory of the Fatherland.

The head nurse, probably in her early fifties, tried to calm down the younger one, mentioning that the students could have been mislead by their professor and clemency might be in order.

My feeling was that execution by a firing squad or even by hanging would have been a preferable choice for execution. I thought like the older nurse that this cruel "French method"[89] of execution was un-German.

I was 14 years old and remembered the time when I was six or seven and had to kill a chicken by chopping off its head. An act of savagery that had seared my soul. Meant to toughen me up, it resulted in the opposite. I was never able to erase this memory.

I lay in my hospital bed imagining what hellish fear Sophie, Hans, and their friend Christopher Probst must have experienced. When later Inge Aicher-Scholl, older sister of Hans and Sophie, reported that her sister and brother appeared to face their executioners fearlessly, it struck me with wonder. Both must have attained great inner strength, most likely convinced that their actions were sanctioned by a higher morality.

Later, I read an account of the White Rose activities and came to admire Dr. Huber. This 50-year-old philosophy professor had heartened and reassured the Scholls that their actions were patriotic by religious standards. They were based on devotion to preserving lives and values.

The members of the White Rose mimeographed flyers predicting that Germany would forever be disgraced unless the youth of Germany rose to overthrow "the dictatorship of evil."

It was a janitor who noticed the Scholls dropping their leaflets from the upper staircases in the University. He went straight to the Gestapo to report his observation. Arrests were made and an inquisition followed at a hasty People's Court trial. It was presided over by the notorious Chief-Judge Roland Freisler,[90] once a fanatic communist turned fervent Nazi.

After the war, a fellow student at the Preparatory Course for Journalists showed me an original leaflet she had picked up in 1943 and kept hidden secretly until the war's end. I felt chills running down my spine when I touched it and read it. I had to admit to her that, had I in Breslau or Prague come in possession of such a flyer, I undoubtedly would have turned it into the authorities.

The information that led to thinking like Sophie and Hans Scholl did not become available to most of us until after the war.

Only those who grew up under totalitarian rule will fully understand how this was possible.

Neither the nurses nor I knew then that White Rose leaflets stated that Jews were being exterminated in Poland—"A crime not to be compared to any other one in mankind's history." Nor was it reported that Sophie Scholl said to her mother just before the execution: "It will make waves." Or that her brother, before putting his head on the block under the henchman's blade had heralded: "Let freedom live!"

We only knew that they were traitors.

***

My training to become a *KLV-Lagermannschaftsfuehrer* took place in Podiebrad (at that time within the so-called Protectorate of Bohemia and Moravia) at a huge barracks-like facility. This facility was called the *KLV Schule der Reichsjugendfuehrung fuer Lagermannschaftsfuehrer (KLV* School of the *Reich* Youth Leadership for Camp Activity Leaders). About 40 miles east of Prague, this spa-city—which is now called *Podebrady*—had many hotels and boarding houses where nearly 10,000 boys and girls escaped the bombing raids in their home city.

After I had completed my training course, I was among those selected to remain as Group Leader, Second Grade, and later as Group Leader, First Grade. I have fond memories of the time spent in Podiebrad. Between courses, we spent time in Prague. A hotel, *Die Goldene Gans,* owned by Sudeten Germans, was where we stayed, taking in the sights of this beautiful city, going to concerts, and frequenting the German movie theater.

One of the films I saw then was *Die Goldene Stadt* (The Golden City). It was disappointing because too little was shown of the "Golden City." A farmer's daughter lives a typical life on the farm until she leaves for the big city where she is seduced and deserted by her own cousin. In her despair, she commits suicide. Kristina Soederbaum, who played the farm girl, was already nicknamed *die*

Reichswasserleiche (The *Reich* Water Corpse), because in so many of her roles she ended up drowning herself.

Another motion picture, *Die Feuerzangenbowle* (Flaming Punchbowl) was funny. It featured Germany's foremost comedian, Heinz Ruehmann. Ruehmann portrayed a published author who decided to enroll in a public high school just so he could experience some of the pranks he had missed out on, having been tutored privately. We laughed throughout the film and had a hilarious time.

I wrote poems at that time, and Werner Frehse, the school leader or head master, took an interest in my creative activities. Without my knowledge, he had sent a selection of my poems to Baldur von Schirach, the former *Reich* Youth leader, and now governor of Vienna. Von Schirach had remained in charge of the *KLV* as designated head of the program that evacuated children from sites of frequent air raids and put them up into boarding school type facilities away from the big cities.

While I was on special assignment in a camp on Lake Tegernsee in Bavaria, I received an important looking letter, forwarded to me from Podiebrad. It was from Baldur von Schirach!

My hands were shaking as I opened the envelope.

Von Schirach had singled out four of my poems he thought quite good, encouraging me to keep on writing. He remarked that he regretted having no more time to write poetry. His many duties no longer allowed time to write.

When I returned to Podiebrad, Werner Frehse made me read the letter in front of all the instructors. He seemed as proud as I was.

After that, I pondered if I should make a photocopy to send to my father. By then, he was serving as a war correspondent. I decided against it, and I no longer know why. Perhaps, it would have been a confrontation. He was against my writing poetry and didn't think my poems amounted to anything, while one of the nation's recognized leaders, a published poet, encouraged me to keep on writing!

I no longer have any of the poems I wrote during this time but I have recreated some of them. I was fascinated with the interrelations of nature and man. I wrote about the river, the waves, the reflection of the clouds, and my perception of natural phenomenon.

The native population in Podiebrad, which I came in contact with, seemed to be very German-friendly, at least toward us boys and girls from the *KLV*, although we almost always wore uniforms. I remember especially the barber who cut my hair. He also was a fan of the comic, Heinz Ruehmann. Besides *Die Feuerzangenbowle*, the barber and I enjoyed *QUAX, the Crash-pilot*. Here, Ruehmann portrayed a madcap who turned into a whacky amateur aviator whose stunts were meant to impress his girlfriend and his whole town.

The barber spoke German quite well. His job, he told us, was not only to cut hair, but also to put every customer, while in his chair, in a good frame of mind.

He always made people laugh, mostly with sexy and scurrilous jokes—but nothing political.

"The best medicine to overcome hard times is laughter. Obtainable without money and without food stamps. Free, but priceless!" was typical of the type of comments he would make.

Even though the Czech barber made us laugh, he also made us talk. Perhaps he was a spy. The barber could have been German-friendly because he felt that way, or he could have been an opportunist merely looking out for himself.

There were, as often happens in situations of conquest or foreign rule, some who cooperated with the subjugators because of the benefits. Not just Sudeten-Germans but also Slovaks and, perhaps, even a few Czechs had seized opportunities at hand because of the power shifts.

Germany, through the Munich Pact in 1938, had obtained the Sudeten territory in Silesia and borderlands of Bohemia. Poland and Hungary shared in the spoils. As Hitler occupied more and more of Eastern Europe, there was little or no opposition to this from other countries. At first, even the allies had given tacit approval with their silence.

When I was in Podiebrad the Deputy *Reich* Protector, Reinhard Heydrich,[91] had already been killed by Czech partisans. For this one murder, the German high command had responded with mass executions. They killed all male inhabitants of an entire village, Lidice,[92] because the "Free Czech" agents (trained in England and parachuted into their homeland) who succeeded in assassinating Heydrich, had supposedly been aided by the local population.

Vengeance's full extent of savagery razed an entire village! Inside the so-called "*Protektorat.*"

***

Until the end of 1944, my mother, a middle-class *Hausfrau* (homemaker), kept what one might describe as a well-regulated household. We were a *kinderreiche* (children-rich) family and throughout the war, my mother was never without a maid.

When, at one time, she was in need of a new one, she turned to the authorities. In the early days of the war, the government had assigned to her a girl who absolved her *Pflichtjahr* (duty year). I am not sure anymore if this service was administered by the *RAD*, the national labor service, or by another party or government agency.

A Youth Service Law existed, but I am not certain if it was expanded to mandate a full year of household duty for the girls.

Whatever the case, we had her for much less than a full year. She came daily to our house, helping my mother with the housework. I don't even recall her name, but I remember her as a very delicate person. She suffered from homesickness although she wasn't far away from her parents' home that could be reached in a few hours by train. Moreover, in Breslau, she did not live with strangers, but with relatives just a block away from us.

She wore an engagement ring. Her fiancé was a childhood friend and the families were friends or neighbors or both. Whenever the girl went back to Ratibor, she visited her future mother-in-law and her mother.

The girl from Ratibor, although still very young (perhaps 17 or 18 years old) expected to get married to her soldier fiancé. When she received letters from him, it made her cry. Every time. Tears came to her eyes even before she opened the envelope, before she ever read what he had written. Ultimately, whenever she was downcast or received a letter, I just disappeared without saying anything. My sister Ute, very concerned, called the letters the maid received *Traenenbriefe*, weepy letters.

Then it happened.

It was not she who received an official notification of his death; it was his mother, who then called her at our house.

The next day she told my mother that she wanted to volunteer to become a *Blitzmaedel*, slang for *Nachrichtenhelferin* (female member of the signal corps).

My mother could not believe it.

Here was a young girl, apparently an only child, pampered, if not spoiled in her youth. She had been overly protected in the past. Now she was struck down by the sudden loss of her lover and yet decided, while in deep sorrow and pain, to volunteer service in the armed forces!

Did she have a death wish?

She told my mother that she wanted to contribute more to the war effort than just being a maid in a children-rich family.

CHAPTER 33

Love and Lust

In Podiebrad whenever we had several days off, I visited my mother in Breslau or my grandmother in Warmbrunn, or both, if there was enough time. Germans observe several religious holidays to which the National Socialists had added some. The latter were designated as holidays of the movement.

We were also entitled to vacation periods during school breaks. I must have had a whole week off and left for home on a late train from Prague to Breslau. I sat across from a beautiful woman. I was 15 years old; she appeared three or four years older. I traveled in uniform with a special railroad pass for *KLV* personnel. She was in civilian clothes and wore a skirt and blouse.

Our eyes met. Once. Twice. We looked at each other, longer and longer.

She started talking. She mentioned that she, too, had belonged to the Hitler Youth as a member of the *BDM*, which gave me a clue that she was already 18 years or older. She insisted that I not use the formal "*Sie*" but the informal "*Du.*" For her it was easier than for me. At least at first. She asked if I were going all the way to Breslau. I was. It seemed to please her.

More questions. First, I answered nervously. I became aware of her full breasts. They moved visibly while she was breathing. Her name, as I recall, was Gertrud but she asked me right away to call her Trudel.[93]

There were other passengers in the compartment, but they did not seem to bother us. Most were tired and tried to sleep.

Trudel told me about her visit in Prague. What prompted it, I forget. I talked about the camp-leader school and Podiebrad and mentioned our occasional nightly boat rides on the Elbe River. I told her that, at the nearby school for female camp counselors, we serenaded the girls occasionally.

Trudel laughed easily. It turned into a lively, late night conversation.

There was light in the car, but the bulb had been painted. The train's window shades were pulled down. This created an almost ghostly atmosphere. Then someone turned off the light completely. We continued our conversation. At times, Trudel reached over to me, touching my arms, even my thighs.

There was a stop. We had reached a station. The dim compartment light was turned on again. The woman who sat next to Trudel had reached her destination and left. I seized the opportunity and sat down beside her. She didn't mind, in fact she seemed pleased that I had done so. We kept on talking. Our bodily contacts increased but so did our laughter. I imagined her expression. Whenever the dim compartment light was turned on, she turned her head to look at me. I noticed her teeth, white and beautiful. She had a habit I found arousing. She kept licking her lips to keep them moist.

Instead of arriving around midnight, as scheduled, we pulled into the station shortly after 2:00 a.m. We discussed the situation; there were no taxis and, for several hours, there was no place for me to go except to remain in the railroad's crowded waiting room—until the first streetcar started operating.

Trudel had a better idea. She invited me to what I thought was her parent's apartment, located within walking distance on a side street between Gartenstrasse and Tauentzienstrasse. I only had one piece of luggage and was able to help Trudel carry her heavy suitcase. As we left the station the street turned darker. I had an uneasy feeling when a policeman appeared, looking us over. I was in uniform and Trudel greeted him as if she knew who he was. His response was friendly and he wished us a good night.

We reached the apartment building where she lived. Trudel opened the front door. There was no elevator. We climbed the stairs. The last flight of steps was very narrow.

It was a small apartment, probably a converted attic. I made an effort to be quiet, not to awaken her parents.

"We are not disturbing anyone," she explained.

It turned out that only her mother was still alive and she was away taking care of an old grandmother who lived in Upper Silesia. Then, with a lowered voice she said that her father was dead. He had fallen on the battlefield. Just a year ago.

This explanation was followed by a moment of silence.

I put down her suitcase and my backpack.

The living room looked cozy, with a couch and armchairs. Trudel went to the windows and pulled down the shades. Even though Breslau had not yet experienced an air raid, *Verdunkelung* (blackout) orders were in force. Then she turned on the heat, which caused a banging noise in the pipes. In the room adjacent to hers— it must have been her mother's bedroom—there was a basket with laundry. From it, she pulled out some towels and asked: "Would you like to freshen up?"

"After you," I replied, sitting down on the living room couch. We took turns using the bathroom.

Then she went into the kitchen.

"First of all, I am going to fix us something warm to drink."

She did and served tea along with cookies.

"Let's make it *gemuetlich* (comfortable) she suggested, went to her bedroom and returned with a white garment, all folded up.

"It's too cold in my room," she remarked. She turned off the light. I was so surprised.

It was totally dark now. I tried to control a sudden wave of excitement. I could hear her undressing.

First I heard her unbuttoning her blouse and pulling it over her head, then unzipping her skirt, sliding it down and stepping out of it.

My whole body began trembling. The rustling sound went

on. What was she changing into? Did she undress completely? Was she now naked?

My heart beat wildly.

She stepped to the lamp and turned the light on. There she was—and so close to me—in a nightgown, almost transparent. For a moment, I saw nothing but her dehiscent breasts, stretching the silky nightgown, moving rhythmically as she breathed. I could see her nipples. Dark pink tits, titillating and arousing. Questions stormed through my head. We had not even kissed. Were we approaching what was known, in contemporary terms, as the highest fulfillment of womanhood?

Something she might be prepared for, but not I? And would I have to prove myself? What if I failed?

In split seconds, I came to realize how little I knew about sex. A classmate of mine and I had, for awhile, researched the biological functions until all of the information contained in the books we had access to had been exhausted.

I had never dared to ask my father questions about sex, and I had never felt at ease enough to talk to my mother about anything that had to do with sexual functions. I don't know why, but it must have had to do with my upbringing. In school or *Jungvolk* there was no sex education either. We were made to understand that attitudes toward love must be healthy, required clean minds, that we should channel our energy into athletic activities. We were, of course, expected to abstain from sex as lust. The purpose of sex was solely to reproduce.

As the young of our great nation, we were expected to maintain, at all times, *eine saubere Haltung* (a clean lifestyle) *und einen starken Willen* (and a strong will). We were never to lose control when alone with a girl.

At the Podiebrad camp counselor school, we had listened to lectures "You and the Girl" by the headmaster. Also to "Loyalty in the Struggle for Purity" written and delivered by Arthur M., the *Schulungsleiter* (Chief lecturer). Both emphasized that sexual behavior is dependent on how strong our will is to keep our actions under control. We were told to maintain comradeship with girls and not physical relationships.

Prior to the war, unwed pregnancy was considered immoral. During the war, however, an official circular stated that it was acceptable for women to become pregnant through relationships with soldiers outside of wedlock. Hitler Youth members were not included in this, nor was there any mention of the *Lebensborn* (Life Source) facilities established for illegitimate children fathered by *SS* members. The Hitler Youth Leadership remained opposed to girls having children out of wedlock. While I was stationed in Podiebrad, all of the instructors signed a letter written by the school's director protesting this circular as immoral.

By all that I had read or heard, I was invariably impressed that by nature a boy's role was to be the initiator and the girl was to be passive. In those few novels I had read that contained romantic passages, the man was always the initiator. Love unfolded in stages, with petting and kissing and, often, much soul-searching and deep commitments proceeding copulation.

It flashed through my mind that I was physically capable of fathering a child. During my long hospitalization, my physician had obtained semen and determined the sperms were potent. He had shown them to me through his microscope, moving through fluid, like long-tailed little creatures.

My hands touched her breasts and she went into a frenzy. She, in turn, clasped me vehemently and scratched my neck with her fingernails. They were sharp; I could feel it. And, suddenly, in my ear, I felt her tongue, wet and rousing. One hand she lowered to open the fly of my pants.

That's when my muscles tensed. A feeling of sheer panic took hold of me.

I freed myself, put my pants in order and grabbed my luggage. She seemed stunned.

"Don't be afraid!" She tried to hold me back.

But I left in a hurry. I left her place, without explanation, not saying anything. I ran down the stairs. She called after me to come back, but I took to my heels until I couldn't hear anymore what she said.

She was a German girl. How could she behave like this? It just wasn't supposed to happen this way. She had turned my inner world around, upside down.

***

For days I lived through the whole experience again and again, with wavering thoughts. Had I been a fool or had I done the right thing?

Among my mother's books was one, *A Beginner's Book for Racial Hygiene*, which I had thumbed through. It was not a primer for sex education but promoted racial improvement through selective breeding. It admonished racial purity through choice of spouse and population growth by having large families.

Trudel didn't exemplify the typical Nordic prototype, but she was a good-looking German girl. She was probably old enough to get married, but I was not.

At one moment, I felt proud that I acted the way I did. At the next moment, I thought of myself as a fool for having panicked. What an opportunity it had been and I had let it go by! What was wrong with me?

Much of what had happened, I just couldn't understand. I kept on reviewing not just my behavior but hers as well. Why had she turned the lights on? I would have been more comfortable in the dark. Why didn't she say anything? I was just about to tell her how beautiful she looked. Why did she plunge her tongue into my ear when I was longing for her mouth?

Was I just a fool? Not man enough to restrain and to conquer her as men did in novels I had read? I had never read of a woman acting as Trudel had. It was always the man who persuaded with great efforts and seduced the woman. What went wrong?

Maybe she was not pure. Purity was a great issue, a moral code for youth.

Could she be right? Was I a coward? For many evenings there was no peace for me. I could not believe that I had behaved as I did. I hated her. I wanted her. I did not know what to think of her, of me. My mind remained filled with turmoil.

One evening, I made myself go back to where she lived. I watched the building. There was no light in any of the windows under the roof. I must have waited for over two hours. She never came. At the end, I was relieved that she did not come. What could I have said to her without coming across like a whey-face?

On my way home, I decided that I had to prove to myself that I was not afraid. The question of courage overcame the issue of purity. I decided to save the money necessary to go to a prostitute. In Hitler's Germany (as is the case now), houses of prostitution[94] were legal.

***

In Breslau, I knew just where to find the *Nutten* (hussies) as they were called. In the rear of Klaus' parents' restaurant, there was an alley called Krullstrasse. It was a designated red light district. Many a time I had observed the women offering themselves for mercenary purposes. I would imagine what would go on after they attracted a male, negotiated a price, closed the window and pulled the curtain. Of course, a *Jungvolk* leader would never feel attracted by a prostitute—or would he?

Occasionally, Klaus and I had talked about them. We decided that it would be below our dignity to pay for something so intimate and to have sex with someone who had done it with hundreds of men before—no matter how attractive she was.

And some of the girls behind the windows on Krullstrasse looked very attractive, at least from the distance I was still keeping.

Klaus, living so close by, knew more about their way of life and how they peddled their flesh. He called the girls "dirty whores." At times they fought with each other, Klaus told me. He quoted samples of their obscenities.

Now, I no longer cared. My confused state and the perplexity of my growing sexual urges kept occupying my mind.

It was a rainy Friday evening. With ten marks and change in my pocket and with a mixture of hesitation and determination, my fortitude finally prevailed. I left the house, jumped on an already moving streetcar heading downtown. I slipped and almost fell off the car.

The drizzle had stopped by the time I reached my destination. The wet pavement reflected the few faint lights of the darkened city and the bright flashes from doors opening.

The two five-mark coins in my pocket weighed heavily. I clenched them in my fist to overcome my nervousness.

No faltering now, I told myself.

Traffic, both ways, was heavy in the small alley. I observed that some men just walked up and down, not even talking to the girls, only looking. Continuously. A few of them were wet and must have walked up and down for some time in the misty weather.

Others, as I did, stayed for a while in one place and looked from an inauspicious distance at what was going on. There were quite a few soldiers who didn't spend much time walking around. Looking the women over, they picked one, without much haggling and were let in the door.

I told myself: "Now!"

Walking down the alley, I stopped at the first one whose window was open. She reached out and touched my arm.

"Come on inside, my darling."

A chill went down my spine.

"How much?"

"For you, only five marks." She grinned. I nodded. She opened the door. I followed her.

When climbing the stairs, I noticed that the steps were uneven and squeaked. Her stockings were not tightly pulled up. From moment to moment, she looked older. She had big, voluptuous, breasts, almost too huge for my liking. Her stomach was also big, a typical beer belly. Her face was nondescript, except for a sheen from a thick layer of skin cream.

What flabbergasted me was that there was a light with a red bulb on her nightstand.

The room was tiny, with just a bed, the small nightstand with the red lamp, a couple of chairs and a very small table. Everything looked crimson. Even the bed. A nightmarish hue. There were some obscene pictures on the wall. They looked ghastly, rather than enticing.

"Where is the money?"

I gave her the five marks.

"Is that all you got?"

"That's what you asked for."

"Give me more and I'll make it nice for you," she encouraged me. I gave her the additional change but not the other five-mark I had in my pocket.

She snatched the money and then said: "Undress!"—almost harshly.

She only took off her skirt and her panties. They looked red. My underwear looked just as red. And so did our flesh.

Her stockings had not been fastened.

Why should that have annoyed me?

All the way into town I had an erection and while I waited, watching what went on. Now it disappeared and I couldn't produce one.

"What's that?" the prostitute asked with a contemptuous smirk.

She took hold of my penis and massaged it. It stiffened, and she kept on massaging it to the point of ejection.

The semen looked red too.

"Not much to it!" she said with a spiteful grin, while wiping the seminal fluid off her hand.

"That's it my boy . . . unless you have another five."

By now, the whole situation had become revolting. There was no more urge.

"Enough," I replied, feeling cheated but in control for the first time.

This all seemed so incredible. A year earlier, when I was hospitalized, the young physician who lived within the complex of the university hospital, had taken me to his small apartment. He had done just what the prostitute did—massaged my male organ. He had warned me that I would "explode."

To do this, I realized later, must have given him pleasure. He had maintained that it was strictly a medical procedure to establish if I had reached manhood and the ability to father a child.

I got dressed and left. Not running as I had from Trudel's apartment. Disgusted at myself, but in a different way, I left her place, wishing for rain outside.

It was drizzling again, with several men still strolling up and down the street.

Most of the windows were closed, indicating that Krullstrasse had a busy night.

***

Following this disgusting experience, I searched through the encyclopedia at home. My previous studies in this regard, clandestinely conducted with a classmate, had enlightened us about the biological facts of life but had not touched on performance and psychological aspects.

Now, after cross-referencing every fact I found on sex and human sexual behavior, I had gathered only a small amount of additional knowledge. It was mentioned that sex drives differ according to personalities, age, circumstances, and even religious beliefs. It was stressed, however, that the stigma of sin had been removed by Hitler's new regime. Sexual intercourse should take place within wedlock and as often as propitious to conjugal life and beneficial to physical well being.

Adolescents had to exercise self-restraint. Self-control, strong willpower, and iron discipline would channel one's energy into positive channels. We would find outlets in athletic and healthy outdoor activities, such as climbing mountains, going on long hikes and the like.

I learned that sex drives differed, that it was natural for me to have one already. But most of my questions remained unresolved. I couldn't even find an explanation of why there were prostitutes.

All I was given to understand was that they were practicing their trade, as old as mankind, under strict medical supervision provided and administered by the government to avoid transmittable sexual diseases. Thus, I determined at the age of 15 (going on 16), that love is a complex matter and love and sex are not necessarily dependent on each other. Biological functions and true inner feelings were not necessarily the same. I decided that Trudel was desirable—the whore was not.

I promised myself that I would never engage the services of a prostitute again.

A year later, when I was being trained for battle, Corporal Schleifer stated with great emphasis: "You can't fuck unless you become soldiers first!" It sounded like an order. First Lieutenant Gutschke overheard Schleifer's outburst and reprimanded him in front of us all.

I would receive my baptism as a soldier in battle before experiencing a relationship that followed my conception of what love and sex were all about.

CHAPTER 34

Total War

On February 18, 1943, a speech by Dr. Josef Goebbels was broadcast which became known as his "Total War" proclamation. He had assembled in the *Sportspalast* an audience of wounded and highly decorated soldiers (including Knight's Cross holders), celebrities, party functionaries, and staunch party members from the civilian population. He posed the question: "Do you want total war?" The crowd answered in unison with a thunderous: "Yes!"

He mobilized the entire nation to participate even more vigorously in the war effort. Goebbels declared that, as a result, fighting would come to an earlier and, of course, victorious end.

I was 15 years old at the time of the speech, being trained to become a camp counselor. I was in a group listening to Dr. Goebbels' speech on the radio. We responded just as his audience did in Berlin. As soon as we boys were asked to fight, we would be ready. He also released in many of us feelings of anger. We had lost Stalingrad. Conditions on almost all fronts were worsening. Drastic actions were needed. Dr. Goebbels had succeeded, very skillfully, to direct our rising rage toward our enemies and not toward our own leaders.

Dr. Goebbels was a master in developing dynamic concepts to pull the masses towards his aims. The results of his manipulations were stunning. He set our hearts on fire and most of the nation rallied behind him and his *Fuehrer*.

I chose to help by writing letters to an unknown soldier as part of a *Heimatfront* (home front) campaign to cheer up servicemen.

The youth program was much more than just ideological indoctrination and military conditioning. It involved hiking, camping, a wide range of sports and competitive events and social activities. These de-emphasized class differences and promoted genuine comradeship. We were, by any standards, healthy, in good spirits, and possessed a sense of purpose. We were the youngest members of a people's community called *Volksgemeinschaft*, a fellowship of mutual support. "All for one and one for all" was one of our mottoes.

Not only Hitler's youth but also millions of adults, in a similar state of mind, accepted the challenge to meet ever-increasing demands. We would carry the heaviest burden. We would support "Total War."

***

Less than a year after this proclamation, the situation had deteriorated to the point that Dr. Goebbels, together with party leader Martin Bormann and *SS* leader Heinrich Himmler, issued a joint appeal to the German people. The appeal asked for a *Volksopfer* (people's sacrifice/sacrificial offering). The new home defense force had to be outfitted. The civilian population was asked to bring to designated collection points, all types of uniforms (police, fireman, railroad, postal, etc.) and shoes, socks, underwear and sweaters, as well as blankets, camping gear and anything else that could be useful.

Hitler had ordered the establishment of the *Volkssturm* (literally: "people's storm," named for the Home Defense Force). All men between the ages of 16 to 60 able to carry a weapon and to defend the homeland were to be inducted. The *Gauleiters* (political leaders of each region) were ordered to draft all males in this age group. *SS* chief, Heinrich Himmler, became the military commander of these units, while party leader, Martin Bormann, was ordered to oversee the organizational procedures. Hitler declared members of the *Volkssturm* to be soldiers under military law that meant that, in case of cowardice, the death penalty would be applied.

The donated clothes were for these men and boys.

***

Horror and devastation, already apparent in those German cities that had to experience barbaric air raids, had not reached my world yet. Neither Breslau nor Podiebrad showed visible signs of any kind of warfare. We could sleep nights.

Meanwhile, without anyone I knew admitting it openly, Hitler's Thousand Year *Reich*[95] began to crack. I was not aware of it and had no suspicions what the reality of the situation was.

Through conditioning, I was still bound to believe. And believe I did. In Hitler, in his "mission" to make Germany great, and in my responsibility to measure up to his expectations. We were "his" youth and, as most of those my age, I had been thoroughly prepared to have absolute faith in him and in his unfailing capabilities as the nation's military leader. I had no qualifications to judge that he had little chance after Stalingrad to win the war.

Temporary setbacks, we were told, did not discourage the German fighting forces but, instead, strengthened their resolve to achieve final victory. It seemed to me that the entire German nation was determined to win this war. We were willing to render the price, even if we had to pay with our own lives.

While the battlefields retrenched and approached Germany's borders, slogans, such as: "The German soldier holds his ground; no one can push him back!" were repeated often enough to have remained, to this day, etched deeply into my mind.

In 1943, Hitler Youth and *SS* leaders entered into a joint undertaking and agreed to make a special contribution to the "total war" effort. Volunteers were sought from the Hitler Youth for the creation of a new section of the *Waffen-SS* fighting corps (not to be confused with the *SS* death head squads).[96] Some of my fellow *Jungvolk* leaders who were born in 1926 were encouraged by our superiors to join this new, elite unit and several did.

Komm zu Uns! (Joins us!) Flyers were distributed among Hitler Youth leaders. They promoted enlistment among those who were old enough. Dr. Schluender and Artur Axmann, my last commander in battle and *Reich* Youth Leader, were instrumental, together with SS leaders, in setting up this crack division.[97] It would be called *Hitler Jugend Panzer Division*. This group developed a high degree of *espirit de corps*.

They were considered daredevils and many were destined to reach the status of hero by the end of the war. The Knight's Cross of the Iron Cross was awarded to no less than 15 of them. But few survived. The blood of these young men, Germany's hope for the future, ended up being shed heroically in battlefields in France and Hungary. In Normandy, the Division fought with tenacity and ferocity.

But even a super-elite force of young enthusiasts could not stem the advancing Allied Forces. They were superior—especially in air power. Only when it became apparent that no relief was forthcoming did the Division Commander pull back his decimated, exhausted warriors. This was done, despite Hitler's orders to fight to the very end.

Some time after the battle of Normandy, its ranks filled again with even younger volunteers (those born in 1927). In February, the Division was transferred to the Army Group South in Hungary and was ordered to recapture Budapest.

The Hitler Youth Division had no chance of accomplishing this. They were swept back into Austria by the overwhelming forces of the Red Army. Those still alive (supposedly less than 10,000)—battle-worn, but still proud, surrendered at war's end, May 8, 1945, to the U.S. Seventh Army.

Two friends of mine from Breslau, who were Hitler Youth leaders and had served honorably, were among the fallen. They probably never realized that their oath had made them soldiers who fought against a mass-murderer, Stalin, and for a mass-murderer, Hitler.

I was too young to join. Late in 1944, some born in 1928 were accepted as volunteers ahead of schedule. I was already committed to join the mountain troops.

To qualify for military mountain-training required proof that I had mountain climbing experience and that I was an accomplished skier. It also required a physical. As it turned out, it wasn't much of one. Completely naked, we had to march up to the doctor. He asked some questions, listened to my lungs and my heart, and signed my papers: "*kv*", suitable for combat. I hadn't mentioned my frequent angina pains and had shortened my medical history substantially. I did not want to be rejected.

For me the "*kv*" was the symbol of a personal victory.

I asked my mother for my father's APO address in order to send him a note. His son was destined to become a wartime soldier and fight for his country and his *Fuehrer*.

I couldn't achieve manhood if I missed the opportunity to become a soldier in battle. So I thought at the time.

First, I had to wait to be assigned to a *WE-Lager*, a pre-military training camp in the high Alps. A year prior, I was declared unfit to become even an air defense cannoneer and had been assigned to a *KLV* camp. I doubted then that I would serve in the *RAD* (*Reich Labor Service*).[98]

Now, there seemed to be a chance that I might end up with a unit almost as famous as the Hitler Youth Division, the *Waffen-SS Gebirgs-Division Nord* (*Waffen-SS* Mountain Division North). It had, together with the Army's 3rd Mountain Division under General Eduard Dietl, distinguished itself as a formidable fighting force in Norway and Lapland. It would all depend on my performance in the Hitler Youth camp. I was determined to give it my all, to complete my premilitary training in the mountains with flying colors.

As alluded to earlier, my friend Klaus and I, when we were 10 and 11 years old, first fantasized about becoming U-boat captains—until we decided to become fighter pilots. I had made inquiries at the Air Force recruiting office and brought home printed information. This was two years before we even could have volunteered. My mother, noticing my enthusiasm, not only reminded me of my age but also pointed out that, to become a pilot, one had to be especially healthy. She warned me that the physical for *Luftwaffen* candidates might be particularly tough.

By 1944, I had given up on becoming an Air Force fighter pilot. I now had my heart firmly set on joining the ranks of the mountaineers. Throughout the war, I wanted to become a hero— to come before our leader and be recognized by him for bravery, an act of selflessness in the service of one's country. I would end up seeing this dream fulfilled, and it would cause me many nightmares later. It all turned into a tormenting irony—not on the morning of victory but on the sunset of defeat.

CHAPTER 35

Family Time

My mother, who believed in Hitler, although in a much less strident way than my father, was nevertheless disturbed by the turn of events and concerned about me. My mother believed in supernatural phenomenon. In Waldtrudering, where I was born, she, *Frau* Himmler (the wife of the notorious *SS* leader), and the wife of the local baker had once gone to a clairvoyant.

All three women, according to my mother, believed in his predictions. He had pleased them with his premonitions of prosperity for their families and for the entire German nation. This had been three or four years before Hitler assumed power. As my mother commented later, he had predicted neither war nor mass-slaughter.

My sister Anje was also already involved in the war effort, actively entertaining wounded soldiers in military hospital with her performance troop.

The only time I remember Anje being upset politically was when she had passed one of her teachers on the street and wished her a "good day" instead of greeting her with "*Heil Hitler.*" The next day she had to come up to the front to face her entire class and was ordered to repeat several times: "The German salute is *Heil* Hitler!"

She found this degrading and henceforth disliked this teacher vehemently, but not Adolf Hitler. I took the time during holidays at home to read my parents' books, among them several about Hitler. They idealized him. These books enchanted my young mind. I remember three: *The People's Book about Hitler* by Georg Schott; *With Hitler to Power* by Otto Dietrich; and *From the Kaiserhof to the Reich Chancellery* by Joseph Goebbels. There were several others whose titles and authors I no longer recall.

Among various periodicals my father received was *The Black Corps* and the *FM-Magazine*. These were both *SS* publications, which I often read from cover to cover. Praise, veneration, respect, and admiration were typically expressed in everything published about Adolf Hitler during the Third *Reich*.

I remember a marching song starting (freely translated): " . . . and today Germany is ours and tomorrow it will be the whole world." I learned only after the war that this was not the right text. According to the original lyrics, we should have sung: " . . . and today Germany listens to us and tomorrow the whole world."

I often heard that God was on Germany's side and protected our *Fuehrer*. My perceptions of Almighty were those of an all-powerful God personified. I believed in God but was without church affiliation as my parents had left the church.

My maternal grandmother, a true Christian not only in words but also in deeds, had planted in me enough of a god-perception that I never doubted God's existence. I had full confidence that Hitler's life and the fate of Germany were being favored by a higher power.

As incredible as it might seem today, in my youthful eyes he was, in a sense, the anointed one—the messiah of our time.

As it turned out, "our time" was short; the image self-destructed. The legacy left behind was that of destruction, of corpses, burnt out buildings, blown up bridges. Total destruction.

I was four years old when the Third *Reich* started. I was only sixteen years old when it reached its end.

***

Less than a year before Hitler's suicide, at some time in the summer or fall of 1944, my father was home on furlough. I came to visit and the question of my *Werdegang*—what should become of me—was on both of our minds.

My father expected that I still wanted to pursue an acting career. Even during my short furlough, I had made a guest appearance at the radio station. Also, I had become an ardent moviegoer often expressing more interest in the actors and their performances than in the plot.

My father was now a war correspondent, sort of a performer himself. But he reinforced his position that a show-business career for me was out of the question.

I don't think that my father overlooked the part culture plays in advancing man's progress, but he had this determination to keep me away from influences of romanticism. He feared they could have a mellowing effect that would make me weaker than I already was.

Writing? He still didn't think I was talented enough to succeed. By now, however, an increasing number of people had a different opinion. Even the former *Reich* Youth leader, von Schirach, thought that I might have the talent to make my mark as a writer. His letter, lauding some of my poems, I valued highly.

Hbfhr. Frehse, the headmaster of our camp leader school, was probably as pragmatic as my father. He came up with the idea that I could use my talent to become a *Schulungsleiter* (social science instructor), one who not only teaches, but writes educational texts as well.

Hbfhr. Frehse talked of the *Zeitgeist* (the spirit of the times) created by the *Fuehrer*, which had elevated all of us who had become unit leaders in Podiebrad. He sketched out a blueprint for my future. "By becoming a *hauptamtlicher HJ-Fuehrer* (professional Hitler Youth Leader), you will have many choices. You could become a writer, one in the service of your nation with a secure and steady income." I repeated this nearly verbatim to my father.

Since I had been unable to qualify for either the *NAPOLA* or the Adolf Hitler School, my father inquired about this opportunity.

"What do you do in Podiebrad?"

I explained my duties.

"How many hours do you attend class?"

"Our high school education is not being continued there. I'll have to make up the classes I am missing."

While my former classmates who had become *Flakhelfer* continued to receive instructions in the major subjects, our training was restricted to becoming proficient camp counselors.

My father was upset by this. He insisted that I request a camp-leader assignment in an evacuated school where higher classes were taught so that I could attend them.

***

My father was frequently at the front either as war correspondent or on one of those special security missions in which he had to participate from time to time. He kept these missions secret even from his own family

The one and only report by my father I listened to during the two years he was a *Kriegsberichterstatter* (war correspondent) was aired on Germany's Memorial Day, in spring 1944. It was titled *The Cross on Acuto Mountain* and was dispatched from the Italian front. It told the story of a hero's death during the battle of Italy.

All I knew of this battle was that the Allied Forces had established a beachhead at Anzio.[99] I knew of the heavy fighting at Monte Cassino but had never heard of Monte Acuto before. I finally discovered, in an old atlas, a map of Southern Italy. A little town named Acuto was located in the Ciociaria region, between Frosinone and Rome. I surmised that there must be a mountain named Acuto.

It had never been mentioned in any of the official reports, so it was my father who drew attention to the fighting there. My father's former secretary, *Frau* Fuhrken, had alerted my mother of this forthcoming broadcast and she, in turn, informed me. There was some static, but I listened intently.

My father described an attack aimed at the battalion's

headquarters to which he was assigned. He and the *Batallionsadjutant,* a first lieutenant, were looking through their field glasses to size up the attacking unit. The cast iron enclosure in front of the window had as its center a cross. While my father spoke into his recorder, the cross and the window bars were hit, and the *Batallionsadjutant* who stood beside him was killed instantly.

At first my father thought that he might have been wounded as well because he had big red blotches on his uniform. But, feeling no pain, he soon found that the blood was that of his fallen comrade.

The battalion commander ordered that this farmhouse be defended as long as it took to bury, in the yard behind the building, the fallen officer. The fighting continued, tanks approached, while a grave was dug—a difficult task because of the stony earth. All of the available Pak-ammunition was used up and the defenders had only a couple of bazookas left.

My father used wood from shelving in the house to put together a cross that was then thrust into the graveside with the officer's helmet put on top.

This report made quite an impression on me. I was proud of my father's accomplishment, the literalness of this gripping story— keeping on fighting to gain time for burial.

CHAPTER 36

Camp Counselor

My pre-military training was scheduled to take place in January 1945. After my stint as instructor at the counselor school in summer of 1944, I had gained enough seniority to enable me to choose my assignment as a camp counselor. The one I picked would take me very close to Niesky. I selected it with great hopes for a reunion with my friend Rudi.

I expected to find him and his menagerie still there where he and his parents had lived when my family had left Waldgut Horka. Although Rudi and I had not corresponded for many years, my memories remained vivid and warm. I did not write to announce my arrival because I had joyous visions of how surprised he would be to see me when I stood suddenly before him.

Prior to my departure, I had a couple of day's vacation and Klaus was at home on furlough too. We went to the Gloria Theater and saw a spectacular film just released, one of the first in color. It was *The Adventures of Baron von Muenchhausen*[100] starring Brigitte Horney, my favorite in the leading role of the rapacious Catherine the Great.

It was a film featuring the adventures of a showoff. With its wild fantasies and stunning special effects, this production took us away for a couple of hours from the reality that soon would drastically change the course of our lives.

German Armed Forces had, on several fronts, experienced decisive setbacks. Hitler, with his stand-firm orders and no-retreat strategies, sacrificed ever-increasing numbers of his soldiers. But wouldn't he follow the Prussian king, Frederick the Great, who, after grave defeats, achieved great victories?

It seems so unbelievable today to realize that not just we—the young—but our parents and even foreigners felt the same way. An increasing number of Czech citizens supported Hitler's dictatorship. At the camp counselor training school, I observed personally that many even raised their hands to salute the swastika banner hoisted in front of our school.

The fact that I remained committed and devoted to the cause and continued on course might also have had a lot to do with the comradeship I experienced. As was the case with high school classmates, many friendships resulted (and have, in some cases, lasted to this day). They are all humane human beings. Thank God, we were not old enough to be given orders to commit murderous acts.

***

In the fall of 1944, I had arrived in Ullersdorf as a complete stranger. I did not know any of the students nor any of the teachers. I knew that I would have to prove myself to the students who were "Berliners" and had the reputation of being prankish.

Sure enough, the first night there, I uncovered my bed and the sheet was filled with a mess of crawling earthworms. I made the mistake of waking up the boys in the sleeping room next to me. I had them remove the slimy, creepy creatures. The next day one of my teachers filed a complaint that I had overstepped my authority by ordering them to clean my room late at night. My action had prevented them from getting enough sleep.

All I remember about the outcome of this incident is that the head of internal affairs of the local *Bann* (district) appeared. It was an awkward situation because my rank was higher than his. I was reprimanded. It was suggested that I keep my room locked. I did not.

I was determined to earn respect from these boys. There was no school on Sunday so I arranged for a full weekend program of hikes, sports, plays etc. This got me off to a good start—although I secretly believed that making them clean up my room had a great deal to do with my success in earning their respect.

***

From the time I arrived in Ullersdorf, I had wanted to visit Rudi. I had to wait until midweek when I could take a day off and pedal to Niesky on my bicycle. On my way, a steady stream of old memories flowed through my mind.

When we left Waldgut Horka in 1935, nine long years earlier, Rudi and I were seven years old—now we were 16. Young men. Soon I would be a soldier. What about him—since he was a hunchback?

I located the school we once attended together. From there, I remembered the way. When I saw the house, I was overcome by an odd feeling. Something looked strange. The front door was locked. There was no response to my knocks. Except for flies, not a living creature was in sight.

I remembered the neighbor woman and went to see her. She didn't remember me. I had grown too much. I asked her where Rudi was.

"Rudi?" she looked at me and then replied, almost disdainfully, "Rudi, the cripple? He went to an institution years ago."

Cripple? It struck me. My first reaction was to ask if he had taken his snakes along. Instead I asked: "Do you know where?"

She shook her head.

"His parents?"

"Rudi's father is dead, fallen in Russia."

Pause: "The mother?"

"Wasn't she a Red Cross nurse?" The old woman seemed unsure. She must not have liked the family. That's the impression I had. I asked: "Where can I find out where Rudi is?"

"I have no idea. He might be in heaven with his pets."

I pedaled to Waldgut—the wooded estate where I had lived.

The road was worse than I remembered. I stopped first at the Geisler house—the only other house in the area. A dog growled. Years earlier, my own dogs would have come running out, barking with excitement to greet me when I came home.

Now, an unfamiliar dog announced that a stranger was approaching. *Frau* Geisler wasn't there. A younger woman greeted me. She did not know who I was. The world of my early childhood was empty now. I had had such high expectations. Now I felt forsaken.

I asked myself over and over again—why hadn't Rudi and I kept in touch. I tried to recall when we had corresponded last and who was last to write. But I could not remember.

I thought of our teacher when he had said of Rudi "What a guy!" He had explained that it was God's doing that he was hunchback. He had asked me: "How would you feel if you were he?" And I hadn't known what to answer.

That night, after my return to Ullersdorf, I wrote Rudi a long letter in anticipation that I would be able to locate him. I never did. Events took over at a rapid pace, and after 1944 came to a close, I would not return to Ullersdorf, Waldgut Horka, or Niesky until 1997.

CHAPTER 37

Christmas, 1944

It seemed as if a miracle had happened. Christmas 1944, our entire family celebrated the holidays together. My father, in a Breslau military hospital due to stomach and gallbladder problems, had received holiday leave.

I came home from Ullersdorf in good spirits. Holidays in our house were always very festive and, even in the fifth year of the war, my parents—especially my mother—managed to make it a memorable event. I knew that right after the holidays I would be leaving for the Bavarian Alps to attend the pre-military training camp for prospective mountain troops. It gave me an additional sense of purpose and a feeling of importance.

Following the Christmas celebration, I would be elevated to a higher level of duty for the Fatherland and then begin training to become a defender of our people and country.

Living at home were my youngest sister, Doerte, who was nine, my brothers Wulf and Ulrich, six and five, together with my mother and our corpulent maid, Hanna. My oldest sisters, Anje (14) and Ute (11), arrived from Strehlen, a small town southeast of Breslau to which they, as students of the Augusta High School, had been evacuated.

Both of the oldest girls played the flute and practiced. They would play for us on Christmas Eve before we all sang some German Christmas songs. Moreover, during the Christmas holidays, they would report to their *Rundfunkspielschar* (radio playing group) and entertain wounded soldiers in local military hospitals.

Right up to Christmas Eve, my mother, helped by our maid,

seemed to be baking nonstop, an assortment of cookies, gingerbread, several almond varieties, and also *Stollen* (a Christmas bread with candied fruit pieces). My father, who had come home from the Mediterranean, had supplied her almonds, oranges, and lemons.

While on this leave and because of his gallbladder and stomach problems, father had to check into one of Breslau's many local military hospitals. The nurses were nuns from Upper Silesia. Upon returning home, our family physician, *Frau* Dr. Petzold, prescribed for him a medication that was no longer available in our local *Apotheke* (pharmacy).

I ended up making a run to obtain this medication. I went from pharmacy to pharmacy without luck. Finally, one pharmacist sent me to a hospital pharmacy. There an *Ordensschwester* (sister of a religious order) still had a supply of this medicine.

My father was determined to get well enough to attend a hunting party with old friends in the woods near Schweidnitz.

Before the trip, he spent many hours looking through photo albums of which he had a voluminous collection. He even made a remark I recall (and found out of character): "I hope that this war will soon come to an end."

On Christmas day I also decided to show him the letter I had received from Baldur von Schirach, encouraging me to continue writing poetry. By now, my father had agreed to my becoming a professional Hitler Youth leader. I figured he couldn't object if I continued to write as long as my future livelihood would not depend on it. I wanted to show my mother the letter, since she would be pleased by it, but felt that I had to show it to my father first.

He was visibly surprised. The letter was short. I think he read it twice.

He looked me in the eyes. "Make sure to keep it."

That was all he said.

It was more than I had expected.

Suddenly, I felt like I was wearing a laurel and it had not been taken from me.

My father left the day after Christmas to go on his hunt.

It seems strange now that going hunting could have been on his mind. But, just before Christmas 1944, optimism spread. The military situation appeared to improve with German troops waging a seemingly successful offensive on the Western front. The Eastern front appeared to be stable. The great Russian winter offensive wouldn't start for another two weeks.

***

We waited for a turn of events caused by the *Wunderwaffen* (miracle weapons) and a falling-out among the Allies. This would happen, we were told, because the partnership between Communist Russia and the Western Democracies was one of natural enemies. It couldn't last.

In 1944 the propaganda escalated about our mission to save Europe from the Bolsheviks. It was a sacred mission and God was on our side. In the end, the *Fuehrer* and his brave soldiers would win this war. The only conception of warfare I had was based on what I saw in the *Wochenschau* (newsreel), heard on the radio, and read in newspapers and magazines.

Later, when studying the history of World War II, I learned that it was at this time that the American forces in Bastogne, France, contemptuously rejected the German demand to surrender, with a single word: "Nuts!" This was uttered by General McAuliffe, Commander of the U.S. 101st Airborne Division.

The Russians on the eastern front, at this very time, were amassing troops upon troops to attack from the Baltic to the Carpathians. They outnumbered the German forces five to one.

This might have been known to the highest military leaders, but was not anticipated by a war correspondent on extended sick leave. His optimism heightened as his health improved. He was able to go on this hunt in the woods of Silesia after all. He had no idea it would be his last one. I left thereafter for the mountain camp, not imagining by any stretch of my imagination that when returning three weeks later, I would come back to an empty house.

CHAPTER 38

Military Training

The holidays over, I reached Garmisch-Partenkirchen on New Year's Eve to begin my pre-military training. I arrived by train with four or five other boys on their way to the same camp. We started hiking together up the mountain. It turned dark when we reached *Toni Huette*, a forest ranger's hut. It was snowing and the others decided to spend the night there.

I decided to go on. I don't recall why. Perhaps because it was New Year's Eve and I expected food and, perhaps, even a party at the camp. There was no storm and the trees had markings to keep me on track. I didn't except any trouble. I had no knowledge, however, of the dangers of hiking in the Alps during a heavy snowfall.

I became very tired and talked to myself for encouragement. Still, I was able to follow the directions given by markings on the trees and reached a clearing called the *Hexenkessel* (Witches' Cauldron). There I walked into a snowdrift several feet high, and suddenly I was submerged up to my chest. I panicked and started screaming as loud as I could, "*Hilfe! Hilfe!*" (Help! Help!).

Despite the blackout, I could see light appear for short moments when the front door of a building was opened. Apparently someone stepped out or in. Nobody heard my shouts, however. My comrades who had remained in the *Toni Huette* became concerned about me when the snowfall became heavier and heavier. They called the camp to check if I had arrived. I had not. Soon after that a ski patrol left and heard my hoarse voice calling. They came to rescue me and took me to the camp.

***

The three weeks went by fast. Although the training was strenuous, it was also fascinating. It took place in a most spectacular alpine setting. We skied on the Olympic downhill slopes. We were taught the basics of mountain climbing, practiced shooting with small caliber rifles, and received theoretical instructions.

The news of the Russian advance reached me there. In Breslau, my mother was alone with my sisters and younger brothers. I worried deeply that she needed me. Despite the risk, I decided to return home immediately—a couple of days before the camp ended officially. I left through a window at 3:00 a.m., descending from the mountains to the Garmisch-Partenkirchen railroad station.

I had no problems reaching Munich, then Dresden. The trains coming from the east were crowded beyond capacity. This was not the case going east. After Goerlitz, the train was nearly empty. In Liegnitz, the train stopped, with orders given over a loudspeaker "Get off the train! Everyone off the train!" No reasons were given. This train had been destined to go to Breslau. The railway station was packed with refugees. They must have been told that this train would take them out of Liegnitz. Before it came to a complete stop, the refugees, their faces filled with despair, stormed this train. Instead of going on to Breslau, it was scheduled by railroad officials to return to Dresden.

The train filled in no time. Many people were unable to get into it, let alone find a seat.

There were some that didn't care anymore or were so exhausted they couldn't move. They lay at the end of the platforms on the icy ground, in blankets, run over by those who hurried to the incoming train. Were some frozen to death, I wondered?

I had to see a *Bahnpolizei* (railroad police) official. It was difficult to get through the masses of people. The officer explained that the train I was on was needed to get refugees out of Liegnitz to Dresden. A military transport heading for Breslau was expected to come through soon. Since I came from a *WE-Lager* and was on my way to join the *Volksturm,* I would be allowed to board.

Then word came that the military transport train had been ordered to pass through Liegnitz without stopping.

A train with secret weapons?

***

Waiting at the depot, I struck up a conversation with a soldier who had an insignia on his uniform that indicated that he served in one of the foreign volunteer units. He spoke German and I wondered aloud if he was a member of Vlassov's[101] Liberation Army.

He was not, but I must have asked some questions that prompted an outpouring of assertions that he belonged in the German uniform he was wearing. He told me about Stalin's great Red Army purge in 1937 when the highest military commanders of the Soviet Union were executed for treason.

Although Stalin's liquidation of his top officers had remained no secret and supposedly reverberated far beyond the borders of the Soviet Union, I was hearing about it for the first time—from this young soldier pouring out his soul to me. This ideological convert, who now fought on Germany's side, didn't have to convince me that he fought for the "right cause." He seemed even more indoctrinated than I was. In the summer of 1944, this Russian or Ukrainian (I suspect the latter) volunteer was convinced that the German Armed Forces were still to turn the tide and defeat Russia. I, of course, thought this too.

We talked about the small Finnish Army that had beaten back the huge Russian *Uebermacht* (superior force) with its mighty tank force and heavy artillery.

I thought German forces, despite the retreats, would launch massive counterattacks, leading to triumphant victories. It was the unbending will of the German soldier and the German nation as a whole that would lead to the *Endsieg* (final conquest).

What I didn't take into account was that combat soldiers need functioning weaponry and sufficient ammunition. Such basic leadership concerns existed among professional officers.

After the war, I learned the truth through firsthand accounts from Stalingrad survivors and from others who had fought in Africa or on various fronts that eventually collapsed. I learned of the desperate conditions in which many German fighting forces were abandoned. They were left to perish with orders to fight to the last man. Their officers were expected to aim their last bullet at themselves. Self-immolation was looked upon as choosing *Heldentod*, a hero's death. We boys looked up to such acts. We revered our heroes as role models for their *Mut* (courage) and *Opferbereitschaft* (willingness to die).

In Stalingrad, the German forces were denied permission to breakout, and with the Air Force unable to sufficiently supply the beleaguered forces, Hitler had created for his own soldiers a cruel concentration camp. The condition of the Germans taken prisoner, especially the many wounded in need of medical care, was abominable. Not only according to Russian reports, which might have been exaggerated, but also from the accounts of German survivors who, at the time of surrender, were starved and freezing, dispirited and dehumanized.

***

More than twenty years later, I met a former Hitler Youth leader known as Gerd. He shared his memories with me in a nightlong talk in the Palmer House in Chicago. He maintained that when General Friedrich von Paulus was promoted to Field Marshal, the defeat of his army was already an absolute certainty.

The reason for this promotion, the ultimate elevation for a German officer, was an ulterior one. The *Fuehrer* expected his *Feldmarschall* not to surrender but to bleed his troops to death and save the last bullet for himself. A captain on a sinking battleship was expected to go down with it. A field commander was expected to die heroically with his troops.

Instead, the just-promoted Field Marshal, a professional soldier and a human being, decided to save as many lives as could still be saved. After surrendering, he was vilified by Hitler. Influenced by my father, I, too, thought of Paulus' action as cowardly behavior. It took an eyewitness over twenty years later, to remove my ignorance and to fully explain the abhorrent conditions in which Hitler had left his troops. By then I could relate to it, having experienced the apocalyptic collapse of Berlin at war's end.

After my talk with Gerd, I checked the *Wehrmachtsberichte* (official war communiqués) and found that on February 1, 1943, the collapse of Field Marshal Paulus' northern flank was announced, matter-of-factly, citing two months of heroic fighting. The next day, February 2, the German people were advised of troop withdrawals to the last stronghold, the tractor plant, admitting that they now lacked ammunition. On February 3, a special bulletin was broadcast over Germany's airwaves. I remembered this. Muffled drums led into several bars of one of Beethoven's fervent melodies (Second Movement, Fifth Symphony). The speaker followed, solemnly announcing: "The fight over Stalingrad has reached the end!"

The German public, the whole world, was told that: "The soldiers of the 6th Army, true to the oath rendered to their flag, fought to the last breath under the exemplary leadership of Field Marshal Paulus. The sacrifice of this army was not in vain! These German soldiers died so that Germany could live!"

Not long after this announcement, my father and his colleagues at the radio station knew that Field Marshal Paulus and nearly 100,000 of his soldiers, among them scores of wounded, had surrendered and become Stalin's prisoners.

Gerd told me something I had never known. Hitler, a soldier in World War I, could not stand the sight of wounded comrades. It made him sick to his stomach. Even the sight of injured animals upset him. Now in his remote headquarters, removed from the battlefield, the sight of a soldier's dying didn't reach him.

Hitler was proud of his accomplishments as a runner in battle that earned him the Iron Cross, class II and I. But, apparently, by the time of the battle in Stalingrad, he had lost all touch with reality. He wanted heroism at a price that, to experts in military strategy, didn't make sense in a situation such as Stalingrad.

Many historians rate Stalingrad as the most decisive WWII battle on the Eastern Front. Although strategists still disagree about best possible alternatives, there seems to be accord that if General Paulus had been allowed to break out, it would have enabled the German forces to regroup. Even in a worst-case scenario, thousands of lives would have been saved.

Gerd, during his emotional outpouring, emphasized again and again how barbarous the conditions were. Casualties were reported to have exceeded 200,000 men. Of the over 90,000 that surrendered with their leader, nearly 85,000 died, already too weak to survive the rigors of Russian POW camps in Siberia.

Individual lives were of little value to Hitler. To Stalin, also, as we know now.

CHAPTER 39

Going Home

I remained with my luggage in the office of the rail police past midnight. A military train passed through at a relatively high speed.

Shortly after that, a railroad official picked me up and took me across the tracks to a short train that had apparently been assembled.

Several refugees followed, but the railroad man ordered them to turn back, explaining that this train would not go west but to Breslau instead. I remember him saying harshly: "Not to Goerlitz, the boy is going to the front!"

I couldn't believe my ears.

I was heading for the front. Right into battle?

Had the Russians advanced to Breslau already?

There were only two passenger cars. The others were freight cars. The conductor invited me into his compartment.

We both tried to get a little sleep but couldn't because of all the noises and sudden stops on the open tracks. Trains going in the opposite direction swooshed by at high speed.

Soon the conductor said, "We are almost there."

Not quite inside the main railroad station in Breslau, the train came to a stop. I wanted to get off as soon as possible. I knew the area where we were.

"Take care!" the conductor said.

I jumped off while the train was still moving, harnessed my rucksack, raised my right arm, and saluted the conductor. The cold air helped me to overcome my tiredness. I crossed over the multiple tracks and walked toward Teichaecker Park. Guards stopped me—two uniformed older men. They had a dog with them.

They checked my papers and were satisfied that I had just arrived and wasn't trying to leave. They handed me a leaflet, a reprint of an order to join the *Volkssturm*. It also spelled out that those who dodged facing the enemy and those who were cowards would face executions.

Although I was willing to fight, it nevertheless shocked me. Down deep I always had the fear that I might not be as brave as I expected. Soon I would be tested.

Most people were on their way to leave town. I had returned.

For an instant I thought of Trudel who lived on the other side of the station. Would she be at home?

The municipal streetcars were still in operation. I took one of them to the stop nearest to our house. No one was at home. One of the neighbors was still there. She told me that our family had left but my mother was expected to be back within four weeks.

The living room, my father's study, and the kitchen—all were in perfect order. The dishes had been washed and the drawers of the dining room buffet where my mother stored the Christmas cookies and the Christmas bread were locked. The beds were made.

On my father's desk were some bills that had been opened and were still to be paid. I searched for my savings book. This she had taken along. Did she expect me to catch up with her? I found another official paper from the local party office in which Hoyerswerda was designated as an assembly point. This somehow reassured me that my mother and sisters and brothers would be all right. We had lived in Hoyerswerda prior to coming to Breslau. She would be well received there. Else Kaspar, the "chocolate aunt," who owned a grocery store there would probably provide quarters for them, as long as my father was not with them. Was he still in Breslau at the military hospital?

I washed up, changed underwear, and put my *Jungvolk* uniform back on, all the while listening to the radio.

"This hour demands total commitment to save the Fatherland," proclaimed the announcer. He stated that Breslau had been designated to become a fortress and that deserters will face a firing squad—instantly! Women, children, and men over 60 years old were ordered to proceed to designated assembly points, with no more than three suitcases per person. All others had to report to the nearest *Volkssturm* registration unit.

Nervousness and real fear stirred my thoughts as I pondered what to do. I left the house and headed to the registration unit nearest to my home. It was the cavalry barracks where I had received riding instructions and "my" riding horse, Fuchs, had his stable. However *Uffz.* Reinecke, my riding instructor, was no longer there. Neither was my horse.

I was informed that I must go instead to the district military office on Gabitzstrasse. I don't remember all of my thoughts but somehow I rationalized that I had to make contact with someone before reporting for duty at the Home Defense Force Assembly Station.

My nearest former classmate was Walther Troeger. He was a year younger and not with the Air Defense group. Would he be in Glatz where the lower grades of our high school had been evacuated, or could he have come home and be there now?

As I learned after the war, he had returned to Wunsiedel,[102] in Franconia, where he was born. Not knowing that the Troegers had left months earlier and that Walther's father had opposed the regime and was in custody, I rang the bell. No answer. The entire house seemed empty. I went on to the old neighborhood using the streetcars. I took Line #18 up to the end station, Admiral Scheerstrasse.

I knew that Kurt had been in Stalingrad. An old woman in the neighborhood told me that Kurt had been missing for some time on the Russian front. This came as a shock. His father was not at home. Most likely he was in the *Volkssturm* already. He couldn't have been older than 60 years. All the rabbit hatches were empty. Kurt's garage door was all locked up. Could his motorcycle still be in there? And my soccer ball?

It crossed my mind, should the Russians advance and come to enter the garage, what would they think, seeing the posters with the runes on the walls. Or had Kurt taken them down before he left?

I knew that Dieter Eberhard Heinrich was in Wartha at the Adolf Hitler School. He might be fighting already. One of the radio reports about the total mobilization had mentioned the battle readiness of the Adolf Hitler School.

If Dieter had returned from school to Breslau as a defender of his hometown, then he would be a member of the fortress regiment. I went on to Kornblumenweg. For sure, *Schuster* Stefan would still be there. It was a big shock. The doors were locked. A neighbor next door told me that *Schuster* Stefan had resoled shoes almost to the day he succumbed. He had suffered a sudden death, probably a heart attack.

His workplace was taken over by the military, but it was locked up.

I went to the houseblock on Kuerassierstrasse where we had lived for almost five years and where I knew several families. But there, all were gone as well. The Binners had left, the Boeses had left, and even the Hausmeister couple was no longer around.

Our family physician, *Frau* Dr. Petzold, who had cared for my father just a few weeks earlier, had closed down her office.

The Prade family, who lived on the other side of Hardenberg hill, was gone too. He was the conductor of the great orchestra. My sisters had been there frequently, playing flutes, taking part in house concerts.

***

I still wonder why I did not go to the radio station to inquire about my father's whereabouts. I didn't know then that my father, officially a war correspondent, was also still working for the *SD* and reporting on the civilian population's mood and behavior.

Announcements blared, coming from a kiosk with a clock and

a built-in loudspeaker. *"Bis zum letzten kaempfen und zum Opfertod bereit sein!* ("Fight to the end and be willing to sacrifice one's life!") was the slogan of the hour. The hour had come. Soon I would have to face death.

I didn't want to be a coward. But was I ready to die?

Although I had been accepted as a volunteer to join the mountain troops, I had not yet been required to pass a real physical. Even in the pre-military training camp at Kreuzeck, I had experienced some dizziness on two occasions—both when climbing.

I decided to ignore the orders given over the radio. I didn't get off the streetcar at the *Wehrbezirkskommando* (Armed Forces District Command Office) on Gabitzstrasse but decided to go to the *HJ-Gebietsfuehrung*[103] to report to the *KLV* office. Perhaps they would return me to the evacuated school at Ullersdorf where I had been a camp counselor. Some boys, unable to return home, might still be there and need my help.

Was this the right decision to make?

Whom would I find to talk to?

On my way, I stopped at home one more time to see if the phone was still working. It was. I dialed the number of the restaurant owned by the parents of my friend Klaus Schauermann. He wasn't there and his parents couldn't be located when I called. The soldier who answered the phone recommended that I call back in the evening.

On my sixteenth birthday, I had assured my mother that I was old enough to make my own decisions. She not only agreed but also, in my father's absence, consulted me in some family matters.

Now I was in an empty house and couldn't decide what to do.

The way she left the house suggested that the block warden told her she could return in a few days. Otherwise, she would have surely taken more belongings. She even left the family photo albums behind. It appeared she departed on the spot and took just clothing and food.

I left a note for her, just in case.

Perhaps she had sent me a telegram at the mountain training camp and I left before it arrived.

I went into the kitchen for some food. I could not bring myself to break open the locked buffet with the Christmas cookies inside.

Then I left the house for the last time. On top of a snow bank, I noticed a dead dog. It saddened me. The first of what would be a very long death toll—of citizens, animals, and countless comrades.

CHAPTER 40

Volkssturm

I had just lined up in front of the office when my superior, *KLV Inspekteur* (inspector) for Silesia, Karl Gutschke, now dressed in an army officer's uniform with the rank of a First Lieutenant, spotted me.

"Armin, I am glad that you made it. We are putting together an elite unit."

I saluted.

Instantly, I was filled with doubts. Gutschke was a disabled veteran. He had lost a lung. Now with two disabled *Unteroffiziere (NCOs)*, he had been given orders to lead into battle the very young who were able to bear arms.

Soon we would have to fire, with our guns and with our souls.

Now we would be tested.

Oblt. Gutschke, together with the noncommissioned officers straight out of a military hospital, assembled our elite unit called *Kampfgruppe* Gutschke. *Kampfgruppe,* translated literally means fighting group. This we would become, a special *Volkssturm* task force, comprised of *KLV* staff members and camp counselors, of students of the Adolf Hitler School in Wartha and of members of a *WE-Lager,* a pre-military training camp.

We were all, to different degrees, conditioned by the Third *Reich's* educational system. My newly issued field-grey *Volkssturm* outfit, actually an army uniform without insignia, did not fit. It was too wide around the shoulders and around the waist. The boots were too big, but I was used to wearing two pairs of socks.

Now I didn't need protection from snakes but from the bitter cold.

Long marches lay ahead of us.

Among the Adolf Hitler School students was my old friend Eberhard Dieter Heinrich. I told him that I had been to his home just the day before but had found no one there. His family had left town with other refugees.

I continued with my efforts to get in touch with Klaus Schauermann. Telephones were still working, and from a farmhouse, I tried again. We were too far away from the city by now and it wasn't a local number anymore. The long-distance exchange was still functioning and a friendly switchboard operator could get me through.

Had Klaus, like I, managed to come home to check on things and to see his parents again? During the past year we had, by complete coincidence, returned home twice, simultaneously, for unscheduled visits. Was there a chance for this to happen again?

The phone rang. As before, a soldier answered. He cut me short. The restaurant kitchen of the Gruener Pollack had become an army facility. He didn't know where any of the Schauermanns were. Click. I was cut off before being able to ask additional questions.

***

"We are off!" *Oblt.* Gutschke announced.

Even those of us who had been instructed in pre-military training camps had only practiced with small-bore (sub-caliber) rifles. Now we would be assigned military carbines, even machine guns, no longer the practice hand-grenades but live ones, and *Panzerfaeuste* (bazookas), hand-held antitank missile projectors.

We were part of the *HJ*-Fortress Regiment Breslau.[104] *Oblt.* Gutschke had received orders to advance. We would meet the Russian forces, southeast of the capital. We were on our way!

The enemy was before us. I looked favorably on fighting in

open country instead of being sealed up inside a fortress.[105] Subconsciously, I hoped for survival. There can be no doubt of that.

My senses stretched time. Yesterday seemed a year ago. Tomorrow, the unknown future still appeared far, far away.

I felt compelled to write. Powerful life-affirming thoughts filled my mind. Those of a soldier to be. In retrospect, I can see the conflict inside my mind when I wrote the following poem:

> *Although war*
> *Is a struggle*
> *For liberty*
> *The road*
> *To victory*
> *Is a row*
> *Of graves*
> *Thus I strive*
> *To be brave*
> *But to survive*
> *To be alive*
> *To come home*
> *Free*
> *To Live.*

This poem I tucked away in my breast pocket.

Looking at it now, it's not even a poem—it is a hastily crafted plea for survival.

While I wanted to live, we followed orders to kill.

And so did the Russians. The gifted writer, Ilya Ehrenburg,[106] implored the Russian fighting men to drench the German soil with German blood: "There is no one who is innocent in Germany, neither in the living nor in the unborn. Follow Stalin's command, smash the Fascist beast in his cave, strip the German women of their pride and take them as your lawful prey. Kill, kill, you brave soldiers, advance death as you conquer!"

Hitler, of course, was as ruthless and brutal a despot as Stalin was. Dr. Goebbels, although more subtle than Ilya Ehrenburg, proclaimed hate as our duty and revenge as our virtue. He challenged us to kill and to bury the Soviet hordes in mass graves.

My desire to live was not a wish to be expressed openly. I should have proclaimed my fervor to fight, my willingness to kill, my readiness to die!

***

When *Oblt.* Gutschke and I arrived at the country schoolhouse, *Uffz.* Schleifer was going through drill practice in the yard. In rapid succession, he bellowed commands, sarcastically commenting on awkward performances. His language was studded with obscenities. "It's no use trying to change him now," Gutschke said almost apologetically and kept me at his side.

"I need you as my *Melder* (courier)," he reassured me.

"You will remain with me." I became the first of his two couriers. The other one was also a *KLV-Lagermannschaftsfuehrer.* His name was Rolf Friebe. The reason for selecting us, and not members of the Adolf Hitler School, might have been that Gutschke knew us well. That meant no drills for me, but also no practice with weapons.

I knew how to shoot a rifle. Several times, I had loaded one of my father's hunting rifles and then taken to the lone woods and discharged it secretly. One night, with school friends of mine, and a few glasses of champagne in our bellies, we had hidden my father's World War I carbine and gone to the Lohe River where we had taken turns shooting at the moon.

Oblt. Gutschke instructed me on how to discharge a *Panzerfaust.* For it's deadliness, it is a relatively simple weapon to handle. He insisted that we use a live one so that I could get the experience. A mixture of anxiousness and apprehensiveness overcame me.

What I held in my hand was a deadly device, far more destructive than its size could possibly show. Gutschke had me aim at an old rusty dung water barrel in front of the farm's manure heap and cesspit.

I positioned the end of the pipe part under my armpit, readied the sighting mechanism, aimed, pressed down the firing heft, and shot through the barrel. The short-lived fire in the dung heap was far enough from the barn not to spread.

We also had a grenade-throwing practice. It culminated with a live one being hurled at an old plum tree. The grenade hit a branch, fell down to the base of the tree and exploded. Jagged, dagger-like slivers, pointed threateningly to the sky.

One of the *KLV-Fuehrers* I knew was another Klaus. Some called him "the Haynauer." This wasn't his last name. The town where he came from was Haynau. Since he had the same first name as my best friend, Klaus Schauermann, I called him "Haynauer" too.

Haynauer was probably the moodiest of all in our unit. His father had been fighting in Stalingrad. Officially, he was missing. Haynauer feared that he was dead. It appeared that he had a very close relationship with his dad, entirely different than was the case between my father and me. I also remember a statement Haynauer once made about his father.

"My father did not hunt. He couldn't kill. It might have killed him," Haynauer stated.

My own father, an ardent hunter, was still alive. But what had hunting to do with war?

Haynauer wanted to become an artist. He was sketching constantly. His pencils lasted him a long time, but he was constantly in need of paper.

Haynauer and I were not the only ones in our group who were artistically inclined. There was another aspiring poet among us— one of the Adolf Hitler School students. I am unable to recall his name, and I am sure he won't mind my remembering him as *der Reimer* (literally: the rhymer).

Knowing that I, too, wrote, he sought my company. Whenever there was a possibility to talk, he told me about his writings. He had his pockets full of poems, short stories, notes and more notes. He wasn't a courier as I was and found more time to put his impressions, thoughts, and fantasies down on paper.

What he really wanted from me, I felt sure, was encouragement and praise for what he had written. *Reimer* had a very handsome Nordic appearance with blond, wavy hair and light-blue eyes. About six feet in height, he was taller than I.

Besides his writing interests, he showed great enthusiasm for soldiering. His aspiration was to write a great war novel based on his experiences. All charged up and ready for battle, he could hardly wait for the action to come.

He would repeat declarations like "Bravery is to fight to the last bullet and then to stand up and show the enemy your clenched fist!" Once I retorted "That sounds arousing, *Reimer,* but if you are killed, you won't get to write your novel." He stared at me.

"Cowards die first!" he responded

He couldn't have thought that through.

I must have had my first inkling that slogans and reality don't always support one another.

In the *Volkssturm*, I would end up being a foot soldier. With the sounds of war in the background, I could see myself belly crawling through hails of artillery shrapnel and gunfire galore.

Even some *Luftwaffe* pilots were now fighting on the ground and not in the air. Since I had volunteered to join the *Gebirgsjaeger,* the mountain troops, I had expected, after putting in my time serving in the *Reichsarbeitsdienst,*[107] to join these elite troops. My intention to serve my country as a *Gebirgsjaeger* was obliterated by the Russians. I ended up just being a *Volkssturmmann.*

In a radio address, *Gauleiter* Hanke, the party district leader for Silesia, had challenged us to harden our will. We were to resist to the extent that it would be impossible for the enemy to break us.

***

I conversed frequently with *Reimer* and not only about topics at hand. At times we talked about Goethe, or Schiller, or Rilke and some of our comrades felt left out. I remember one of the *WE-Lager* members referring to us as *Eierkoepfe,* the German term for "high brows." I resented the remark, but *Reimer's* eyes lit up, he even laughed and slapped me on the back.

"This heroic war will be survived by two great writers."

On the other hand, it became apparent that my education, in some respects, was no match to that of the Adolf Hitler School students.

Dieter Heinrich, with some of his classmates, discussed Carl von Clausewitz's[108] book *Vom Kriege (On War).* I knew that von Clausewitz, a Prussian general and military writer, had assisted General von Scharnhorst[109] to create the army that in the war of 1813-15 contributed greatly to Napoleon's downfall. But I had never read von Clausewitz's book so I couldn't participate in the discussion about this soldier-philosopher. Obviously, these Adolf Hitler School students were better read on military literature than I was.

A lively discussion took place over von Clausewitz's doctrine of total war and what did and what did not apply to Germany's present situation. War was not to be restricted to soldiers fighting against each other but rather to affect the enemy's entire territory, its citizens, and possessions. But now both sides were completely involved in total warfare. With everyone, except very old people, fighting or fleeing, the situation by far exceeded the magnitude of von Clausewitz's doctrine. Later, I learned from members of the *Fuehrer's* inner circle that Hitler was of the opinion that the best had fallen already. He thought the German people had failed because they were not worthy of his aims.

***

We reached a schoolhouse and members of both *Zuege* (units/platoons) were put up in different classrooms. *Oblt.* Gutschke asked the corporals, *Uffz.* Schleifer and *Uffz.* Hinkel, as well as Rolf and me, his two couriers, to quarter with him in the adjacent teacher's house. I would have preferred to be with my friends. However *Oblt.* Gutschke wanted his NCOs and his couriers right at his command post.

The nights since I had left Kreuzeck had offered little sleep. Tonight I seemed to be on the brink of absolute exhaustion. Two beds and one couch were all the furniture that was in the teacher's house. Gutschke selected the couch. I fixed my bedding on the floor. The *Oberleutnant* did not undress. Neither did I, nor did Rolf. The heat from the tile stove did not carry far. The wood was green and at the time it sounded as if firecrackers were going off. There was also an unrelenting draft. I moved closer and closer to the stove. My blanket did not hold much heat and even with my uniform on, I did not feel warm.

But I fell asleep almost immediately.

When I awoke, my face felt flushed and I was very hungry. Had we eaten last night? The first morning light entered the room. Everything emerged in gray silence. The stillness made me uneasy. Rolf was still sleeping.

But where was *Oberleutnant* Gutschke?

Cautiously, I raised my head. The couch was empty. I got up. The door to the bedroom was open.

The beds were empty and the two *Unteroffiziere* were gone. I heard voices outside.

Cautiously I stepped out into the dawn. Hinkel was pumping water.

Despite the freezing temperature, Hinkle and Schleifer had removed their uniform jacket and shirts and, bare-chested, washed up.

"You are next!" Hinkel shouted.

Shivering, I washed. After rubbing myself dry, I felt warm for the first time.

We ate in one of the classrooms. Breakfast consisted of hot *Muckefuck,*[110] *Kommissbrot,*[111] and canned liverwurst. We sat on benches that had been pushed along the walls. Rolf, looking at the dirty floor, called it a pigpen.

Oblt. Gutschke returned from a briefing. Soviet forces had reached Pomerania. They were increasingly invading German soil. German troops were now pushed back on all fronts.

We waited for tanks.

Kurt Ruppelt, also 16 years old, had secured from the Schweidnitz weapon depot: automatic rifles; machine guns; hand grenades; bazookas; and 7.65 mm pistols. He also had been to Breslau and had succeeded in getting shoes, uniforms, and snow capes for us to wear.

By *Volkssturm* standards we were outfitted better than most.

Uffz. Hinkel, who had lost his left leg in battle, limped noticeably with his prosthesis. Occasionally, Hinkel would refer to his wooden leg affectionately.

"It's the safest part of my body," he would say. "It will take any hits without a whimper!"

Hinkel was better liked than Schleifer, who was a tough drill sergeant.

Everyone, including the Adolf Hitler School members who had become group leaders, respected *Oblt.* Gutschke.

I believe it was January 29 that we were picked up by trucks and driven to the front. We were unloaded in a small village in front of a *Gasthaus*, where we were fed a warm soup. The last stretch we had to advance by foot.

We wanted to stop and help the animals that roared in agony.

Livestock tossed their chains, kicked stable walls for lack of food. Some of the sounds were heartbreaking. Cows, unmilked for days, mooed in agony. Some that had been able to free themselves roamed around and even sucked each other. Horses, goats and sheep had broken loose and strayed about. There was no time to attend to any of these animals, and we were not allowed to feed any of them or to open the stables. We were told that supply unit personnel would follow us and take care of these abandoned creatures. One of the comrades, an apprentice butcher, suggested to the *Oberleutnant* that, as we were resting for a while, we slaughter a couple of calves, cut them up, and take along fresh meat. That was not our job, the *Oberleutnant* replied, we had to advance.

The unit of old men following us would do the butchering to provide fresh meat for the field kitchen.

We marched on.

A horde of hounds followed us, barking and growling at each other. Some dogs, not having been fed in days, seemed quite aggressive. *Uffz.* Schleifer shot one of them. We had no food with us except emergency rations. There was nothing we could share with this famished pack of mongrels. I remember so clearly how distressed I was since I loved animals—dogs and horses above all. If only the *Oberleutnant* would allow us a couple of hours to do something for these animals.

But there was no time to lose. We had strict orders to move on. Camouflaged with the hooded snow capes, we trudged through the snow, ever more wearily under the weight of our weapons. The longer we marched, the heavier they became. After two hours, we stopped for another rest and looked for food in a deserted farmhouse. We quickly lit the stove to warm up. Some dogs had followed us into the houses and created havoc. Schleifer became irritated, drew his pistol, and shot again, this time killing two. The others fled. When we marched on, most of the pack came back, but remained at a distance or circled us widely.

Toward the afternoon, we reached a larger village. I was the first to notice a white flag hoisted from the church belfry.

As we came closer to the first houses, a group of elderly people approached us, including the village pastor. One woman with erratic behavior clapped her hands. The other women, all much older, were holding baskets with loaves of bread, slabs of smokehouse bacon, and other foods, even some bottles of Schnapps. They had gathered around their pastor to surrender. In our white hooded snow capes they had mistaken us for approaching Russians.

"Feed the dogs!" was *Uffz.* Hinkel's initial reaction.

When they realized that we were Germans, expressions of terror reflected from their faces. Some women fell to their knees and begged for mercy.

"We have no weapons with which to defend ourselves," the pastor explained. "Only women and disabled men remain, too advanced in age and too ill to serve in the *Volkssturm*. All others are gone."

"We couldn't fight!" another of the men emphasized, visibly shaken.

Oblt. Gutschke agreed. These people were too old and without weapons and, therefore, unable to fight.

The erratic woman still applauded our arrival. She appeared to be slightly deranged. I can still see her, her face drawn, her eyes staring. She was dressed in dark, long flowing peasant garb. She shouted suddenly, approaching *Uffz.* Hinkel: "Children, children. Oh, God! These are just children."

Uffz. Hinkel responded by putting his right hand on his Mauser revolver and kept her at bay. With his left arm outstretched, he pushed her away.

She fell.

The pastor helped the woman get up, and explained her behavior to *Uffz.* Hinkel, saying that she had lost her mind when her only son was killed. *Oblt.* Gutschke turned to his two couriers, Rolf and me, and ordered us to climb up the stairs of the church tower to bring down the white flag.

We left for the church. The stairs were old and in bad repair. Rolf and I assisted each other when climbing up and down.

We brought back a bed sheet and gave it to *Oblt.* Gutschke, who handed it to the pastor. He didn't say a word.

The insane woman was no longer there, but a car drove up with the *Volkgrenadier* (National Rifleman) commander in it, dressed in a police officer's uniform.

"These people should be shot!" he yelled, grabbing the bedsheet from the pastor. *"Fuehrer's* orders! Surrender is punishable by death!"

His rank must have been higher than *Oblt.* Gutschke's. He was in charge of the *Volksgrenadier* unit that was following us, the unit of old men *Oblt.* Gutschke had mentioned.

Oblt. Gutschke, despite his lower rank however, must have

been in command. He took the older police officer aside into the entrance of the farmhouse where they conferred briefly.

The lives of the pastor and all those at his side were spared.

Without exception, we all had sided with *Oblt.* Gutschke. He took great pains to explain that only those able to bear arms and to defend themselves could be court-martialed. Not women and tottering old men, some, perhaps, already senile. They were all older than 60 years, he pointed out.

Had another officer been in charge, we might have had to witness an execution. Just four months later, a comrade and I would be in a similar situation.

We left this hamlet and its people behind. Our march continued. We approached the village where we were to spend the night before attacking the Russians. Rolf and I were given our first dangerous assignment.

We were sent ahead to make contact with anyone who had remained in the village to find out what they knew about Russian positions.

"Could the enemy be already there?" *Oblt.* Gutschke didn't think so, but told us to be on our guard.

Now, our training had to be implemented. For real. We advanced quietly each on opposite sides of the road. We reached the first houses. Not a sign of life. I signaled Rolf to advance further from farm to farm. At the seventh or eighth house, I was greeted by an old farmer. He said there had been women in the house I had just left. I had not seen any.

"You didn't go down in the cellar. That's where they are hiding," the farmer explained. Rolf noticed that I had made contact and crossed the street to join us.

"What are you boys doing here?" the lone old farmer inquired.

We told him that our unit was approaching the village.

He asked how old we were.

"Sixteen," we replied in unison. We must have looked younger in the unlit hallway.

Then he assured us: "No *Iwans* (Ivans) yet!" referring to the Russians.

He predicted that they would be arriving the next morning. A disabled veteran from World War I, he was the only one from his family who had stayed behind. He had thought that no one would come to defend the village.

"I will be at your commander's disposal," he emphasized when we parted.

As we returned to our group, shots were heard from a village still ahead of us. They weren't fired in our direction.

Rolf and I reported back to *Oblt.* Gutschke. He commented: "*Gut gemacht!*" (Well done!), and it made us feel good.

I remained at the side of *Oblt.* Gutschke. We were the first to reach the village.

"No dogs," someone remarked.

These farmers must have taken all their dogs along when they left, I thought. Or did they kill them?

The stables seemed empty, too. No horses, no cows. Some stray hens and a couple of cats were visible.

The Adolf Hitler School students became group leaders and different groups were housed in different farms.

Oblt. Gutschke talked to the farmer who recommended a big *Bauernhof* (farm house with stables and barn) as command post. *Oblt.* Gutschke followed his advice.

There, he, Rolf, and I took quarters. This time the NCOs were housed with their respective platoons. During the evening, Rolf and I were sent to the various group leaders with orders to establish watches and periodic patrols. As couriers, we were exempt from guard assignments but were kept busy with dispatches.

In one of the farmhouses someone played a *Mundharmonika* (mouth organ). In another one, everyone had assembled in the kitchen where there were huge food supplies, rings of smoked sausages, slabs of bacon, and loaves of bread and even beer.

An old woman, who had come out of hiding, prepared sandwiches to eat, enough for all of us. She was stooped, with tremulous hands, and in the midst of all the commotion, she cut herself.

Oblt. Gutschke had a first aid kit and put a bandage over her cut.

She told him that her husband was no longer alive and explained why she had refused to flee with her daughter-in-law and her grandchildren.

"I would just have been a burden and someone should remain on the homestead no matter what happens."

Oblt. Gutschke nodded.

"Where are you heading?" she asked.

"To the next village to hold off the Russians," he replied.

"Yes, we heard them last night." Then she added, haltingly, "We also heard shots from other directions. Since yesterday we thought that the Russians had surrounded us already."

I continued my delivery of orders. Dieter Heinrich had become a group leader. We visited briefly.

Uffz. Schleifer and Uffz. Hinkel had been quartered strategically on different farms.

I delivered orders to both of them. Schleifer didn't say a word. I wasn't used to him being so quiet. *Uffz.* Hinkel, with his leg prosthesis, was noticeably in pain. He mentioned he needed a night's rest to recover.

Oblt. Gutschke who already had lost one lung in the war, prepared for next morning's situation conference that was scheduled prior to our attack.

Before lying down, I stepped out one more time and observed some distant flares. In the rear I heard heavy artillery fire. Could Breslau be already under barrage?

***

I wondered if I should write to my grandparents to tell them what had happened to me in case my mother got in touch with them.

"Herr Oberleutnant," I asked, "do we have a field post number?"

He shook his head.

"We can't send any letters?"

"Not right now. But field postal service will soon be in place. Presently only the fortress headquarters in Breslau knows of our existence. Should we be returned to the fortress, we then can use the field post number there."

There were three or four last dispatches I had to deliver.

After I returned, *Oblt.* Gutschke told me to get some sleep.

"Soldiers sleep whenever and wherever they can. Sometimes just for minutes."

"Tomorrow it will be them or us," Rolf remarked.

He asked if I were ready to go into battle.

"We have to fight," I replied. "We have to be brave soldiers." Then I added, "and I hope we will not get killed."

The moment I said it, I wished I had not. However, *Oblt.* Gutschke put me at ease. "I don't want to be killed either." He put his arm on my shoulder.

"Yet, the Russians have to be stopped or the war will be lost." And, as if it was an afterthought, he added: "We are greatly outnumbered!"

"Tomorrow we shall try to surprise them," he continued. "If we succeed, it will reduce losses."

Oblt. Gutschke explained that he didn't expect the Russians to have had enough time to dig tank traps. The frozen soil wouldn't have made it possible for them to dig trenches. We were in a war of flexible fronts, he explained. Tank warfare was no longer trench warfare.

"Good night."

"Good night."

I had located several blankets, a quilt, and a pillow and wrapped myself into as much warmth as I could.

I lay down in the darkness, on the floor with my boots and coat off, my pants pockets emptied and my gear right beside me, including my revolver. Rolf and I were the only ones of the enlisted *Volkssturm* members who had received pistols as weapons. When delivering dispatches, we did not have to carry rifles, enabling us to run faster.

I was proud to be a *Melder* (dispatch runner), always being with the *Oberleutnant,* always at the center of things. It had other advantages, too. We were excused from guard duty and guard patrols.

My feet still hurt. Although utterly exhausted, I noticed every movement anyone made and heard every sound inside and outside the house. I had visions of enemy soldiers crawling on the snow, approaching the farmhouse, surprising and overpowering us. I remembered our maid at Waldgut Horka, who always found noises at night alarming. She often had awakened me to check that there were no intruders inside or outside the house. Now, my senses, too, were on a high pitch and reacted supersensitively to noises and motions.

Most of the time I remained in a fatigued drowsiness without finding real sleep.

The enemy was out there—and not very far.

CHAPTER 41

Into Battle

The attack was scheduled for 5:30 a.m. We had to be up by 4:30 a.m. and ready by 5:00 a.m. Despite troubled sleep, the next morning we all were up ahead of time. Our column assembled in the barn and *Oblt.* Gutschke spoke, with a low voice and matter-of-factly.

We had to fulfill our duty—we had a job to do. Silesia had to be saved for Germany to survive.

The enemy had to be thrown back. We were lucky that the enemy hadn't attacked us during the night.

He spoke of us as soldiers. He expected us to do honor to the Fatherland and reminded us to be brave, yet not to be careless. "There are the Russians," he said, pointing in the direction of the village we had to capture. "They are after our lives and we are after theirs. They are tempered soldiers and they can be very tough. We have to show them that we will be even better fighters, indomitable, unfaltering, resolute."

Oblt. Gutschke explained that we would be supported by three Tiger *Panzers* on each flank. Two companies of older, seasoned *Volksgrenadiere* would follow the tanks. We were not alone.

This was the crack of dawn. The Russians couldn't possibly see us, unless they had a *Spaehtrupp* (a small observatory unit) in the field. There were no noticeable movements ahead of us. The tanks were held back at first, to keep our attack as silent as possible for as long as practicable. Then they were to advance at both flanks.

Under the thick snow-blanket the ground was frozen and stone-hard. But there were drifts. We had not been trained for infantry attacks. We belonged to a *Panzernahkampfbrigade* (close-range tank attack brigade), a crack unit armed with bazookas. The bazookas were portable, hand-held, antitank, armor-piercing rockets called *Panzerfaust* (tank fist) because they could knock out tanks at close range. We had been instructed, ever so briefly, in how to use them. This morning, however, our objective was to storm the village, in a surprise attack, if possible. We had to take it and hold it. If they came with tanks, we would "crack" them with our "tank fists."

My stomach started to grumble. I suddenly realized that we had not had breakfast.

I remembered reading that soldiers in World War I had a saying. "A good breakfast keeps body and soul together!" My stomach was empty but I carried an iron ration with me. It made me think of the survival exercise of a couple of years earlier and how proud I was when my group came in first.

My earliest understanding of what approaching battle would be like were those of a horseman, riding through day and night, as told in *The Tale of the Life and Death of Cornet* Christoph Rilke by Rainer Maria von Rilke.[112] It is a wistful, rhythmical narration of a warrior in love who charges, holding up his flag, into the sabers of the enemy.

This type of warfare had taken place almost 200 years ago. But Rilke's sorrowful poetic tale had romanticized and glorified in my mind the death of his hero and of all heroes who sacrificed their lives in battle.

If we perish, would our families ever know? We didn't even have a *Feldpostnummer* (APO address). Our families had become refugees. We didn't know where they were.

Just two nights ago, someone had mentioned how wars had changed. Now, sabers were only worn on dress uniforms and no longer used in battle. But we had bayonets that could be mounted on our carbines should enemy soldiers be encountered within stabbing distance.

We advanced slowly over the rugged winter soil in a pyramid

formation with *Oblt.* Gutschke and me at the apex. *Oblt.* Gutschke jumped forward in short intervals. He kept advancing and I followed close behind.

Nothing happened at our flanks at first.

The early light of dawn heightened.

The first shot that sounded came from behind us, not from the Russians in the village ahead.

I heard *Oblt.* Gutschke curse: "Idiot!"

Soon, I heard tanks rolling. But only on the southeastern flank.

What had happened to those supposed to be on the other side of us?

Suddenly there were shots everywhere. Machine-gun fire.

Everything happened so fast.

The earth, with its icy snow-crust, shook, quivered, and trembled. *Oblt.* Guschke was down on his belly. I was down on mine. We both were in the midst of a barrage of shelling, fierce detonations, blasts, grenades bursting into pieces, bullets whizzing by.

Instinctively, I crawled up next to *Oblt.* Gutschke. He shouted as loud as he could: "We will wait here a short while and let them squander ammunition. When our tanks come, we'll move on."

Our tanks did not come and the fire increased.

The Russians had sharpshooters up in the church tower.

Right next to me a heavy shell exploded. My head banged against the icy snow on the ground. My left leg jumped. A sharp, burning pain seared through me. I put my hand on the wound. When I lifted it, it was full of blood.

"Damn! I'm hit!"

Oblt. Gutschke crawled back and pulled me behind a snowdrift. "Remain here!"

He went ahead alone.

It seemed like an eternity. The hail of fire kept increasing.

I tried to dig deeper into the snow. It was too icy. I lifted my face and it burned.

There was no halt to the downpour of bursting shells. Sharp

whining bullets cut through the air over my head. It made no sense for me to shoot. The enemy wasn't in sight.

Our corporals, who had first-aid-kits, were not near. Amid the battle clamor, there were cries of pain. I saw badly wounded comrades.

Although *Oblt.* Gutschke had ordered me to remain where I was, I could not stay. I had to pull some of the wounded into the more protective ravine. I knew enough about first aid to grasp that bleeding limbs had to be tied up.

I always carried a pocketknife. I cut up some cloth. One of the wounded looked okay; I couldn't even tell where he was hit. Then blood came out of his mouth.

Another had no hand. I placed a tourniquet on his upper arm as tight as I could, to arrest the bleeding.

I pulled more wounded into the small gully. By the time I lacked the strength to get up again, there were four or five of us there.

One, apparently a Catholic, made the sign of the cross and closed his eyes.

His last gesture prompted me to think of God.

God could not be watching over all of us individually, I thought. God most certainly would not control the path of every bullet shot, of all the shrapnel from every exploding grenade or bomb. *Oblt.* Gutschke had reminded us to set forth with a *starke innere Haltung* (strong inner bearing), to be vigorous!

Now was the time. But, I had lost most of my strength.

When I lifted my head I could see through the embrasure of the bell tower the silhouette of an enemy soldier, the barrel of his rifle up on a sill, aiming at us. This sharpshooter became my very first human target. He failed to hit us and I, apparently, failed to hit him, since he didn't disappear. I kept bleeding and ceased shooting to keep my hand on the gash. It felt like a fist-size hole in my left buttock. The snow around me had turned red.

Another close hit. My head, again, thumped on the ice. Shrieks. Groans.

Two of my comrades yelled for help. Out of nowhere, *Uffz.* Hinkel appeared followed by some boys. Hinkel wanted to catch up with *Oblt.* Gutschke. He looked ashen and was breathing heavily, pushing himself to the brink of exhaustion. It must have been his leg. "How badly are you hurt?" he asked me.

"I don't know. It might only be my left leg. I have to stop the bleeding."

"Press against it. Keep on moving your body or you will be frostbitten on one side."

"Where is the *Oberleutnant?*"

"Way in front. He must have reached the village by now."

We were very close to the first houses. "The Russians are still in there!" Hinkel yelled.

He got up and motioned with his arm for the ones behind him to follow. Even though I was wounded, I couldn't just remain inactive. I decided to move forward along with *Uffz.* Hinkel. I checked my hurting thigh again. My torn pants were increasingly soaked with blood. In front of us more and more smoke was rising. Houses in the village were burning.

Soon a lightheaded feeling overcame me. I lost my balance. Pain pierced through and throbbed in my thigh. It shot up as far up as my heart and as far down as my toe. I could still crawl, very short stretches, resting in between.

Finally the artillery fire seemed to let up. Some dull 'plub-plubs' from mortars could still be heard as could machine-gun fire at both ends of the flanks.

My pain increased but, peculiar as it may seem, with the increase of pain, I regained some strength. Pressing my right hand at my wound, I limped forward.

Now the village appeared to be much closer. At least six houses were burning. Flames, bright red and yellow created clouds of smoke. The battle sounds, even the machine-gun fire and rifle shots, lessened. Just awhile ago, with detonations and fire all around me, I had remained unruffled. Now, every shot startled me.

The Russians had retreated. There were comrades behind me—

fallen ones and wounded ones. I approached a dead Russian soldier. His skull was shattered and bloody, and his brain spattered the area. Why hadn't he worn a helmet? It was a physically painful sight, and made me feel sick to my stomach. I swallowed back the acid that came up my throat. I closed my eyes and demanded of myself not to collapse.

I passed out anyway and only regained consciousness when *Uffz.* Hinkel arrived with a horse-drawn cart, apparently one that a local farmer had used for transporting coal. Small pieces of *Steinkohle* (anthracite) and a layer of black dust had remained.

Uffz. Hinkel, with his wooden leg, sat up front holding the horse's reins. Two of the *Volksgrenadiere* (older soldiers of the Home Defense Force), not even medics, picked up the wounded and the dead, placing them on the coal cart, tightly, like sardines. My thoughts wandered through pain and gray dreams. To blend in with the winter landscapes, we had worn snow-capes over our uniforms. My poetic mind called them "soul capes." A row of fallen soldiers entering heaven?

The next one loaded into the cart jolted me out of my daydream. Dieter?

"Um Gottes willen?" (Oh, my God). It was the handsome straw-blond youngster, my friend. I recognized him at once, Dieter Eberhard Heinrich, my boyhood buddy. I didn't see any signs of injury. But he was gone. Dead.

"Dieter!"—My voice cracked. I felt the impulse to cry and had to bite my lips. A *Hitlerjunge* doesn't cry! I had just turned into a soldier.

I still can't describe the depth of my despair.

The next body put on the cart had a faceless head, consisting of blood, raw flesh, and bone fragments from the torn off nose. His eyes had been smashed and seeped out of the sockets.

The sick feeling increased. It became so acute that I had to throw up, right on the cart, soiling two of my comrades, one dead, but the other one still alive.

Although conditions were horrendously sickening, I was

appalled at myself for not being able to control what I viewed as war-sickness. We had been conditioned in so many ways, but I was totally unprepared for warfare's abominable, ghastly cruelties. I was unprepared for the helplessness I felt at not being able to master the situation.

Not capable of control seemed bad enough, but being the only one on the cart who couldn't stomach the unnerving sights of the mutilated bodies, devastated me.

There were no blankets, nothing to cover the gory head, facing down into the coal dust on the cart. I kept on choking and vomiting. At final count, there must have been ten to twelve bodies on this horse cart, at least five of them dead. Along with Dieter Eberhard Heinrich, another two showed hardly any sign of a hit, no blood, no mutilation, just frozen facial expressions.

One appeared to be even younger than I was. I didn't know him. The other was the petrified countenance of *Uffz.* Schleifer.

Uffz. Hinkel remarked: "I believe he knew."

I remembered how quiet and withdrawn *Uffz.* Schleifer had appeared during the last day before battle. Of course, he was a veteran and understood all about combat. He knew that the outcome would be deadly for some of us and ghastly for the rest.

By now my stomach must have been empty. My nausea finally subsided, but I did not regain control over my nerves. My body quivered. The sound of every shot, no matter how far, made me jerk. The wounded and fallen in our cart and in others (one of them was a *Panjewagen*—a small carriage drawn by a pony) were taken to the local tavern, set up as an emergency dressing station. The fallen were declared dead and their dog tags, pay books, and personal belongings—such as watches and billfolds—were removed. They were taken to the cemetery for burial.

I mumbled: "*Auf wiedersehen*" (See you again) to Dieter.

See you again?

Where?

If there was a comforting thought about Dieter's death, it was that he had not been mutilated.

In heaven, will all the bodies be restored?

The repulsive, unnerving image of our faceless comrade was by far the most gruesome sight I had had to view in my young life.

We were told he had activated a hand grenade but then froze, not throwing it, and it exploded in his face. Someone even commented, "That's what happens to cowards!" This I did not believe.

I learned later that the Russians were shooting with *Knallerbsen,* bullets that exploded on impact. I am convinced that this comrade was hit in the face by such an explosive and that it tore his countenance to shreds.

Feeling sick and frightened, brought death so very close and in a much more heinous way than I had ever imagined. My thoughts drowned in an abyss of horror.

Uffz. Hinkel stated later that I seemed lifeless. But then he saw my arm twitch. And, I was breathing. Did I have a chance to survive, he wondered?

CHAPTER 42

Among the Survivors

I was lying on the floor. I don't remember sighing or complaining, but I was in pain and surrounded by others, moaning and groaning. I shivered uncontrollably. The floor was cold. At first there were no blankets, nothing to provide warmth—to comfort us who were suffering. There were no medications to numb our pain. Only cups filled with water were being handed out. There were desperate cries for help.

We were told that a doctor would arrive and see us soon. It didn't happen.

We were transferred, I believe, in a truck filled with straw from the *Gasthaus* (local pub) to a *Hauptverbandsplatz* (main dressing station). By then my leg was stiff and had turned blue. Someone predicted that it would have to be amputated. Where we were now, there were medics but still no physician. The medics had some medications, but were out of anesthetics already. I remember that my wound had to be cleansed, that it was very painful, and in order not to scream, the corpsman who performed the medical work put his belt in my mouth with the words: "Bite into the leather!"

A *Kumpel* (pal) lit a cigarette for me, and I started smoking to find relief from the pain. With bleeding lips lacerated from biting the leather belt, I lit cigarette after cigarette, using the end of one to light the next. I kept on smoking until I finally passed out. Hours later, I was told that a medic had taken the last cigarette from me. Had I dropped it into the straw matters, I could have burned to death. He had counted the butts. I had smoked 17 in a row.

This *Kumpel,* only slightly wounded on the upper arm, was clever at *organisieren* (an expression used for getting things by nifty means, short of stealing). He helped even more in easing my suffering. He brought me some *Schnapps* (home-made spirits of high alcoholic contents). I drank straight out of the bottle. It burned my throat, but I gulped down several swallows. I inhaled even more deeply. The combination of alcohol and nicotine continued to take the edge off of my increasing, gnawing pain.

Vorschriften fuer Hitlerjungen im Kriegseinsatz (a set of orders prepared for *Hitlerjungen* in action) either did not yet exist or we were unaware of these regulations not allowing us to smoke or to consume hard liquor. In my case, I started smoking and gulping down *Schnapps* because of lack of medication.

***

Ordensschwestern, (nuns trained as nurses) arrived at our *Hauptverbandsplatz,* a local hospital with staff quarters nearby. A few days later, one of the youngest and prettiest nuns disappeared and so did a corporal, one of the medics. We were made to understand that, should they be caught, they would be executed. This thought disturbed me. I wondered why this corporal, who frequently had made off-color remarks when she was present should have attracted this young nun. I thought the remarks embarrassed her. I had noticed how a couple of times she had blushed.

For the first time in many days, we received a copy of a newspaper. I believe it was the *Silesian Daily* or the *Daily Observer* of Schweidnitz. I clearly remember reading a bold-printed notice that the death penalty now applied not only to deserters but also, in the case of those who refused to follow orders.

Published excerpts from a *Fuehrer* speech again emphasized his belief that *Vorsehung* (Providence) had saved him from the assassination attempt on July 20th of the previous year. Thus he

HM

would lead Germany to victory. He challenged all Germans to harden their spirit of resistance and to fulfill their duties.

The *Fuehrer*, once more, brought to the fore that everyone able to fight had to fight so that the great German nation would emerge victoriously. Having just faced my baptism of fire and lying here among the wounded, I felt that I, indeed, was doing my duty. In his speech, he had mentioned how much Germany had shrunk already. Although I realized that the Russians were less than 50 kilometers away from us, I didn't comprehend in any way how hopeless the overall situation had become.

Another news item caught my attention. I was familiar with Klettendorf, a village near where we had lived, with a plant that produced syrup from sugar beets. My parents knew the plant manager and the party officials there, including the *Ortsgruppenleiter* (district leader), Paul Glueckel. I was shocked to read a notice that Glueckel had been executed. Instead of mobilizing the men in his village to form a home defense unit, the newspaper article stated, he had left Klettendorf. Upon being located, he was shot on the spot. Someone I knew had been executed! I trembled.

An entire series of *Todesurteile* (death sentences) were published, no doubt as a deterrent for anyone thinking of retreat. I didn't recognize any names beside Glueckel's, but I noticed that among those executed, Glueckel had not been the only one who held a high party office.

How deplorable that some of Hitler's followers would desert him now, at this critical stage of the war, when everyone's total commitment was needed to turn the tide. That was the way I thought at the time and the so-called *Abschreckungsmassnahmen* (deterrence measures) reinforced my thinking.

A few days later, a train arrived for us to be taken to Dresden, by then known as a hospital town. Schools and other public buildings were used as emergency medical facilities. This city was considered to be relatively secure from air raids. We were reassured that it would be a safe place for us to recover. The nuns stayed behind. So did my *Kumpel*, the organizer. His wound didn't require

an operation, just dressing and healing. In a week or so, he would
be well enough to be returned to the front.

Less than 30 of us could be transported. A *Feldunterarzt* (junior physician) and three or four older medics came along. We left
behind some who had died and some others who were close to
death. There was hope for us who departed.

CHAPTER 43

An Ocean of Flames

The military hospital train reached the main railroad station in Dresden on February 12, 1945. We expected to be unloaded and taken to a school building, designated to become an emergency military hospital, a common practice then. It had happened in Breslau with my high school.

We waited.

We had a kitchen car on the train. By the time we reached our destination, it was closed down—probably already without provisions. Girls from the *BDM (Bund Deutscher Maedel* the girl's branch of the Hitler Youth) and women from the *NSV*[13] came to comfort us, serving coffee, even hot soup.

The attending physician on our train, who had left upon our arrival, had not returned. It was announced that the school we were meant to occupy had, in a desperate move by the officials, already been assigned to a refugee group from the East. Many of these people were very old and too sick to be moved again.

Other quarters had to be found for us. Until then, our train could not be unloaded. We had to wait for orders. Where they would come from, nobody seemed to know. Our medics became frustrated. The supplies were depleted. We were hungry, but there were no meals.

The mood on the train became one of increasing despair. Most of us were in pain and some expressed their miseries with agonizing sounds that affected all of us.

Some refugees from other treks, apparently hardship cases, were admitted to our train that was already overcrowded.

Among them were two boys who had lost their mother and one young, pregnant woman in great pain, probably already in labor. The *Sanitaetsfeldwebel* (medic sergeant-major) was at a loss for what to do. Every sentence he uttered seemed to start with *"schrecklich"* (awful).

"Awful, we are out of water."

"Awful, we used up all of our food."

"My god, these boys. How awful, they lost their mother."

"How awful, this woman is ready to give birth."

Awful—awful—awful!

When would our doctor return? Supposedly, he was still in the city, assisting party or military officials in the search to find a place where still another emergency military hospital could be established, one to house us.

We already had spent too much time packed in the train. Most of us were in great pain and downcast because we felt so miserable. Our water was depleted. The kitchen remained closed. In dire need of medical supplies, our medic kept on repeating this one expression that summed it all up: "Awful…"

I can still hear his gruff, throaty voice.

He wanted to take better care of us and help the young boys who were starved. The pregnant woman he put in another car in a cot of a soldier who had died and been removed. He had died of gangrene, we were told. Some boys from a fire-fighting unit had come to pick up his body.

"Why can't we get off too?"

"They are taking him to a cemetery."

The young soldier on the bunk bed below me remarked: "Whatever happens, we have to pull through!"

The medic continued with remarks expressing how dispirited he felt.

"I am here to help you, but I need dressing supplies, medications, food, and water."

Finally, one of the medics decided that he would take things in his own hands. He left the train and reassured us that he would be back soon. I felt uneasy from the moment he was gone, sort of abandoned. This feeling of having been deserted increased as time went on.

Late at night he returned. Water and food would arrive soon, he assured us.

This was a sure sign we wouldn't be unloaded soon.

Very early the next morning, February 13th, before daybreak, we were awakened by our car knocking and banging us painfully around.

The medic explained that the cars of another hospital train were being added to ours. Apparently the locomotive had broken down or had been destroyed by fire from an enemy plane, stranding all the cars filled with injured and sick soldiers. While these hospital wagons were added to our train, a lot of moving forward and backward, tugging and yanking took place, affecting the seriously wounded most of all. The jars and jolts were dramatized by the sounds of agony.

When, finally, all these cars had been added to our train and the physician having returned, we were moved from the main railroad station to an *Abstellgleis* (railway yard) outside of Dresden, perhaps 15 to 20 kilometers away from town. We were told in which direction we were traveling. Heading for Chemnitz and Plauen made us uneasy, because Chemnitz, an industrial city, had by then become a constant target of air raids.

***

We all could have died in the carnage of Dresden. Not just my comrades and me, but my mother, my sisters, brothers, and my father too. I had no clue whatsoever that on this crucial day our entire family was near or inside this very city, soon to be doomed. None of us knew of the others' presence.

My mother, with my sisters and brothers and our maid, Hilde, had arrived at Dresden in a refugee train. They had pulled into *Hauptbahnhof* (main railroad station) apparently on the same day our hospital train had arrived.

My father, on his way to the Dresden radio station, had no idea that the members of his family were there also. He expected me to be in Breslau inside the fortress. His younger sons, his daughters and his wife, he thought to be with relatives or, by now, in a refugee camp, possibly in Hoyerswerda.

My sister Ute wrote a summary based on their remembrances while in Dresden:

> We were all dead-tired when we arrived in our crowded train at the main railroad station in Dresden. Wulf and Uli (Ulrich) were deeply asleep, almost as if in a coma. Mother tried to wiggle them out of their languid slumber. We took turns dragging them and carrying them along to the station's huge air raid shelter. Crowded with refugees, we were lucky to find enough space for all of us to lie down on the floor. Around 11:00 a.m., a hot chicken soup was served, a meal from heaven. This, and the opportunity to rest, encouraged my mother to stay for a while.
>
> We all wanted to remain except for Anje. She urged mother to get out of the shelter.
>
> 'Please let's go on!! Let us leave, please, please!!'
>
> A local woman overheard Anje's pleadings and reassured my mother that it was safe to stay. "Dresden has never been bombed," she told them. "Nothing will happen here. Here you have a roof over your head and you won't starve with the soup kitchen being maintained for the refugees."
>
> However, Anje kept on insisting that we should leave. With additional refugees constantly arriving, the bunker became more crowded and stuffy, even ill-smelling. The best argument for leaving in mother's mind was the news that a train would soon be leaving for Bavaria. The train route to Mecklenburg via Berlin experienced almost daily air raids. Interruptions in rail traffic were common, with tracks being hit and torn apart. Rail traffic to Bavaria, however, was less disrupted and less dangerous.
>
> In a small village on that route, lived Opa Lehmann, the

grandfather who had lived with us in Waldgut Horka. More-over, as a minor party official and as mayor, he might be influ-ential enough to help us until we could return to Breslau.

Mother and, of course, we children still believed that we would return home. It looked now as if it would take longer than what mother had been told originally. Thus, Bavaria seemed to be the most sensible place where we could wait until we could go back to Breslau.

We left the station house. The platform was crowded with people, mostly refugees and soldiers. The trains coming in were filled already beyond capacity. Legs dangled out of windows. Bodies adhered to the doors, unable to get in.

There seemed no chance for us to get on. The situation seemed hopeless. In this frenzy, with people pushing recklessly, we not only had problems staying together, but discovered that our big suitcase was missing. Mother and Hilde wanted to search for it. Anje, however, pleaded to let it go. Secretly, she had taken along coloring pencils and her flute that she carried in her ruck-sack. In the missing suitcase was only clothing and food. It mattered less to her. Mother, off course, valued the food and garb highly, especially under the circumstances.

In this mass of people, chances seemed slim enough to find the suitcase. It might have been picked up by strangers and shoved into the train that was leaving. People were desperate.

What saved us was the decision of one official. He gave our mother, because she had five children, special permission to board a military hospital train. Although also overcrowded, we were pushed through the windows, above wounded soldiers, some of them moaning and groaning in pain. We were squeezed in between their cots. For quite awhile, we were separated, but, eventually, ended up all together in the same car.

A young mother who had left to get water for her baby was thought to be lost. She had found some water just as the train left and jumped on the last car. It took her hours to make it through the cars to where we were and where she had left her baby.

> *We departed at about 14:00 (2 p.m.), just hours prior to*
> *the devastating air raid that would follow on that night. The*
> *destruction included the station. Anje's premonition probably*
> *saved our lives.*
> *Very slowly, at first in a stop-and-go, go-and-stop fashion*
> *the train left the city. By dusk, we were finally rolling, still at a*
> *slow speed, destined for Wuerzburg.*

While my mother, sisters and brothers were on their way out of Dresden in a train also filled with wounded soldiers, the hospital train in which I lay was still sidetracked and on hold. It was a very cold day. Although steam heat kept our car warm, every time the door was opened, an icy breeze could be felt.

I was in an upper berth with enough clearance that I could look through the window. I looked out and saw many trains rolling by. In one of them must have been my family.

More than two hours passed before our *Zugoffizier* (train commander) returned. He conferred with our *Begleitartz* (attending physician). The news spread fast about our new destination. We were to go to Bayreuth, capital of Upper Franconia, known as *Richard Wagner Stadt* (City of Richard Wagner).

Thus, the two trains in which, unknowingly, members of the Lehmann family traveled passed each other headed in the same direction!

***

My father, too, was in Dresden on the 12th and 13th of February 1945. He was the only one of us to remain, as a patient in a provisional aid station set up downtown at a school. There he experienced the massive bombing raid that started around 22:00 hours (10 p.m.) on the fateful night of February 13.

After the war, my father, having told his wife and children the story many times, committed to paper his experiences. Fifty years later, I translated the paper, without much editing, as follows:

> *The streets of Dresden, on February 13, 1945, were so*

congested with cars, trucks, horse carriages and refugees that without common consideration and exemplary discipline it would have been impossible for me to maneuver my Dienstwagen (official car) through the four-lane refugee treks and reach the Lazarett (military hospital).

I approached in need of treatment. Passenger trains, hospital trains, and freight trains in never-ending chains also passed through the city. They were mostly overcrowded with women and children whose husbands and teenage sons were left behind in Silesia to defend their homeland.

Dresden, city of military hospitals and, by now, also a refugee assembly point, had increased its population of 650,000 by 500,000. Over one million civilians and wounded were attacked by British and American bombers in successive raids that destroyed over 13 square kilometers, including all of the historical old-town. In the evening, after I had finally arrived at the Lazarett, I was unable to reach the air raid shelter because wounded soldiers on stretchers blocked the entrance. Through a window on the ground floor, I attempted to get to the air raid shelter in the next building. But already in these very first minutes of the attack, the Lazarett, in a school building, had been hit by high-explosive demolition as well as by incendiary bombs. I ran between houses that were on fire, jumped over burning phosphor and found, briefly, some protection from the raging flames in the empty air raid shelter of a house already aflame.

In this cellar, I discovered a bathtub filled with water. Before the burning house collapsed, I was able to grab two blankets from the cots. I soaked the covers in the stale water. The cracking sounds of the burning house increased, a warning that at any moment it might collapse and force me to leave.

Back on the street between the flames, I could see a mother with her daughter, running as fast as they could to find protection. I figured that they were local residents and knew their way around. When I had caught up with them, I asked the frantic mother if there was a park nearby or at least a large place, a square or court, an opening where there might be no fire.

Gasping, she explained that a nearby school, now being used as a Lazarett (military hospital) had a big yard. That's where I had come from. Thus we turned back. The Turnhalle (gym) and the main building with the markings of a big Red Cross symbol on its shingles, were burning fiercely, soon to collapse, buried by the roof's raging flames. Everyone inside must have burned to death. The three of us, still in the open, wrapped the wet blankets around us like a package with six legs. We didn't know where to go. We saw two wounded soldiers partly shielded by the huge trunk of an old tree. The fire was so close already that our blankets became hotter and hotter and started steaming. We seemed at the end when I, through a break in the smoke, saw that there was in the corner of the schoolyard a betonierte Muellgrube (concrete garbage pit).

In there, we might be shielded from the flames, I thought. But would there be enough space for the five of us?

I crawled to the trash-bin. With my wounded hand, I was not able to lift the metal cover, but with the other one I succeeded. My heart jumped. The concrete pit was empty. The other four followed behind. We all stuffed ourselves into the concrete disposal trap fall and, despite smoke and intense heat, we all survived the night. In the early morning, however, the smoke became thicker and ever more constricting. We all coughed harshly, choking and gasping, but not for long. Soon I was the only one still conscious.

Just able to muster enough strength to lift the cover and climb out of the concrete pit, I noticed men wearing gas masks belonging to a search and rescue unit. I yelled as loud as I could: "Here in the garbage pit.... "

That's my last memory. Days later, I regained consciousness in a hospital in a nearby mountain village. I learned that the rescuers that had saved my life had been dispatched from Pirna to the burning city of Dresden.

They must have rescued me, provided transport to this hospital, and then returned to the inner city.

No one from the nursing staff knew more details and I was unable to ascertain if the other four in the pit were still alive and if they had been saved. As soon as I was on my feet again, I checked the hospital room-for-room, searching for the mother and the child and the two wounded soldiers. None of them were in the hospital here. Probably all four had died. The mother obviously had saved my life. That she might have lost her life and that of her daughter's disquieted and saddened me.

Most of the wounded in the wards of this hospital were native Dresdeners. Some had, as I, sustained severe burns and suffered from smoke inhalation. Astonishingly, the majority of the casualties had been hit by bullets! Yes, they had shot wounds! Lacking shelters, thousands had fled to the banks of the Elbe River to escape the wild fire-storms. Following the bombardment, both embankments, carpeted with people, came under heavy machine gun fire from low-flying enemy aircraft engaged in mop-up actions. The river turned red.

These were my father's recollections prompting him to observe that: "Murder is murder and mass murder is mass murder whether committed in Auschwitz or Dresden. Never forget it!"

Except for stating that "one does not excuse the other," I didn't discuss this point of view with him. To my mind, there are no valid excuses for the deliberate, at-will extermination of human beings. The "final solution" for the Jewish people and the killing of the people in Dresden were both terrible slaughters.

Although my father remained mum about many things I was to ask him, the horror-night of Dresden was not one of them.

At any occasion that presented itself, he would tell the story of his survival, over and over again, always emphasizing that, among the hundreds of patients and nurses in the *Hilfslazarett,* he was among only three that survived.

After the war he explained that he had transferred confidential materials from Breslau to the radio station there. He didn't elaborate on what kind of records those were; neither did I find out why he, officially a war correspondent, once again, was on such a special mission.

Interestingly enough, the Director of the Breslau radio station, Hans-Otto Fricke, after leaving his post in Breslau, was looked upon as a deserter because he didn't arrive in Dresden but had left for Prague instead. After being sentenced to die, he was offered the opportunity to serve in an *SS-Bewaehrungsbattallion (SS* probation battalion). Most of its members ended up sacrificing their lives in a typical suicide mission. Aware of the fate that awaited him, Fricke committed suicide instead.

The leading musician of the Breslau radio station, Ernst Prade was with a larger convoy on the way to Dresden. He didn't reach the city prior to its destruction as my father did. The entourage of the music department had, supposedly for lack of fuel, come to a halt in the city of Cottbus. Most of this crew was among the Breslau radio station's few survivors.

Some personnel in Vienna's radio station were investigated during the last two months of the war. According to one of the survivors, my father had been assigned to a *Saeuberungsaktion 05* (Depuration Mission 05), which was responsible for the dismissal of many of them. Despite extensive research, I have been unable to uphold claims of executions alleged to have taken place as part of this last minute, clean-up operation.

During the last years of his life, among old comrades, my father reminisced and shared memories of these past secret missions. One who initially belonged to this *Kameradshaftskreis* (inner circle of old comrades), and who survived him, mentioned at his funeral that all who belonged to this informal group of veterans held my father in high esteem and considered his war record honorable. Until they died, these veterans rationalized that "orders were orders" and had to be followed. Those who issued the orders were responsible, not those who carried them out.

There was never any indication that my father suffered under psychological burdens. He was always good at explaining things away. He maintained that horrible things happen in horrible times. All participants in the war are responsible for its horrors.

In the fall of 1946, when we had an argument, he yelled at me, stating that Jews had to blame themselves for their fate. I was so shocked, I choked. After all that had happened, how could his thoughts have been so demented, his mind so bent?

I am certain he was a very intelligent man. But what had happened to his reasoning ability? I am sure that he was not a sadist by nature. With his fellow hunters, he had deplored the torture of animals. He had compassion toward fellow human beings. When we were children, he always demanded consideration and courtesies toward grown-ups.

Whether he knew about the "Final Solution" and what went on in concentration camps, I am still not certain. I have always given him the benefit of the doubt. But, after the war, when the horrible deprivations, repulsive persecutions, and abominable mass-murders came to light, he should have deplored what happened and expressed his feelings.

He only countered with arguments that the enemies also engaged in mass killings, naming Hiroshima and, especially, Dresden.

To his way of thinking, I remained naïve.

Why, after I had served as a soldier as he had, after I had participated in just as much bloody combat—if not more—by the time this internecine, slaughterous war had come to its end, why, he asked, had I not matured to his way of thinking?

My answer: "War causes but never sanctions crimes against humanity. Justifying terrors of the past would invite terrors in the future."

***

What was my own experience of the devastating air raid on Dresden? I was wide awake in the hospital train—probably about 20 km south of the city—and could clearly hear the undulating sound of air-raid sirens warning the citizens of approaching enemy aircraft.

"That cannot be!" remarked one of the wounded. "They (he meant the Allies) won't bomb Dresden!"

"It could be Russians! Coming from the East," someone remarked. But I commented, "They would destroy Breslau before hitting Dresden."

"Breslau might already be in rubble."

"I hope not, most of my classmates are there!"

I listened anxiously, every muscle straining to hear.

Far away, a humming of heavy engines in unison soon escalated into a vibrating, droning sound. I envisioned, high in the sky, the approach of a mighty phalanx of metal birds.

There were also some sounds of faster planes criss-crossing. We thought that German fighters had taken off and were up in the skies to attack the approaching enemy. But none of us could see any planes or hear any shots being fired.

I noticed flares, some in the shape of small Christmas trees, falling from heaven and illuminating spheres of the firmament.

Most fizzled out before hitting ground.

Then there were some flaming flashes. Fire bombs?

Suddenly I could hear "plub-plub" sounds.

But instead of increasing, these bursts decreased.

Heimatflak (home defense anti-aircraft guns) units had to be stationed in Dresden, as in Breslau. Most of my high school classmates had become trained crews of 8.8cm flak guns: Klaus, Werner, Martin and all the others. I imagined how they would fire relentlessly at approaching enemy aircraft, shooting down as many as they could hit.

Why was there nothing of the sort happening here in Dresden?

Bombs were falling in jam-packed succession. It felt as if we were closer now than 20 kilometers to the sites of the impacts. Much closer.

How many planes could there be up in the sky? From several directions, hissing sounds cut into the roar of the bombers' engines.

On the ground, strangely enough, there seemed to be few explosions on impact. I didn't know then that firebombs don't explode like demolition bombs, but ignite upon impact like flame-throwers.

One of the other wounded soldiers in our car also had a view through a window. He yelled "Incendiary bombs!" over and over.

By now, it must have been close to 11 p.m. Through the smirchy glass, the sky in front of me was totally afire. In the confines of our train, we weren't aware of the firestorms, the whirling heat twisters. But, through my small window, huge glowing tongues spit up spirals of smoke.

Without a doubt, a beautiful city, thought to be safe, crowded with people, was being scourged before my eyes, and blown into fragments.

I was overcome by the sight of the sea of fire.

It had always been my greatest fear—death in flames. Fire, I was convinced, caused the highest degree of excruciating pain.

A whole city was being turned into a blasting furnace, scorching living people, frying them, reducing them to ashes.

The explosions made the ground tremble. In my cot, I could feel the earth shake. An ocean of flames expanded and approached our location, increasing my fears. Why wasn't our train being moved?

Didn't the enemy suffer any losses? Only once did I observe what looked like a flaming comet crashing down to earth. Had one of their planes been downed, a single plane out of what must be hundreds?

While I kept watching, overtaken by fright, others in the car wanted to get out. Some who could walk, got up, opened the door, and left the train. Nobody stopped them. They ran to the field and threw themselves into the dirt. Several, with their hands, scraped out enough soil to find some protection.

Hours went by. Only after the second attack, did my comrades return. Fortunately, the firestorms had not reached us and our train had not been bombed.

***

We would be hit the next day. Already in motion, we were probably closer to Chemnitz than to Dresden. In the distance, signs of the burned down city were still visible.

My only memory of Dresden was as a boy, when I had traveled by train through this beautiful city twice or thrice. Once I had spent a weekend in this city which was named by Johann Herder,[114] "Germany's Florence."

During my assignment as councilor at the camp *Schloss* Ullersdorf, I received papers for a weekend leave to visit my grandparents in Goerlitz. I don't recall why I changed my mind. But even during the war, I always had the desire to visit new places.

I loved my grandparents, but I had been to Goerlitz many times before. Dresden, I had only traveled through. I had heard, again and again, what a magnificent city it was, full of splendor, with its famous Winger Garden,[115] museums, and extensive artistic, literary, and scientific collections. Thus, I decided—on the spur of the moment—not to visit my grandparents, but to travel to Dresden instead.

I didn't have my papers changed and encountered problems at the Youth Hostel. A local *Hitlerjugend* leader, a year younger than I was, not only made it possible for me to stay, but with great pride, showed me his city on the next day, a Sunday. His mother (his father was in the service) served us a delectable, satisfying *Mittagessen* (dinner eaten at noon).

The young man's name was Helmut, and I couldn't help comparing him with the ruffian, Helmut, from Klein-Berlin in Hoyerswerda. The Dresdener, Helmut, was soft-spoken, with a melodic Saxonian dialect. He was as caring and as considerate as my boyhood friend, Rudi from Niesky.

I was unable to determine the fate of all three after the war. But there seems to be little doubt that my short-term friend Helmut from Dresden had been among those who burned to death in the firestorm. I thought of him as I watched through the window from the upper berth of the hospital train that had just moved far enough to enable us to escape.

***

Suddenly, we were attacked. I had not noticed any markings when we were loaded, but our *Sani* (short for *Sanitaeter*, the German word for medic) insisted that on top of our cars were huge Red-Cross markings. They identified our modified bunk bed coaches as a hospital train—a transport of wounded soldiers.

Nevertheless, after we had survived the two-day, three-wave air attack in Dresden, we were suddenly, in open country, attacked by low-flying enemy aircraft. Not only was our locomotive hit and put out of order, bullets strafed through the cars, shattering windows and perforating walls and partitions.

Holding on to a handle above my berth, I was hit in the left elbow, grazed by what must have been a machine gun bullet. I also sustained severe cuts from broken glass. My face bled.

Some bombs were dropped, too, because I remember huge fountains of dirt spouting up on the farm field in view. There were casualties on the field because some *Sanis*, and a few of the wounded that could walk, had left the train.

One of the boys was killed. *Sanis* brought him back into our car, his shirt removed, the small chest torn open, with two broken rib splinters piercing through the flesh. There was blood, blood all over. I could see him from my bunk. He lay there with his eyes open, as if his face had turned into wax. Although he must have been dead already, some blood still trickled down.

His brother was even younger (I guessed his age as six). I was baffled by his behavior. He didn't cry. He just clung to the *Sani*, who lifted him up and cradled him in his arms for a while, but then had to set him down again because he had work to do.

The troubled boy looked up. For seconds he stared at me stonily. Then he threw himself on the floor face down. No sobbing, no tears.

I tried to stop the bleeding on my face by pressing my washcloth against the cuts. It soaked up the blood in no time and soon was dripping gore. Finally, the *Sani* came, put iodine and gauze on my wounds and taped them up.

There were others who had been injured more severely than I. Opposite me a comrade was being attended to. Blood drooled out of his mouth and his breathing caused a gurgling sound. His left hand was pressed on his chest. The *Sani* had lifted his blanket; there was blood on his chest too. Not near the heart but on the other side.

While we were waiting for the tracks to be repaired and for a new locomotive to arrive, our *Sani* prepared us for the funeral. He passed around a bottle of *Weinbrand* (a brandy), restricting each of us to one swallow. "We must leave the dead here," he said.

My throat throbbed and I coughed. My dressing slipped down and my face bled again. When the bottle made its second round, it was nearly empty by the time it reached me. The very last drop burned on my lips.

I wasn't awake when the graves were dug. I don't remember anything of the burial.

Our train was moving again, slowly and in short distances. The boy who had lost his brother remained in our car. Gradually, he broke out of the confines of self and became a contributing member of the crew. One of the *Sanis* had given him a medic armband with the emblem of the Red Cross. He wore it proudly. It turned him into an orderly, probably the youngest ever.

For the remainder of our journey together, he never mentioned his fallen brother. Not even once. Neither did any of us soldiers.

Word reached us that in the other car, among the wounded soldiers, the pregnant woman had given birth. It was a boy. I thought back seven years when my mother and I were alone at our apartment in Breslau and Wulf was born. He would be seven years old soon, just two or three years younger than the boy that was killed.

Where were my brothers and sisters and my mother now?

I had no idea, of course, that they had been in Dresden and had left in a train, too, just in time not to have perished in this terrible inferno.

CHAPTER 44

Anne-Maria

It must have been two days later when we reached Hof, located on the Saale River. There the most serious cases were to be discharged from the train. We were told that an emergency military hospital had been set up downtown in an elementary school and we would be taken there for emergency care.

I was among those to be left in Hof because my fever exceeded 40° Celsius. Surgery must be performed right away, so that my leg could possibly be saved. There wasn't enough time to wait until we would arrive in Bayreuth.

I noticed how badly wounded some of those being taken off the train were.

We were carried into a room at the station, and put on the floor. Some remained on the stretchers; a few sat up on chairs. None of the *Sanis* remained with us, they all went back to those left on the train destined for Bayreuth. At first it seemed that there was no one in Hof to receive us. A *Bahnpolizist* (railroad police officer) made room for us, then took a count and filled out some papers. I was able to raise my head and take a look at the others.

If my leg was saved or even if it had to be amputated, I would be among the lucky ones. I still had two arms, both of my eyes and ears. I could see and hear. The superficial cuts on my face, I had been assured, would heal without leaving me scarred. There were at least twenty of us waiting, most, apparently, much worse off than I. One had his head completely wrapped up with bandages. How could he breathe?

All of us were supposedly in desperate need of surgery whether
we suffered from lung shots, perforated guts, damaged livers, kid-
neys, spleens, or other injuries. Gunshots and shrapnel wounds
required debridement.

Battlefield casualties on a dirty floor, in an overcrowded train
station. Victims for the cause we believed in—to insure a great
future for our Fatherland.

Because of the delay caused by the air attack after Dresden,
the dressings and bandages applied to our wounds were full of pus
or blood-caked. The room filled up with foul smells of purulence
and decay. Sounds of pain and suffering increased.

We were dehydrated and hungry.

Finally, some women arrived from the *NSV* with large containers
of grain coffee. We were told that soup would come later. The *NSV*
women were very concerned and made every effort to comfort us.
But before the soup arrived, we were picked up in a *Holzgaser*
(truck fueled with charcoal gas) and taken on the bumpy ride to
the school that was to serve as an emergency military hospital.

***

Of Hof, I have many recollections, kaleidoscopic at the beginning
but becoming more sequential, detailed, and to the point, because
of a love affair with *Schwester* Anne-Maria. *Schwester* means sister
and, in Germany, nurses are commonly addressed as "sisters." Thus,
Schwester Anne-Maria was not my sister but our very young Red
Cross nurse. Not as young as I, though.

The nurses worked shifts, although *Schwester* Anne-Maria was
mostly on duty during the day because she became the charge
nurse of our room.

A classroom had been vacated when we arrived. Old men had
moved the school benches into the hallways where we had been
waiting. Along with the shrieks of pain now came curses and
complaints about the cold draft coming through the hall. We
shuddered and shivered.

I was taken straight from the hallway to a makeshift operating room. I don't recall anything about the surgery. Obviously, medications and anesthesia had arrived together with a surgical team.

When I regained consciousness, the first thing I checked was to see if they had amputated my leg.

It was still there; they had only removed the shrapnel.

The young Red Cross nurse, in a blue-striped dress covered with a white apron, had introduced herself: "Good morning, I am *Schwester* Anne-Maria."

She carried a pot of coffee and a tray with slices of bread covered with marmalade. She went from cot to cot.

When she reached me, I only took the cup. My hands were shaking.

"No bread?" she asked. After the surgery, I still felt nauseated.

"No thanks," I replied and spilled some coffee.

She looked deep into my eyes.

"How old are you?"

"Sixteen."

She stroked my head.

I felt infused with warmth and gentleness. The surroundings appeared to be more hospitable. The sizeable classroom we were in had been converted into a patient's ward and 16 cots had crammed into the room.

Our *Stubenaeltester* (NCO-in-charge/room steward) was a *Feldwebel* (sergeant-major) from the famous regiment "Grossdeutschland."

Schwester Anne-Maria referred to him only as the one from *Grossdeutschland,* and he became "*Grossdeutschland*" when talked about. It wasn't meant to be disrespectful to the fame of this distinguished military unit. It might have been a tribute of special respect. I can still hear *Schwester* Ann-Maria's voice: "*Grossdeutschland* is in charge!" "*Grossdeutschland* is jealous." "*Grossdeutschland* is looking for you." "*Grossdeutschland* reported you to the *Stabsarzt!*"

He was, indeed, a good example of the soldier from a crack unit: tough, self-assured, and somewhat presumptuous. He had a crush on *Schwester* Anne-Maria and how did anyone dare to compete with him? Almost everyone in our room seemed to love *Schwester* Anne-Maria.

She was a 19-year-old beauty, thoughtful and caring, despite the enormous hardships she and her fellow-nurses encountered.

In the beginning, as Anne-Maria told us, they had no quarters and slept in the school's cellar on straw, crowded like cattle. They found potato sacks and stuffed them with chaff that turned out to be too prickly. Thus, they ended up sleeping on the straw that was more comfortable than the husks-sack mattresses. The first nights they also had no lights, except for flashlights.

Several of the nurses were, as were their patients, plagued by dysentery, with insufficient medications available. Normally, as nurses, they would have had their own personal first-aid kits. But all of their luggage was missing and was still being searched for at the railroad station. Except for what they carried in their purses, the nurses assigned to us had arrived in the vacated school building without belongings.

At first, no medicines were available other than what was in the hands of the surgical team for the emergency operations. The city's hospitals and pharmacies were also in dire need of medical supplies. "Total war" had caught up with the wounded, too. There were so many reasons for our morale to be low. However, Anne-Maria and the nurses who weren't sick kept us from sliding into downright despair. They did it just by being there, by talking to us, by instilling hope that "things are under way," that "medications will get here soon," that "a kitchen is being set up and you will get a warm meal before long," (at first we received cold canned food only).

"We take care of our soldiers," the nurses emphasized, obviously convinced that the worst was over.

Soon they had reason to be optimistic. They were billeted two to four to a room, and their luggage, finally found, had arrived.

Anne-Maria told us that, except for the bunk beds, a military-type locker, and a couple of chairs, there was no other furniture in their rooms, no nightstands, no desks, not even shelves. A "community room" was furnished with a large table and chairs, a shelf with magazines, a radio, and a desk, meant to provide a writing corner.

According to Anne-Maria, one could hardly concentrate in there to write letters. "It's our *Quatschzimmer* (gossip parlor) instead," she said.

When they had guests, they called it their "tea room." Later, I would be one of the occasional guests, and I remember a *Tauchsieder* (immersion heater) with which they brewed herbal tea. The nurses were not allowed to have guests in their bedrooms. I remember *Schwester* Anne-Maria, who shared a room with *Schwester* Irene and two others commenting that it looked so cheerless. Nothing could be bought anymore to fix up the place. All they could do was pick up little green branches and put them in cups. It was too early for wild flowers.

For our room, a local woman had brought a potted plant.

The nurses who were ill had recovered. Most of them were good looking. One of them even a "femme fatal" type, leggy and flirty. Another one, when off-duty, wore a very tight sweater. She had voluptuous breasts and reminded me of Trudel, stirring my young mind with her flaunting seductiveness.

But such incitements did not divert my heart from longing for Anne-Maria. From the first moment I had seen her, I had fallen in love with her. Increasingly, she seemed to respond, giving me more attention, an extra touch, a devoted look sometimes a whisper—a few words meant only for me to hear. It made me happy, but at times I also felt awkward or embarrassed.

The first week after my operation, I had to observe strict bed rest, even having to use a bedpan. I managed not to ask for it while Anne-Maria was on duty. Then the day came when I was permitted to use the toilet located down the hallway. That evening I put on my pants and borrowed a uniform jacket (my own had probably been left on the train) from a roommate who had also a walking cane. Painful as it was to walk, I left the room and went in the schoolyard to get some fresh air.

On the next morning, I told Anne-Maria that I had taken my first walk.

First she thought that I was pushing my luck, but I convinced her to meet me that evening, after her shift was over, for a walk. I had no pass. *Grossdeutschland* and most of my room-mates didn't approve. Nevertheless, I was daring and I left.

Anne-Maria and I walked to the Saale, which became "our" river, and the topic for a couple of poems. I had the desire to write again.

Our excursions became a nightly occurrence. I returned later and later until, one morning, *Grossdeutschland* openly scolded Anne-Maria: "*Schwester,* how can you get involved with a child?"

She turned red and didn't reply.

I felt angry and ashamed but also kept quiet.

In a sense, *Grossdeutschland* was my superior.

Most of the others in the room also disapproved of the apparent romance going on between the *Junge* (kid) and this vivacious young woman. All in our room felt attracted to her.

Grossdeutschland must have reported me to the *Stabsarzt* because I was ordered not to leave the hospital without permission. Anne-Maria was reprimanded severely. When she told me about it, she cried. Then, still sobbing, she said, "I am a wild cat!" It broke the ice and made us smile. My feelings had been just as agitated as hers.

Outraged, I confronted *Grossdeutschland,* with everyone in the room witnessing my outburst. "I am not too young to die."

"But you are too young to marry!" he replied. Was he right?

Although only 16 years old, as a *Volkssturmmann,* I was a soldier. I had been wounded in battle and then wounded again on the way to this hospital. I smoked. I had proven, several times by now, that I was able to hold my liquor. What else could make me an adult?

How could anyone, no matter how superior in rank, be able to restrain me from associating with a nurse, especially one who was also in the service of the Fatherland? If I wanted to marry Anne-

Maria, and she was willing to become my wife, why would we have to wait until I turned 18? What were my chances to be alive then?

The Russians were advancing toward Kolberg. Soon to return to the Front, my chances of survival were ever so slim. I was suddenly consumed by the thought that I should have an heir, that I should exemplify my manhood not only by being a soldier, but also by being a progenitor of ongoing life. I wrote about the rightness of my cause—of our cause—because Anne-Maria wanted my child. Hers was a vision of love and patriotism.

Should I soon be among the battle dead, my blood would continue in the veins of our child. I wrote with flaming idealism about my wish to secure my place in the eternal river of life. I described the river as filled with the blood of the fallen soldiers, to which my own blood might be added.

Anne-Maria was impressed by what I had written. We both were willing to forgo our lives, as a sacrifice for *Fuehrer und Vaterland.* In the great scheme of things, we had been taught, our individual lives belonged to the nation. Not for us to live on, but for the nation to survive.

***

An orderly had pulled a small table up front and placed on it a box.

"*Stubenappell*" (room inspection) shouted *Grossdeutschland.* Since the daily doctor's visit was already behind us, something special was to take place.

Those who could get up, had to put on their uniform. By now I had been issued a jacket. Although too big, I had to wear it. Orders are orders and *Grossdeutschland* ruled.

The important visitors who arrived were the *Ortskommandant,* the local commander, an *Oberstleutnant* (Lieutenant Colonel), and his adjutant or aide-de-camp, a *Leutnant* (lieutenant). After the official greetings, the *Oberstleutnant* spoke to us. He addressed us as "*Kameraden*" (comrades) and it struck me that such a high-ranking officer would call me a comrade. He mentioned that we were deserving of the nation's gratitude and that, in the name of the *Fuehrer*, it was his honor to award some of us with decorations.

Anne-Maria knew of it but had kept it secret from me. I was among the ones to be decorated.

Oblt. Gutschke, after his unit had been pulled out of the fighting, was successful in locating some of the medical facilities where his wounded were being treated. He had found out that I was in Hof. Since it was uncertain when I could be released, he had informed the officer in charge of the hospital that, in addition to the Black Wounded Badge, I was to be awarded the Iron Cross, Second Class.

One of the two Silver Wounded Badges was awarded to *Grossdeutschland*, who wore already the black one and who also had previously been the recipient of the Iron Cross, Second Class and the Iron Cross, First Class. In fact, several of my roommates were highly decorated soldiers, but on this occasion, after the Silver and Black Wounded Badges had been awarded, I was the only one to be decorated with the Iron Cross.

I became a *junger Held*, a young hero.

It seemed that, thereafter, all of my roommates treated me with some respect. I remained the *Junge*, but now was often referred to as *der mutige Junge* (the brave kid), the one with the Iron Cross.

The citation had been impressive. It praised my courage and the fact that I had saved some of my comrades' lives.

***

After the bulk of the surgeries had been completed, two military physicians were stationed there and attended the entire hospital. One was referred to as the *alte Doktor* (old doctor). He might have been a civilian recalled to service in the medical corps, assigned to service in Hof, instead of preparing for battle with a *Volkssturm* unit.

ARMIN D. LEHMANN

We saw him in his long white coat and polished riding boots, which suggested that he wore a uniform underneath. Once or twice weekly, he made rounds in our ward. I had taken an instant liking to him. Grandfatherly, with noble demeanor, he was very imposing in appearance. He had a full head of silver-gray hair and projected an image of mature manhood.

He must also have been a very sensitive man.

I thought that doctors and nurses were hardened to suffering and dying, but both Anne-Maria and the old doctor, from time to time, appeared affected by their painful chores.

Anne-Maria had one expression she used now and then: "I had to bite my lips!" It meant that she had to hurt herself to keep from weeping.

"I can't break down in front of others and cry," she explained.

"It would look as if I were faltering!"

More of a surprise was that the old doctor, too, could be overcome by his emotions. Once, in our presence, he had to fight off signs of discomposure. One of our roommates had died unexpectedly. He came and checked with his stethoscope, confirming that his heartbeat had stopped. It was a young soldier, probably two or three years older than I. His handsome face was unmarked. I watched when the old doctor pulled the cover over his face.

With his head lowered, without saying a word, without seeing anyone else, he left the room.

The comrade who had died was left in our room for several hours. It was such an eerie feeling to have him remain with us. We kept on whispering, although nothing would have disturbed him anymore. We were told that a chaplain would come, but he never arrived. When two *Sanis* finally removed the dead, we all saluted. No one said a word.

Meanwhile, it became obvious that the old doctor was not, or not anymore, a supporter of the "Total War" effort. In fact, he was the most critical of anyone I had ever come in contact with. He called the retreating soldiers "poor devils." Had I not liked him as much as I did, I might have been angered by his comments.

Interestingly enough, no one in our room ever said anything to his face. Only after he had left, some comments were made. Anne-Maria was present. She pretended not to hear what was being said. When we were alone, she said: "The first thing nurses learn is never to disagree with a doctor!"

At his very first visit, he had read my chart, looked at me, smiled and said, "You'll make it!" But then, he had turned to the *Stabsarzt* and *Schwester* Anne-Maria and said, *"Kindersoldat"* (child soldier), with a lowered voice, but still loud enough for me to hear. I was sure it wasn't meant to put me down, but inside it pulled me up short.

I wasn't a child anymore!

The young boy in the hospital train, who had lost his brother during the air attack, was what I thought of as a child soldier. A kid dressed up as a soldier or one amidst soldiers, blending into the milieu. The hospital train had become his home, his playground in which he imitated the grown-ups, acting like an adult.

I learned, after the war, that many partisan groups in various countries had young children involved in actual fighting. Many— the younger the better—were used for spy missions. They were sent to villages and enemy formations and returned with valuable information.

Here I was, a young man, member of an elite home defense unit, who had encountered combat in battle, who was wounded and who was decorated for bravery. Didn't all this measure up to manhood? Regardless of age, I was a true soldier, not a child soldier!

By now, full recovery for me seemed to be assured. I would return to the front. This was important to me, for, at that time, I was still committed to the *Fuehrer* and the Fatherland. Moreover, having fallen in love with Anne-Maria, I longed to be recognized as a brave soldier, as a man.

As time progressed and new patients arrived, the physician remained devotedly committed to his patients but, increasingly, he openly decried the *verdammte Krieg* (damn war) for the sufferings he encountered and the miseries near and far.

"He better be careful. If party officials hear him make such comments, he could end up in Flossenbuerg!"

"What's in Flossenbuerg?" I wanted to know.

"It's a concentration camp. There they put *Meuterer* (mutineers), *Miesmacher* (defeatists), and other *Volksfeinde* (enemies of the people)."

The only concentration camps I had heard of were at Dachau and Buchenwald. Thus, Flossenbuerg was only the third concentration camp I was aware of by name at the end of February 1945!

In just a few months, newspapers were published by the victorious occupation forces, revealing the locations and depictions of many facilities, including the extermination camps, whose images would stay in my head forever with recurring nightmarish horrors. Names like Auschwitz, Belzec, Maidanek, Sobibor, Treblinka, Chelmno, Mauthausen, Theresienstadt, Bergen-Belsen, and the many others. A human tragedy of staggering proportions. Shortly after the war and once more in the nineties, I would visit Dachau. The latter time, I went also to Flossenbuerg. Wilhelm Canaris,[116] chief of the German *Abwehr* (counter intelligence), who had joined the resistance movement, was executed at Flossenbuerg two weeks after I left the military hospital in Hof. At that time, I didn't even know who he was and that he was a prisoner there.

In February 1945, newspapers were still filled with reports of the failed plot by the generals to assassinate Hitler. Editorials repeated again and again that the soldiers were behind the *Fuehrer* unshakably.

There were reports about the killings, mutilations, and rapes committed by the Russian hordes in the eastern provinces. It was up to us, soldiers of all ages, to repel the Bolshevik madness. There were interviews with fighting men, declaring their determination to keep up the battle spirit, but there were also separate notices about those who were executed for cowardice, disobedience, resistance or any derogatory behavior, punishable by death. The condition of total war demanded that cowardice be liquidated ruthlessly!

***

I belonged to the *Volkssturm* and never received any pay. Anne-Maria would buy magazines and newspapers for me. Once in a while, she got hold of an old paper she knew would interest me. It included news about the fighting in and around the Fortress Breslau. In the worst way, I longed for information about my hometown where classmates and friends were putting up a valiant fight. The Russians had still not been able to capture this city.

In the middle of February, an old paper was circulated in our room that featured Hitler's 12th anniversary[117] speech in its entirety. Previously, I had only read an article with short excerpts. *Grossdeutschland* made sure that everyone in our room knew what the *Fuehrer* had said. But even if he had not insisted, I would have gone over every single word anyway, sought assurance that soon the tide would turn. With the help of the new miracle weapons, a final victory would soon be achieved!

I longed for hope, for encouragement, for confirmation of what *Grossdeutschland* had been talking about: that we had new *Duesenjaeger* (jet fighter planes), new types of invincible U-boats, and, of course, new V-3 and V-4 rockets able to cause wholesale destruction not only of major cities, but of whole armies. *Wunderwaffen* (miracle weapons) were frequently on our lips and constantly on our minds.

In his speech, however, Hitler didn't mention any new weapons. More than 50 years later, I re-read this oratory.[118] The *Fuehrer* started with telling the German people that the ghost of Eastern Bolshevism had threatened Germany when he became chancellor and that this had not changed. He emphasized that the gruesome occurrences in the East were destroying people by the ten and hundreds-of-thousands.

He assured us that—despite all of the setbacks—the enemy would be stopped.

"In this struggle for survival only one command is to be followed: Who fights with honor can save his life and that of his loved ones. Who, however, of weak or cowardly character stabs our nation in the back, will, under any conditions, find a disgraceful death!"

He declared that we had two choices: die honorably by fighting or dishonorably and face an execution squad.

Then he stated that he put great confidence in Germany's youth. Being committed like this, he said, gives us the right to step before the Almighty and ask Him for His mercy and His blessing which will be extended if everyone fights who can fight, and everyone works who can work, and if, jointly, we are willing and determined to sacrifice everything for freedom, the nation's honor, and, thus, life's future.

There was never a doubt in my mind that I would seek the upright way out. To be obedient was the moral thing to do, to follow the *Fuehrer* and to fulfill his expectations was what honorable service to one's country was all about.

The old doctor was probably the only one around us who saw it differently.

***

The nurses received one day off per week. I applied for a day-pass on Anne-Maria's free day, which would have allowed me to leave the hospital. It was denied.

My facial cuts had healed, my wound on the arm was still open, but I could bend my elbow again. Only my upper thigh still caused concern. All of the big shrapnel pieces had been removed. However, I still had a fever in the low 39's (Celsius) and required strong pain medication.

That I had been able to leave the hospital several evenings in a row was due to the fact that there was no security. There were no guards. Only my roommate and the night nurse knew, until *Grossdeutschland* decided that he had to report me.

We had made plans on Anne-Maria's day off to make a trip to Marktredwitz, my paternal grandmother's hometown.

My leave denied, I considered leaving without a pass. One of the older roommates, who liked both of us and thought that we should get as much enjoyment out of life as we possibly could, nevertheless discouraged me from just taking off on Anne-Maria's free day.

"You could be stopped and without papers you would be a deserter and you could be shot!"

He pointed out that we couldn't check into a room in a hotel or rent a *Fremdenzimmer* (room rented out in a private home) since whoever rented it to us would commit a crime called *Kuppelei* (procuring/pandering).

I have since researched this to see if he was right. He was. According to ¶180 of the German Penal Code, it was a crime and carried a jail sentence.

Grossdeutschland had also hinted that I might be taken to Flossenbuerg. Deserters ended up there to be shot. Did he know for sure or just surmise that this could be the case?

For Anna-Maria and me, the seriousness of the situation began to sink in.

We didn't leave town, but escaped within the school complex. At air raids, those who could walk had to leave our building and assemble in the cellar of a nearby high school building that served as a shelter and as an underground storage for turnips.

In this school building, the upper classrooms, when not occupied, were left open. In such a classroom, in the early evening, we found privacy.

I had told Anne-Maria about my experience with Trudel. "But we love each other," she replied, "and I want your child. You will be leaving soon to return to the front."

My first attempt to fulfill our longing was a poor performance with a premature ejaculation but the disappointment didn't last long. We were amorous, continued to caress and made love until sexually, too, my manhood had asserted itself.

When, eight months later, in October 1945, I saw Anne-Maria again, she was with child, but only in the third month of her pregnancy.

***

The intensity of our relationship escalated because we knew we had so little time. While my condition improved, Anne-Maria's heavy workload increased even more.

A new arrival of wounded, an assembly of misery with some of these soldiers, almost as young as I, trying in vain to fight off their pain, yelling in distress, as if stabbed.

My own recent experiences on the battlefield caused phantasmagorias. Nightmares invaded my head. Again and again, the horrible sight of the faceless head appeared, without nose and eyes, flesh mixed with blood and bone fragments and slimy fluids.

Anne-Maria and I were able to see some films, light fare, shown in a theater with the peculiar name of *Weisse Wand* (White Wall). Both of us had been looking forward to seeing *Traeumerei*, a highly acclaimed feature film with Hilde Krahl, portraying Clara Schuman, this great pianist, who was married to the famous composer Robert Schumann. We both loved classical music and expected the film to feature recitals of some of Schuman's romantic piano concertos.

As happens in wartime, with transportation problems, the film did not arrive in time as scheduled. Shown instead was *A Woman For Three Days*, a bittersweet comedy of falling in love and breaking up. We were disappointed.

Another film we saw at the *Weisse Wand* was *Passion*, a murder mystery in a forest setting with a plot that involved aristocrats and a brilliant attorney.

As mentioned already, as a *Volkssturmmann*, I never received any pay. Regulations for disbursements for *Volkssturm* members were never received at the military hospital or at my unit, for as long as I served.

In addition to buying me newspapers and paying for theater admissions Anne-Maria, secretly, passed on to me most of her cigarette ration. I had become a chain smoker since the first night after being hit. All of the wounded in our room seemed to smoke heavily.

Anne-Maria did not smoke regularly. On special occasions, she enjoyed an occasional "treat," together with a cup of coffee. She only smoked one or two cigarettes a day, and it was I who became the lucky recipient of the rest of her tobacco apportion.

What I read in the newspapers didn't make me realize how strong the Soviet forces were. Over a 300 km wide front, they had invaded Pomerania, pushing back our troops. The Army Vistula was now under the command of *SS*-chief Heinrich Himmler, known for his unwavering loyalty to the *Fuehrer,* but lacking military training. We waited for victorious counterattacks. Instead, the Soviets kept advancing. General Henrici later replaced Himmler.

After the war, I, too, would learn of Himmler's utter incompetence in matters of military leadership. The great and cruel organizer had, as a military strategist, been a complete failure. That I would meet him soon, in person, I could not even have imagined.

Meanwhile, Posen (now Poznan) had fallen after a month-long battle. In Silesia, Russian troops had reached the Neisse River. Only in Breslau did our forces, including the *HJ*-Regiment (Hitler Youth regiment) keep on defending the fortress successfully. What I still did not realize was what many adults already knew, that we could no longer win this war.

One day, it was announced that our *Stabsarzt* would return to the front, to be replaced by an *Assistenzarzt* (assistant physician), referred to by the nurses and by us as "*Assi.*" The old doctor remained a visiting physician. He probably was the one who, more than anyone else, understood the reality of the situation.

Anne-Maria kept me supplied with notebooks and pencils. During our time together, I wrote many poems (mostly for her), several short stories, and even a few short fairy tales. Having an address now, and with mail service still being provided (except to the areas of Germany already occupied), I wrote to all of my grandparents, aunts and uncles, to everyone whose address I could remember. I also wrote letters with incomplete addresses to Klaus Schauermann and others.

My grandfather, *Opa* Lehmann, who lived in Upper Bavaria,

received my letter and his reply was the first one to reach me. The envelope was fat and contained another long letter, written by my mother. She and my sisters and brothers had found temporary shelter at *Opa's* house in Seefeld-Oberalting in Upper Bavaria.

It must have been the middle of March. A short recovery leave was being contemplated for me and it induced a bold idea. Wasn't Anne-Maria entitled to vacation, too? We could travel together. I could introduce her to my mother. Anne-Maria could meet all of my family now residing at my grandfather's.

My camera had remained in Breslau and, together with our house, was probably destroyed by now. But my grandfather had a camera and, as the town's mayor, could probably still secure film. I would take pictures.

My excitement grew. I had this vision of a holiday in the beautiful Bavarian mountains. Away from dying, away from suffering, surrounded by nature's tranquility. Repeatedly, I imagined asking my mother to photograph Anne-Maria and me. We would embrace, laugh, and our life would be spirited for a few precious days—as if there were no war.

To sustain the fleeting bubbles of my daydreams, I sat down and wrote to my mother that I would soon be coming and not alone. The ravages of war had left my mind and I couldn't wait until Anne-Maria and I had a chance to be alone.

"We will go on a short furlough together!" I said with certitude as if I had the authority to make this decision and handed her the letter, expecting an outburst of joy. Instead, she shook her head and said: "How wonderful it would be!"

Then she explained, " I wish I could come with you, but I can't. None of us can go on leave right now. We are too short-staffed. Gisela's mother died last week and not even she got permission to attend the funeral. It's out of the question."

"When did you have your last vacation?" I asked.

"I haven't had a vacation since I became a nurse. None of us has."

"Ask the old doctor, he will give you a break, even if just a few days."

"He has nothing to do with us nurses."

"Who does?"

"The *Assi!*"

"He is young."

"He makes fun of emotions and he is a fanatic."

"Will you ask anyway?"

Suddenly her face lit up. " I could be pregnant." My face lit up, too.

The following day she asked to see the *Assi.*

Not only was her request denied, but he also became very angry with her. She should have made a better selection in choosing the father of her child. She should be ashamed.

The following day, when my discharge was being discussed at my bedside, the *Assi* emphasized that he needed beds for newly arriving wounded.

Although still limping, I was now free of fever. My leg was no longer blue, only some yellow blotches could be seen. It was somewhat slimmer than my right one. The wound was healing.

The old doctor, who wanted to keep me at least another week or two before allowing me to travel, assured me that both legs would look the same again after a while.

Not he, but the *Assi* made the final decision. He asked me where *Kampfgruppe* Gutschke was located and if, with the proper marching orders, I would know how to get there.

"I'll get through, no matter what!" was my reply.

"Well, before you do, you get a short *Genesungsurlaub* (recovery leave)!"

He slapped me on my shoulder and shook my hand.

Then he raised his arm and said, "*Heil*, Hitler!"

I did the same. I remember this, because, for the very first time, I felt the salute was not fitting. Snappish, I added "*Danke*" (thank you). He turned around.

"Report back to me for a final check-up. Your papers will be ready to return you to your unit on that day."

I disliked this younger doctor. He had denied Anne-Maria's

requests for a couple of days off and he had belittled me.

Now, a final blow. When I return, I won't be able to spend a last night with Anne-Maria.

Except for the bitterness I often felt as a boy toward my father, for the first time in my life I felt real enmity toward a superior and a doctor at that.

***

Anne-Maria did succeed in changing her schedule so that she could accompany me to the train station. Baggage was no problem. I had none. All I possessed was the uniform I wore, a small bag of toiletries, two notebooks which contained some of my writings I wanted to save, and a pill box with the medication I still had to take. Anne-Maria had also fixed me some sandwiches.

I carried everything in a shopping bag made out of netting

There we were. A Red Cross nurse arm-in-arm with a young soldier still limping slightly, both downcast. Intermittently, Anne-Maria said, "You will be back!"

"Yes, in just a week," I replied, knowing already that it might be for just a few hours. I kept the *Assi's* orders to myself, hoping for something to change.

We reached the station; Anne-Maria wiped her eyes with her handkerchief.

I wanted to say one more time how much I loved her, but I had this fear that I might be overcome by emotions. I was in public. I was in uniform. I had to control my feelings.

"Can't we part smiling?" I asked, pressing her hand. She tried to smile and so did I.

"I miss you already," she said, "and you are not even gone." One last hug.

"*Tapfer sein!*" (Let's be brave) were her last words. She turned around and left, not turning her head back but still waving.

***

I elbowed myself into the overcrowded train, remained at the door, waiting for her to look back just once more. She didn't. Still, I kept waving and didn't stop until she was completely out of sight.

The old rickety train shuttled through town, picked up speed when we reached the country. It was a miserable ride. The vintage passenger cars were filled, exceeding capacity, mostly with soldiers and refugees.

A veteran with an artificial leg took it off for all of us to see.

"Damn it," he swore. "I will need crutches again." The stump was too sore and, for the entire train ride, he didn't put his artificial limb back on.

The train suddenly lurched, jolted and we stopped. Were enemy planes approaching? Would I experience another air attack? My first thought was to get off. I was one of many. But we were ordered to return immediately. There were no aircraft in the sky. Instead, ahead of us a freight train had to be side-tracked so that we could pass.

We passed a seemingly endless train of brown, rusty box cars. There were distant sounds, stifled and susurrus, and I thought it to be strange that animals might be in these closed wagons.

Now of course, I wonder if it could have been human beings. What appeared to be sounds from animals in misery, triggered commiseration. But months later, after I had seen the first documentary about liberated concentration camps, I would think back and be overcome by shock.

These cars could have been filled with prisoners! Some already dead, others dying—surviving in a state of near starvation and utter exhaustion. It didn't cross my mind that freight trains with locked cars required less guards.

Before the *Hauptbahnhof* (main railroad station) in Munich, the train stopped again and then inched forward very slowly until finally, we reached the terminal.

Aside from having to change trains, I had no desire to see the by now heavily bombed city again, the city which, years prior, I had visited with my grandfather. This was where I had learned how to take photographs, where I had seen the locations of some of the events important to the Party's history.

There was smoke in the sky.

I had long ago eaten the sandwiches Anne-Maria had given me and I was hungry. But I didn't take time to search for a field kitchen or a place where I could get something to eat but got on the next train to Murnau. On this train, I even got a seat.

I thought of Anne-Maria constantly. The intensity and radiance of her personality, the brightness of her eyes, her wavy, often wind-blown brown hair, the sensuality not only of her body but of her face. On the stretch from Munich to Murnau, for the first time in my life, I thought about the various types of love and how they expressed themselves in different types of feelings.

From as far back as I could remember, at home, in school, and in the *Jungvolk*, it had been ingrained in me to love our *Fuehrer*, and I thought that I did. I did not realize how much of a make-believe emotion it was, a child's adoration of an inspiring leader to be worshipped.

While growing up, I didn't think of boys loving each other. Our perception was that, as youngsters, we created bonds of comradeship. We believed that they were much stronger than the bonds of love.

To have a comrade is to have found someone to rely on. Combat fellowships were comradeships of the highest order.

I never thought of (or had the feeling of) loving my father. He was an authority figure and I looked up to him. I had been fearful of him, but I can't remember ever having had feelings of affection for him. I knew he liked it that way. According to Hitler's vision, the next generation of Germany's soldiers was to "maintain sentiments as hard as steel."

I considered my love for my mother as a dominant, strong, and everlasting devotion.

Now, passionate love had entered my life, a new force I experienced that had ignited my soul, my mind, and my body. Was the love between a young soldier and a Red Cross nurse a bond of comradeship interwoven with a bond of love?

CHAPTER 45

The Furlough

My memories of the time I visited my mother, sisters, brothers, my grandfather, and *Tante* Musch (the woman he lived with) make me realize today how well conditioned I had been to cope with pain in body and soul. I had become accustomed to looking upon destruction and situations of chaos as just another reality of life. It was all part of war and, thus, to be accepted.

I was in the presence of my beloved mother, my sisters and brothers, and my grandfather, whom I had adored since childhood, but in my thoughts there was only Anne-Maria most of the time. Our moments of parting kept recurring in my mind, over and over again.

Throughout my entire recovery furlough, my soul resembled the needle of a compass vacillating between two magnetic forces. My family constituted one pole, the other, far stronger one despite the distance, was Anne-Maria.

My grandfather, *Opa* Lehmann, as *Ortsgruppenleiter*, was the local party official, aside from being the mayor of the small town where he lived. He still believed in his *Fuehrer* and that we had to defend our country and destroy Bolshevism.

For his grandson to have become a soldier at such a young age—moreover a decorated one—filled him with pride. My grandfather was highly intelligent and, as an engineer, a very practical man. He was also very close to my heart since he had lived with us in Waldgut Horka.

Although of advanced age (he was now 73 years old), his duties remained a challenge to him and he fulfilled them tirelessly, day after day. Proud to have been trusted with such great responsibility, he truly cared for people and since, as a Prussian, he was liked and respected by the local conservative Bavarians, he must indeed have done an outstanding job. His values of ethics and honor, by any standards, were high. But he, too, was a blind follower. In March 1945, his devotion to his *Fuehrer* seemed still unshakable.

My mother, with five children and the maid, appreciated having found shelter there. However, seven additional people crowded this two-bedroom house. The situation became very burdensome for the old couple. My grandfather never mentioned anything, but *Tante* Musch, as my sister Anje told me, was quite outspoken about the hardships and inconveniences with which she had to put up.

Still hopeful, mother read all the news about Breslau, the fortress the Russians were unable to capture. As late as March 1945, she, too, believed that the time would soon come when she and her children could return home. And, despite all, I, too, had encouraging words for her. So far the only battle I had participated in, we had won.

During this time of my short furlough, my sister Ute was hospitalized. We depended on public transportation, a local bus, to visit her. It took a whole day to do so. Anje had drawn a picture for her of a dwarf riding on a snail.

I had nothing to take to her and quickly wrote a short poem.

On her delicate face, tears rolled down her cheeks. Tears of joy, she said. It became apparent that there existed a strong bond between us siblings even though we had been separated for over two years by now.

My youngest sister Doerte, good-natured and very mild-mannered, seemed among all the most saddened. She was ten years old then and most affected at being so far away from home. She mentioned she was afraid that something might happen to me. "If there was just something I could do for you," she said. It touched my heart.

My young brothers, Wulf and Ulrich, 5 and 6 years old, took life in stride but were not at all fond of *Tante* Musch and the feeling was mutual. I, in turn, thought that my brothers, for boys of this age, were well behaved. Nevertheless, I had a talk with them, pointing out that they were guests, that it was *Opa's* and *Tante* Musch's house. I still remember Wulf's brazen reply: "Here we are all people of parity, with equal rights!" A typical expression of the times which demonstrates how indoctrinated even a six-year old was already.

Before my departure, the question of money came up. My mother was desperately waiting for some to arrive. She had hardly any to give to me. My money was at a *Sparkasse* in the fortress Breslau. However, my grandfather gave me several 20 *Reichsmark* bills, some of which I would take to Anne-Maria to repay her.

The week in Seefeld-Oberalting went by fast, too fast for everyone. On the other hand, I couldn't wait to return to Anne-Maria. With my mother, I had long talks about Anne-Maria. She wasn't shocked, in fact, she thought that any feelings of happiness should be treasured. Her only concern was: "Wait until the war is over before tying the knot!"

To which I replied "We will belong forever to each other."

Obviously, I didn't anticipate what the future would have in store for us. On the day of my departure from Oberalting, it rained. When the goodbyes were said, once more, tears flowed. I was able to hold mine back. *Tante* Musch was out of sight, my grandfather didn't cry and neither did the boys. But my mother and my sisters wiped their eyes with handkerchiefs. I still remember my mother kissing me on the forehead and saying: "*Machs gut!*" ("Do well!") Then she embraced me and added, almost defiantly: "I just know that you will return." My mother's attitude, a combination of caring and stoic endurance, was so typical of her. She pulled off her silver ring with a lapis lazuli, a semiprecious, azure-blue stone, and put it on my finger as a talisman. She wished for the stone to have magical, protective qualities.

I have hardly any recollections of the train-ride back to Hof,

except that most of the way, despite the inconveniences and crowd-
ing, my head was filled with erotic thoughts. Anticipating seeing
Anne-Maria again, I looked forward to the warmth of love and the
fire of sex. I closed my eyes for long stretches. My senses and
thoughts reeled tempestuously. My body was recuperating. For a
whole week by war's standards, I had eaten well. I was rested and
my longing for Anne-Maria had never ceased.

The next day mattered. The uncertainty of the long-term future
should not cloud our reunion.

Station after station, more and more soldiers entered the train,
several on crutches. One of them remarked: "Once more we were
able to escape from this hell!" I think he was referring to having
survived an air raid.

The southern front was still on the other side of the Alps. On
the western front, however, U.S. Forces already occupied Aachen.

The train was delayed and I arrived in the early evening. I had
not been able to reach Anne-Maria by telephone, but had sent her
a telegram and expected her to be at the station despite the belated
arrival. She was not.

Anne-Maria had tried to switch shifts with another nurse to
have the day and the night off, but this nurse suddenly became ill
and couldn't fill in for her. She had sent a telegram to my
grandfather's address but it must have arrived after I had left.

I realized that I was here to get my orders to leave and my
return to Hof turned into one of disarray and disappointments.

When Anne-Maria finally finished her shift, we walked and
walked and walked through dark streets on this drizzly, dreary,
dreadful night.

We felt—and it was true—we had no way and nowhere to go.
Finally, we returned to the nurse's quarters. It was too late to go in.
We stood in front of the big entrance door, embracing each other
until we were soaking wet.

"Until tomorrow" were our parting words, but it was after
midnight and tomorrow had started already. Soon I would be gone
and we both would be alone.

In my old room, there was no space available. Every bed had been taken. I ended up, with interruptions, sleeping a few hours in the hallway, with strangers, newly-arrived wounded, most of them still experiencing great pain.

I awakened at an uncertain hour, before dawn. I felt sick. Nightmare-prone, I must have had a terrible one that night, perhaps one in anticipation of death. I woke up in a cold sweat—shivering and longing for Anne-Maria.

What would the future hold for us?

Anne-Maria came to the hospital early. We went to the kitchen to talk together for the last time prior to my departure that day.

She hoped that she was pregnant. My feelings were mixed. Should I die, flesh and blood of mine would live on, but then, not being alive anymore, mother and child would be without support.

"Don't worry about it, as a nurse I will always be able to make a living, even if we lose this war."

My God, what did she just say?

"We are still going to win this war!" I countered.

"All I see are the wounded that are coming in and then I have to hear about the many fallen comrades they left behind. It's getting worse and worse."

She was also worried sick about her parents who lived in the Protectorate (the old Czechoslovakia), expected to fall to the Russians any day now.

I psyched myself into making a statement of sorts, saying: "We have to remain strong. All the great sacrifices, the bravery, and determination, has to lead to victory."

Suddenly overcome, Anne-Maria's emotions overwhelmed her.

She saw my mother's ring and pulled off her finger a small gold ring with a coral. It fit only on my little finger. We said good-bye that morning in the hospital's kitchen. She had to start work and I had to get my papers. The doctors were too busy with newly arrived wounded; I didn't even get a discharge physical. I had hoped that the old doctor would see me but he wasn't in the hospital that morning.

What were Anne-Maria's last words?
I remember them to this day. She said: "You can't leave me!"
But I had to. And she knew it.
We kissed and she cried. I kept my tears inside.
Suddenly, we were apart and my arms were empty.

CHAPTER 46

Coming Back

On the way back to my unit, *Kampfgruppe* Gutschke, I had to change trains in Goerlitz. I utilized the connecting time of several hours to briefly visit *Grossmuttel* and *Grossvatel*, my grandparents on my mother's side, who lived not far from the railroad station.

My grandfather had closed his shop. Deep in his mind, he must have sensed that Germany's total defeat was near. "We will remain here," he said, "no matter what happens. *Grossmuttel* is suffering too much already." He referred to my grandmother's heart disease. I remember how swollen her legs were and how long it took her, with a walking cane, to climb the flights of stairs to their apartment. She was the grandmother who had read Bible stories to me.

Now we all felt that we might be seeing each other for the last time. The most treasured possession in her pantry was a slab of smoked ham her daughter (my Aunt Isa,) had sent her. The three of us sat in the kitchen eating rye bread with sliced-up ham and drinking an herbal tea.

Both wanted me to stay overnight, but I had marching orders and had to return to the station and take the next train to Hirschherg, which would get me there late in the afternoon.

Grossmuttel asked if I had with me a photo of my mother. I didn't. She gave me one with me, as a baby, in my mother's arms. "Remain alive and trust the Lord!" were her parting words.

The train was on time, and for the first time in a long time I traveled in a railroad car that was not crowded. I had a whole wooden bench to myself. I was dead-tired but unable to fall asleep. My head was filled with thoughts about mortality. My grandparents, whom I had just visited, were 76 and 63 years old. They seemed close to death, especially my grandmother who was the younger one. But then I might even be closer to death than either of them, because I was on my way back into battle.

***

I couldn't relax.

Anne-Maria, my mother, my sisters and brothers, my grandparents, all occupied my mind. I had said good-bye to all of them except *Oma*. I decided that in Hirschberg, before proceeding to the *Jugendkammhaus* (final destination), I would risk a short side-trip to Bad Warmbrunn to say good-bye to my *Oma* as well. Did I need official permission to do so? If stopped by the military police what would I say?

It was evening already and I wanted to make sure that my grandmother knew what to do if evacuation orders were given.

When I arrived, she complained about a toothache and that her dentist was no longer in town. I asked her where she would go if the Russians came.

"Nowhere! I remain here! What can they do with an old woman like me?"

"Haven't you heard about the cruelties?"

"I have a gun! If it comes to that, I'll shoot myself!" I couldn't believe it. She pulled out the drawer of her night stand and there it was, a lady's handgun, the grip inlaid with mother-of-pearl. She showed me that it was loaded.

Here was my *Oma*, this tiny, delicate woman with the black eye-patch, 72 years old, determined to remain where she was and prepared, if necessary, to shoot herself.

Oma had a small, one-bedroom apartment in this nursing home owned and medically supervised by a physician whose name was Dr. Hoffmann. She talked me into staying overnight, and I slept on the sofa in her small, cramped living room. This was against regulations, and I could have been charged with desertion had anyone in the *Sanatorium* reported me to the authorities. These were all people in my grandmother's age range and probably would have hidden me had I not wanted to return to the front.

But this was not the case.

I simply rationalized that the *Jugendkammhaus* would have been difficult to reach late at night and I remembered when, months earlier, I almost lost my life in a heavy snowdrift as I approached Kreuzeck.

My commander, whom I knew so well, would have supported my arriving in good condition one day late rather than to risk catching the last street car to Giersdorf and then having to take the perilous two-hour hike late at night.

Oma thought that I should spend the holidays with her. It must have been the night of March 28/29 when I visited since Easter was approaching. I explained to her that soldiers have to follow orders, even on holidays, and my orders were to reach the *Jugendkammhaus* and report to my old unit.

In the morning, we got up early. She boiled the last egg in her tiny pantry for me, and surprisingly, had some pastry in her breadbox, which she served us both with tea. Since she didn't have *Bohnenkaffee* (real coffee), she chose herbal tea.

After breakfast I had to leave.

She told me: "Take anything you want from here, anything!"

It was an easy decision for me. I went to her bookshelf and picked an *Insel Buch*, a small volume of a series published by Insel Verlag in Leipzig. It was the first in the series by Rainer Maria Rilke and titled, *The Tale of the Love and Death of Cornet Christopher Rilke*. It tells the story of a soldier's love and death.

No other book would I read so many times, with the possible exception, at a much later time, of Antoine Saint-Exupery's translation of *The Little Prince*, the small volume by the French aviator and warrior-turned-poet.

When *Oma* saw the little book I had picked as her good-bye

present, she insisted that this wasn't enough. "Take something else too!"

Without thinking, hurried and intuitive, I took a framed Duerer[119] picture from her wall. I believe it was a *Kupferstich* (copperplate engraving). It depicted a mature girl-angel and a little boy-angel, surrounded by chaos.

"Please wrap it up and send it to my girlfriend!"

"Girlfriend?"

"Yes, *Schwester* Anne-Maria, I'll write down her address."

"That's impossible that you have a girlfriend already, you are still a child!"

"I am a soldier."

"*Du lieber Gott!*" (Oh, dear Lord!)

We parted, both with mixed feelings, discouragement to say the least, overshadowed by deep sadness. I left her with a sinking heart.

CHAPTER 47

To Berlin

At the *Jugendkammhaus* in the Riesengebirge, Silesia's major mountain range, departure activities were in full swing at the time I arrived. I was told, confidentially, by one of Gutschke's new couriers that we would be flown into the Fortress Breslau to join the Hitler Youth regiment we were part of, but from which we were cut off.

There were celebrations because I had returned. *Oblt.* Gutschke explained why he had instructed the military commander in Hof to award me the Iron Cross.

He did not think that I would be back. Now he wanted to read, in front of all, the citation:

After being wounded, he pulled other wounded into a snow ravine for protection and, despite heavy loss of blood, he was among the first and the bravest who captured the village.

There was applause and jubilation and I was expected to make a speech.

I remembered having pulled the wounded on the field into the snow concavity. However, I made it only to the edge of the village before I collapsed and later was thrown on the horse-drawn carriage together with wounded comrades and others who had fallen. What was I supposed to say?

I organized my thoughts and I said something like: "I am glad to be back with you my old comrades. But my feelings are dampened by how many from our fighting group are missing." Of our original unit—120 strong, only 30 or 40 were present. Of the 80 or 90 missing, I knew a few and I mentioned all I could think of by name.

They responded, shouting out: "Fallen! "Wounded!" or "Missing!" I wondered how anybody could be unaccounted for since we hadn't retreated and all the territory of the battle had remained in our hands.

I looked into so many strange faces. After our first battle, these boys had been attached to *Kampfgruppe* Gutschke. Some were survivors of a Hitler Youth Home Defense Unit that had fought valiantly at the bridgehead of Steinau on the Oder River. Our fighting unit was back to full strength again ready for its next battle assignment.

I closed my remarks by stating: "We will defend our beloved Silesia and our Fatherland, even if we have to die." It was not a rousing speech, but I had not expected this ceremony honoring me.

On Easter Sunday, we celebrated with a distinguished guest. The native writer Hans Christoph Kaergel[120] visited us. He read from his works and then made a speech, emphasizing with big words that it was our holy duty to defend our beloved homeland. We were blessed to have the great *Fuehrer*, the nation's first soldier, as our leader.

He closed with the demeanor of an actor, shouting: "Save Silesia! It is our homeland!" That, of course, was our mission, and we all thought that shortly we would be flown into Breslau, our Silesian capital, where already many comrades in the Hitler Youth Fortress Regiment Hirsch[121] were putting up a valiant fight.

The poet Kaergel had among his papers a clipping with good news. It was read by *Oberleutnant* Gutschke: "The last attempt by the Soviets to take Breslau was, once again, repelled, with the destruction of 64 enemy tanks, most of them by *Panzerfaust* (handheld bazookas)."

We applauded. The *Panzerfaust*, after all, was "our" weapon and required firing at the heavy armor from very close distance. It was a weapon for the brave.

***

In Germany, Easter Monday was then (and still is) the second of a two-day legal holiday. Most of Sunday night, I spent at a corner desk in the recreation room, writing and rewriting a long letter to Anne-Maria. The only paper that was available was the official stationery of the youth house with the Hitler Youth national emblem—an eagle holding the HJ-diamond with the swastika. Not the type of writing paper usually used for intimate letters.

I wrote briefly about my visits with *Grossmuttel* and *Grossvatel* in Goerlitz and with *Oma* in Bad Warmbrunn. I mentioned that *Oma* would send her a package. A surprise.

I mentioned also how old-fashioned my *Oma* was because she scolded me for having a girlfriend already. Indignation and sadness had overshadowed our parting. I told her about *Oma's* gift to me, how Rilke's *Cornet* kept my mind stimulated with poetic images that, again and again, I visited mentally. "To ride, ride, ride, through the day, through the night, through the day." Had I been born into an earlier generation, I might have shared Cornet Christoph Rilke's experiences, and after a day's ride on horse-back, witnessed: "The hour streaming out of dark-red wine and thousand roses rustling into the night's apparition."

By the time I had finished, it was past midnight. Was I one day closer to death?

Where was the front?

Would mail still be delivered?

There was no envelope and I would have to wait 'til morning to get and address one.

This was the morning we were ordered to exercise (despite the fact that it was Easter), and shortly thereafter the news broke. We would not leave for Hirschberg's airport, as originally planned, to be transported in a Ju-52 into the fortress Breslau. Instead, we would head to the railroad station to board a train.

We had been assigned to defend another fortress—Frankfurt/ Oder. I was among the first to learn that *Reichsjugendfuehrer* Artur

Axmann, personally, had telephoned *Oblt.* Gutschke, ordering our unit to report to the *Panzernahkampfbrigade Artur Axmann.* Why?

Oblt. Gutschke explained that we were battle-experienced and therefore selected to set an example for the Hitler Youth Defense Forces there. Like us, they were looked upon as an elite unit. It incorporated students of Adolf Hitler Schools and students of National Political Education Institutions.

Bearing the name of Artur Axmann, this brigade was expected to set additional shining examples of bravery. Among those of the combat-experienced core of *Kampfgruppe* Gutschke, six had been decorated with the Iron Cross, and several with the Infantry Assault Attack Badges. Those who had been wounded and returned, fully or partially recovered, wore their Wounded Badges.

Our mission was to instill courage into our comrades in Frankfurt/Oder who were still wet behind their ears.

At our new assembly point in the township of Klein-Koeris, we were joined by other Hitler Youth units, now designated to become *Panzernahkampfbrigade Frankfurt.* Some were Frankfurters and expected to be returned to the fortress. Others were from the Wartheland, formerly Polish territory, but from our standpoint, liberated German territory.

Once again, we were conditioned for battle by sergeants from Austria. I experienced severe angina pains but bit my lips and kept going. Had I reported ill and asked to see a physician, I was sure it would have looked like an excuse to get out of having to fight again. I did not want to be suspected of cowardice, and of course, I wanted to remain with *Oblt.* Gutschke and my comrades.

Our training program in Klein-Koeris ended rather abruptly. Completely unexpectedly, we received the most startling and drastic change our unit had to undergo.

We were moved to the Mars-la-Tour barracks in Fuerstenwalde an der Spree, where a recruiting team from Spreenhagen near Erkner had arrived to induct us—with no questions asked—into the *Waffen-SS!* Yes, the *Waffen-SS!* This, we were told, was done by orders received directly from the *Fuehrer!*[22]

According to *Oblt.* Gutschke, a specific directive to our unit to "voluntarily" join the *Waffen-SS* had come, once again, from *Reichsjugendfuehrer* Artur Axmann himself. This, as far as I can remember, was the only instance that *Oblt.* Gutschke seemed upset over orders received from Axmann.

He was beside himself.

"It is out of the question!" was his response. It wouldn't apply to him. He would remain an army officer. We, however, were given no choice; he couldn't prevent it. We were inducted into the *Waffen-SS.*

It did not upset me. As long as *Oblt.* Gutschke would remain our commander, I would gladly serve under him as a member of the *Waffen-SS.* Had I not wanted to join their mountain troops in the first place? Would not my father be proud of me now, that I, weak as I always appeared to him, was able to join the same elite *Waffen-SS* of which he was a member as a war correspondent?

Wouldn't I, from now on, be entitled to recognition as a soldier? I would be respected by people, especially older comrades such as the *Feldwebel* from Grossdeutschland, my former room-steward in the military hospital in Hof.

At no time had I an inkling that after the war during the Nuremberg Trials, the *SS*, including the *Waffen-SS*, would be declared criminal organizations.

We were asked to turn in our *Vokssturm* pay book for a *Waffen-SS* pay book. I remarked, "Finally, we might get paid." (So far we had never been issued any compensation for our services whatsoever.) Although not realizing at the time how smart it was, I asked to hold on to my *Volkssturm* pay book as well since it contained official entries of my decorations—the Iron Cross II and the Black Wounded Badge. I think it also listed the dates, places, and types of the war injuries I had suffered on the front and in the hospital train.

These certifications would be transferred, I was told, by the physician who would administer our physicals. I was permitted to keep both until that time. We never received a physical and, thus, we were never tattooed. (Every member of the *Waffen-SS* had his blood type tattooed under his armpit.) So, I also remained in possession of two pay books.

Bannfuehrer Peter Kiesgen, who previously had made an impassioned speech while in the *Hitlerjugend* uniform, now exchanged that uniform for one of an Army officer. Having prior service in the Army, like *Oblt.* Gutschke, he put on his officer's uniform with rank of *Hauptmann* (Army captain). Decorated with the Knight's Cross of the Iron Cross, he also had a sleeve covered with tank destruction stripes. (By the end of the war, I, too, would have earned one. He, however, had six already and earned one or two more after he had taken over as our commander.)

We remained in the Mars-la-Tour *Kaserne* several days. There, the emphasis shifted from being drilled to being instructed. In Klein-Koeris, we had been rigorously exercised to get back into shape physically. Now, our minds were being conditioned with just as much intensity. We welcomed it because, in comparison, it was painless.

We had several classroom sessions of instruction. One stressed that the *Waffen-SS* attracted idealistic, intelligent and, above all, brave men. Surprising, at least to me, was the large number of those who were not from Germany but were nationals from other European countries. A long list of *Waffen-SS* units was reviewed in which foreigners that served voluntarily was listed. (See Appendix B)

This gave us a sense of belonging to a multi-national brotherhood, sharing a common world view where we jointly opposed Communism.

We were also shown photographs and one of the instructors read eyewitness reports about cruelties committed by the invading Russians to German civilians, especially women. Thus, we were incited to fight with extreme determination against the approaching enemy.

We were taught to think of the enemy as "faceless monsters" and ourselves as belonging to a comradeship of the highest order, a team of unquestionable reliability. We could depend on each other's help and support in any situation and under the severest of circumstances.

"All for one, one for all" was stressed, as was "Loyalty is my honor." We were told that loyalty runs through the *SS* from *Reichsfuehrer* to us, the youngest recruits. An invisible bond connects us as comrades and, mutually, we strengthen each other. We shall all follow our *Fuehrer*, fearlessly, to final victory.

I thought of my grandfather's teachings as we learned that those who belong to the *Waffen-SS* do more than their duty and achieve more than what is expected of average men.

Not a word was said about the *SS*-Death's Head formations. I didn't even know that they existed and am sure that most of my comrades didn't either. (They were set up as early as 1933 and consisted of *SS* volunteers assigned to guard concentration and detention camps.)

What was often told to us at the Mars-la-Tour *Kaserne* was that we were involved in a "life or death struggle." We fought to preserve the new social order, which eliminated all social differences and regional and sectarian rivalries, establishing the ideal of a genuine national community.

Last but not least, we were instructed that Adolf Hitler's greatness was unmatched in German history, that a sacred trust existed between him and us who were chosen to serve in the elite *Waffen-SS*. Our Commander-in-Chief had the right to continually demand from us the utmost fighting spirit. Victory was assured if we followed our sacred oath to our *Fuehrer*—to obey him and, if necessary, to die for him.

There were no question-and-answer periods and the only explanation offered for the retreat of the German forces was that all of our allies, except Japan, had failed in decisive battles and didn't match up to our troops militarily. The tide would turn soon, we were assured. The *Fuehrer* had learned that he could depend only on his own troops—tough, battle-tried and courageous—with the *Waffen-SS* leading the way. And now we belonged to the *Waffen-SS!*

We had very little free time. Our last lecture ended at 9:00

p.m. and curfew was at 10:00 p.m. Still, some took off.

There was a wall surrounding the barracks, but probably from past air raid damages, there were stretches with breaks big enough to get through. These ruined sections of the wall were not watched over by the sentries on duty who were stationed at the main gate.

While I had discovered the writing room and continued to commit to paper my thoughts for Anne-Maria, some of my comrades had made contacts already with local girls. Long after curfew, they left through one of the gaps and returned the same way without getting caught and then bragged about their exploits.

I had spent the evening hours writing, right up to "lights out" time. Convinced that by belonging to the *Waffen-SS*, we would now get an APO address, I was waiting anxiously for this to happen. I asked repeatedly about it, always being told to hold on to my letters. We would be assigned an address any day now. The day never came.

I finally mailed the letters, listing as return address only: Home Defense Force Man A.D. Lehmann, enroute to the frontline. I couldn't even write "Frankfurt/Oder." To reveal any location was forbidden even that late in the war.

I did not write *SS-Mann* or *SS-Schuetze* (soldier/private) A.D. Lehmann either. My reason for not identifying myself as a recruit of the *Waffen-SS* was simple. I didn't want to worry Anne-Maria or my mother. *Waffen-SS* units were known to be among the most elite with the highest casualty rates. And even though we had now, without our concurrence, been inducted into the *Waffen-SS*, our unit's name was not changed. On one hand, *Reichsjugendfuehrer* Axmann had facilitated our joining forces with and becoming part of the *Waffen-SS*, on the other he and *Oblt.* Gutschke effected that our designation remained "*Kampfgruppe* Gutschke." Recognized as a Hitler Youth unit. One of great valiancy, a shining example for other boy troops.

As I would learn later that summer, neither Anne-Maria nor my mother received any of my letters. Mail was still being picked up, transported and delivered, but, apparently, many trains containing mail were attacked by low-flying enemy aircraft and went up in flames.

Anne-Maria, I learned later, wrote me every day and waited anxiously to hear from me and to receive my address. My mother had also written a letter with notes added from my siblings. For lack of an address, it was never mailed.

Most of the time, the breast pocket of my uniform jacket contained communications for Anne-Maria, as well as notes I had made and wanted to save. It was my "poet's pocket"—almost always bulging.

***

It must have been April 10th or 11th that we were ordered to leave the Mars-La-Tour *Kaserne*. *Oblt.* Gutschke seemed puzzled since we were taken straight south to Bad Saarow. There, the regimental headquarters was located in the villa that belonged to Dr. Robert Ley, whom Hitler had appointed earlier (28 March 1945) as commander of the *"Freikorps Adolf Hitler."* This was a motley, motile, partisan-like volunteer corps on bicycles. How this organization and its aims differed from the *Volkssturm* and the *Werwolf*[23] is unclear. As was the case with some of the most fanatic Nazi leaders, Dr. Ley now had the chance to sacrifice lives for his *Fuehrer.*

In the courtyard of Dr. Ley's villa, a steaming field kitchen was situated and a warm soup was waiting for us. *Oblt.* Gutschke attended a briefing inside the house. Before we left, *Hauptmann* Kiesgen made another short speech, urging us to find the spirit of Langemarck[124] and to follow the example of the *SS Panzerdivision Hitlerjugend* and its leader, *Panzermeyer,*[125] who had earned the reputation for exceptional courage. Among our *Vorbilder* (role models), were the heroes of the Hitler Youth *SS*-Division.[126] The speech was short but impressive.

An inspiring send-off.

At Muellrose was a *Waffen-SS* check point.

The officer in charge had some directives that were contrary to the orders *Oblt.* Gutschke had received.

Once more, we had to turn south and arrived in Biegen, south of the Berlin-Frankfurt *Autobahn.*

We established temporary quarters. *Oblt.* Gutschke chose as his command post a large landholder's estate. To our surprise, we were ordered to prepare for a visit from *Reichsminister* Dr. Goebbels.

He and his entourage never arrived.

Instead (it must have been April 16), a *Kuebelwagen* (jeep-like military automobile) drove up with *Reichsjugendfuehrer* Axmann. He was accompanied by *Oberbannfuehrer* Otto Kern, our brigade commander in a major's uniform, and *Hauptmann* Peter Kiesgen, our regiment commander. Axmann, I recognized at once, having seen many photographs of him. Kiesgen, I had met previously. Kern, I saw for the first time.

My Iron Cross ribbon caught Axmann's attention and he asked who else from our unit had been decorated for bravery. I didn't know how many there were altogether, but knew that eight from our old unit had been awarded the Iron Cross, two posthumously. Then, with his right, wooden hand, he pointed to my wounded badge. "So you are back for action?"

"Jawoll, Reichsjugendfuehrer!" I blurted out. *("Jawoll"* is the military version of *"jawohl,"* meaning "yes, indeed," with maximum emphasis).

Axmann wanted to know of my combat experience. I mentioned that I was *Oblt.* Gutschke's *Melder* (runner). "In the first World War, our *Fuehrer* was a *Melder* too!" he pointed out. I replied: "Yes, I know!"

"I want you and two of your comrades to come to Berlin, the day after tomorrow, to join a delegation on the *Fuehrer's* birthday!"

I was speechless. I just couldn't believe it. Me? Being ordered to go to Berlin to be introduced to our *Fuehrer* Adolf Hitler? The man I was in awe of and had been for as long as I could think back? At this crucial time, when he was just about to turn things around, to lead us to final victory?

Here I was, a sixteen-year-old *Volkssturmmann*—now, a *Waffen-SS* soldier—soon to meet our great leader, who, according to what

I had been taught, was the most supreme human being on this earth! Me!

Hours after the *Reichsjugendfuehrer* and his staff had left, a war correspondent arrived and interviewed *Oblt.* Gutschke and those of us who would soon leave for Berlin. My thoughts went head over heels.

Didn't I always want to be a hero?

Now, Anne-Maria would read about me.

So would my mother, sisters, and brothers. So would my friends and classmates, those who were still alive. But most of all—so would my father.

As Axmann had reminded me, Hitler, in World War I, had been a regimental staff runner. Now I, a runner in World War II, would meet the once unknown soldier who had become Germany's leader.

***

The day before we departed for Berlin, in the distance, the rumblings of the enemy's heavy artillery fire increased. *Oblt.* Gutschke announced that along the Oder main defense line, the Russians had achieved several breakthroughs and were penetrating en-masse, north and south of us. He expected to receive orders to relocate our unit north from where we were, to reinforce Hitler Youth Home Defenses units located in the hills of Seelow.

Their southern flank needed to be strengthened to avoid encirclement by the Russians.

We were on our way to Falkenhagen, *Oblt.* Gutschke, his driver, his adjutant, and me—his courier. However, near Petershagen, hits from long-range heavy cannons began to increase. *Oblt.* Gutschke was briefed by the local commandant. The soldiers we encountered there belonged to the Army Division *Kurmark,* although some documentary evidence exists that the *Waffen-SS Panzer-Abteilung 502*[127] was stationed there under the command of Lieutenant-Colonel Kurt Hartrampf.

HM

I had remained with the driver and only *Oblt.* Gutschke, accompanied by his adjutant, conferred with the leader of the unit stationed there. He was apparently ordered to return because we did not proceed on to Falkenhagen but returned to Biegen.

Hurriedly, from there our *Kampfgruppe* was moved south of Petershagen, into the village of Petersdorf. Near the church, next to the cemetery was a large building, probably a great agricultural estate too. It was still inhabited, and *Oblt.* Gutschke did not evict the occupants. We moved into the cellar where storage rooms had to be vacated, except for the cellarage that was declared off limits, because of the wine stored there.

To this command post of *Oblt.* Gutschke, I was to return from Berlin along with a newly assigned motorcycle driver on the day after Hitler's birthday. The three of us, my two comrades and I, were to experience history in the making. We became witnesses of Hitler's last appearance outside of his Bunker before his suicide.

***

The trip to Berlin started on the morning of April 18th. My two comrades and I were picked up by an army bus, now used as a supply truck hauling provisions from depots in the capital and taking the wounded and those with special orders into the city. We, of course, had special orders to see the *Fuehrer. Oblt.* Gutschke's parting words, I still remember: "Reassure the *Fuehrer,* that we will fight to the last. We wait for the deployment of the miracle weapons. Urgently!"

This was a clear indication that *Oblt.* Gutschke, too, believed that we had secret weapons soon to be deployed, which would be so devastating as to turn the tide. As if it was an afterthought, he added: "Before it is too late!"

"*Jawohl! Herr Oberleutnant!*" I replied, speaking for the three of us.

We almost didn't make it since the old bus broke down twice.

Our driver and his buddy must have been mechanics because both times they were able to fix it.

It became apparent that we never would make it to Berlin by noon, and we didn't. For long stretches, the *Autobahn* was clogged up with military troops and retinue as well as with refugee treks. The latter were not supposed to use the *Autobahn* but were desperate enough to disregard orders.

This day, as we would learn afterwards, the Russians, after bitter fighting, captured the Seelow Heights. Hitler Youth forces had been among the defenders who fought valiantly and suffered heavy losses.

South of where we were, Russian advance troops had crossed the river Spree. Worse than that, a Russian scouting unit had advanced from Storkow and had crossed the *Autobahn* south of Fuerstenwalde. At a checkpoint, our driver had to leave the bus and report to an officer.

He returned and we pressed him for news. He was not at all optimistic.

"We might not make it this time."

"How come?" I asked.

"Shit! Everywhere!" He had been told that the Russians were pushing forward at a rapid pace. It was uncertain how far they had advanced. "They could reach Berlin before we get there!"

"But we have to make it, we have to see the *Fuehrer!*"

He had just learned that some sections of the city were already under artillery fire.

(Not until after the war would I learn that 2,200,000 enemy troops with more than 5,000 tanks, over 15,000 mounted guns of heavy artillery and multi-barreled *Katyushas,*[128] supported by nearly 6,000 aircraft, were facing less than 1,000,000 German troops.)

The Russians were in better physical shape, charged up emotionally due to recent victories, and they were well supplied.

Most of our troops, in turn, were battle-worn, poorly reinforced with insufficiently trained old men and young boys, greatly outmatched in weapons, and lacking adequate supplies of ammunition.

The treacherous ride only increased our exhilaration. All three of us were excited, of course. I must have been glowing with pride.

As we traveled to the *Fuehrer,* the Allies were finding horrors still unknown to us. It was not reported on German Radio or in German newspapers. Though we might not have grasped what was happening in the concentration camps, the slaughter of Germany's own should have aroused our minds. Throwing the very young into this last losing battle was the final act of a dictator who had concluded that the best had fallen and those still alive were not worthy of him—never mind how young they were!

On our way to Berlin, we were almost killed. Shots were suddenly fired at or near us. After swearing like a stevedore, the driver of the bus questioned why we were traveling without weapons. It was against regulations, he maintained. We could be looked upon as deserters.

No one had told us to take our carbines with us to see the *Fuehrer.*

Weapons were in short supply. Local boys who joined our unit had to be armed. Obviously, there would be weapons in Berlin that could be issued to us if needed. We were sure that when presented to Hitler we would not bear arms. And no one had thought of Russians catching up with us on our way to the capital.

It seemed there were soldiers and refugees everywhere but no fighting troops. Who, then, was shooting at us? Our own troops? Civilians? Local Communists wearing red armbands?

Or, could a Russian reconnaissance unit have advanced this far already?

The driver accelerated and almost lost control of the bus. We barely avoided an accident with a horse-carriage. The horses, apparently scared by a sudden sound or motion, turned, cutting into the path of our bus. The fierce, unexpected stop threw us out of our seats. There were no seatbelts then.

The movement caused me to feel the gun in the lower right

pocket of my uniform jacket. As a courier, I had been issued a pistol.

"I have a Walther with me!" I yelled to the driver who took another sharp turn into a side street.

We entered Berlin through Blankenburg passing smoldering ruins on our way to Wedding. Even on the streets inside the city, it seemed that refugees were everywhere.

My God, all these homeless people! Misery everywhere. There was nothing we could do. We were on our way to see the *Fuehrer*. Did he know about them? He had remained in Berlin. He had to know!

Perhaps on his birthday he will speak to all these folks and give them hope.

Or, even better, he might put the miracle weapons into action, turning the tide on this national holiday, forcing the Russians to retreat. Then all these people can return home–or what was left of their homes.

My mother, sisters, and brothers were waiting, too, to return home, as soon as Breslau became an open city again with the enemy retreating.

It occurred to me for the first time that, if new devastating weapons were to be used on German soil, wouldn't those that stayed behind be killed too? If they had not already been killed by the Russians or killed themselves as my *Oma* intended to do.

Besides soldiers and refugees, we noticed women and children with pails, buckets, and pitchers, queuing up for water. An even longer line led to a bakery that apparently was still in operation.

Increasingly, we were slowed down, not only by people, but by obstacles and barriers as well. Disabled trolley cars, trucks and automobiles that had been hit during air raids were plentiful. Some were now being used to create tank barricades, forcing our driver to make detours.

All the streets, whether wide or narrow, were pitted with deep craters. Some our driver could not circumvent and the jolts were so severe we were afraid that the old bus might not withstand the shocks and break down, leaving us stranded in the middle of all this chaos. Repeatedly, he voiced concerns.

"I know, I know, you have to get to see the *Fuehrer*," the driver said, rubbing it in that he might have done better without us.

There was black smoke and yellow smoke; there were burning houses and ghostly structures of ruins. In houses still harboring people, with most of the glass shattered, many windows were boarded up with wood panels, clapboard or even cardboard. "Our walls may break, but never our hearts" was still legible on a badly shattered brick barrier in front of a burned out hospital. We reached our destination, aching from the rough ride, and starving since we had not eaten. We arrived in the early evenings hours (April 18, 1945) on Kaiserdamm 86, where the *Reichsjugendfuehrung* (the head office of the Hitler Youth) was located. We had, indeed, made it.

We thanked our driver and he said, "Take care!" Then he added, "Now don't you forget to tell the *Fuehrer* that we need the miracle weapon now—before it is too late!" He headed to a supply depot and we entered the Hitler youth headquarters. There, *Amtschef* (chief of staff) Gustav Memminger had been anxiously waiting for us. Six other decorated Hitler youth members had gotten there already. Three others selected for the Hitler youth delegation had not arrived. I was told that one of them would be my roommate. The decision was made not to wait for them. We were officially welcomed. Then an assistant of *Amtschef* Memminger interviewed us individually.

We were served sandwiches and tea and then taken to an in-house storeroom and clothed in new uniforms. To my great surprise, we were not outfitted as *Waffen-SS* or *Volkssturm* soldiers but given *Jungvolk* or *Hitlerjugend* uniforms, as this was all they had available. I was disappointed, wanting to be soldierly in appearance. *Volkssturm* cuff-stripes were to be ordered and to be sewn onto our lower sleeves, but this never happened.

Thus, I became a *Jungvolk* leader again. Not visible were the two paybooks in my pocket. One from the *Volkssturm* and one from the *Waffen-SS*.

There was another reason for the uniforms. The *Reichsjugendfuehrer* wanted us decorated *Jungvolk* leaders in *Jungvolk* uniforms, as guests of honor at the celebration when 10-year-old boys and girls would, on the next day, be inducted into the *Jungvolk* and *Jungmaedel.*

I requested to be issued a *Fahrtenmesser* (the official knife that belonged to the uniform) but knives were no longer available. I ended up with black *Jungvolk* trousers and a matching waist-length jacket, displaying on the left arm the round, single *Siegrune* patch below the black district triangle with the letters *RJF* (initials of *Reichsjugendfuehrung*). Thus, it gave the false impression that I was a staff member of the *Reichsjugendfuehrung.*

Some wore their *Leistungsabzeichen* (proficiency badge). Mine had remained at home in Breslau. What counted now was the ribbon that indicated that I had received the Iron Cross 2nd class and the black badge with the steel helmet and the crossed swords. It showed that I had been in battle and that I had been wounded.

***

The three others who were expected never made it. They would be declared casualties. Killed on the way to see their *Fuehrer*. They had been dispatched from a Hitler Youth unit that fought north of Seelow in Gusow. Since they never reached Berlin, it was assumed that somewhere along the way they were ambushed and killed or taken prisoners.

From the Hitler Youth headquarters, we were driven to a guesthouse for foreigners in Gatow. The nine of us were assigned two to a room. I ended up being the odd one and had a room all to myself.

Shortly after check-in, there was an air raid alarm and, together with *Reichsjugendfuehrer* Axmann who had just arrived, we went to a shelter located in the garden.

Axmann talked to us informally, emphasizing that never before had German youth been able to participate as much in the nation's fight for survival as we. He said that, as early as 1943, members of the Hitler Youth acted heroically during air raids and were awarded *E.K.*'s (Iron Crosses) and *Kriegsverdienstkreuze* (War Service Merit Crosses). He wanted us to know that, during the times of Frederick the Great, cadets only 12 years old participated in battle. He told us about one of his favorite books authored by a boy our age. He had participated as a volunteer in World War I and written about it.

One of us asked the *Reichsjugendfuehrer* how he had lost his arm. He was hit on the first day of the Russian campaign, he said. Attacking an elite unit of "Stalin-cadets." They advanced. He was hit . . . it all went that fast! He stressed that Hitler had outwitted Stalin by attacking first. The *Fuehrer* himself, Axmann told us, had explained to him the necessity of the action, code-named *Barbarossa.*[129]

After the all-clear signal, we left the air raid shelter and were given the choice to retire or to view a feature film. The guesthouse had its own projection room. Always an ardent movie-goer and charged up enough to stay awake, I joined some of the staff and a few of my comrades for a showing of *Kolberg*, the last major film produced in Hitler's Germany. It was an epic production, in color. The leading actors were none other than Heinrich George, Kristina Soederbaum and Horst Caspar. When, during Napoleon's siege, the Prussian army failed to defend this seaport, a forceful civilian militia (similar to the *Volkssturm*) took over under the mayor's leadership.

It is believed that Dr. Goebbels, who commissioned this film, saw a parallel between the situation in Kolberg in 1806-07 and the challenge faced by Germany in 1945. He wanted to demonstrate that people survived who held out heroically to the very end. The film, a masterpiece, made a great impression on me.

***

Up to the very last word that was printed during the Third *Reich*, I never noticed a revision of the view of Hitler and what he meant to the nation. Hailed as the great leader chosen by Providence to unite and elevate Germany to its deserved glory, he was to remain in our minds a supreme historical figure and a great warrior of Napoleonic proportions. Since we had become members of the *Waffen-SS*, which had a multitude of volunteers from other European countries, it was also stressed that Hitler had arisen for all of the Aryan people, to create a new Europe. People of Nordic stock, healthy and life affirming, were in a struggle in which only the best would survive. They would form an ideal alliance under an ideal leadership—Hitler's leadership.

In a newspaper, following the final glorification of Adolf Hitler, a succinct message from Dr. Goebbels was printed mandating that we not surrender, but fight on to the victorious end.

Shrewdly, he placed on our shoulders the responsibility for the outcome of the battle for Berlin. He called it a final challenge, a most difficult test. It can only be passed, he said, with unfaltering belief in the genius of Adolf Hitler.

Years later, I remember a discussion with my mother. She speculated what times and conditions would have been like if Hitler had not started the war, if the Jews and others had not been persecuted, if he had been a benevolent ruler.

Before the war started, except for Jews and Gypsies or those who had physical or mental handicaps, he had provided several "good" years for Germany's youth and most of the population. Yet, as soon as he assumed power, he had become a despot. Most of the excluded were already in concentration camps. The political prisoners were culpable of not supporting Hitler and his party. Most were not guilty of a criminal offense. In the very end, even not to bear arms and not to kill became a crime for boys my age. I would soon come to view such a victim with my very own eyes.

***

Amtschef Memminger took us on a sightseeing tour of Berlin (or what was left of it). He then treated us to a *Mittagessen*. The dinner consisted of London broil, red cabbage, boiled potatoes, and, for dessert, sorbet. This was a meal out of the ordinary for us, and we savored it.

In the afternoon, he drove us to the stadium complex where, in the dome-shaped enclosure, Axmann inducted the 10-year-olds into the Hitler Youth as *Jungvolk* and *Jungmaedel*.

It was an eerie experience. The majority of the boys wore white shirts. They reminded me of my induction seven years prior. My shirt then was ivory-colored, not brown, and I had felt very much out of place, like an outcast.

Now the situation was reversed. The few who had brown shirts, probably handed down from older brothers, looked like black sheep. All of the other boys wore white ones with most of the girls wearing whitish blouses as well. In my case it had been a question of money. Now, for these inductees, the materials for the uniform shirts had been lacking. Moreover, most of them didn't have their *Fahrtenmesser* (camping knives) either. (I would, of course, notice this!) This official blade, for a ten-year-old, was an important status symbol. I wondered what went on in the minds of these boys. Did any, as was the case with me, feel slighted? Or, had the war conditions wiped out such embitterment?

My comrades and I wore *Jungvolk* uniforms, also without *Fahrtenmesser*. I, however, carried a pistol, a Walther 6.35, concealed in my coat pocket.

The Hitler Youth's own chamber orchestra had performed prior to Axmann's speech. He told the boys and girls that they were Germany's future. *Rjfr.* Axmann still spoke of winning this war. In fact, he impressed upon these ten-year-old boys and girls what the future held in store for them: " . . .there is only victory or annihilation!"

He promised these youngsters inclusion into the *grosse Kameradschaft* (great comradeship), providing for common support. *Rjfr.* Axmann wanted them to show boundless love for their Fatherland and on the other side he wanted them to generate intense, limitless hate for the enemy. *Rjfr.* Axmann challenged

Germany's youth to resist the enemy's advances fanatically, thereby demonstrating unshakeable loyalty and love to the *Fuehrer*.

I asked him after the war, if he had still believed what he said. He did not reply with a yes or no but remarked that, to say what he had said, was his duty. That was his answer. Fifty years later, Axmann wrote in his book: *This Couldn't Be the End*[130] "It was difficult for me on this day to find the right words. Where could one still find hope? Nevertheless one kept on planting, even on a grave."

On April 19, 1945, I still idolized Axmann and both of us idolized Hitler, and we were dedicated and committed to follow his path unerringly. We were convinced we would be part of the "New Order" destined to last a thousand years and benefiting all of Europe.

How difficult it must be for all those who live in a democracy, used to a free press and to open exchanges of opinions, used to a multiple party-system or, at least, to a two-party system, to understand the one-track mind of youth in a dictatorship.

I hope that in this new Millennium, the world will reach a level of humanness that even military strikes to prevent wars will no longer be necessary! Above all, common people should never be made to suffer for their leaders' criminal acts.

When Axmann finished, the applause was faint. A song concluded the ceremony. We, the Hitler Youth soldiers, seated in the front row, were the first ones to leave. I assisted one of the wounded who had come from a military hospital. Down the row, a soldier with only one leg, hobbling on crutches, tripped, fell on the floor, and was hurt.

"We need a wheelchair!" his accompanying nurse called out.

"We don't have an extra one," another nurse replied. Two medics carried him out.

One of the white-bloused girls followed him, carrying his crutches. A girl next to me, about 10 years old, remarked: "My father lost both legs and hasn't gotten a wheelchair yet!" She said it so matter-of-factly and shrugged her shoulders, as if to convey, that's just the way things are.

Not once did it cross my mind that, in the future, I might need a wheelchair or crutches and there would be none.

CHAPTER 48

Hitler's Birthday Reception

The Broadcasting House on Masurenalle was Berlin's major radio station. It had survived all of the Allies' bombardments.

Amtschef Memminger had written *Felecitations* (birthday salutations) for Hitler, and I was chosen to record them for later broadcast. Early in the evening of April 19th, I was taken to the radio station where one of the technicians recognized who I was because he knew my father.

The reception with Hitler, originally scheduled for midnight, was cancelled and rescheduled for the next morning at 10 a.m. *Rjfr.* Axmann would extend his congratulations over the radio live at midnight.

That night, still without a roommate, I sat down on the table and wrote a letter to Anne-Maria, describing what had happened and what would take place tomorrow.

After finishing the letter to her, I was still too keyed-up to go to sleep.

There was a radio in my room, but I couldn't get a station, not even the local one, without interference. Thus, I had turned it off and not watching the time while writing, I missed the midnight broadcast. When I was finished with my story, it was nearly 1:00 in the morning.

I never found out if Axmann's and my message were aired. I was curious, of course, as to whether Hitler had listened to any of the birthday greetings that were broadcast that night.

The *Magnetophonband* (tape) of Goebbels' speech remained

in the station's archive. The short messages Axmann and I had recorded were apparently played over or destroyed.

The next day, April 20th, Hitler's birthday reception was postponed once more, from 10:00 a.m. in the morning to 5:00 p.m. in the afternoon. I doubt that we would have been able to sleep late because of all the excitement. Suddenly, we seemed to be in an entirely different world. Being treated like young heroes of the nation and being put up in a guesthouse like the *Auslandshaus* (usually used for foreign diplomats) made it such a stimulating occasion.

Amtschef Memminger seized the opportunity to give us a briefing, which sounded encouraging. I remember his mentioning Breslau, the battle between Goerlitz and Cottbus and the frontline between Zwickau and Hof. On all three battlegrounds, according to Memminger, Hitler Youth were fighting side-by-side with regular troops and attacks by the enemy were being repelled. Thus, my friends and classmates in Breslau; my grandparents in Goerlitz; and Anne-Maria in Hof were being defended valiantly by our forces. (Only after the war did I learn that the occupation of Hof began on April 15 and was already completed by the 20th. All my comrades in the military hospital were POWs by now.) Nor was there mention of the breakthrough of the Russian Army north of us, where they advanced rapidly.

The deep breach that had opened up allowed these Russian troops to turn south toward the *Autobahn* where *Kampfgruppe Gutschke* was located. The three of us in Berlin had no idea that our comrades were being attacked already.

Amtschef Memminger showed us a Russian flyer, supposedly an order from Stalin to his Russian soldiers. It threatened to kill every single German, old people and babies included, even the unborn. (Most likely it was one of Ilja Ehrenburg's[131] inflammatory epistles, since no records exist of such leaflets with orders from Stalin himself.)

Less than two weeks prior to the total collapse of his might, Hitler was described by the German press as follows: "The *Fuehrer*, as a person, rises today more shining and purer than ever, as a fearless and unblemished knight amid a world in danger of being overthrown by Jewish Plutocrat Bolshevist War Criminals into a chaos of destruction, hunger, epidemics and slavery."

It was Dr. Goebbels who had been able to create in our young minds a belief structure that securely harbored the Hitler myth. He had hoodwinked us into believing that Hitler was a genius, if not a demi-god, who could do no wrong. Aside from being Propaganda Minister (chief of the Department of Propaganda), he was, at present, also *Reichsverteidigungskommissar* (*Reich* Defense Commissar). He commanded that we not surrender but fight on to the victorious end!

Shrewdly, he placed on our shoulders the responsibility for the outcome of the Berlin battle. He called it a final challenge.

Throughout Europe, even in countries that opposed Germany, Hitler had found followers. Among his last defenders were *Waffen-SS* volunteers from France and Scandinavian countries. Hitler was their idol. Among those who survived the war, there were those who had to face a firing squad and those who survived, often because they were able to change their identity. But did they change their beliefs? And, if so, did they change theirs as drastically as I changed mine?

In my case, not a German but a foreigner would gradually emerge as my most revered leader, one who moved the masses without making inflammatory speeches, one who did not threaten to arm his people and lead them into battle. Instead, if necessary, he would "fast unto death."

In April of 1945, I didn't even know of Mahatma Gandhi. Ironically, after surviving the war, I almost lost my life in Calcutta at the hands of militant Indian students as I traced Gandhi's footsteps. I wish I had met him prior to his assassination. I was fortunate to meet, prior to his death, Dr. Albert Schweitzer, who cared for people Hitler considered to be sub-humans. Unfolding truths caused a metamorphosis in my mind.

But it was months before this transition would commence.

Meanwhile, the platform was being built to provide Adolf Hitler's heroic departure from the stage of world history. His adoration of Richard Wagner had, no doubt, expanded in our young minds the myth of belonging to a *Heldenvolk* (nation of heroes), deserving of a *Goetterdaemmerung* (dawn of the Gods). A Wagnerian-type spectacle was about to unfold. Blood was being shed—thousandfold.

Even *Amtschef* Memminger, in his address to us prior to the reception, reminded us of the great responsibility Hitler was burdened with and alone able to handle.

Then, from Fichte's[132] *Addresses to the German Nation*, he read selected excerpts. It all added to our excitement in anticipation of the great historic event.

After the war I would study all of the different leaflets dropped by Russian planes on the Eastern Front and by Allied aircraft on the Western Front. Some referred to Hitler as a criminal, but most pointed merely to the hopelessness of the situation, urging German soldiers to save their life as well as others' lives and to surrender, promising fair treatment according to the Geneva Convention. As *Waffen-SS* or *Volkssturm* soldiers, we had no access to BBC broadcasts. It is my understanding that neither the BBC nor other foreign broadcasts ever revealed that Hitler was a mass-murderer. Only in the very last days of the war was some light shed on the concentration camps and the horrific, inhuman conditions discovered by those that liberated them.

***

The manager of the guesthouse and his daughter were also introduced to us. Their name was Keppler. He said that he was proud to host us and that following our visit, he expected to host the commanders of the Hitler Youth brigades from every *Gebiet* (province). They would attend a summit scheduled by *Rjfr.* Axmann. The Hitler Youth units in Breslau were to serve as shining examples. I remember this distinctly since I asked if *Gebietsfuehrer*

Herbert Hirsch was also expected to come here to Berlin. He was the commander of the Hitler Youth brigade in Breslau that was named after him. *Kampfgruppe Gutschke* had originally belonged to it.

As we learned days later, due to the fast advance of the Russian troops, this conference never took place. Instead, a contingent of Navy cadets arrived, among them some trained for suicide missions. They were housed there for a night before being attached to *Kampfgruppe* Mohnke[133] to help defend the *Fuehrerbunker*.

We left the guesthouse for the *Reich* Youth Head Office around noon. We had lunch at the canteen. There was no menu. But, at least, it was not the typical soup waiting for us. It was Friday. We had fried herring in a can and a freshly boiled potato, another real treat.

After lunch, we were given a tour of the building and introduced to those still on their jobs, including *Gebietsfuehrers* Grimm and Schroeder and *Reichsaerztin* (*Reich* physician) Dr. med. Gertrud Huhn.

Finally, the time came to leave for the reception. When we arrived at the *Reich* Chancellery, I remember distinctly some civilians at work, cleaning up rubble from the latest bombing raid. I, as did *Rjfr.* Axmann, believed that they were *Fremdarbeiter* (foreign laborers). Hitler's adjutant, Otto Guensche, disputed that the *Fuehrer* was ever exposed to the potential danger of foreign laborers near him.

In the garden of the Chancellery, the three delegations were arranged with the Hitler Youth positioned in the middle. To the right of us was the *Frundsberg*[134] delegation, even smaller than ours, consisting of four or five delegates and, to the left, a slightly larger delegation, with ten to twelve representatives that had come from Kurland.[135]

Axmann had originally selected twelve for our group but with the three that hadn't arrived, we were only nine. I do not remember whether Axmann selected three other boys from units inside Berlin to bring us back to twelve. By no stretch of imagination were there twenty of us—as has been reported. That was the number presented to the *Fuehrer* a month earlier on March 20 when Axmann appeared with twenty boys, some decorated by Hitler himself.

Hitler appeared, surrounded by many of his top functionaries. I recognized at once Dr. Joseph Goebbels (Propaganda Minister), Heinrich Himmler (Chief of the *SS* and *Waffen-SS*) as well as the prominent military operatives: Wilhelm Keitel (Army Field Marshal) and Alfred Jodl (Army General). Martin Bormann (Party Chief and Hitler's Secretary and Chief of Protocol) appeared to me to be fat and seemed out of place.

By Hitler's side were Adjutants *SS-Obergruppenfuehrer* (Lieutenant General) Julius Schaub and *SS-Sturmbannfuehrer* (Major) Otto Guensche. I knew neither of the tall officers at that time. They stayed close to the *Fuehrer* until he reached the first group, then remained several meters behind.

The delegation from the 10th *Waffen-SS Panzer Division Frundsberg* wore a *Frundsberg* cuff title (the unit's name embroidered on sleeve) and a special emblem, a capital "F" with an oak leaf as background. As I know now, they were led by *Obersturmfuehrer* (Lieutenant) Bachmann, who proudly wore his Knight's Cross. The three or four other officers who accompanied him were highly decorated as well.

Obstf. Bachmann presented Hitler with a *Winterhilfe* (winter relief) donation, a check reported to be in the amount of 3,000,000 *Reichsmark* (an American equivalent at the time of $700,000). Little did Hitler know when he received this delegation and the generous winter aid donation that, at that very time, the commander of this division, *Brigadefuehrer* (Brigadier General) Heinz Harmel was about to disregard Hitler's latest command sent to him from the *Fuehrerbunker*. It ordered him to immediately attack and repel the advancing Russians between Spremberg and Cottbus. This widening gap constituted a great threat for Berlin.

In typical Hitler fashion, his military directive concluded with a threat: "You will be held personally responsible for carrying out this order. You will lead a victorious attack or fall in front of your division!"

Succeed or die!

Brigadefuehrer Harmel knew that he couldn't carry out this order. Two thirds of his forces were already in the Spremberg region and the remaining third was immovable—out of fuel and totally exhausted. Hitler's mandate had completely ignored the reality of the situation. But even to refuse an order that could not be carried out was considered disobedience and a punishable offense. Facing a possible death sentence, *Brigadefuehrer* Harmel opted for the only choice that made sense and would save lives, a breakout attempt to the west.

In Berlin, the birthday reception took place punctually at 5:00 p.m. and probably lasted about 20 minutes. It was followed by a situation conference that Axmann attended. (Thus, it is in error when, in some of the historical literature, it is stated that the situation conference took place at 4:00 p.m. I estimate that it was close to 5:30 p.m.)

When Adolf Hitler approached the *Frundsberg* delegation, his two adjutants remained behind. Although not allowed to move my head, I looked as much to the right as I could and soon had my eyes fixed on him. Here he was, our nation's great leader, destined by fate and infallible, at his 56th birthday. He looked much older. I had seen him in peace-time, seven years earlier, when he radiated power and looked healthy and strong. When he had spoken then, he mesmerized the entire audience.

Now, he even appeared to have shrunk, with his head set deeper between his shoulders. His steps appeared somewhat uncoordinated, insecure. It was my impression that his entire body trembled, even his head, but most obvious was the shaking of his left hand which he tried to control by holding on to his coat-flap in the back.

The well-known photo showing him in front of a Hitler Youth delegation, dressed in a heavy overcoat, with his collar put up, often attributed to the April 20 reception, was taken at the reception a month earlier. When we met him, he was wearing a field-gray uniform jacket with his Golden Party emblem, the Iron Cross First Class and below it the Black Wounded Badge, all pinned onto his left chest pocket. The pants he wore were black.

Out of the corner of my eye I could see the fidgeting Hitler take the check and, with his hand trembling, pass it on to either Schaub or Guensche.

Now he reached us.

Close up Hitler looked much older than my grandfathers. Both were in their 70's.

Axmann raised his left arm, apparently looked Hitler straight in the eyes and, judging from his exalted voice, spoke with great intensity, staccato-style: "My *Fuehrer!* In the name of Germany's youth I congratulate you on your birthday. I am proud once again to introduce to you young fighters whose courage and valor is typical of the readiness for action of the Hitler Youth. They stand the test on the home front with an iron will to achieve the final victory."

"Thanks, thanks, Axmann," Hitler replied: "If in battle only all were as brave as these boys." By now, *Rjfr.* Axmann had lowered his arm. Now Hitler took steps toward me. I thought that Axmann would introduce me. Hitler, with his right hand grabbed my upper left arm and held on to the sleeve a second or two.

I recalled that *Amtschef* Memminger, at the morning briefing, had told us to each tell the *Fuehrer* our name, what Hitler Youth unit we belonged to, and where we participated in combat.

The moment had come. I trembled. Hitler quivered involuntarily.

It affected his entire body.

I could feel it when he let go of my arm to shake my hand, actually enclosing my outstretched right hand in both of his. (He did not pat my or anyone's cheek in our group. This, too, happened to others a month earlier.)

However, he came very close. His eyes, with a lambent, capti-vating brilliance, seemed surrounded by moisture as if irritants had produced tears or if they had been treated with eye-drops. Black sacks under his eyes added to the effect caused by his wrinkled, ashen face.

I stammered my name. Before I could continue, he started to query me using the familiar '*Du*' instead of the formal "*Sie.*"

"Where did you fight?" was his first question, spoken rather softly.

"In Silesia, south-east of Breslau, my *Fuehrer,*" I replied. He wanted to know the exact location. As I described it, my nervousness subsided.

"And you were brave and earned the Iron Cross?"

"I was wounded, pulled other wounded into a snow-ravine and kept on fighting..."

Before I could finish, he asked the next question, "What was your injury?" I was not sure what words to use to answer this question as a large piece of shrapnel had pierced my left behind.

In the hospital my room-mates had often remarked that I had been shot in the ass and for a split second this teasing remark crossed my mind, causing a short hesitation, until I said: "I was shot through my upper thigh, my *Fuehrer!*"

He patted me once more on my upper left arm, but looked at *Rjfr.* Axmann who was still standing next to me and said: "More-over, a brave boy!" I would rather have heard him say, "soldier" instead of "boy," but in Hitler's eyes, I, too, was looked upon as one of Axmann's boys.

My comrade next to me was the same age but shorter, and Hitler asked him if he and I were from the same unit.

Not just we two, we are three here from the *Kampfgruppe Gutschke* was his answer. He pointed to the comrade on his left to include him.

By the time Hitler had finished shaking hands with each member of our delegation, Axmann stepped out front to join the *Fuehrer's* entourage, and I felt free now to move my head. I kept watching him as he greeted the highly decorated members of the *Kurland* delegation, and it appeared as if he took more time to talk to each of them.

From there he walked back to a center position, just about six to seven meters (20 feet) in front of our group. Now his voice was strong.

His address was short and poignant. He spoke to all of us.

(Since no transcript has as yet been located, the speech presented below is solely based on my memory and some of the notes I made more than fifty years ago. Therefore, what I report that Hitler said is not verbatim but merely analogous. Nevertheless, I am using italics, as I have previously, to signify the passages that were spoken. What I don't recall is in what manner Hitler addressed us as a delegation—if at all. I certainly would have remembered had he referred to us as *Meine Kameraden* [My comrades in arms] as was suggested once long ago in one of the tabloids. I am sure that the delegates in front of him were captivated and listened intently to every single word he uttered).

> *On all fronts heavy fighting is taking place. Here in Berlin we are facing the great, decisive battle. Germany's destiny will be decided by the performance of the German soldier, his exemplary steadfastness and his unbending will to fight. You are witnesses to the fact that with dogged resistance even an enemy that outnumbers us can be repelled. Our belief that we will win the battle for Berlin has to remain unbroken. The situation can be compared with that of a patient believed to have reached the end. Yet, he does not have to die. He can be saved with a new medication, discovered just in time to save him, which is now being produced. We just have to be determined to hold out until this medication can be applied, to achieve final victory. That's what counts, to keep on fighting with an iron will! Heil Euch!*

His "*Heil Euch!*" meant, "I salute you." It remained unanswered. There was no response. Absolutely none.

Although *Amtschef* Memminger had briefed us beforehand to respond to Hitler's parting salute with "*Heil mein Fuehrer,*" no one replied. No one from our delegation. No one from the *Frundsberg* delegation. No one from the *Kurland* delegation. No one from his entourage. No one at all.

Did he mean the miracle weapons when he referred to the new "medication" that would save the patient thought to be dying? That patient was us.

Axmann in *Das kann doch nicht das Ende sein* also described Hitler's address, but in a more generalized fashion: "He [Hitler] made a short speech. He compared our nation with a very ill patient for whom scientists discovered a life-saving medication. However, it is decisive that the patient maintains his will to live. The battle for Berlin has to be won."

Axmann also observed that: "Hitler ended his remarks with '*Heil Euch!*' Silence prevailed. No answer. A sign of shock!"

What had shocked us? Hitler's appearance, no doubt. His condition appeared to be that of a dying man.

If any of those in attendance felt deceived by what he said, I was not among them. For me, he had just reinforced what I believed and wanted to believe.

***

After the reception, the *Frundsberg* delegates were unsuccessful in finding *Brgdf.* Harmel and the remnants of his unit who were by now attempting to cross the Elster River at Plessa. Some local Hitler Youth members had attached themselves and were used as scouts. The Russian troops in Plessa were routed and the bridge, still intact when captured, could be crossed. On April 28, *Brgdf.* Harmel learned that he had been relieved of his command for having disobeyed Hitler's orders. He expected to be court-martialed. Instead of facing execution, he was, surprisingly, sent to Klagenfurt in Austria to form still another *Kampfgruppe* (fighting unit).

Obstf. Bachmann with the other members of the *Frundsberg* birthday delegation were finally able to locate the remaining divisional survivors and, with *Brgdf.* Harmel gone, commanded the remnants of the armored forces during these very last days of the war.

The *Kurland* delegation is believed not to have made it back to their unit. Army Group *Kurland* was holding out on the eastern shore of the Baltic Sea. This encircled army, as was the case with the forces inside the Fortress Breslau, was one Hitler took great pride in. They were in a hopeless situation, but Hitler had justified his strategy by claiming that enough Russian units were held down to delay the attack on Berlin. He cherished the fact that neither the Army Group *Kurland*, nor the twenty-two divisions of the Sixteenth and the Eighteenth Armies, ever surrendered.

It explains why, on his 56th birthday, he specifically had insisted on recognizing Army Group *Kurland* for its heroism, by receiving a delegation of some of its bravest fighters.

Even after Hitler's death, they kept on fighting! Encircled, they held out. It was not until May 9th upon ratification of the German surrender that the units of Army Group *Kurland,* 208,000 strong, commanded by *Generaloberst* (Colonel-General) Karl Hilpert, met the terms of the armistice. They marched into Russian POW camps nine days after Hitler's suicide.

Hitler, supposedly, had also requested to see heroes from inside the Fortress Breslau. For lack of aircraft and take-off capability, his wish to honor *Breslauer* could not be fulfilled. From Kurland, sea and air routes were still open. In fact the forces there were amply supplied, better equipped than the defenders of Berlin. Trained, battle-experienced soldiers did the fighting.

This was not the case with most of the formations assembled to defend Berlin. *Volksgrenadier* and *Volkssturm* divisions (civilian forces) were created everywhere. New fighting groups were established instead of reinforcing existing units, decimated by heavy losses. Most divisions consisted now of only five to six battalions with a total manpower of 5,000 to 6,000 officers and men. In the *Volkssturm,* battalions were designated as brigades and regiments as divisions.

HJ-Panzernahkampfbrigaden were often companies of cyclists, each armed with a *Panzerfaust* (hand-held-bazooka).

For the *Kurland* delegates to Hitler's Birthday Reception to return to their army group required transportation by seacraft or by aircraft. They had headed north instead. It is believed they never returned to their unit but were taken prisoner in Merwick near the Baltic seaport of Flensburg, close to the Danish border.

***

The British historical periodical, *After The Battle* No. 61/1989, on page 61 contains a two-page facsimile of an article published in the German magazine *STERN*, with a photo of *Rjfr.* Axmann and the following caption: "He [Hitler] should see that we were at the end." This was Axmann's explanation as to why he brought Hitler Youth members from the front to introduce to the *Fuehrer.* Axmann was then 32 and the *Reich* Youth leader.

My memory, however, differs. I was under the distinct impression that *Rjfr.* Axmann wanted to impress Hitler with the loyalty of the Hitler Youth and welcomed this opportunity to bring their brave performances as young fighters to the *Fuehrer's* attention. Axmann presented us to Hitler to demonstrate how loyal and brave the Hitler Youth were.

Whether or not Hitler was pleased to see us, I couldn't say. Watching him it appeared that the whole reception was a painful experience for him.

Rjfr. Axmann maintained that the miracle weapons existed but couldn't be used in Berlin since they would kill soldiers on both sides.

As it turned out, the casualties on both sides were enormous with just the conventional weapons on hand. The Russian superiority, in numbers alone, caused catastrophic death statistics as the battle went on.

Armageddon had come upon us.

Between April 20 and April 30, Hitler held on to life and power for a few more days.

Still able to impose his will on most of those under his command, especially the very young, he kept instilled in us a volition to unceasing doggedness. We overcame exhaustion and kept on fighting, stretching our efforts beyond sensible limits, therewith securing him the additional time. Another ten days and ten nights.

To the reader, this continuous portrayal of Hitler, as I saw him then, might seem redundant and unnecessary—more than enough to make my point. But it reflects precisely the way the image-making of this absolute leader was being maintained, with his "greatness" permeating every facet of every medium of our lives.

After Adolf Hitler had finished shaking hands and spoken to all of us, *Reichsfuehrer-SS* Heinrich Himmler came up to greet the *SS-Frundsberg* delegation.

I overheard a few words, spoken to the *Frundsberg* delegate standing next to me, about how critical the next days would be and that Hitler had been assured by him (Himmler) that the *Waffen-SS*, as always, would battle heroically, "willing to make the last necessary sacrifice."

"*Jawohl Reichsfuehrer!*" replied the last *Frundsberg* delegate.

Now, Himmler had stepped in front of our delegation. He stretched out his hand and used the formal *"Sie"* addressing me: "You will, of course, become a cadet of the *Waffen-SS* and we will see each other again in Toelz!"[136]

"Yes, *Reichsfuehrer,* I am already a member of the *Waffen-SS.*"

"What? Aren't you a *Hitlerjunge* in the *Volkssturm?*"

"It was when I was awarded the Iron Cross. Meanwhile, however, in Fuerstenwalde we became part of the *Waffen-SS.*"

Himmler seemed visibly taken aback. "Why then did you not appear here in a *Waffen-SS* uniform?"

"Yesterday, in the *Reich* Youth headquarters, we were allotted *HJ*-uniforms for this reception."

He seemed baffled and turned to his adjutant:[137] "This, I will take up with Axmann."

Himmler looked almost feminine with shiny, soft skin. His appearance was not soldierly or even athletic. Had I not known who he was, I would have thought of him as a "softy." That's the impression he made. Only *Reichsleiter* Martin Bormann looked less appropriate among all these officers. Goebbels, who had a clubfoot, nevertheless had a hawkish face and fire in his eyes.

Hitler's entire entourage descended into the bunker and the delegations were dismissed. Elated because of our appearance on the stage of world history, we had no idea that the perspective of this memorable event would soon change drastically.

***

Rjfr. Artur Axmann attended the situation conference in the *Fuehrerbunker* afterward and obtained—from Hitler himself—authorization to attend, henceforth, the daily *Fuehrer* briefings. In the evening, he seemed in high spirits when he came to the *Auslandshaus* to say good-bye to us.

Amtschef Memminger had mentioned already what a good impression we had made on the *Fuehrer*. Axmann repeated it, using more glowing words. He added how very proud he was of all of us. He wished us well and told us to take personal greetings from him to our comrades.

Before leaving, to my great surprise, he asked me to follow him into the manager's office.

Had I done something wrong?

First he inquired about the impression the *Fuehrer* had made on me.

I was frank.

I told him how surprised I had been at his looking so old and walking stooped, with his head shaking and his body trembling, especially his left arm and hand.

"But isn't it amazing what strength of will he still radiates, how clearly he thinks, and how much on target his decisions are? Every detail he takes into consideration. Nothing escapes him."

Then Axmann asked me: "Weren't you impressed by the *Fuehrer's* speech?"

"Yes I was!" I replied and Axmann said, "So was I!"

I wanted to know why Axmann, too, had not returned Hitler's salute after the speech. Before I could ask, Axmann told me that after the *Fuehrer's* speech given to the Hitler Youth *Volkssturm* delegation a month earlier, all in unison had replied with a fervent "*Heil mein Fuehrer!*" (Hail to my leader!)

What had Adolf Hitler conveyed in his speech then, I wanted to know.

"Basically he said the same that he did today," Axmann replied. (Axmann erred. In my research I located a *Deutsches Nachrichten Bureau* (German Press Agency) report that cited Hitler's short speech given on March 20, 1945. At the end, he had emphasized:

What it is like to fight you already know from your own experience and you know that this struggle will determine the German nation's continuance or its demise. I am convinced, however, despite the bad times that we will emerge from this battle victorious, especially in view of the German youth and above all you boys! Hail you!

After this, the response had been enthusiastic. There was no mention of new weapons, no mention of newly discovered medication for a dying patient, only confidence in victory, especially in view of Germany's youth.

Now Axmann wanted to know if I had an explanation why today no one responded to Hitler's parting salute.

"I froze, perhaps the others did, too."

He shook his head and then changed the subject, asking whether I knew how to drive a motorcycle (I did) and if I knew my way around Berlin (I didn't).

Then he pointed at my left hand and the two rings I was wearing, "My mother's and my girl-friend's," I explained.

He asked me to send in whoever was next in line. I saluted and left. I had no idea what this meeting was all about and wondered all evening. Could it have been the two rings? He hadn't asked me to take them off.

Finally after supper *Amtschef* Memminger said good-bye to us, announcing that he, too, would be leaving the next morning. He was heading to the Western front on special assignment. Then he stepped toward me, grasped my arm and pulled me aside. With a low voice, for no one else to hear, he said to me: "You will remain here. The *Reich* Youth Leader has added you to his staff. *Oblt.* Gutschke will be informed accordingly. *Rjfr.* Axmann needs a courier."

That explained the meeting.

Once again, I couldn't believe that I was chosen. Axmann, surrounded by so many members of his staff and by Hitler Youth Leaders with whom he was acquainted, had selected me to be one of his *Melder* (couriers). Why me?

The two comrades from *Kampfgruppe Gutschke* had retired already. I wanted them to know what had happened. They would have to return without me.

Emotionally, I felt placed in the middle of a whirlwind, a torrent of cross-currents. I felt pulled apart by foreboding and disquietude, but also by excitement and pride. It seemed like a big promotion. *Oblt.* Gutschke's runner had become one of *Rjfr.* Axmann's couriers. He was a member of the *Fuehrer's* top echelon.

That night, my feelings kept me awake. What should I expect? What tasks would the *Reich* Youth Leader assign to me? It didn't cross my mind at all that I might end up having to deliver some of Hitler's last dispatches.

I realized that this might be the last night for some time I could sleep in a bed in a house not yet ravaged by war. Above all, in a room I had all to myself, a place of solace and comfort.

Then I was struck by another sudden realization. I had a return address now—the Hitler Youth Headquarters in Berlin. The address was listed on my orders, which had brought me here.

Thus, I wrote, not envisioning that this would be my last letter to Anne-Maria and not knowing that the city of Hof was occupied already by American troops.

I stated how fortunate I felt and described in very general terms what had happened to have placed me where I was. Sensitive to the wartime conditions, I didn't say that I expected soon to see action again. I merely wrote that, for the time being, I would remain in Berlin and could be reached in care of the *Reichsjugendfuehrer's* address. Then I hesitated. Could I put on paper that I loved her? I added *in Liebe* (with love) and experienced a rush of elation. Then I went to bed and slept, seizing the last night away from the battleground.

***

At the *Auslandshaus,* we had received copies of *Vorschriften fuer Hitlerjungen im Kriegseinsatz* (Regulation for Hitler Youth in Service), apparently prepared for the *HJ*-brigade commanders that were expected at the meeting scheduled to take place in a few days. We all had read these guidelines with amazement and some of my comrades had openly joked about certain provisions. I was horrified, realizing how much in violation I was already with these formal orders issued by *Rjfr.* Axmann who had just chosen me to become one of his couriers.

We were forbidden to consume alcohol. (On my 14th birthday, my own father had served me, with ceremonial gestures, my first glass of wine.) Members of *Kampfgruppe Gutschke,* my age and younger, had beer before and after our first battle. The *Unteroffiziere* (non-commissioned officers) had joined us and proposed toasts: "*Glueck auf!*" (A coal miner's salute of "fortune upwards") and then, of course, we drank "to victory" and not just once.

The regulations stipulated as well that we were forbidden to smoke. I had cigarettes on me and *Rjfr.* Axmann must have seen me smoke. I wasn't the only one in our group. He had never said anything.

For over two months now, I had chain-smoked. I had been handed cigarettes when there was no medicine available. It had become my pain medication.

In fact, as I read these *Vorschriften,* I smoked, inhaling even more deeply than usual.

Should I stop smoking?

Instead of cigarettes, we were entitled to special rations of sweets.

Apparently unbeknown to Axmann, all members of *Kampfgruppe Gutschke*, regardless of age, received rations of cigarettes, just as the older men in the *Volkssturm* did. But we had also received an allotment of what was called *Fliegerschokolade* (flyer's chocolate). The name indicated that these had been "energy bars" for pilots.

With hardly any *Luftwaffe* left but air force K-rations still in ample supply, we, the last ditch fighting units, became the beneficiaries of such special treats.

The *Vorschriften* directed that we were not allowed to patronize brothels.

I had had my one and only experience with a prostitute long before I became a member of the *Volkssturm*. Now I realized that in the eyes of my Commander, I had conducted a dishonorable act, even before I had been called to arms.

What shocked me the most, however, was the fact that intimate relationships with girls were explicitly forbidden. Did the *Reichsjugendfuehrer* think that I had merely a platonic relationship with the girl whose ring I was wearing? He had inquired about the rings, and I had explained that one was from my mother and the other from my friend[138]. I had not felt comfortable to elaborate further, but he asked me who my friend was.

"A Red Cross nurse at the military hospital in Hof where I recovered from my wounds."

"In war time, that's what happens," he had replied.

Anne-Maria's gold ring held a small red coral with a secret ensconced—our love. Did it reveal that I was in non-compliance with Axmann's codes for Hitler Youth fighters? When I fell in love with Anne-Maria, I didn't even know that such *Vorschriften* existed.

Although I had become a chain-smoker, I was not one with a thirst for alcohol. The Austrian *Waffen-SS* NCOs, our instructors in Fuerstenwalde, were, in their free time, always "organizing" booze. This meant that, even if not quite legal, they would find ways to get their hands on beer and Schnapps, any of several liquors distilled from grain, with high alcoholic content.

I would soon be assigned a motorcyclist, a few years older than I, who carried a flask with Schnapps. When he put it to his lips, he often explained: "to warm up my soul." Although I disliked the taste and the burning sensation in my throat, I would soon encounter situations, when I, too, would take a swallow to "warm up my soul."

I had become a member of the *Waffen-SS*. I had the *Waffen-SS* paybook in my pocket. Wouldn't that exempt me from regulations issued for the Hitler Youth? Even though *Rjfr.* Axmann, head of the Hitler Youth, was now my new commander, my *Waffen-SS* status was not reversed.

Reichsfuehrer-SS Heinrich Himmler had thought that I should be wearing a *Waffen-SS* uniform. *Rjfr.* Axmann kept me in a Hitler Youth uniform. Two of the highest leaders had taken an interest in my status. For a 16-year-old—what a remarkable situation to be in.

What I did not realize was that, so close to the end of the war, none of Axmann's *Vorschriften* ever became an issue.

I kept wearing my mother's and Anne-Maria's rings and kept on chain-smoking. Moreover, in a few days, we would be out of drinking water and would have to turn to *Sekt* (champagne), and I would have access to hard liquor as well.

CHAPTER 49

Hannes

My recollections of the events that follow resemble a cyclone of exploits, actions, and events. In retrospect, the reality appears stranger than far-fetched fiction.

Even now, I ask myself, was it possible for all this to have happened or could I have been shell-shocked and dreamt what I remember so intensely?

The experiences I recall are reflected in images, some striking and clear, others not. The portrayals of events are disconnected fragments, loose beads of a broken chain. I have spent much time and made great efforts to thread them again, but cannot be sure to have arranged them correctly and in consecutive order. Time in memory often rearranges itself by highlighting some events, veiling others, and shifting sequences around.

Under these circumstances, I am writing what I and surviving comrades remember, waiting for historical research to make adjustments and amendments.

***

Rjfr. Axmann remained a stickler for following regulations, even that late in the war.

Previously, he had asked: "Do you know how to drive a motorcycle?" And with pride, I replied: "Yes! *Reichsjugendfuehrer!*"

Now he inquired: "Do you have a *Fuehrerschein* (driver's license)?"

"No!"

"Then I will have to assign to you a driver."

Although there was a great shortage of manpower, I wasn't allowed to drive, even on military missions, without a driver's license!

I lucked out, however, with the driver he would assign to me on the next day. Never could I have performed alone what the two of us were able to accomplish together.

His first name was either Johann or Johannes, but he went by Hannes. Not only was he a mechanic and a member of the *Motor-HJ* (motorized Hitler Youth), but also he was a Berliner and knew the city inside out.

His *Kraftrad* (motorcycle), I believe, was a *Zuendapp*. We referred to it as *das Krad*.

Hannes, his *Krad*, and I would become a firmly bonded three-some, two men and a machine, a daredevil team, not by choice, but because of the assignments that were given to us.

Hannes had a dry sense of humor, typical of Berliners, but he was also an idealistic member of the Hitler Youth. Throughout this one week we spent together, he was the most steadfast and trustworthy comrade, confidant, alter ego, and fellow adventurer that I could have wished for.

He was a skillful, courageous driver but he had not seen combat as yet. A selfless and dependable veteran of the city's devastating air bombardments, he knew war from the perspective of its apocalyptic dimensions, home-front destruction, suffering, and death. As a member of a fire-fighting team, he had been exposed to danger again and again and had risked his life in many a rescue effort.

We talked about some of our past encounters with death, experiences that had impacted both of our lives and now brought us together. Hannes reminded me in many ways of my friend Kurt in Breslau. Both had only a *Volksschul* (elementary school) education but expressed a wealth of thoughts—and had a lot of practical knowledge and the ability to fix things.

Both loved their motorcycles and their interests were not confined to things technical. They also were captivated by the rituals and symbols of the regime and were much more knowledgeable about runes and ancient wisdom than I was. Both must have had a penchant for occultism.

Both were of medium height and had wavy hair.

Above all, they were daredevils.

The drives with Kurt through Breslau were in peacetime and had been exhilarating experiences. Driving with Hannes through war-torn Berlin, often maneuvering between shell-holes, barriers, and other obstructions, became life-threatening adventures. Nevertheless, even under these most dangerous conditions, I would be overcome by a high sense of intoxication, a tingling rush of excitement, whenever we took off.

***

Hannes was familiar with the layout of the Hitler Youth head-quarters and knew some of the staff members personally. Before we left on our first mission, he helped me find a key official, a disabled war veteran who knew Werner Frehse, the headmaster at the Podiebrad camp leader school where, just a year ago, I had been an instructor. I wanted to find out if the school had been moved or dissolved. However, the *KLV* coordinator had no concrete information. I also inquired about Ullersdorf Castle, where I had been camp leader from October until Christmas of 1944.

"The boys from Ullersdorf were sent home at the time the camp was dissolved," I was told.

"When was that?" I asked.

"In the middle of January!"

He had no records of the names of pupils, only of leaders. Apparently, I had never been replaced since my name was still listed as the last *Lagermannschaftsfuehrer* (camp counselor) there. I wondered what might have happened to a couple of boys I had felt very close to. They were war orphans; their fathers killed in battle, their mothers at home during enemy air raids.

For those two, as for others, the *KLV* camps had been orphanages.

It must have been on this day, April 21, that Hannes and I became acquainted with Dieter Schroeder, a 13-year-old from East Prussia. *Der Kleine*, as he was called, was exemplary of the blind devotion and preparedness to serve under any condition, obediently and efficiently. He, too, was an orphan.

CHAPTER 50

Our First Mission

Later that day, Hannes and I were assigned our first courier mission.

I couldn't believe it!

Axmann wanted orders forwarded to no other than to *Kampfgruppe Gutschke*, the very unit I belonged to.

I would see *Oblt.* Gutschke again and my Silesian comrades— not only the two who had been with me at the reception, but also Rolf, Kurt, and all the others!

There were at least 20 different *HJ-Kampfgruppen* in action by now on the eastern front and within Berlin. What a coincidence that *Rjfr.* Axmann had picked my unit to receive his first order.

Once again, *Kampfgruppe Gutschke*, battle-experienced and a heroic, elite unit, was expected to set a glowing example for bravery and to achieve victory as had been the case at the end of January at Wansen.

After the briefing, no time was lost and Hannes and I headed toward the battle east of Berlin already in progress.

Rjfr. Axmann had explained to us in no uncertain terms, that *Oblt.* Gutschke was not to retreat from his position. He had to face the already approaching Russians head-on and hold the Biegen-Jacobsdorf-Petersdorf-Petershagen line with its strategically important road.

"We will not disappoint the *Fuehrer*," Axmann declared.

I agreed.

I had no idea, of course, how weak our forces were compared to the Russian's. Hitler's mania was such that his immediate reaction to any defeat was to blame cowardice or even treachery on the commanders in the field, while ignoring shortcomings in manpower, deficient weaponry and lack of ammunition.

***

Hannes and I left on our first mission, heading from Kaiserdamm to Petersdorf.

Berlin was already a city of mostly ruins. Now, buildings not previously hit were aimed at by heavy Russian artillery. Not only could the explosions be heard, but also they could be felt. It appeared that the ground was trembling. In the distance, flames burst up and smoke rose into the clouds. Obviously, the city was about to turn into a fiery, gutted battleground. Would we be able to get back?

Although refugees were not supposed to use the *Autobahn*, shortly past Fuerstenwalde we encountered a congested, chaotic condition caused by a mass of helpless people, many apparently hungry, freezing, and desperate. Horses needed rest and feed, some of the carriages were in need of repairs. Overloaded handcarts had broken down. I remember babies crying and an old, old man who addressed Hannes and me as *Landser*.[139] He pleaded with us to give him a "coupe-de-grace."

"I can't cope anymore," he beseeched us. "Please, please, release me from my suffering."

"Oh, my God," I said to Hannes, "what can we do for him? We can't shoot him?" A real *Landser*, an NCO, approached the pleading old man.

"Grandpa, I can't shoot you, but for one shot you can use my pistol." Hearing this, Hannes and I were stupefied.

We stepped away, but heard the shot.

Hannes surprised me. He made the sign of the cross. I had thought him to be a heathen because of his interest in occult practices and mythological beliefs. Earlier, we had talked briefly about death and exchanged addresses of whom to inform if one of us should fall and the other survive.

I remarked: "If death catches us both, then we'll be reunited in hell." To which Hannes replied: "We have reached Hell already, and if I have to bite the dust, then I want to end up in Valhalla."[140]

The shot must have triggered Catholicism deeper inside him than the mythology he professed.

I noticed that the *Unteroffizier* reclaimed his revolver, while a young woman came running from behind the covered wagon, screamed and threw herself over the body of the old man as if to protect him.

Hannes thought that he might not be dead since the woman's blouse was drenched with blood.

"The dead don't bleed," he remarked

"We have got to go!" I urged.

Hannes revved up the *Krad*, with little effect. Hardly anyone moved out of the way. Hannes yelled. I yelled. Very slowly, we penetrated the throngs of desperate refugees. Finally, we gathered speed and were off. The next congestion we encountered was caused by army vehicles brought to a halt by a military patrol.

With courier orders from *Rjfr.* Axmann, we were cleared to proceed, soon to be exposed again to enemy fire. With artillery barrages increasing, it became doubtful that we would reach our destination. But, as it happens in war, the shooting suddenly stopped and we whizzed along a stretch of the *Autobahn,* which was completely empty, concerned that the *Krad's* whirring sound would attract attention. What an eerie feeling.

It made us stop, and we debated whether to remain on the *Autobahn* or continue on a country road instead? I took off my two rings and slipped them into my shirt pocket. Holding tightly onto the handle of my seat caused the metal of the rings to bite into my fingers.

It was during this short rest stop that Hannes retrieved from his gear his liquor flask and, suggesting that we warm up our souls, offered me a drink.

I took a swallow and handed the bottle back to him.

He said a toast: "To the poor *Opa,*" and then gulped down several swallows.

I was more disturbed by the distress of the woman with the bloody blouse.

My mind was suddenly flooded with memories of the gruesome casualties from my first battle. The Russian soldier's cracked head with his brain spattered around; the comrade who had been hit by a bullet that must have exploded in his face. Since then, had I become tougher? Was Schnapps the answer to getting through these ghastly images?

The rat-tat-tat of a Russian plane we called a "sewing machine" stopped the flow of these thoughts. After looking up for a while, we both thought that the pilot hadn't spotted us. The plane was gone. Or that's what we thought.

We each lit a cigarette, relaxing, when out of the sky machine gun bursts splashed nearby into the field. We threw ourselves on the ground and were lucky. We were not hit.

We spotted the plane again, but had no weapons to shoot at it. Just our pistols, which were not far-reaching enough. The plane disappeared; we decided to drive on and remain on the *Autobahn* until Briesen. There we took the turn-off and proceeded on a muddy road toward *Oblt.* Gutschke's command post in Petersdorf.

After a stretch through no-man's land, some single shots out of a wooded area seemed to be aimed at us. Hannes increased the speed, and I was almost thrown off my seat. The heavy fire, farther away, seemed also to intensify.

We encountered a group of local *Volkssturmmaenner,* older men of the home defense force. Under the leadership of a schoolteacher, they were digging a tank barricade. This was west of the village, while the Russians were already attacking from the opposite, southeasterly direction.

Obviously, the danger of a rapid encirclement already existed.

I inquired about *Oblt.* Gutschke's whereabouts. No one knew of his location.

Noticing open straw silos on the field, we turned off the road and stopped behind one to decide if we should both continue onward. We didn't want to drive straight into a line of fire.

It was late afternoon. We decided that I would advance alone. Hannes would wait here for me for four hours and if I didn't come back, return to Berlin without me. He would report that, with an attack in progress, I had proceeded on foot and not returned.

I continued on the quest alone. I expected *Oblt.* Gutschke to be at his command post. Because it was near the church, it was easy to find.

To my surprise, the place was deserted except for a lone, young soldier, receiving orders over a field telephone. I showed him my dispatch envelope addressed to *Oblt.* Gutschke.

He explained that he, too, had messages for him, handed them to me and said that I would find Gutschke at the schoolhouse where he and *Bfhr.* Koeck had combined their command posts. *Bfhr.* Koeck's *Kampfgruppe* had joined up with Gutschke's experienced fighting troupe.

I reached the schoolhouse.

The corridor resembled a small weapon's depot. It was filled with bazookas, hand grenades, and munitions boxes for machine guns.

In one room, the benches had been pushed against the wall. Two women, wearing aprons, sat at a table near the door, peeling potatoes.

I continued to look for *Oblt.* Gutschke.

Instead, a Master Sergeant from another unit appeared and yelled at me: "What are you doing here? Why did you leave your fighting post?"

I saluted and explained what I was there for. "I have a dispatch to *Oblt.* Gutschke!"

"Gutschke? Gutschke? He's not here, he must be on the road to Jacobsdorf."

"Then I am off to Jacobsdorf!"

"The road is under heavy fire!" he yelled after me. I was on my way, running hunched over.

I headed south and, when I reached the end of Petersdorf, crossed the street so that I could duck into a ditch that provided some protection.

The distance between the two villages was about two miles. In the ditch, I passed a Hitler Youth Leader with a platoon of young men walking single-file. I was disappointed that it was not Gutschke leading the group. It might have been *Bfhr.* Koeck, however. He cursed: "Damn it, the 'Ivan'[141] is out to kill us!" He then told me that Gutschke was advancing further south.

There were stretches with no one in sight and the road to Jacobsdorf seemed never ending. With stabbing chest pain, it took stoicism and determination to reach the village. Under fire, with the roar of war increasingly unnerving, it reminded me of the march to our first battlefield because of the agonizing sounds from frightened and injured animals. Hurting and worn out, my thoughts were tormented, so much that I felt overcome by terror.

Explosions. Shells and bullets flew in lethal profusion.

At last, I reached Jacobsdorf.

With the village under heavy attack by Russian artillery, I darted from house to house.

No one there seemed to know where *Oblt.* Gutschke was.

Finally, someone directed me to a farmhouse, and there he was, in the garden with a platoon of boys. They were shooting through hedges at attacking Russian soldiers.

I yelled "*Herr Oberleutnant!*"

He turned around.

"What are you doing here?"

Before I could answer, he put another clip in his *MP*-40, an automatic weapon, and kept firing. South of us, a machine gun shot continuously to ward off the enemy.

Was it Kurt, I wondered?

Keep it up, keep it up!

There were hits all around us, and I was trembling. By Gutschke's side, a boy pointed to a gun next to a fallen comrade. I picked it up, fired, and finished the clip.

The fallen comrade lay face down, his legs positioned grotesquely, bloodied and mutilated.

It crossed my mind to turn him over to make sure that he was dead.

I remembered in Wansen where the wounded were not collected until after the battle.

As if he was reading my mind, *Oblt.* Gutschke shouted: "Shot in the abdomen. Dead!"

Another unit, attacking the Russians from the flank, forced them to withdraw from their attack.

The fire died down and to my great astonishment, Hannes with his *Krad* arrived to pick me up. Having driven on the road, which the Russians kept shelling, he had put his life on the line to get me out. But *Oblt.* Gutschke decided that I should remain in Jacobsdorf for the night.

He also determined that Hannes should return to the open silo and wait for me there.

To reach him there on foot would be a long way for me. I was alarmed by *Oblt.* Gutschke's decision but didn't say anything. An officer's order was never to be questioned.

"Eat something and get some sleep," *Oblt.* Gutschke told me.

The fallen and wounded were collected. I held on to the gun but took off my helmet.

Several girls appeared with fresh milk and sandwiches made from freshly baked bread. I didn't know where the people were who lived in this farmhouse and if they would come back. Thus, I avoided the living quarters and crumpled up in a heap of straw and must have fallen asleep instantly. I was probably in a pigsty or stable that connected the farmhouse with the barn.

What I remember next resembles a dream.

Face down and sleeping on my stomach, I was awakened by boots kicking me in the back. A Russian solider attempted to roll me over. Did he think I was dead? Instinctively, my body must have stiffened. I kept my eyes closed. He ripped the watch off my wrist and took my gun.

I expected a shot.

I expected to die.

Although keeping my eyes closed and playing dead, my mind and my senses were wide awake now and razor-sharp. I felt heat, heard the crackling of fire and flames shooting off. I realized that the barn must be on fire.

The Russian soldier will shoot me. I will burn to ashes. Nothing will be left of me! These thoughts raced through my mind. No one will be able to notify Hannes. Neither *Oblt.* Gutschke nor *Rjfr.* Axmann will ever know of my death. Anne-Maria, my mother, my father, my sisters and brothers, my friends, my classmates, whoever survives and keeps waiting for me, will ever learn of my fate. Forever unresolved, "missing" will be the verdict. Unless my burned skeleton would be found with my dog tag not melted down. My thoughts were rushing, pleading! Pull the trigger! Stop my thoughts! Shoot! Shoot! Get it over with!

The scorching heat spread out. My skin burned. My throat seemed in flames. That's when my body snapped out of its rigidity. I turned my head around and opened my eyes. The Russian soldier had left. I choked. The smoke was suffocating, and with great speed, I fled from the heat, escaping the flames. Were Russians waiting outside to shoot me as soon as I ran through the door?

A shot grazed my upper left arm, ripping off a shred from my uniform.

In front of me the smoke seemed to be filled with silhouettes, semblances and shadowy profiles. The first face turned out not to be a Russian soldier but a comrade of mine. The Russians had been repelled.

In the very early morning hours, before dawn, *Oblt.* Gutschke handed me my orders: "Enemy driven back. We are holding out. In urgent need of reinforcement!"

The last three words Gutschke spoke to me were: "Reinforcement! Reinforcement! Reinforcement!"

In my memory remains the urgency with which he shouted! I never saw him or heard from him again.

He must have fallen, together with the thousands and thousands of the very young, palpably insufficient to repel the superior forces we were fighting against.

***

After an hour of frenzied dashing across grounds and pastures, I approached my first goal—a plot of trees.

It blocked the view to the mid-field where the straw silo was. I hoped Hannes would still be waiting for me.

After running for such a long time, intermittently slowed down by chest pain, I looked forward to a breather. I would seize the opportunity and hide in this grove before racing the last stretch to reach Hannes. Behind me increasing artillery fire indicated that the Russians were launching still another attack against Jacobsdorf. Had I left just in time? Would they succeed today and capture the village?

It never entered my mind that an enemy reconnaissance troop could have advanced during the night and may already be ahead of me.

I ran right into a trap.

The moment I reached the first trees, someone shouted "*Stoi!*" What had seemed unimaginable until now happened. I lifted my arms.

I had received absolutely no training for what to do or what to say in a situation like this.

We were not to become POWs. We were expected to fight to the last and then die.

My comrades were in a battle. I was a courier. I had been careless, had not recognized a trap.

Even if I had wanted to kill myself now, I had no weapon to do so. I had left the *MP*-40 behind, as I had no more ammunition. My own pistol had been taken by the Russian soldier.

I was alone. In a hopeless situation and overcome by sheer terror.

Now death would come. How brutal would it be?

What sounded like commands were given in Russian. I did not understand Russian. What was I supposed to do? Remain standing? Walk with my raised hands toward the voice?

I still couldn't see anyone, although more voices now shouted.

Once again visions of horror tormented me—that death might not be swift but drawn out and torturous.

We had been told, over and over again, the Russian soldiers are barbaric—not ever to expect to be treated humanely.

Two enemy soldiers emerged from the woods. I couldn't believe what I saw. They looked almost as young as I, and they were not steady on their feet. Had I stumbled into an early victory celebration?

They must have bivouacked there all night. I noticed a camp-fire that had been put out, but light smoke was still rising. Had they caught Hannes and already killed him?

Now, one grabbed my collar and tore it as if he wanted to rip off my uniform, yanking off several buttons. He yelled at me in Russian.

He reeked of vodka.

Then another one, also smelling of vodka, grabbed me, checked my wrists, and then hit me. My arms were bare and that must have incensed him.

The only visible thing of some value was my satchel—a leather-pouch that contained, in a courier envelope, *Oblt.* Gutschke's reply to *Rjfr.* Axmann's orders, Gutschke's urgent request for reinforcements.

I realized that I had been captured by a leaderless group. Two of the Russian soldiers began to quarrel over possession of my leather satchel.

I didn't notice any casualties. No wounded or dead soldiers in sight.

Only live ones, six as far as I could tell, and all were in high spirits.

What could their mission have been? In their minds, probably, the war had been won already.

They had taken a prisoner, but they seemed disappointed.

So little booty.

In the breast pocket from which one of the soldiers had lifted my fountain pen, there were also the two rings that I had taken off, but he didn't notice them.

After a few more pushes and kicks, a bottle made the rounds. To my utter surprise, I was offered a drink and angered them even more when I refused. I can't explain my reasoning. Perhaps I declined out of fear. In any case, it was a grave mistake and it almost cost me my life. I remember being thrown down, kicked in the ribs, stepped on in my face, and one of the soldiers fired with a submachine gun into the ground, so close that the dirt from the impact sprayed over my body and hit my face. They emptied the bottle and threw it against my head. Surprisingly, it did not knock me out or kill me. They kept shouting and it sounded threatening, but not able to understand what I was being told, I just remained lying where I was. Less than an hour must have passed when the clamoring stopped.

One of them, probably an observer, must have spotted something alarming. Movements of approaching Germans? At the edge of the grove, they had positioned a machine gun and camouflaged it. They started firing.

Despite their inebriation, or perhaps because of it, they fired relentlessly. I couldn't see anything except this Russian machine gun nest. Two of the soldiers were at the machine gun. The others fired in the same direction with submachine guns. No shots seemed to come our way. Nevertheless, I took cover.

Then, with little planning, I seized the opportunity.

No one seemed to be watching me. I rose up, leaped behind a tree, lowered my pants and squatted, pretending to have a bowel movement.

My captors, while firing, had lost sight of their prisoner, at least long enough for me to take off.

When facing death, it's easy to risk death. Without hesitating, I took my life in my own hands.

Keeping as close to the ground as possible, I distanced myself from the encampment. The shooting continued, I pulled up my pants and then started running toward the silo.

I did not expect Hannes to still be around, but thought that from there I might have a chance to make a big swoop to return to the village, to *Oblt.* Gutschke and his *Kampfgruppe.* I didn't think that I would ever get back to Berlin.

I reached the heap of straw and saw a wheel of the *Krad,* then Hannes. I was amazed!

Hannes seemed just as astounded as I was. "My God! What happened to you?"

"I made it! I can't believe that you are still here!"

"Your face?"

"The Russians beat me up!"

"Russians—where?"

"Over there." I pointed to the grove.

"How did you get over there? There is a machine gun nest there. I have been watching them. They celebrated after they took the grove. No one was there—they seized it without resistance."

I briefly told him of my capture and escape.

The Russian machine gun fire was still going on, aimed toward the *Autobahn.* We were closer but heading in the opposite direction. Because of the trees, we were unable to see anything except great clouds of black smoke in the direction of the *Autobahn.*[142]

Hannes started the engine. "Off we go!"

"How will we get through?" I wondered.

"We just have to," Hannes replied, and then he added: "I'll run over everything!"

Still protected from view by the silo, he started slowly through the muddy field, but as soon as we reached the road he took off like a madman. Ahead of us was a forest and we wondered if enemy soldiers were waiting for us there.

We went with hazardous speed, jolting and bumping on the forest road. With all the strength I could muster, I held on to the handle on my seat.

As far as I could tell, we were never shot at. The Russians in the grove kept firing in the opposite direction.

The first stretch of the forest turned out to be a no-man's land. We encountered neither Russian nor German soldiers. Then after several kilometers, we ran again into convoys, German military retinues, and refugee treks.

I was in pain from the beating by the Russians. The bumpy

ride increased my misery. My head hurt and even more severely, my left rib cage. I was convinced that I had broken ribs.

It was a frenzied ride. We left the *Autobahn.* Past Fuerstenwalde, we encountered dense congestion. The roads were clogged even more than the day before with soldiers and home defense force fighters of all ages, most on foot, some with bicycles.

The sights of misery abounded with refugees, horse-drawn wagons, hand-pulled carts, and baby carriages, some with a child or even two children inside, others brimming with belongings. Sheep and goats tied to carts were dragged along, yammering. There were dogs, many running loose, yipping, yelping, and barking.

Scenes of misery, distress, and desolation.

I feared that most of them wouldn't survive and was thankful that my mother and siblings had found refuge at my grandfather's in Bavaria.

I was hurting physically to the point that I was almost numb.

I wanted Hannes to halt. He drove into the courtyard of a farm for a rest stop. The house seemed deserted, but then a very old woman appeared and asked us a startling question. It made my blood run cold. She thought that we might want to desert.

She inquired matter-of-factly: "Are you looking for a hiding place?"

"*Nein!*" Hannes replied emphatically, "We need to go to the bathroom."

This farmhouse still had an outhouse and the old woman showed us where it was, not giving up on the idea that we might want to stow away until the war was over.

"On the upper floor in the barn there are refugees who can't go on, men among them."

"We have to get back to Berlin," I explained.

She shrugged, but insisted that we have something to eat and drink before going on. She brought a side of smoked pork, sliced some bread, and heated up some milk for us. She also turned on the radio. The reception was poor, and while eating I didn't pay much attention to the music until it was interrupted and an announcer cut in with an announcement. It was directed to those guarding the capital, proclaiming basically the following:

> *Defenders of Berlin! The Bolshevists have assembled for the decisive attack on the German capital. Supported by every available means, they are now approaching the final goal of their mighty offensive: BERLIN!*
>
> *Toward Berlin! These words even resurrect the dead! With the promise "just one more city to conquer and then the war is over and you can go home," the Jewish commissars of the Red Army incited their soldiers.*
>
> *At stake is the Reich capital.*
>
> *At stake are countless German women and children. They look to Berlin's defenders. They look up to you! They expect you to fight with fanatical hatred to beat the Bolshevists. Make them bleed to death! Turn every house into a fortress! Turn every street into a mass grave! Bury the red horde!*
>
> *Top their hatred with even greater hatred for them!*
>
> *Fight to the last!*
>
> *Seek bloody vengeance and thousandfold revenge for the atrocities committed by the Bolshevists in our homeland!*

Then the announcer went on to list assembly points for civilian home defenders.

The old woman listened, too, mumbling: "Poor devils."

Hannes and I thanked her and took off.

She mumbled: "Tomorrow the Russians will be here," and sort of waved good-bye. It looked almost like a wave of disgust.

At the outskirts of Berlin, anti-tank barricades slowed us down again. Not very far from us, Russian artillery shells exploded. By the time we reached the *Reich* Youth headquarters, *Rjfr.* Axmann's command post, it was late afternoon and as was typical of Hannes, he remarked: "Lucky break! We made it against all odds." And then he observed sardonically that we were down to the last drops of gasoline.

CHAPTER 51

Dr. Gertrud

I was taken aback when I realized that Hannes was a Catholic. Now, he surprised me even more. He didn't want to accompany me to report to *Rjfr.* Axmann.

"You go!" he urged, "I have to look after the *Krad.*" Hannes saw in Axmann "a big shot" and avoided coming in direct contact with him. I am sure that it was not fear. But for some reason he felt uncomfortable having to face him. This was not the case with me. I looked forward to it and I wanted Hannes to accompany me. I prodded him to back me up when I had to explain our delayed return. But Hannes wouldn't budge. Unless the *Reichsjugendfuehrer* specifically requested his appearance, he insisted that I go alone. He was my driver and I was Axmann's courier. That's the way Hannes saw it and I couldn't change his mind.

As it turned out, *Rjfr.* Axmann was in conference, and it was his adjutant who asked me for a full report.

Before I had finished, *Rjfr.* Axmann stepped out of his office, took a look at me and asked if we had been in an accident. Apparently, I looked as if I had been thrown off the *Krad.*

"No!" I replied but before I was able to explain what happened, he asked: "And how does it look with Gutschke?"

"He urgently needs reinforcement!" And, just as Gutschke had done, I repeated: "Reinforcement! Reinforcement!"

Rjfr. Axmann lifted his artificial arm, signaling that he had to leave, but as if to reassure me, said sternly: "Will be taken care of!"

He left, obviously in a hurry, with a small entourage joined by the adjutant who had started to debrief me.

He never learned the whole story. Sent to the infirmary, I ended up telling it to the physician, a young woman I addressed as *Frau Doktor,* until I became aware that everyone else called her Dr. Gertrud. She was the female physician I had been introduced to previously. I became closely acquainted with her in the next week as the fighting progressed.

She treated my bruises and contusions with a black ointment. It looked and smelled like tar.

In her sickbay, Dr. Gertrud had already two or three patients waiting to be transported to a hospital. I believe they had been wounded during the last bombing raid. She wanted me to be transferred too, but I refused, maintaining that the *Reichsjugendfuehrer* needed me, even though I was injured. That was my decision and she accepted it, even praised me.

I needed to locate Hannes, get some sleep, and recover sufficiently for our next assignment.

My belief then was that *Rjfr.* Axmann would be able to strengthen *Kampfgruppe Gutschke* and that very shortly, support units would be on the way.

As it turned out, without reinforcement, they repelled another Russian attack. *Rjfr.* Axmann was notified of this through army channels. He shared the news with me, as if it constituted a major victory. How very proud he was of *Kampfgruppe Gutschke*, with its Hitler Youth elite fighters, and with its accomplishments.[143]

***

I was never superstitious, but since Hannes had a medallion he thought protected him, I reached for my two rings in my pocket. The Russians had not detected them. I decided that these two rings should be my talisman and put them back on; my mother's ring on my ring finger, Anne-Maria's on my little finger.

Our next mission (it must have been the afternoon of April 23) was to make contact with the advance unit of *Waffen-SS* General Felix Steiner's forces that were being pushed toward Berlin from the North. From there we were to head southwest toward Berlin and make contact with General Walter Wenck's advancing troops. A tall order for a rookie courier and his daredevil driver.

Hannes had given me a gasoline canister to take along on this ride.

"Just in case," he explained. "It might turn into a long trip."

With his usual recklessness, he raced through the streets, taking in stride all of the obstacles. In the outskirts, all kinds of troops clogged the highways. The word was that the Russian encirclement had been completed. There was no more way out.

But Hannes and I were not to be discouraged. Darkness approached and with just a slit-light (a headlight covered except for a slit), Hannes had to slow down. Even at lower speed, he didn't notice an oncoming motorcycle soon enough. He had to turn sharply to avoid a crash and lost control. We ended up in a ditch. My head somehow banged against the gasoline canister and my right leg was squeezed underneath the *Krad*.

More bruises, no broken bones.

Hannes made sure we retrieved the gasoline canister.

What now?

We approached the next village. There, in the *Gasthof* (restaurant), a group of *Reich* Labor Force girls were housed and served us a split-pea soup.

The girls were packed and ready to go, but the vehicles to pick them up were long overdue, causing concern and bedlam.

Some yelled at each other, a few were crying.

Hannes and I were mobbed with questions. Some of the girls gave us cigarettes and chocolate.

They wanted to leave on foot but where to?

I have no recollection what they decided to do. Hannes and I got a few hours of sleep in the *Gasthaus* and took off again before dawn.

We didn't get far on our way to Oranienburg. Artillery thunder surrounded us, and suddenly we were in the midst of an enemy attack with bullets whizzing by, right and left.

We tried to find cover.

As we would learn later, we were shot at by Polish soldiers. The *Krad* was hit. Holding on to the handle of the back seat, my hand was pierced by a bullet; the little finger practically shot off, dangling on tendons and skin. Anne-Maria's ring was gone. I was bleeding profusely. Hannes stopped, tied a cord around my hand joint to reduce the bleeding. In the wheels of our *Krad,* some spokes were cut and bent but there was still air in the tires. We decided there was no chance to complete our mission and we would return to headquarters.

With the motor still running, Hannes took off like mad hitting pot holes and circumventing debris. It turned into a wild and painful ride. At one point retreating soldiers on bicycles were stopped and assigned to a local, last-ditch fighting unit, but we were cleared to proceed and returned to Hitler Youth headquarters at Kaiserdamm.

This time, Hannes had to report to *Rjfr.* Axmann's adjutant.

I rushed right to Dr. Gertrud's treatment room. She aligned the bone of my small finger on the left hand, dressing it with a wooden splint as support. She gave me two injections. One was for pain; the other one was a tetanus shot.

Dr. Gertrud thought that I needed a blood transfusion. No blood was available. I did not want to be transferred to a military hospital.

Rjfr. Axmann had made it known that he needed Hannes and me. Dr. Gertrud was present when I, wanting to impress *Rjfr.* Axmann, assured him with "I am up to it!" while she insisted that, in my condition, I could not yet be released.

The outcome was that I would remain in Dr. Gertrud's care, but with a job to do. In a day or two, we would relocate.

Rjfr. Axmann put me in charge of transferring her, her patients, and her nurses and nurses' aids, to Axmann's new command post at the Party Chancellery on Wilhelmstrasse, across from the old *Reich* Chancellery.

***

During the days and nights from April 22 to May 2, 1945, crucial events followed each other in rapid succession throughout the days and nights. My existence was thought by the decision-makers to be insignificant, ready to be sacrificed together with so many others. Men and women. Boys and girls.

Of all the girls helping Dr. Gertrud, I still recall the first names of three: Renate and Gudrun and Lotte (or Charlotte).

Renate, always at Dr. Gertrud's side, was her helping hand, a physician's assistant, probably a medical student aspiring to become a doctor. I remember her emotional bursts. "What have the Russians done to you?" she would ask a new arrival and then bite her lips. Or: "Isn't it horrible how they have hurt you? And then shake her head. Those wounded severely, she would touch, putting her hand on a forehead or caressing a cheek. She kept holding the hand of one who had just died.

Gudrun was a nurse's aid assigned the duties of a "sister." As mentioned before, nurses were (and still are) called "sisters" in Germany. I believe that she was from Bremen, a no-nonsense type of person with great physical strength. She lifted and carried the wounded onto the truck when we evacuated them from the infirmary on Kaiserdamm. Days later, she volunteered to help out in the *Reich* Chancellery emergency ward, which was overcrowded and understaffed.

Lotte emerged out of nowhere.

Aside from these three, there were so many others, unsung female heroes, sucked into the hellish cauldron of one of the war's last battles.

Had they been members of the conquering forces, they would have been looked upon, historically, as heroines. Their names would be emblazoned on monuments, memorializing their heroism.

But they happened to be Germans. Germans in Hitler's Germany. Germans at the very end of a lost war, disintegrating in the final destruction of matter and minds.

***

Before the transfer of Dr. Gertrud's sickbay, Hannes and I took another ride with orders to facilitate defense positions, keeping thoroughfares open for expected relief forces.

Notifications had to be delivered to *Kampfgruppen* at Spandau, at the Pichelsdorf bridges and in the Olympic stadium. In various sections of Berlin where *HJ-Volkssturm* units were positioned, decimated forces had to be consolidated. At Axmann's headquarters, over a dozen *Melders* (couriers) had been assembled to dispatch these orders. With Franz-Karl, *Der Kleine,* Hannes and myself included, there probably were as many as twenty.

Most were Berliners and we were called the *Melder Brigade* (Courier Brigade). "Platoon" would have been a more appropriate designation.

A bicycle had been assigned to most. The only exceptions were Franz Karl Kepler, who brought along a small motorbike and Hannes and I, with our *Zuendapp.*

Axmann himself had a *Kuebelwagen* (military version of the Volkswagen). I don't recall the name of his first driver. He had been wounded near the park of Charlottenburg Castle and Erich became Axmann's next driver, at least until we had moved into the cellar of the Party Chancellery. Hannes and Erich knew each other. They seemed to be friends.

Neither was still with us a week later at the breakout.

I remember that Axmann's adjutant, who had assigned all of the destinations and who had individually handed out the orders, waited impatiently for the return of the couriers—mostly in vain. Only two or three of the couriers returned.

We had parted in good spirits.

We had been told what orders our envelopes contained, in case we had to destroy them.

Hannes and I delivered commands to hold out to the very end.

***

Among the Hitler Youth leadership, it was not a secret but discussed openly that "with General Weidling there had been trouble" and that "Axmann was upset."

But what about?

We couriers did not know and I doubt that the *Kampfgruppen* leaders were told. I am certain that only his closest associates, high-ranking Hitler Youth leaders, were informed what the dispute was all about.

Now we know, based on interrogation reports published in a Russian military journal, that General Weidling had asked *Rjfr.* Axmann to dissolve all of the *Volkssturm* Hitler Youth troops. He had wanted to send the boys home and save their lives!

Not so *Rjfr.* Axmann. His intent was to hold out to the end. He was determined to prove to his *Fuehrer* that the youth would keep on fighting and remain loyal until victory or death! I can attest to this.

Axmann had expressed frequently in my presence that "the *Fuehrer* can depend on his Hitler youth." In Axmann's eyes, we were "Hitler's youth;" our lives belonged to him, and whatever he asked of us, we had to fulfill.

Rjfr. Axmann must have known by then that there was no new miracle weapon ready to be deployed, but he did not tell us.

Hitler, who at the end felt betrayed by his generals, never felt betrayed by Axmann and the Hitler Youth. Among Hitler's last thoughts was how to reward *Rjfr.* Axmann.

The nation, or what was left of it, was hemorrhaging.

Rjfr. Axmann's last orders to his units—bypassing Gen. Weidling—were delivered as orders from the *Fuehrer,* the Commander-in-Chief. They were given after *Rjfr.* Axmann had participated in situation conferences with the *Fuehrer.*

When later on, in discussions with historians I pointed out that Axmann gave orders directly to Hitler Youth units defending Berlin, no one believed me. Finally, Carl Diem, the then Secretary of the German Olympic Committee, who had joined the *Volkssturm,* mentioned in his memoirs a dialogue with Dr. Schluender, stating clearly that orders for Schluender came directly from the *Fuehrer.* The couriers were Hannes and I.

There can be no doubt that the two dispatches Hannes and I delivered did not contain orders issued by the military but by *Rjfr.* Axmann, who had received them from Hitler directly or had issued them the way Hitler had wanted them to be promulgated. Not only was the military commander being by-passed but also Bormann, who otherwise had all of Hitler's last orders dispatched through his own radio station in the Party Chancellery.

It was obvious to me that Axmann and Bormann disliked each other. Bormann felt superior because he had unrestricted access to Hitler.

Only following the birthday reception did Axmann gain access and he used it to demonstrate his absolute loyalty. To disband the Hitler Youth as Gen. Weidling had requested would have been treason.

***

The transfer of Dr. Gertrud's infirmary was performed at night. I thought it to be safer to move during darkness. I am not sure of the date, but most likely it was the night of April 23/24. A major offensive by Soviet forces was expected, but prior to this attack, our forces were anticipated to arrive from the West and from the North. We became familiar with the names of General Wenck and General Steiner.

Hannes had to repair our motorcycle. My left hand was in a cast.

Some of the staff of the *Reichsjugendfuehrung,* much higher in rank, had been assigned to assist me with this mission to move the sickbay.

We were unable to find an ambulance and, finally, located an old delivery truck called a *Holzgaser* because it ran on charcoal.

The transfer turned into an all-night operation because with only one *LKW* it required six runs, three each from the Hitler Youth headquarters to the police building and then another three from there to the Party Chancellery.

Our last departure was delayed. Two of the wounded were to be picked up by a military hospital ambulance.

We waited. It never arrived.

We couldn't leave those two behind all alone in the infirmary, and with Dr. Gertrud gone already, I decided to take them along, despite their serious conditions.

We were also asked to take along the last remaining supplies and even weapons—some submachine guns and *Panzerfaeuste*.

Delayed by over an hour, the situation had changed drastically. It was Hannes who suggested the alternate route. He was a Berliner and knew his city. We followed him. I sat next to the driver in the *LKW*. Before we had completed our detour, just at daybreak, we were caught in a sudden barrage of fire. Unable to make a U-turn, we had to stop in a driveway of a partially demolished corner house. We carried the wounded to temporary safety.

I told the driver to stay with the injured and with the girls. Then, armed with a submachine gun and a bazooka, I crossed the street.

I could see two Russian tanks, wide-tracked T-34's with sloping armor, followed by several infantrymen. A startling sight. I decided to run through backyards into the cellar of the house the first T-34 was approaching. The tanks fired into the buildings ahead, including the one where our wounded and the girls had found cover.

The sub-basement room I entered was small with narrow windows at street-level height. The glass had been blown out. Just a few sharp edges remained in the frame.

Now I couldn't see the Russian foot soldiers anymore. Did our *LKW* driver or even some of the girls shoot at them? Had they sought cover? Could they already be in the house above me?

I kept looking.

Apparently, no German Pak or artillery was located anywhere near.

The first T-34 rolled again, following a shoot-and-go pattern. When nearing the building where I was, the cellar floor and walls trembled. The noise caused by the chains was horrid. For seconds I was terribly frightened. Now, the distance between the tank and me could not have been more than 20 feet.

It was more than flesh and blood could bear. There I was—not calculating; just following my instinct; using my cast to raise the bazooka. I aimed then pressed the handle with my other hand, closing my eyes for just a fraction of a second...Boom!!! There was no recoil.

Hitting the tank appeared to be more like a burst than an explosion. The cellar cubicle was small and the bazooka's exhaust, repelled from the wall, had cauterized the skin of my neck and singed my hair. The smoke made me cough and my eyes tear.

The Russian tank, engulfed in a black cloud, didn't move anymore. I saw flames leaping through the smoke and a soldier running to the other side of the street. Was my bazooka discharge a direct hit?

I did not know how many men made up the crew of a T-34. I saw only the silhouette of one. He got away. There must have been more inside such a big tank—two, three, perhaps even four?

Although it had been instilled in us to hate our enemy, ever since I had seen the faces of the young Russian soldiers whose prisoner I had been for an hour or so, I thought of them as human beings. Even though they had beaten me up badly, my concept of the enemy had changed from abstract, abominate beings to be despised, to soldiers who fought as we. Of course, I still believed that God was with us and we, guided by our great *Fuehrer*, fought for the right cause.

Since to burn to death was my greatest fear, I wished that the tank crew wouldn't experience a tortuous death in their blazing tank but hoped that all would be able to get out. Once I had felt blameworthy after I guided the blind Jewish woman across the street, now I just wished that the enemy soldiers wouldn't burn to death.

***

Shaking, I ventured back to the *LKW* to get another *Panzerfaust*.

From there, I entered the corner house. There was smoke all over. In the hallway I made out three or four girls, each with a bazooka.

"No! Back down into the cellar!" I demanded sternly. But they ignored me.

I turned to Hannes for help, but he turned his back on the girls.

"If they want to fight, let them fight!"

"They are nurses' aides."

To Hannes it did not matter.

Hannes and I climbed upstairs; I went ahead with an automatic assault rifle navigating through heavy debris. Not all of the steps held up, several were loose and some were missing.

Hannes carried two bazookas, his and mine.

Through a hole in the brick wall, I looked down the street. On the other side on the sidewalk, leaning against the building, a few Russian infantry soldiers could now be seen. In this position, they fired wildly at the windows in the corner house. I aimed and shot at them. Soon they were out of sight. Had they found cover in a cellar shaft or were they retreating?

Now, only the second tank was in sight, passing the burning one, almost ramming it. The street was hardly wide enough for two T-34s to pass.

Although this tank was not yet within *Panzerfaust*-range, I signaled Hannes to bring me mine.

Then something unexpected happened! I couldn't believe my eyes. Lotte suddenly appeared on the street. She carried a *Panzerfaust*.

She raced into the middle of the street.

"Back off!" I shouted as loud as I could. It wasn't loud enough.

She stopped for a second, aimed, fired the bazooka, ran to the other side of the street and disappeared as fast as she had appeared.

With the Russian soldiers near the tank, and she having crossed their firing line, I thought that surely she would lose her life. She had scored—point-blank! A direct hit with a single, handheld bazooka. She also reached the other side of the street, found cover and survived.

***

Two or three days later, *Rjfr.* Artur Axmann received the Golden Cross of the German Order. The date was most likely April 26. Hitler surprised him with this, Germany's highest decoration. Hitler personally awarded it to Axmann who later reported the following dialogue:

"Without your boys, the battle could not be continued, not just here in Berlin, but in all of Germany."

"Those are your boys, my *Fuehrer!*"

I was present when Axmann, wearing this order like a Knight's Cross, returned to our room in the Party Chancellery. His words to us were *"Fuer Treue! Fuer uns alle!* (For loyalty! For all of us!).

A day after *Rjfr.* Axmann received his Golden Cross of the German Order; I was awarded the Iron Cross First Class and the silver badge for the wounded. I also was awarded a tank destruction stripe. Lotte received the Iron Cross Second Class and her tank destruction stripe as well. Axmann decorated me. Dr. Getrud decorated her.

I would see Lotte occasionally in Dr. Gertrud's new quarters with the wounded and remember seeing her for the last time during the night of the breakout. She again carried a *Panzerfaust.* Most of the other girls did not. Within hours, according to historical accounts, Dr. Gertud and several of her girls were killed. I don't know whether Lotte was among them.

CHAPTER 52

The Party Chancellery

Axmann was impressed that we had succeeded without a single fatality to transfer Dr. Gertud's wounded, her nurses, and aides from the *Reich* Youth head office to the police precinct office on Sophie-Charlottenstrasse and from there to the Party Chancellery.

Martin Bormann was the party's leader and, as such, head of the Party Chancellery at 64 Wilhelmstrasse. Now it became the command post for *Rjfr.* Axmann, who occupied the air-raid shelter of Bormann's office building. Bormann was functioning as Hitler's right hand and stayed mostly in the bunker with him.

When we arrived we realized that we had not been expected. Storage boxes and rummage had to be cleared out. One of Bormann's department heads objected to us taking records into the backyard. But we needed space. There were no field cots anywhere; we had to get them from the air raid shelter in the cellars of the Propaganda Ministry.

Dr. Gertud's new sickbay would soon become a first aid station and turn into an emergency hospital on a smaller scale than that under the *Reich* Chancellery.

Space was at a premium. In fact, *Rjfr* Axmann did not occupy a private room. He lodged in his command post and shared his quarters with three members of his staff; his adjutants, Boldt and Weltzin; and me, his staff courier.

The Navy personnel that staffed the radio room located in the air-raid shelter had their own officer-in-charge at the Party Chancellery. Their commander, Vice-Admiral Hans-Erich Voss, the

Navy's liaison officer at Hitler's headquarters, was in the *Reich* Chancellery. I didn't know him, but because of his uniform, I would have noticed him had I seen him. Apparently, during the last days of the war, he never set foot into the navy's radio station for which I had become a back-up runner. The dangers crossing Wilhelmstrasse had become too great and the Vice-Admiral remained in the safety of either the *Reich* Chancellery or the *Fuehrerbunker.*

The Party Chancellery was located across from the old *Reich* Chancellery. Hitler's architect, Albert Speer, had built the new *Reich* Chancellery adjacent to the old one. All of the Chancellery buildings were still recognizable despite hollowed windows and damage caused by past air attacks, as well as recent impacts.

Portions of the garden's stone wall had also been blown away. In the Chancellery garden, small fires generated smoke that concealed some of the corpses; twice I stumbled over stiff bodies that had not been buried.

In some of the historical literature (e.g. *Berlin Now and Then— After the Battle,* London, 1992), an underground crossing is shown between the *Vorbunker* and the building next to us occupied by personnel of the *Propaganda Ministerium. Rjfr.* Axmann and his staff, myself included, did not know of a subterranean tunnel below Wilhelmstrasse.

If there was such a pathway below the street, by the time *Rjfr.* Axmann had moved with us into the Party Chancellery, it had either caved in or been totally obstructed. No underground access remained unused. Had we been able to reach just the adjacent cellar and from there been able to use a tunnel below, many casualties would have been avoided.

Wilhelmstrasse was under almost ceaseless barrage from Russian Katyushas. The stretch we had to use for crossing had become a burial pit. *Rjfr.* Axmann, who was proud of each of his boy's bravery, wanted to avoid—as much as possible—our exposure to open fire on our ways back and forth from the *Fuehrerbunker.*

From the time we moved into the cellars of the Party

Chancellery to the night of the breakout, at least 30—if not 50 or more—of them lost their lives. *Hitlerjungen,* Navy personnel and other soldiers—including several officers—were killed or wounded, including almost all the couriers of the Naval radio station.

Various Berlin Hitler Youth leaders, such as Hamann, Bartel, Siebert, etc., were among those who came to see Axmann and were killed either coming or leaving on deadly Wilhelmstrasse. Bodies covered the pavement in a variety of uniforms and in varied conditions, some maimed beyond recognition. Whenever we thought that the enemy firing must have reached its peak, it increased still further. The rain of metal caused candescent specks on impact, creating carpets of sparks.

Some bullets or shrapnel must have exploded upon impact and when they hit people, tore them to shreds. Of those badly wounded, we pulled several to safety and treatment by Dr. Gertrud. Some she could not save.

Care of the wounded was becoming increasingly oppressive. There was no more space to put them, and there was a shortage of bandages and medications. What seemed to frustrate Dr. Gertrud the most was the lack of water.

"Get water!" she would shout in desperation.

Water could only be gotten from the other side of Wilhelmstrasse. We started out using bulk marmalade containers, but their covers were not tight enough and they were too heavy; too cumbersome for running fast across Wilhelmstrasse. Finally, we got hold of some 10-liter metal containers.

I only carried water two or three times, as I had to deliver ever more frequently, urgent dispatches. But until the end, the youngest of the runners—including *der Kleine* (13-year-old Dieter Schroeder) and some of the *BDM*-girls—faced the dangers again and again and continued to get water across Wilhelmstrasse. While transporting these canisters with the all-too-precious water, several lost their lives or were wounded, including *der Kleine* who, despite his own injuries, helped rescue one of the wounded girls.

There were no body bags and no blankets to spare. The dead

were put near the stairs and intermittently taken into the back-yard whenever the shelling subsided. But once it did not let up long enough and a direct mortar hit killed the two carriers, a *Hitlerjunge* and a *BDM*-girl, as they hauled their young comrade out to be buried.

In the end, I must admit, most of the fallen were left where they fell. I believe that *Rjfr.* Axmann's own brother was among them and *Adjutant* Theilacker's courier, a boy my age whose name I don't remember. Four or five of us crowded the exit, waiting for a pause. At the moment of a near-by explosion, Theilacker's courier made the sign of the cross and started running. Seconds later, in front of our eyes, he was hit.

"Straight into heaven!" commented one of the boys standing next to me.

"Let's get him!" I said, "He might still be alive!" Three of us took off, two to look after the fallen comrade; I went straight to the emergency entrance of the *Fuehrerbunker.* Once again, I made it.

Later, I learned that Theilacker's courier had died instantly.

When I reported it to *Rjfr.* Axmann and *Adjt.* Theilacker, there was no comment. For a moment, it grew silent in the command post.

Of the ten to fifteen boys, ages 13 to 16, who had come along from the Hitler Youth administrative offices, we were down to three: Dieter Schroeder, now a patient himself in Dr. Gertrud's emergency hospital; Franz Karl Keppler; and I, constantly on courier runs.

Franz Karl was the son of the manager of the Gatow-guesthouse. Once we talked about the book *Rjfr.* Axmann had brought to our attention, written by Richard Arndt who, at the age of 15, had participated in the First World War. Titled *"At The Age of Fifteen at the Front-Line,"* it described the boy's experiences in the Battle of Verdun.

In World War I, Richard Arndt was an exception. At the end of World War II, fifteen-year-olds fought bravely in great numbers.

In a conversation with Franz Karl, we reassured ourselves that we matched Arndt's bravery and naïve as we were, thought we also deserved a glorious page in the book of history.

As insane as this may appear today, we remained determined to live up to our *Fuehrer's* expectations. Our mood was numbed but we kept going, still driven by great faith and idealism.

***

Many survivors' memoirs and historical accounts, place at the end of April 1945, a radio station inside the Propaganda Ministry. There might have been one, but if so, I doubt that it was still functioning. Or, if still in operation, it must have lacked access to the then all-important Navy and Party ciphers.

According to *Rjfr.* Axmann, both *Reich* Press Secretary Lorenz, and *Reich* Secretary Dr. Naumann, used our radio room in the Party Chancellery to dispatch and receive messages.

Rjfr. Axmann might have known to whom they went and what they contained since both Lorenz and Dr. Naumann had had private conferences with him at his command post in the cellars of the Party Chancellery.

Lorenz had legal access to enemy broadcasts and kept Axmann advised, although I have no recollection of having seen him in person. However, he was talked about a lot. I did see and even talked to Dr. Naumann who came to see *Rjfr.* Axmann several times. I left the room when they conferred. The location of our *Funkstelle* was so close to the Propaganda Ministry that by some it might have been thought of as being located in Dr. Goebbels' domain instead of Bormann's.

It is known that Bormann kept matters concerning his activities as confidential as possible. He might not have wanted Army and Air Force officers to know that there was a Navy facility in his Party Chancellery. The Navy might have taken over the radio station in Bormann's Party Chancellery as a military necessity. From the very first time I appeared there, only uniformed Navy personnel were present, never a party functionary.

CHAPTER 53

Last Missions with Hannes

Hannes and I were not able to complete two courier missions. We were unable to reach the spearhead unit of General Steiner's troops because they had not arrived. Our attempt to reach *Kampfgruppe* Heissmeyer in Spandau was prevented by a *Waffen-SS* officer who, at a barricade on the highway leading to Spandau, ordered us to return. I could have continued on foot but after my experiences at Petersdorf/Jacobsdorf, I decided not to.

It was customary for Axmann to call a Hitler Youth fighting unit by the name of its leader and he made no exception with the *Jungmannen* unit from the *NAPOLA* in Potsdam. He called them *Kampfgruppe* Heissmeyer just as *Kampfgruppe* Gutschke had been assigned the name of its leader.

The *NAPOLA* fighters themselves had no knowledge of Axmann's designation, especially since their commander, *SS-Gruppenfuehrer* August Heissmeyer, had left them already. It never crossed Axmann's mind that Heissmeyer could no longer be in Spandau. But he wasn't! After a rousing "keep on fighting" speech he had left his boys.

Hannes and I frequently returned with valuable information, especially in regards to how far Russian forces had already advanced in those areas *Rjfr.* Axmann believed were still under German control. Spandau, we were told had already been encircled by the enemy.

Spandau, as I recall, was of special interest to Axmann. He envisioned a major battle to be fought there to end with a decisive defeat for the Russians.

Kampfgruppe Gutschke, as we knew, had been able to repel the Russian advances southeast of Breslau at Wansen and Weigwitz. *Kampfgruppe* Gutschke was a *Volkssturm* unit that was comprised of Hitler Youth leaders, members of a *WE-Lager* (pre-military training camp), and of students of the Adolf Hitler School in Wartha. In Spandau, there were no students of an Adolf Hitler School, but *Jungmannen* youth of the Spandau and Potsdam NAPOLAS. Their fanaticism, degree of bravery, and willingness to sacrifice themselves for their leader and the nation seemed identical. Axmann expected once again the elite of the German youth to be instrumental in repelling the Russians.

Heissmeyer was a much more prominent man than *Oblt.* Gutschke.

According to a historic novel, *Praised Be What Strengthens One (GELOBT SEI, WAS HART MACHT),*[144] Heissmeyer appeared in Spandau, and as just mentioned, addressed the boys to perform well in battle, and then took off in one of the last planes from Gatow to join his wife.

Rjfr. Axmann had, at that time, no knowledge of this, thinking that Heissmeyer would lead his boys into battle as Gutschke had done at Wansen, Weigwitz, and Jacobsdorf.

Both Hitler and Axmann kept pinning unrealistic hopes on what the Hitler Youth fighting units could accomplish, especially those comprised of predestined heroes.

The situation in Berlin was quite different from that in Breslau. The Silesian capital had been turned into a real fortress. The *Reich* capital instead had remained an open city, engulfed in flames and smoke, crowded with refugees, and mostly exhausted soldiers in need of sleep, food, and ammunition.

When a body is exhausted and starved, the mind inside this body eventually succumbs to a similar state. Hitler didn't see it that way. He believed in mind over matter regardless of circumstances.

I felt I was being put to the test. I was exhausted. We still had sufficient food and a cot for the few hours of sleep. And, I, of course, felt close to the center of power from where the order for the deployment of the secret weapon would come. Yet I had my moments. Periods of total numbness. Instances when I felt dragged down, ready to collapse. Usually, it was *Rjfr.* Axmann who pulled me up again.

***

Only years after the war would I know for sure that there had been no new weapon ready to be deployed. That since the end of March even the production of the so-called vengeance weapons, the V-1s, the "buzz bombs," and the V-2s, the first and only ballistic missiles in action, had ceased.

These were manufactured underground, mostly by slave laborers and by *KZ*-inmates, and the advancing Allied Forces had ended production at least three weeks prior to Hitler's birthday when he had talked of a life-saving medicine for a dying patient.

In the sixties, through a relative in Communist East Germany, I was given access to Julius Mader's account of *The Secret of Huntsville,* published by Deutscher Militaerverlag. I learned of Camp Dora, an underground tunnel factory where rocket science had its origin.

It was not a typical factory, not even a typical concentration camp, but by terms used today, the mother of all concentration camps. It was a place where enslaved people of various nationalities, Germans included, were tormented, tortured, abused to the utmost! Deaths occurred in cruel and inhumane ways.

Having been warned that this East German publication might be Communist propaganda, I engaged in some research and located a civilian engineer who had first-hand knowledge of Camp Dora and was captured on April 11,1945. He was very hesitant about sharing recollections, but he confirmed the camp's existence. At times, he said, the frightening losses of life increased to the point that, for short periods, production was slowed down until new *"Menschenmaterial"* (humans, seen as matter or substance) arrived. They could be driven harshly to catch up with the quotas.

***

A couple of days before I received the Iron Cross First Class, Hannes and I came close to being executed—put to death for desertion! We were returning from a run to the Pichelsdorf bridges where Dr. Schluender and his *Kampfgruppe* were located. On our way back, we had to deliver an order for the Berlin *HJ-Leader,* Otto Hamann. He was not at his command post. Short of time, we left Axmann's orders with a member of his staff. Axmann had told me the nature of this order—"If and when needed, send reinforcements to Dr. Schluender." Schluender, in turn, was advised that, on demand, reinforcements were available and he was not to retreat regardless of casualties.

We continued back to the Chancellery and Hannes, as he so often did, chose side streets.

The controversy over how many *Hitlerjungen* were in combat near the Havel bridges, at Heerstrasse and other locations of bitter street fighting, is still going on. Based on what Hannes and I saw, those located at the Havel bridges probably were in the hundreds. But if all other *HJ-Kampfgruppen* in the area, especially the fortress regiment in the *Reich* Athletic Field, were added in, I find the number of 5,000 quite realistic. The Athletic Field was a huge complex, including not only the Olympic Stadium but also many administration buildings. At the time we drove through there, we saw many members of the *Reich* Labor Service and several large formations of Hitler Youths, as if assembling for a mass rally. (The Hitler Youth fortress regiment from Koenigsberg was also expected but had not yet arrived.)

This afternoon, as always, the streets were clogged with apparently leaderless formations—civilians and animals among them. Repeatedly, we ran into a congestion of soldiers and refugees; of homeless with their belongings reduced to what they could carry; of children, probably with many orphans among them; and of animals, most of them abandoned.

My devotion to animals, and especially dogs, caused me great pain as I saw how cruelly the war that man waged affected them. Many memories I now have of this war are so grisly; they still make my stomach churn, like those of a horse being cut up before it was dead. An old woman with a tin cup collecting blood from a slaughtered dog.

***

I will never forget the sight of the big bucket. A laundry tub from the medical operating room filled with putrefied dressing, blood, and amputated human limbs. Someone had put the tub in front of the old Chancellery exit and left it there, awaiting a break in the bombardment to be disposed of.

In the streets, several headless bodies were most likely the result of decapitation.

Compared with these, the sight Hannes and I encountered that afternoon was relatively innocuous, but shocking because it was a boy. He dangled from a post. A lad, in a torn *Volkssturm* uniform was hanged with a clothesline, his right ear half torn off, with blood all over his right side. No poster explained why. His neck had apparently been broken after the hangman had put his head in the noose and pulled up the rope. His hands were tied behind his back; his legs were tied together at the ankles. He had the face of a teen-ager and could have been anywhere from thirteen to sixteen years old.

There was no *HJ* armband on his sleeve. Perhaps it had been removed. It would have suggested that a Hitler Youth was a coward.

I remembered when *Rjfr.* Axmann was informed that some boys had been hanged, his response had been: "For sure not any of our boys!"

Now I wonder—who were "our boys?" By law, all of Germany's boys and girls belonged to the Hitler Youth.

This youthful, rundown "deserter" Hannes and I viewed brought home to us that the publicized directives from Bormann, Goebbels—or whoever—were not mere threats but, indeed, carried the death penalty. It applied to all who failed to defend the city—including youngsters like us.

For a moment, I remembered the radio announcements we had listened to in the farmhouse when returning from Petersdorf, and also the recent proclamations published in the *Panzerbaer* (literally *Tank Bear,* a newspaper for the fighting troops):

Whoever, at this moment, doesn't fulfill his duty is a traitor, a traitor of our nation . . . And when the point is reached that the weak think the end has come, then the strong have to carry on . . . The fight has to go on and harder and more fanatical than ever . . . Where the Fuehrer is, there is victory! There can be no more consideration of one's personal fate. Fight, die or be declared and treated like a traitor!

How many were executed?

Neither near the *Reichssportfeld* nor on the last day of the war in the Voss Strasse did I see boys hanged in rows. However, since Hannes and I were almost hanged, too, there might have been many.

Looking down the street, Hannes and I saw the many white flags (mostly sheets) hanging out of windows and from balconies.

How did it happen?

We were stopped by a young *Waffen-SS* NCO. He asked us for the password. We had not been informed by anyone about a password.

Behind the young NCO was an older man who appeared to be wearing a long coat without insignia. It might have been that of a police officer. However, on this coat, he wore an Iron Cross First Class. One didn't wear medals on an overcoat. It seemed so out of place, even to Hannes, who remarked: "This he most likely swiped from a fallen comrade." There were no other medals on his coat and no Iron Cross Second Class stripe. One had to be awarded the Iron Cross Second Class, before qualifying for the First Class Iron Cross.

Something seemed phony about this old man and the way he behaved. He shot at the white flags along the street. We didn't see any fall. His aim must have been poor. He made a nonchalant

ARMIN D. LEHMANN

remark: "From here you either end up on the gallows or you return back into battle."

"We are couriers from the *Reich* Chancellery," I explained.

The NCO gave me a push, saying, "Don't lie to me!"

"I am not!" I replied emphatically.

He got angry and now our troubles began.

Hannes didn't have a pay-book. He produced as identification a membership pass of the motorized *HJ* and his driver's license. He explained how he became my driver at the *Reich's* Youth Leader Headquarters on April 21.

The NCO didn't believe him, commenting: "Retreating from battle, no doubt about it!"

Then he asked me for identification and I had two paybooks on me, one as a recruit from the *Waffen-SS* and the other one as member of the *Volkssturm*. The NCOs immediate conclusion: I was a deserter from the *Waffen-SS*, now pretending to belong to the *Volkssturm*.

He decided that we did not have the proper papers and were not authorized to retreat on a motorcycle. Even my entry permit to the *Fuehrerbunker* signed by *Gruppenfuehrer* Johann Rattenhuber, Hitler's last chief security officer, didn't seem to make much of an impression. Hannes whispered: "He has his eyes on our motorcycle."

The only weapons Hannes and I carried were pistols. After the Russian soldier in Jacobsdorf had taken my small caliber Walther, both Hannes and I were issued one each of the model worn by high-ranking Hitler Youth Leaders.

I no longer had a courier pouch. It had remained with one of the Russian soldiers who had briefly captured me west of Petersdorf. But I had in my breast pocket a folded dispatch from *Obergebietsfuehrer* Dr. Schluender. I didn't feel authorized to open it, but it was clearly addressed to *Reichsjugendfuehrer* Axmann. Once again, I came across someone who insisted that our *Reichsjugendfuehrer* was Baldur von Schirach, and who was unaware that, for almost five years now, Artur Axmann was in charge of the nations' youth.

Had Axmann's name not been constantly in the news since the Hitler Youth had entered the war? What was the matter with this guy?

Could someone that ignorant make a live-or-die decision about Hannes and myself!

I had escaped the Russians twice. Now, we were on an important mission with military orders from Axmann that might even have originated with Hitler.

And here we were, stopped by whom? An old police officer whose behavior seemed questionable and a *Waffen-SS Unterfuehrer* who did not appear to be disabled in any way. He should be fighting in the battle zone and defending the women and children of Berlin, I thought.

"Follow me!" the young sergeant ordered.

I, with my two paybooks, and Hannes, with his papers in hand, were taken inside the corner house down into the cellar. There were several women and, behind a makeshift desk cluttered with records, a field telephone, and a briefcase, sat a really fat man (overweight people were a rarity in Germany during the last years of the war). He was an Emil Jannings type but with a facial expression more similar to Bormann's. He was also dressed in what appeared to me a "mystery" uniform of dark gray pants and a flock coat with the collar resembling those of Catholic priests. Was this a World War I uniform?

Why would an officer of a Home Defense Auxiliary unit be the superior of a *Waffen-SS Unterfuehrer?* Was this fat official a man of the law? Could he have ordered the hanging of the boy outside?

I told this officer what I had told the NCO, and to my surprise and great relief, he used the telephone and apparently was able to get through to the *Reich* Chancellery and checked out that what I had told him was true.

He warned us: "The Russians are listening in and know that you are coming." Hannes replied that we would take an alternate route back. I had no idea where the Russians would be waiting for us and was glad that Hannes, the Berliner, was with me.

The female volunteers in the cellar were not young *RAD* girls as Hannes and I had encountered days ago at the *Gasthaus.* These were middle-aged and older women, some of them in uniforms I was not familiar with. They probably belonged to relief agencies, maybe to the Labor Front or some other *NS*-organizations. Not until long after the war, when I read an appendix in Prof. Schenck's book, *The Emergency Hospital Below the Reich Chancellery,*[145] did I learn of the existence of a *Freikorps* Adolf Hitler, whose members were empowered to execute deserters.

***

Hannes and I were in urgent need of gasoline. But so was every-body else. As Axmann's couriers, we believed we deserved some preferential treatment. Even *Rjfr.* Axmann agreed. He ordered his chief administrator, *Gebietsfuehrer* Ludwig Grimm, to sign a requi-sition for a tank full of gasoline for our *Krad.* We went directly to the underground motor pool facing Hermann Goering Strasse. Lt. Col. Erich Kempka, Hitler's personal chauffeur was there but with-out paying much attention to our all-important requisition, he declared brusquely; "We are out of gasoline! Period!"

On Kempka's totem pole, *Rjfr.* Axmann's position must have been very low. Perhaps in Kempka's mind, too, Baldur von Schirach was still the head of the Hitler Youth.

I had orders and I took it upon myself to point out that Hannes and I carried dispatches directly from the *Fuehrer* to outposts such as the *Pichelsdorfer Bruecken.*

Once more, this time with even greater vehemence, Lt. Col. Kempka sized us up and stated sharply: "Not you two!"

Thereupon, Hannes made a mistake and turned to the garage manager. I believe he was *SS-Hauptsturmfuehrer* (Capt.) Karl Schneider. Hannes pointed to some barrels.

"Out of the question!" he was told angrily.

Hannes was sent to the Tiergarten to get gasoline. He never returned.

I don't even know if Hannes arrived there. Or whether or not he received gasoline and where he went from there. Did he have a *Schluck* (drink from his flask) to warm his soul and decide, like so many others, that the war was over?

Now we know why we could not get the gasoline from Kempka. Hitler had already requisitioned all of it to store in the underground garages so that his and his future wife's bodies could be burned beyond recognition.

Although Hannes did not return, I held on to his letter. If I am not mistaken, it was addressed to his mother. I never had a chance to post his letter. It must have been lost with all of my papers at the end.

The letter I had given him was addressed to Anne-Maria. The school in Hof that served as a military hospital still existed. The wounded and nurses remained there for several months after the war. It never found its way there. No doubt Hannes never posted it.

Months later, Anne-Maria told me that, having not heard from me and with the way things were going, she became convinced that I was no longer alive. She grieved. She kept all of the letters she had written to me but had been unable to post for lack of an APO number.

In Hof, there was no battle. The city surrendered. Anne-Maria had no indication that I was in Berlin, assigned to being Hitler's last courier. She was by then a prisoner but being a nurse, was kept on to continue her job. Her patients were now POWs as well. Later she would fall in love with an American G.I. whom she married. I, in turn, married an American school teacher.

M

CHAPTER 54

New Responsibilities

Since the move, my runs led through the Voss Strasse entrance into the emergency hospital and the adjacent air raid shelter that was also open to the public.

A lengthy subterranean passageway led to the upper bunker. From there, descending steps connected with the guarded main entrance of the lower bunker—the deepest one—Hitler's last quarters.

In the cellar adjacent to the air raid shelter on Voss Strasse, there were guard stations, the emergency military hospital, the telephone exchange, and officers' and guards' quarters.

What we—Axmann's staff, called the upper bunker and the lower bunker (the *Fuehrerbunker*) were actually located below the Chancellery garden, somewhere between the Old Chancellery and the Foreign Ministry. My memory is that there were two levels: the upper bunker in the garden, in my estimation, was on the same or a very similar level as the bottom cellar below the New *Reich* Chancellery, and deep down, one flight below, was the *Untere* bunker, Hitler's bunker, the *Fuehrerbunker.*

The subterranean garages could not be reached from Wilhelm Strasse but from Hermann Goering Strasse.

At the end, most of my missions delivering and receiving dispatches were between situation room and radio room. I also obtained and delivered medical supplies for Dr. Gertrud's makeshift first-aid ward located below the Party Chancellery from the emergency hospital below the new Chancellery.

It was a Navy ensign to whom *Rjfr.* Axmann had offered my services as a back-up courier. The Navy had lost most of their runners. Communications from Hitler, Bormann, and others in the *Zitadelle* (citadel) to be sent off to outside military commanders, as well as to party district leaders, were increasing at a rapid pace.

Despite the dangers looming with each run, I remained filled with pride, being given such important assignments, delivering messages right into the bunker headquarters of the Commander-in-Chief. To my indoctrinated way of thinking, we could be near the victorious end of the war. To my mind, the Wenck and Steiner armies were on their way and the secret weapon was finally being readied for deployment.

The Navy ensign who instructed me on strict delivery procedures and who stressed the urgency factor, was aware that *Rjfr.* Axmann had pledged the life of us *Hitlerjungen* to take Hitler into our midst and then break out of this cauldron. Thus, he was quick to express that he was sure of my stout-heartedness, but then he stressed that courage alone was not enough. Courier assignments required an understanding of how important each run was and an unswerving determination to succeed. Obviously, the ensign saw in me an immature youngster whose bravery had been established but whose sagacity was that of an adolescent.

From a historical perspective, my becoming one of Hitler's last couriers, if not the last, certainly goes to show that the manpower level of his fighters had reached rock bottom. It would take a couple more weeks before I came to realize how pathetically puny conditions were at the time Hitler's and Bormann's last radio dispatches were entrusted to me. I ran—ran my heart out. No unnecessary time was ever to be lost under any circumstances. If I, for example, was also expected to return with medical supplies, I would not get them first from the emergency hospital, but only after I had delivered the dispatch envelope to the ante-situation room.

Which of the now famous orders—such as those that told when to expect Wenck's attack and advising Doenitz that he was to become Hitler's successor—I delivered, I am not certain.

However, I know for sure that I took the incoming telegram from *Gauleiter* Karl Hanke, party district leader, to the Goebbels family. It must have been on the 27th or 28th when *Gauleiter* Hanke from Breslau sent a telegram to the Propaganda Minister and his wife. The Goebbels family had quarters in both the upper and the lower bunker. In the lower bunker, Dr. Goebbels had an office. In the upper bunker, the family occupied a suite of two or three rooms, their last living quarters. It was up to me to decide where to deliver the telegram, and I decided on the upper bunker. As it happened, Dr. Goebbels was just coming up from the lower bunker as his wife approached me with two of her children, the oldest girls, I believe.

I saluted and handed the envelope to Dr. Goebbels. He tore it open.

I still remember his reaction and that of his wife, probably verbatim.

Why?

Perhaps because this telegram was sent from Breslau. My father knew *Gauleiter* Hanke well, and now as political commander of the fortress, he had been constantly in the news. What I did not know at that time—and no one in my presence had ever talked about it—was that at the same time Dr. Goebbels was having an affair with Lida Baarova, (famous Czechoslovakian-born movie star), Mrs. Goebbels had a liaison with Hanke.

If Hitler himself had not intervened, the Goebbels would have divorced and married their new lovers.

Standing next to his wife, I became aware of how short Dr. Goebbels was.

He ripped open the envelope, took out the telegram and remarked: "Ah, from Hanke."

Mrs. Goebbels looked over his shoulder, saying: "Poor Karl, New Year's Eve all of us were still together."

Days later, I was directed to pick up a transmittal at the anteroom in the lower bunker.

Reichsleiter Bormann was there, but he didn't give it to me.

Despite the fact that he had seen me several times before, picking up dispatches, he asked as if refusing to believe: "Is this the courier?" "Yes," said the staff officer present, who took the dispatch envelope from Bormann and handed it to me.

I never knew what the contents were in the envelopes I had to deliver, but I can still see the radioman who opened this one shake his head in disbelief, saying: "My God, these children too!"

I saluted and left. Only after the war did it come to light that Bormann had directed, perhaps even ordered, his wife to kill their children—all ten of them—and then herself. (The oldest boy, however, was at a boarding school and not with his mother).

Even though I was in the bunker, I didn't know that Dr. and Mrs. Goebbels had decided to kill their children and then to commit suicide. They must have made this decision before April 28. On this date Hanna Reitsch left the bunker and Mrs. Goebbels gave her a letter addressed to Harald Quandt, her oldest son from a previous marriage. She informed him that:

> Our glorious ideas are approaching the end and therewith everything beautiful and venerable, noble and virtuous I have known in my life. The world that will succeed the Fuehrer and National Socialism will not be worth living in...

That, apparently, was what she believed to the very end.

M

CHAPTER 55

The Pilot

There were many service women in various uniforms as well as civilians in the cellars below the *Reich* Chancellery.

The first woman I recognized was the famous test pilot Hanna Reitsch, whom I had met when visiting her parents' house with my *Oma* in Hirschberg. What was she doing in this bunker? How had she come here?

I took a second look. No doubt, it was she.

Hanna Reitsch, looking not like a pilot at all but like an exhausted fighter who had just emerged from a foxhole, stood next to an Air Force officer on a stretcher. Apparently he was wounded, in fact, badly hurt. His eyes were closed. Although covered by an army blanket, he was still in his uniform. I noticed right away that in front of his collar, partly visible, was a Knight's cross of the Iron Cross with Oak Leaves and Swords covering the *Pour le Merit* (highest order for bravery awarded in WW I). He was a high-ranking officer with a Bismarck-like face and a huge nose. I knew what many of the war heroes looked like from pictures in magazines and newspapers. I didn't recall ever having seen this face. Who could he be?

The lower part of the blanket was drenched in blood and folded over by a physician or medic who, with a splint and bandages, was attending to the General's right foot. I couldn't tell if the foot was still firmly attached to the leg or if he would lose it. The General kept his eyes closed. He could have been unconscious. Behind me, two of the guards who had carried him on the stretcher through the passage to the *Notlazarett* (emergency hospital) were waiting for the dressing to be completed so they could carry the General to the *Fuehrerbunker* where Hitler was waiting for him.

One commented: "The little doll won't leave his side." She was still holding the General's hand and frequently stroked his forehead. I must have been the only one there who knew that this "little doll" was Hanna Reitsch, the courageous, highly decorated aviatrix. I saluted and said something like: "*Frau* Reitsch, I met you in Hirschberg..."

Indignant, she sharply interrupted me: "I am not *Frau* Reitsch, I am Air-Captain Reitsch!" She was the famous test pilot and I had extended military honors to her by saluting. What could have made her angry?

She looked ragged, but didn't we all who came from the outside? Close-up, I noticed some grease on her hands and face. As far as I can remember, she wore a plain leather jacket. It might not have been hers since it looked oversized and loose on her petite figure. Her white blouse underneath, smudged where visible and partly torn, didn't look like Air Force attire. I am sure that there were no emblems on the jacket and she did not wear a single medal. Many had been awarded to her—flying badges and the Iron Cross Class II and I. In fact, as far as I know, she was the only woman who had been awarded the Iron Cross First Class.

I didn't dare to say anything further, let alone ask questions. Instead, I withdrew, as I did a day later when I saw her in the upper bunker's hallway talking to the Goebbels' children animatedly, more like I remembered her from Hirschberg.

By then, I had been made aware that she and her wounded companion had arrived under most hazardous circumstances and that the Air Force Colonel General was Robert Ritter von Greim. Despite his superior rank and high decorations, I had not known him nor heard of him and, thus, had been unable to recognize him.

He had arrived on direct orders by the *Fuehrer*. Hanna Reitsch was the General's mistress. This was obvious to me, a 16-year-old, but not admitted or even talked about openly by anyone in the bunker. She had decided to accompany him and succeeded in doing so. How? By her own account, she had been in hiding in the aft of the aircraft, not revealing her presence until after the plane was airborne. Thus, Ritter von Greim had no choice but to take her along. As it turned out, Hanna Reitsch's bold decision to accompany him on this visit to the *Fuehrer* resulted in her saving his life.

After they had arrived unharmed in Gatow, Ritter von Greim permitted her to accompany him on the last leg so that she, too, could see the *Fuehrer* once more, should they succeed in reaching him. A *Fieseler Storch* (a "stork," a 2-man short-range reconnaissance plane) was at their disposal, and with Ritter von Greim at the controls, they took off against all odds hoping to reach a provisional airstrip. With increasingly heavy fire, one of the hits resulted in an injury to the General.

Hanna Reitsch would testify later that she was prepared for such a predicament. She took over and was able to navigate the crippled aircraft with its wounded pilot through the Russian flak cannonade. She managed to land in front of the Brandenburg Gate, near the Chancellery.

After a short ride in an Army motor vehicle, they reached the Chancellery. She became hysterical because Ritter von Greim, unconscious, was not immediately attended to. She stated that she feared he had been wounded critically and that she might lose him.

Over 50 years later, I was able to locate Prof. Dr. Schenck. He and I corresponded and even met on May 10, 1997, in Aachen. We reviewed thoroughly the Ritter von Greim/Hanna Reitsch arrival. We concluded that Hanna Reitsch erred when she wrote in *Flying my Life*[146] that von Greim was transported straight to the operating room of the *Notlazarett* and treated there by Dr. Stumpfegger.

Prof. Schenck left the bunker for the last time on April 26th to secure provisions from the bakery. He returned to the *Notlazarett* by evening. He relieved Prof. Dr. Haase in the operating room where he performed several emergency surgeries, but none on Colonel-General Ritter von Greim. Of this Prof. Schenck was sure. At no time had the young Dr. Ludwig Stumpfegger ever performed surgeries in Haase and Schenck's operating room or anywhere in the *Notlazarett* below the *Reich* Chancellery. Dr. Stumpfegger had, in Hitler's bunker, his own treatment room— the one previously occupied by Dr. Theodor Morell, the physician whose drugs, according to Prof. Schenck, had been undermining Hitler's health.

Even though a great need existed in the *Notlazarett* for an additional surgeon, Dr. Stumpfegger never pitched in. He maintained that since Dr. Morell left Berlin, he (Stumpfegger) now was Hitler's exclusive personal physician, requiring him to be at his *Fuehrer's* side at all times, being on call 24 hours a day, seven days a week.

The 30-year-old Stumpfegger actually ended up treating Ritter von Greim, but only after the General had seen Hitler and from there was taken to Stumpfegger's own treatment room. The other exception, by Hitler's own order, was that he treat *Frau* Goebbels, which he did. (However, Prof. Dr. Schenck seemed to have doubts about Dr. Stumpfegger's involvement in the murder of the six Goebbels children. Schenck had received information from once-secret files in Russian archives that *Frau* Goebbels is believed to have called their family dentist, a Dr. Kuntz, and that it was he who administered the injections that killed the six Goebbels children.)[147]

At least once Dr. Gertrud asked Dr. Stumpfegger to come to her treatment room to perform complicated surgery on a badly wounded *Hitlerjunge*. The request was denied and the boy died.

Prof. Schenck told me that he and Prof. Haase had learned of Ritter von Greim's arrival only after he was already in the lower bunker (the *Fuehrerbunker*). Both physicians were informed that the wounded Air Force *Generaloberst* had been promoted to Field Marshal. He was Hitler's choice to replace the "traitor" *Reichsmarschall* Hermann Goering.

The newly appointed Field Marshal had been granted special quarters adjacent to those of Dr. Stumpfegger, with Hanna Reitsch remaining. Somehow, she had held on to the stretcher for her to sleep on, after taking it upon herself to assume round-the-clock private nursing duties for which her only qualifications were that she had studied medicine for two semesters.

They spent three nights in the *Fuehrerbunker*. During this time I never saw him again, but got a few glimpses of her in the lower bunker and also in the upper bunker where the Goebbels' children roamed around.

I made no attempts to once more introduce myself. I now did the opposite and made efforts to avoid her. There is no doubt that the pair arrived in the *Reich* Chancellery on the evening of April 26, the first day Axmann had occupied his new command post at the Party Chancellery. Hanna Reitsch's father, my grandmother's ophthalmologist, would take his own life too. Hanna spent time in internment but chose to keep on living, escaping back into flying without ever publicly addressing the horrors her *Fuehrer*, once greatly admired by her, had left behind.

CHAPTER 56

Martin Bormann

The German historian, Prof. Dr. Guido Knopp, in his book *Hitler's Helpers*,[148] wrote about Martin Bormann, Hitler's secretary and "shadow man," and stated that I witnessed and studied Bormann during the last hours in the *Fuehrerbunker*. Witnessed—yes—studied, only in that I thought about him more than about the other bunker people, except Axmann.

Bormann was a relatively hidden figure among the leaders of the Third *Reich* and not well known publicly. During just eleven days, he left memories in my mind that somehow became dominant.

In appearance, Bormann and Himmler were the least militant of the men surrounding Hitler but, after the war, we learned they were among the most death-dealing and the most conniving of the *Fuehrer's* closest associates.

On April 20, at Hitler's birthday reception, Bormann was barely visible and soon I had lost sight of him in this gathering of mostly military officers. He must have remained in the back of the crowd and simply vanished.[149]

During the entire time from April 20 until the night of May 1, 1945, whenever I encountered Martin Bormann, he seemed oblivious of my presence, despite the fact that twice he had handed me a dispatch to be delivered to the Party Chancellery.

My memory may have retained so many more detailed impressions of him than of many others, because of Bormann's relation to a friend of my grandfather's.

My grandfather, *Opa* Lehmann, an old party member, had

connections to some of Hitler's earliest followers. The one who ranked highest in the party hierarchy was Martin Bormann's father-in-law, *Reichsleiter* (*Reich* leader) Walter Buch, a former major in the Kaiser's army and later a Volunteer Corps member. Among the earliest followers of Hitler, he distinguished himself during the *Kampfzeit* (time of struggle). One of only 12 Nazis elected to the parliament, Buch became known nationally. My grandfather met him in Nuremberg at a party function. They struck up a friendship and kept in touch with each other.

I don't recall my grandfather ever mentioning what they had in common or if they shared any interests others than their political commitment to National Socialism.

Most old party members never ceased dwelling on the past. The feeling of belonging to the movement that had seized the country and the old bond of comradeship probably prevailed.

Only as the war progressed and conditions worsened did their relationship begin to dissipate.

In the late thirties, the Buch family must have resided near Munich, because I recall that my uncle, Dr. *med.* Hans Lehmann, who had his practice not far from Munich in Utting am Ammersee, was once called to the Buch residence. He was not their family physician. But known for a special gift to correctly diagnose baffling cases, often intuitively, he was probably consulted for a second opinion.

By 1934, *Reichsleiter* Buch had risen from presiding over the party court that dealt with disciplinary infractions. He became Supreme Party Judge.

Neither my grandfather nor my father or anyone else had ever mentioned that Buch was at Hitler's side during the "Night of the Long Knives" when, in Bad Wiessee, *SA* leader Ernst Roehm was arrested. Hitler had asked Buch to have Roehm taken to Stadelheim prison and forever silenced. Buch supposedly placed a gun in Roehm's cell, suggesting an "honorable" parting.

When Roehm refused to commit suicide, an execution squad was assembled who silenced the "traitor and conspirator" for good and all.

This, too, I learned only after the war. In our family, it had never been mentioned and in the *Jungvolk* we had learned that Hitler himself put down the *SA* revolt and that the guilty had been punished.

In the Third *Reich,* education glorified its leaders in power. Biographies were changed as time went on and voided of all negative information.

I never felt at ease with Bormann. Not at any time did I have the desire to step up to him and declare that my grandfather and his father-in-law were friends or that my uncle once treated a family member.

I did not know at the time that in the early twenties, Bormann had served under Roehm (while the *SA* was outlawed) in a paramilitary unit called *Frontbann* and had masterminded the killing of the suspected assassin of Leo Schlageter, famous German freedom fighter in the French-occupied Ruhr district.

It was a vigilante killing and also involved Rudolf Hoess, later to become the Commandant of the Auschwitz Concentration Camp.

For a short time, Bormann and Hoess are believed to have shared a jail cell.

I never knew anything about Rudolf Hoess until Germany had a free press again following the occupation.

Another interesting piece of information about Martin Bormann emerged after the war while I attended the journalism school in Munich. A fellow student, son of an attorney, was familiar with police records of the suicide of Hitler's niece, and possibly his mistress, Geli Raubal. The name of the detective in charge of the investigation was Mueller. Martin Bormann is believed to have intervened and paid off detective Heinrich Mueller; a name I never knew until the last days in April 1945 in Berlin when *Rjfr.* Axmann had a message for *SS-Gruppenfuehrer* Mueller. I was ordered to deliver it to the *Gestapo*[150] headquarters. Heinrich Mueller was *Gestapo* Mueller.

***

Why did I have these anxious feelings about Bormann, the official, the man, the father of ten children?

Even my grandfather didn't care much for Martin Bormann, referred to him (probably not publicly but within family circles) as "the gray eminence," instead of "the brown eminence." "Gray eminence" meant prominence of questionable reputation while "brown eminence" would have signified distinction among Hitler's followers.

I also remember my mother referring to Gerda Bormann as "the poor woman," a remark probably caused by the frequency of her pregnancies.

As far as I can recall, in the Hitler Youth Bormann was hardly ever mentioned. It had come as quite a surprise when in late 1943 or early 1944, *Hbfr.* Werner Frehse, the headmaster of the camp counselor school, wrote a letter addressed to *Reichsleiter* Bormann to protest Bormann's proclamations that German women, regardless of their marital status, should bear children to secure Germany's future. *Hbfr.* Frehse, very definitely, opposed the single motherhood concept. He was a married man. Most of us, voluntarily, signed this letter and it is my recollection that *Hbfr.* Frehse had cleared this protest with the titular head of the *KLV* (*Kinderlandverschickung*—children's evacuation program), Baldur von Schirach.

To take on Bormann was in fact a risky undertaking. *Hbfr.* Frehse obviously wanted to be assured of von Schirach's support should Bormann in response take action against Hbfr. Frehse and us. As far as I recall, Bormann never replied. Apparently, he received similar reactions from other party branches and some distinguished leaders as well.

By the time *Rjfr.* Axmann had moved his command post into the cellar of Bormann's offices located at the Party Chancellery, Wilhelmstrasse 64, Bormann was functioning as Hitler's right-hand man. He had indeed become "the gray eminence" and advanced over his rivals, Goering and Himmler included, with one exception: Artur Axmann. *Rjfr* Axmann, instead of leaving Berlin, was determined to remain with his *Fuehrer.* He wanted to prove to Adolf Hitler that his youth, the Hitler Youth, would remain fiercely devoted and fight courageously to the bitter end, not giving up, willing to sacrifice their lives.

"Unconditional allegiance to the *Fuehrer!*" had become Axmann's motto. He was proud that the Hitler Youth in the most difficult of times would, through deeds of bravery, demonstrate its loyalty to Hitler and his ideas!

There was no last minute decoration for Martin Bormann, Hitler's chief of staff; in charge of his secretariat and, most of all, his appointment schedule; the *Fuehrer's* all-important protector from bad news; a mind-guard of sorts.

He decided who had direct access to Hitler and who had not. He also slanted incoming and outgoing messages, at times altering the meaning for Hitler, so that he would react in a certain way. This was, according to Axmann, the case with the telegram sent by Hermann Goering, Hitler's designated heir.

The *Reich Marshal* thought that, with Berlin almost encircled by Russian forces, the *Fuehrer* was no longer able to fully function as head of state. Thus, Goering had sent a cable to Hitler seeking the *Fuehrer's* consent to assume the leadership of what was left of Germany. Bormann had interpreted this as an act of treason. Hitler than ordered Goering arrested. Axmann told me later that he, too, was deceived by Bormann's misinterpretation and, only after the war, learned all of the facts. They changed his mind and he realized that Goering had acted properly and in good faith.

CHAPTER 57

Glimpses of Hitler

During the period from April 20 to April 30, I caught glimpses of Hitler numerous times, but I really only saw him close-up on four occasions. Twice he was within touching distance. Except for the birthday reception, he acted as if he didn't know I was there—yet he must have seen me.

My first close encounter with Hitler had taken place on April 20, 1945 (his birthday) between 17:10 and 17:20 Berlin time as described earlier.

I am not as certain, however, of the dates and times of my second and third close encounters with him inside the bunker. Days and nights had merged into a flow of destruction, such that I did not even try to keep track of time. There was no more set times for meals or for sleep; dispatches came and went around the clock.

The next time I saw him could have been on April 26 or 27th, definitely after I had received my bunker pass. Some military officers and couriers, I among them, were waiting in the anteroom, described by some as a waiting room or hallway. On both sides were several doors.

Unexpectedly, Hitler entered. He stepped into the hallway from one of them. Most likely the one from his study, by some called the map room. Whatever its name, it was crowded with people on this occasion. I noticed that they were packed in as tight as sardines.

When Hitler left them he seemed to be in deep thought, no longer taking notice of anyone. He was by himself. Somehow this startled me. He just walked into the room where most of the dispatches were issued and received.

When Axmann's liaison officer—I forget if it was Dietrich or Weltzin—came out to hand me the dispatch to be delivered to the *Funkraum*, Hitler was no longer in sight.

On the third occasion, I encountered Hitler as I entered the bunker through the emergency entrance, and I saw him leaning against the wall. He had at his side *Reichsleiter* Bormann and on the other side an *SS*-officer. I am not sure who it was.

Some guards passed by carrying out boxes. I wasn't close enough to hear what Bormann was talking about, making expressive gestures to emphasize what he was saying. By the time I received my dispatch, Hitler, Bormann, and the other officer were gone.

SS-guards continued to carry out boxes. However, while I turned right to climb the stairs to the emergency exit, they turned left. That's why I am so sure that a second exit must have existed that led to the observation tower.

In the garden above, these records were being destroyed under not too favorable conditions. Loose pages flew away before they burned. If, as is to be assumed, these were secret documents, then some got away.

In connection with the burning of secret documents, a dispatch was received containing the news that *SS-Obergruppenfuehrer* Julius Schaub, who had left Berlin in one of the last courier planes, had destroyed Hitler's train. This was probably an attempt to demolish the records stored there. Most of those in the Bunker belonged to the inner circle and at one time or another had been on the train and were sad and disconcerted to receive the news of its destruction. Hitler, however, was relieved, according to Major Weltzin who was present when the news was received.

In historical literature, it is pointed out consistently that no records exist of Hitler having given orders in regard to the "final solution." Perhaps they were destroyed at the very end in the Chancellery gardens or blown up with his train somewhere near the Berchtesgaden Station.

Most of the dispatch envelopes I carried to and from the bunker had a big rubber stamp imprint *NUR DURCH OFFIZIER* (via officer only). This shows how deteriorated the situation was around Hitler these last days. I wasn't an officer, not even an NCO. I wasn't even wearing a *Waffen-SS* uniform, but that of the *Volkssturm* with a *HJ*-sleeve band. As a 16-year-old, I was entrusted with these dispatches. Most of them were marked *Chefsache*, some even *Fuehrerbefehl* (Commander-in-Chief orders). They came directly from Hitler. Bormann had his own dispatch envelope with the eagle holding the swastika in a wreath. I also remember that his signature was weird, an illegible scribbling.

***

The fourth and last time I saw Adolf Hitler close-up was on April 30th. There can be no doubt that this date is accurate.

I am also certain that it was during the very early morning hours, some time between 4 a.m. and 6 a.m.

In the hallway, the teacart—usually filled with open-faced sandwiches—was empty now. During the day, it was Bormann most of all whom I observed coming out, grabbing sandwiches, always more than one. Hungry, too, I never dared to help myself and no one ever offered me one or told me to help myself.

It must have been an important dispatch that I delivered so early in the morning from our obscure radio station next to Axmann's command post, which was still functioning. I remember being told by one of the dispatchers in Navy uniform that there was still contact in the east with the fortress Breslau and in the west, to my great amazement, with the Channel Islands.

The message I handed over before dawn on April 30th to a duty officer with red stripes on his pants, must have been shocking news, judging from his reaction.

"This on top of everything!" was his reaction. I was told to stay—an immediate reply would be forthcoming. He retreated and seemed to be gone for the longest time. Utterly exhausted physically, I dozed off sitting on the bench.

Two or three hours prior, on that same night, I had been on an emergency run to the *Notlazarett* and crossed though the upper bunker's corridor which held the often-mentioned oak dining room table. Credible survivors have reported that it is here that Eva Braun, by now Mrs. Hitler, had partied through the night. Supposedly, she had been there with some of the "inner circle" still in the bunker, playing a gramophone and dancing through the whole night—her wedding night—until daybreak on the day Hitler and she would commit suicide.

I maintain that if the party took place, it must have been at another location, because I had passed through the upper bunker not once, but twice during the night. In adjacent rooms, the Goebbels' children were sleeping.

All I remember seeing were some of the *Waffen-SS* guards, a few of Rattenhuber's men. Thus, if a party was going on, it could only have been in one of the canteens below the *Reich* Chancellery.

There was commotion in the public air raid shelter and a flurry of activities in the emergency hospital, but nothing that could have been a private party of high dignitaries. Still, I was only familiar with the rank-and-file canteen. There must have been an officer's mess, too, perhaps away from any of the passages with which I was familiar. Namely the one through the Voss Strasse entrance to the underground hospital and pharmacy, and from there, via a subterranean gangway to the two separate bunkers connected by a stairway. It was often described as a cast iron spiral stairway, which wasn't the case either. There was a sharp turn, but these were concrete and not metal steps.

In the small "upper bunker," the eating area next to the kitchen could hardly qualify as a canteen or mess hall. The room was just big enough for one table, probably seating six to eight at the most. I had sat there myself a couple of times, once talking briefly to *Oberscharfuehrer* (sergeant) Rochus Misch, a friendly fellow-Silesian. Misch, however, has no recollection of this, and I wonder now if I mistook him for someone else. There were several Silesians among the mostly Bavarian detachment.

We ate canned sausage and canned bread. Although preserved, the bread tasted stale. We weren't served open-faced sandwiches like officers and Bormann and his staff received.

Across the street, *Mutti* Lehmann had served fresh bread from a nearby bakery for a day or two. This bakery was supplied with flour by no other than Prof. Schenck who as a physician, had access to and control over supply depots. It was a sensational event when Hannes arrived with a rucksack filled with loafs of bread. *Mutti* Lehmann cut them up so that everyone received a slice— including our three wounded foreigners: the Russian prisoner and the two Frenchmen.

The fresh bread was of short duration. Perhaps, the smell from the bakery reached the nearby Russian soldiers. They lost no time in capturing the building. The story goes that the baker kept baking now for the Russians, but I couldn't find anyone to confirm this.

Mutti Lehmann's staples were soon down to sardines, zwieback, and champagne. Yes, we were without drinking water, but we still had an ample supply of champagne. Her small canteen had two, possibly three tables moved together. This is where Lotte and I received our medals. Other ceremonial activities, all involving decorations, had been performed here as well. One involved the wounded French volunteer. He received the Wounded Badge.

Gebietsfuehrers Grimm and Schroeder, both World War I veterans, arranged for these award ceremonies, a daily event to the very end.

Why they (Grimm and Schroeder) were exempt from *Volkssturm* duties, spared from having to join the nearest *HJ-Kampfgruppe*, I never knew.

Down the street our block was being defended by what Axmann called *unsere Jungen* (our boys). It was under the leadership of *Hauptbannfuehrer* Otto Wuerschinger, who was younger than Grimm and Schroeder, probably in his late twenties, or early thirties. *Rjfr.* Axmann seemed to be soft on some of the old-timers. I don't think he involved them anymore in any of the decision-making processes. They obviously were department heads and, as such, bureaucrats. There was nothing left for bureaucrats to do.

They knew of my carrying last orders, my unexplainable fortuity, my luck as a runner—not just with dispatches, but also when having to get urgently needed medical supplies.

"Again, lucky as a pig!" was the expression they constantly repeated.

Aside from the brief, austere award ceremonies, no partying was going on in our canteen, and if there was a doomsday mood, I was too busy and worn out to observe any of it. Only after Hitler had committed suicide did I become aware of the "let's-live-it-up-before-it-all-ends" mood across Wilhelmstrasse at the public air raid shelter.

***

In the early morning hours an officer tapped me on the shoulder.

It startled me and I became embarrassed.

From the corners of my mouth, spittle had dribbled down my chin. "Only a few minutes more," he said. I wiped my mouth and now made an even more determined effort to avoid catnapping again.

Finally, I was called from the anteroom into the situation room where officers were sleeping on the floor. The officer on duty gave me the dispatch in reply to the message I had delivered earlier. Just as I was ready to leave, one of Axmann's liaison officers, Dietrich, appeared. He must have stepped out of Hitler's study or map room.

"Keep waiting a moment—don't leave yet," Dietrich demanded, projecting a sense of great urgency. He went in the room that, during the day, Bormann shared with his secretary, *Frl.* Krueger.[151] I vaguely remember a small switchboard, actually what looked like a portable box, and a teletype machine, but this equipment could have been in another room as well.[152]

As a rule, I got only glimpses of what was inside the rooms, having to wait most of the time in the situation room or in the anteroom.

Neither Martin Bormann nor his secretary Else Krueger, were present that early. Besides Dietrich, two staff officers were on duty and there was a guard at the steel door.

Then suddenly Hitler appeared—like a ghost! Now no one awake was in sight, except he. Exiting his study, he walked toward me without looking up. I was so stunned I didn't salute.

At last he looked up, gazing, as if lost in deep thought. He almost stepped on one of the officers sleeping on the floor. It appeared as if he looked right through me.

At this very instant, a tremor shook the bunker.

Hitler lifted his right arm, visibly shaking, stretched it out until his hand touched the wall to find support. Was it a hit above the bunker's ceiling? If Dietrich had not delayed me down here in the bunker, would I have now been blown to pieces? Down came dirt of some type, mortar, or plaster. Hitler didn't look up. He said something to himself. It sounded like "Again a hit!" He, too, went into the room where Dietrich and the on-duty officers must have been huddling. They must have discussed whatever late development was urgent enough that Hitler, himself, took an interest in or had to be informed about.

I could have taken one—two steps forward and touched him. I had been standing less than four meters from the door.

Hitler had appeared even more deteriorated than I remembered from ten days earlier at the birthday reception. It might have been caused by the bunker light, but he struck me as having jaundice. His face had looked sallow and the white of his glossy eyes appeared to have turned yellow.

CHAPTER 58

The Mistress

The fact that Adolf Hitler had a mistress and that she was in the bunker really astonished me. It came as a complete surprise. It just didn't fit my perception of this all-powerful leader. We had been told over and over again that all of his energy was devoted to leading the nation. In fact, I even remember assertions to this effect made by my mother. "The *Fuehrer* can't afford to be married!"

Therefore, I was stunned when, after returning from my first run to the bunker, I was asked by Dr. Gertrud if I had seen Eva Braun?

"Eva Braun?" I asked. "Who is she?"

"You don't know?" Dr. Gertrud explained: "The *Fuehrer's Geliebte* (lover)."

"What nonsense!" crossed my mind, but only as a thought. I couldn't say it. It would have been disrespectful toward Dr. Gertrud.

Instead, I expressed my disbelief by blurting out "Impossible!" I looked into Dr. Gertrud's eyes. "The *Fuehrer* doesn't have a paramour!"

"I didn't know it either," she replied.

But Dr. Gertrud portrayed her as a heroine, telling me that she had come from Berchtesgaden to be at the *Fuehrer's* side, refusing to leave him.

Still not convinced, I asked *Rjfr.* Axmann. He, too, knew that our *Fuehrer* had a mistress—and one of long standing.

As far as I remember, I saw Eva Braun, who became Eva Hitler, three times close-up. Never accompanied by the *Fuehrer*. Always in the presence of other women.

The most memorable, but embarrassing event happened in the anteroom. Still out of breath after having crossed through a barrage of fire, my smoke-filled eyes made out the semblance of three women in front of me.

How ragged I must have looked, with pieces of my uniform torn to shreds. My face, dirty and unkempt, undoubtedly shocked them. Since we had moved into the cellar of the Party Chancellery, I had not had a change of jacket and pants, let alone of underwear or socks. I must have appeared "crusty." Taking notice of me, the one with a dark dress and a golden brooch, gave me a silken handkerchief, neatly folded. With it, I wiped my eyes. She handed me a glass filled with water. *Sprudel,* a cold drink.

It was Eva Braun.

The moist glass slipped out of my hand, fell to the floor and shattered. I felt awkward, must have blushed and wanted to get away, but she reached out for another one from a cart.

"Calm down!" she said.

Meanwhile, *Frau* Goebbels put a hand on her own forehead as if she had a headache. The third woman in the background, I did not know. She remarked: "Isn't it horrible how these boys have to fight."

Frau Goebbels kept her right hand on her forehead, while Eva Braun continued her efforts to comfort me. She even cleansed my stinging eyes.

This encounter with the three women had happened before I delivered the telegram for Dr. and Mrs. Goebbels from *Gauleiter* Hanke. I had seen *Frau* Goebbels close-up for the first time on this day when I dropped the water glass. Later I delivered the Hanke telegram and knew what she looked like and recognized her, while I saw her husband close-up, very close-up, for the first—and for the last time.

I became curious, even inquisitive. Dr. Gertrud was even more curious.

"Did you see her again?"

"Yes," I replied.

"How old do you think she is?"

I was never good at guessing people's ages.

"*Mitte Zwanzig?*" (Mid-twenties?), I replied hesitantly.

I was wrong.

She was 33 years old, I found out after the war. I had just witnessed Hitler's 56th birthday a few days earlier, and he had looked much older than his years. With Eva looking younger than she was, I couldn't picture them as a married couple and never saw them together.

CHAPTER 59

The End Approaches

Even when I was present, *Rjfr*. Axmann talked very openly about some of his concerns. Never in my presence did he address Hitler's chances for survival. It was our job to hold out. As far as I knew, Generals Wenck and Steiner were still expected to slash open the encirclement and to get him and us out of Berlin.

If they didn't succeed, the bodies of Hitler Youth boys would provide the *Fuehrer* with a human shield to spearhead through the Russian front and reach our troops. They expected to take their leader to the Alpine fortress. At no time, did *Rjfr*. Artur Axmann or anyone in his entourage ever mention that Hitler might commit suicide or even that he would be getting married.

Axmann left for the *Fuehrerbunker*.

I must have gotten in an hour or two of sleep. But I was awake when he returned, and I remember it clearly.

"The *Fuehrer* and Eva Braun were married!"

I was stunned.

My reaction was as naïve as could be: "Then we'll include her in our midst, too, when we break out!"

In my head we still kept on fighting for the "patient" to survive until the "miracle cure" could be administered to save us all.

Word spread, however, that Hitler was writing his testament. This seemed understandable. Even if we provided a human shield, he could be killed. A successor should be lined up. And this was even truer now that Goering and Himmler had emerged as traitors.

SS-Gruppenfuehrer Hermann Fegelein, the liaison between

Himmler and Hitler, I had never heard of, and I never met him during those last days in the bunker.

When *Rjfr.* Axmann dispatched me to a high ranking officer, *SS-Gruppenfuehrer* Heinrich Mueller at the *Reichssicherheitshauptamt (Reich* Security Headquarters), I didn't even know that this was the headquarters of the *Gestapo.* Mueller, of equal rank as Fegelein, was *Gestapo*-Mueller, head of the Secret State Police.

Gruppenfuehrer Mueller was not at the *Reichssicherheitshauptamt.* An officer there directed me to the *Bendlerblock*[153] where I got a glimpse of Gen. Weidling, but Mueller wasn't there either and without having my mission accomplished, I returned to *Rjfr.* Axmann.

When Hitler learned that *Reichsfuehrer* Himmler was negotiating behind his back, he became suspicious and had Fegelein arrested. He ordered a court martial.

Realizing that Bormann was known to have been Fegelein's friend, he wanted Axmann to take Bormann's place on the panel to judge Fegelein. Axmann, ostensibly, wanted no part of it. He conferred with Gen. Mohnke, who agreed that only military officers should sit in judgment of a fellow officer. Mueller seemed the ideal man.

When Fegelein was caught he was with another woman, most likely a spy. As an *SS*-officer, he was sworn to absolute loyalty—to *Meine Ehre heisst Treue* (My honor is devotion).

Since Mueller could not be found and Hitler insisted on a speedy trial, Axmann, after all, became a member of the panel that condemned Fegelein to death.

He was Mrs. Hitler's brother-in-law and he left behind a pregnant wife.

Interestingly enough, *SS-Gruppenfuehrer* Fegelein's name appears on the manifest of the so-called "Barcelona flight." A flying ace and highly decorated bomber pilot, Lt. Col. Werner Baumbach was a close personal friend of Albert Speer. According to *Gestapo* files (genuine or forged, I am unsure), he had been selected to fly the Nazi elite to neutral Spain.

According to my research, Baumbach's JU-290 never took off from Hoerching (how could the Berliners have gotten to this airfield, located near Linz in Austria?). Baumbach's arrival in Spain remains undocumented. After the war, he emigrated to Argentina with his family. He crashed on a test flight in 1952 and was killed.

Nevertheless, in Gregory Douglas' book, *Gestapo Chief*,[154] a document is reproduced, signed by Heinrich Mueller. It stated that Adolf Hitler and a party of ten (Mueller included) were scheduled to depart on a special trip to Barcelona, Spain, on April 26, 1945.

If the flight took off, then Mueller might have been the only passenger from this list who was on board, since in addition to Hitler, almost all others listed are known to have been in the bunker and never departed for Austria.

Eva Braun and Martin Bormann were certainly still in the bunker after April 26. I saw them with my own eyes and both talked to me. Hanna Reitsch and Ritter von Greim were definitely the last among the top Nazi leadership to leave the bunker and succeed in taking off in a small plane during these last days of the Berlin battle.

***

At the time I received my Iron Cross First Class there must have been a lack of certificates, because with the medal I received a typewritten certificate with Axmann's real signature.

With the other two decorations, the Silver Wound Badge and the stripe for having single-handedly destroyed an enemy tank, I received certificates with my name typed in and with facsimiles of Hitler's signature.

Since Axmann had a wooden arm, I remember that Dr. Gertrud assisted him. It was she who actually pinned the Iron Cross First Class on my breast pocket and also replaced the Black Wounded Badge with the new one, in shining silver.

Lotte was there and had, ahead of me, received the Iron Cross

Second Class on a ribbon that Dr. Gertrud had attached to her nurse's uniform. She also received a tank stripe and it was she who would later sew mine on the upper left arm of my uniform.

Axmann and Weltzin had left already, but Dr. Gertrud was still there when *Mutti* Lehmann, the lady in charge of the canteen, served us champagne. She referred to Lotte and me as young *Panzerknacker* (tank destroyers).

The awards ceremony in *Mutti* Lehmann's canteen, although austere, had made a lasting impression on me. *Rjfr.* Axmann had said words of high praise.

One of Dr. Gertrud nurse's aides had a small camera and took a picture of Lotte.

Had a photograph been taken of me with my face injury, my left hand in a cast, and on my chest the Iron Cross First Class and the Silver Wounded Badge, I would have wanted this picture to somehow reach my father. He would realize that his "weakling son" at 16 had become a fighter and had been decorated. My father had no war medals, not even the Iron Cross Second Class. He had been severely ill several times but never wounded in battle.

I didn't know then of his experiences in Dresden. Under constant threat of being killed, acknowledged as a young hero by most people with whom I came in contact, I had an urgent desire to let my father know that I must be meeting his expectations—even exceeding them.

I wasn't fearless, but able to conquer my fears. I was miserable but like a soldier I didn't buckle under the cries, the screams, and the shouts around me. I parted with those horrors inside me and maintained as valiant a state of mind as possible.

I never knew until after the war that Hitler had told Axmann that the best had sacrificed their lives on the battlefields already. Those who survived were the inferior ones. Even though it was a lie, what an insult to the German people—to those surviving!

Erich Baerenfaenger, the youngest of Hitler's generals, had great praise for the boys under his command. He attended one of the

situation conferences in the bunker, and Axmann introduced me
to this war hero, taking great pride in doing so.

Axmann and Baerenfaenger[160] were friends and on a first name
basis. I remember Axmann saying: "I want to introduce my courier,
Lehmann, received by the *Fuehrer* on his birthday."

Gen. Baerenfaenger shook my hand and then actually patted
me on the back—not a customary gesture at that time.

I had just received my Iron Cross First Class. He had been
decorated with the Knight's Cross of the Iron Cross with Oak
Leaves.

CHAPTER 60

Aiding the Wounded

When Dr. Gertrud was not wearing her physician's coat but was in her *BDM*-uniform, she looked, at least to me, not much older than the girls in her health unit. Dr. Gertrud's medical group of girls—aged 14 to 18 years if not older—were all experienced nurse's aides or orderlies. Their training included all aspects of first aid. They even treated severe battle injuries. Most of them were from Berlin and had provided emergency aid called *Unfallsdienst* (literally: accident service) after air raids. I remember seeing on their uniforms life-runes of white crosses on red round patches. The older girls who wore white armbands with a red cross must have been full-fledged nurses. They were probably not even volunteers but professionals, as were *Schwester* Erna and *Schwester* Emma, the surgical assistants of Prof. Dr. Haase and Prof. Dr. Schenck in the *Notlazarett*.

The evening before we had transferred the wounded from Kaiserdamm to Wilhelmstrasse, Dr. Gertrud wore an *Aesculapius* patch. Otherwise, until we readied for the breakout, I remember her only in a physician's smock with just a *BDM*-emblem. She did not need any identification. Everyone seemed to recognize that she was the doctor. She acted with the authority of a physician, although she didn't look old enough to be a doctor. The performance, dedication, and devotion of all of the girls under her command were exceptional—beyond depiction. Even when all came to an end, they still performed beyond what seemed humanly possible.

It was pointed out to me by a veteran that Dr. Gertrud's treatment room in the Party Chancellery bunker could not be called a *Notlazarett* (emergency hospital). By military standards it barely passed as a *Hauptverbandsplatz* (major first-aid field station).

It was space in an air raid shelter, unfurnished except for some wooden benches. We had brought along some stretchers, plank beds, chairs, and the table new arrivals were treated on.

With Russian air activity escalating, artillery fire increased above and grenade fragments showered upon those outside like hailstorms.

Dr. Gertrud had started out with 12 to 14 patients. The count increased rapidly after street fighting flared up nearby. Reports about Russian sharpshooters increased, although I wondered where they could have found sufficient coverage not to be exposed to the shelling of their own artillery.

By the time of the breakout, Dr. Gertrud's sickbay was overcrowded with 30 to 40 wounded, several very severely. Some had died and been carried out in the yard to be buried when the fire subsided. It never happened. The Russians must have found the exposed corpses there when they arrived.

Meanwhile, in the emergency hospital across the street, several hundred wounded were attended by the two physicians. During the first two days and nights, we had carried some of the injured requiring surgery that Dr. Gertrud was unable to perform—whether for lack of surgical instruments or knowledge, I don't know.

In the *Notlazarett*, they had an operating table with a bright light above from what appeared to be a sun lamp usually used for tanning. To me, it appeared to be a small but fully equipped clinic.

In comparison, Dr. Gertrud and her aides had essentially brought along only first-aid supplies. She had what looked like a vanity case with a Red Cross emblem on it. The instruments in this bag appeared to be the only ones at her disposal.

There was a constant flow in and out of her station. Diarrhea had become a problem. For me too. At both stations medication was soon depleted. I chewed Zwieback and had some Schnapps thinking it might kill the germs. It didn't. Toilets were in putrid conditions, especially those below the Old and New Chancelleries. Ours, in the Party Chancellery cellar, experienced some flooding too. I remember the stinky smells. However, the toilet in the bunker occupied by Hitler was kept in working order and unsoiled to the very end. I had discovered a restroom near the exit and no one prevented me from using it.

Throughout the trying experiences, my left hand was in a cast and my little finger became infected. Dr. Gertrud insisted that I see Dr. Schenck. His nurse, Emma, gave me injections. Ironically, one too many. It caused blisters all over my body. (An apparent overdose of tetanus vaccine).

Gudrun urged me to "Remain here!" trying to keep me safe. I went on. I could still walk.

In the *Notlazarett*, the wounded count increased so rapidly. The two physicians, nurses, and aides worked practically around the clock with Prof. Haase, in poor health himself, periodically resting in the small pharmacy.

The last names of two other nurses were later released by Russian authorities: *Schwester* Flegel and *Schwester* Tscherwinska. Named also was a *Schwester* Rut. She, as I recall, was also one of Dr. Gertrud's nurses.

The two highest-ranking Hitler Youth leaders in Berlin were Gisela Hermann and Otto Hamann. Hermann was the district leader of the *Jungmaedel* (young girls 10-14 years) and *BDM*-girls (14-18 years) Hamann was the district leader of the *Jungvolk* (boys 10-14 years) and the Hitler Youth (14-18 yrs.). They had come from the *Reichssportfeld* to see *Rjfr.* Axmann and were struck by weapon fire while crossing Wilhelmstrasse.

Dr. Gertrud, although short-staffed, insisted that Gudrun provide extra care for the two *HJ*-leaders in the *Notalzarett* and transferred her. Both would soon be visited by *Rjfr.* Axmann. I had shown him the way.

Hamann died within hours, while Hermann survived.

Renate, who remained with Dr. Gertrud, could have been an

Assistenzaerztin (assistant physician) or the charge nurse. But as an assistant physician, she would have been addressed as Dr. Renate, I believe. Yet I only remember her as Renate, not even as *Schwester* (nurse) Renate.

This suggests that she might have been a medical student. If so, she certainly was very assertive. She gave orders like a physician, and it was she who decided that an attempt should be made to secure needed supplies no longer available in the pharmacy of the *Notlazarett.* I was to go to the Military Hospital in the Zoo Bunker.

"You can do it!" she challenged me. It turned out to be a run through hell and back. I still remember the hailstorm of exploding "Stalin Organ" *(Katyushas)* shells, the *Flammenmeer* (sea of flames) in the background, and close to the bunker, blinding smoke.

I was surprised when I arrived at the Zoo Bunker. It appeared to be a *Luftwaffe* (Air Force) facility. With soldiers and civilians jammed in, discipline was lacking. I could hardly move. The hospital was not in the cellar, but up a couple of flights.

Fortunately, some of the supplies requested were still on hand, but I had to wait.

It occurred to me that Hannes might be there and I looked around. But only for a very short time because, even if he was, chances to detect him would have been very slim. The crowd was merciless. I had to push myself back down and to the exit and was almost glad to cross through fire once more.

My hellish run was successful.

Renate rewarded me with an injection that mitigated my pain and the itching from the blisters. The Zwieback and the Schnapps didn't take care of my intestinal pangs. For a day I didn't eat. I drank only water. Had I not had access to the *Fuehrerbunker* where drinking water was still available, dehydration might have taken its toll.

Eventually my cramps subsided, but now I was a human wreck. It must have been more than mere willpower that kept me going. My instincts must have warned me that, if I gave up, it could be the end of me.

***

If, at this very last stage of the war, a "no prisoners taken" order existed, it was not observed by the fighting *Hitlerjungen,* because one of the wounded among Dr. Gertrud's patients was a Russian soldier. He probably held a sharpshooter's position when, most likely, shrapnel from Russian artillery injured him. He was picked up by some of our boys. Dr. Gertrud treated him as if he were one of us. I remember seeing him—blond with curly hair and a boxer's nose. Some time earlier in his life, it must have been broken or injured.

This face, with the hooked nose, attracted my attention because one of my *Berliner* comrades from the *Reichsjugendfuehrung* (Youth Headquarters) support unit, had a face with similar features—a crooked nose, just as contorted.

Then after the war, former *Stammfuehrer* (unit leader) Bert Hartmann and I corresponded. He maintained that a Russian spy had been among us. He asked if I remembered the name Alex Kapp. I did not. To me the name did not sound familiar at all. I was then (and still am) sure I never met anyone with this name.

Fifty years later, when I read the book of Petrova and Watson, *The Death of Hitler,*[156] a "spy in the bunker" was mentioned. His undercover name, supposedly, was Sasha Kvap. His real name was Alexander Kvapishevski. The book contains a picture of this alleged spy. It's a photograph of a young man's handsome face, with a straight nose and dark, straight hair.

With absolute certainty I can say this was not the Russian soldier treated by Dr. Gertrud. He, by the way, was dressed in a Russian uniform and wore three or four medals on his jacket. Several of us, including Dr. Gertrud, made comments about the medals—they included gold stars.

We had been informed about so-called "Seydlitz soldiers,"

EHM

supposedly German Communists wearing German military uniforms. I learned later that this was probably not true. General Walter von Seydlitz, chief of staff to Field Marshal Friedrich von Paulus, was second in command at Stalingrad. He survived the defeat but was taken prisoner. Disillusioned by Hitler as military leader, he became one of the co-founders of the resistance group *Nationalkomittee Freies Deutschland* (National Committee to Free Germany). He then formed in Moscow the "German Officers' League" with the aim to overthrow Hitler and his regime. Discouraged by the failure of the July 20, 1944 plot, he then encouraged formation of a "Liberation Army." Sufficient numbers from among the captured German officers and rank-and-file soldiers joined. They fought, however, under Russian leadership in the battle of Berlin. Their aim, upon liberation of the city, was to establish a free democratic Germany.

That it would become a socialized state and a Russian satellite became apparent as soon as the war had ended.

Once Hannes and I, when returning from Petersdorf, encountered some stray soldiers, and Hannes thought that they were either German Communists shooting at us or at Russians in German uniforms. It could have been Seydlitz troops. General von Seydlitz, however, did not see the troops bearing his name in action. He remained in Moscow. Stalin, for unexplained reasons, kept him in prison. There he endured detention for another ten years.

In Germany, Hitler had, in absentia, sentenced him to death. This condemnation remained in effect after the armistice. A court of the *Bundesrepublic* of Germany (then West Germany) after Konard Adenauer was elected Chancellor, had to officially annul Hitler's death sentence.

In reverse, of course, we had on our side the Russian commander Col. Gen. Andrej Vlassov who, after his capture in 1942, wanted to free his country of Stalin's rule. He became the founder of the "Free Russia Committee." Later, under his command, two divisions of Russian soldiers fought on Germany's side. Recruited in POW camps, these Russian soldiers had rationalized that having joined the enemy by opposing Stalin, they fought for the better cause. So did their German counterparts who, after the Stalingrad fiasco, turned against Hitler.

Gen. Vlassov, captured by the Allies at war's end, was extradited to the Soviet Union and executed as a traitor in 1946.

In the early seventies, the office next to mine (in Los Angeles on La Brea Ave.) was occupied by a tour operator who specialized in travel to Africa. In the travel industry, his company was well known and so was he as an individual. His name was Pierre C.T. Verheye. Pierre was also a hobby historian.

From him I learned, 30 years after the war, about the multitude of mercenary units there had been. Countries such as Albania, Bulgaria, Czechoslovakia (which, during the war, had become a German "protectorate"), Estonia, Finland, Hungary, Latvia, Lithuania, Poland, Rumania, and Yugoslavia fought in separate Foreign Legions for Hitler and must have believed in him and his cause just as strongly as most Germans did.

In Berlin, volunteers from France and the Scandinavian countries fought to defend the area around the *Fuehrerbunker*. With some of these fighters I had talked occasionally. I remember one who arrived wounded and was treated by Dr. Gertrud. He spoke broken German, but with French enthusiasm he kept reminding us: *"Wir muesseen das Abendland retten,"* (We have to save Western civilization!) as if to cheer us on.

CHAPTER 61

The Suicides

During these very last days, whenever I used the emergency entrance and exit leading directly into the garden, the guards recognized me and without looking at my permit or checking for my weapon, they let me pass. My pistol remained in my coat pocket. When I saw him for the last time, I could have shot Hitler!

Years later, when I talked to a history class, a high school student asked: "Why didn't you kill Hitler, you could have become a hero?"

"I would have been a dead hero, almost instantly!" I replied, "My name would be in your history books, but I wouldn't be standing before you. Even if I had lived, I probably wouldn't have been able to have lived a life that, at least for me, turned out to be meaningful!"

It was difficult for me to explain that during this time period (April 20-30, 1945), though I encountered Hitler at very close range, I had absolutely no inclination whatsoever of killing him, not even of opposing him. He was still the *Fuehrer*, the great leader, and my belief structure had not as yet collapsed.

I had no knowledge that he was a mass murderer. I still believed that holding out was our duty as soldiers. I did not realize that, for some time already, he must have known that he could no longer win this war and thus, irresponsibly and heinously, sacrificed the lives of his soldiers and now the lives of young boys as well.

Had I known everything that I know now, would I have been

able to make a life or death decision and kill him? I will never know.

A few top-echelon members remained absolutely loyal to the very end: Axmann, Bormann, Dr. and Mrs. Goebbels, members of his personal staff, and a handful of military officers. Others such as Keitel[157] and Jodl[158] were gone, even Speer,[159]his favorite. The number of women who had remained was amazing: Eva Braun, now *Frau* Hitler, three secretaries, his cook[160] and, of course, Mrs. Goebbels, who had arrived with her husband and all of their children. Consequently, she had received from her *Fuehrer* a last and very special gift. According to historical accounts, Adolf Hitler had given his Golden Party Badge to Mrs. Goebbels.

When, over 50 years later, I corresponded with Hitler's former adjutant, Otto Guensche, I mentioned that I had gotten a very good look at the *Fuehrer* and nothing seemed to be missing on his uniform. Guensche confirmed that Hitler had given Mrs. Goebbels his *goldenes Partei Abzeichen*. But he was also sure that Hitler had duplicate badges and that the one presented to Mrs. Goebbels was replaced immediately on his uniform.

Therefore, I wouldn't have seen him with a badge missing.

On this very early Monday morning, both Captain Baur and General Mohnke in their accounts describe seeing Hitler in a robe. Guensche disputes this, stating that Hitler would never have received anybody while not fully dressed. Not even on the last day of his life.

All I can attest to is that he was still in uniform in the very early morning of the night that was his wedding night—his last night alive.

In the evening (April 29) until shortly after midnight, activities between the radio unit and Hitler's situation room had peaked, probably caused by Bormann who sent out messages all over to military and party leaders. The reason for that might have been a devastating radio message received from Field Marshal Keitel. He advised Hitler that Gen. Wenck was unable to advance further, that the 12th Army had come to a standstill and thus, was unable to liberate Berlin. The news about the 9th Army was even worse; it was totally encircled by Russian troops.

I don't know if I was the bearer of this catastrophic news. Axmann was briefed by Major Weltzin and asked to report any advances the Russians were making within 300 yards of the bunker. Bormann was suddenly gone, reportedly with a bottle of cognac under his arm. He was not among several high-ranking officers I saw sleeping on the floor. Bormann's uniform would have given him away. He, as was rumored, had a girlfriend to sleep with.

Except for dozing off a couple of times, it was a night without sleep. It would become a long night of criss-crossing thoughts, cross currents of abnormal duress. I was dead tired but unable to find restful sleep. My mind kept overflowing with anticipations, imaginations, and reflections, resulting in questions upon questions upon questions.

Earlier, when I had crossed Wilhelm Strasse, someone standing in the doorway observing the hail of metal said: "Boy, it's just insane!"

In war, insanity becomes a common occurrence in all its forms.

The battle that was fought, the actual street fighting from house to house, I did not participate in. However, by having to run through heavy shellfire and seeing so many of my comrades killed and wounded, I, too, must have been in shock. It's difficult for me now to assess the condition I was in.

In the early afternoon of April 30, I returned from the *Fuehrerbunker* to Axmann's command post. Axmann wasn't there for about two hours. When he returned, he was visibly distraught.

With a cracking voice, he said: "The *Fuehrer* shot himself."

I was just stunned.

The *Fuehrer* dead! It was beyond belief.

Almost immediately the question: "What about the miracle weapons?" crossed my mind. I felt as panic stricken now as I had thirteen years ago when my father had left me on the sidewalk and driven off. Now I didn't cry.

With Axmann visibly crushed, I did not dare to ask it out loud. He reached for paper and, with his left hand, jotted down some notes.

I recalled that just months ago, we had been told that Divine Providence had saved the *Fuehrer's* life after he had survived the July 20, 1944 assassination attempt.

If guided by Divine Providence, how could he have taken his life? Nothing seemed real anymore.

Axmann sent me to get Dr. Gertrud. She sensed immediately that something terrible must have happened. She grabbed my arm and held on to it as we walked to Axmann's desk. I left the room.

After a few minutes, I saw her come out sobbing.

She seemed even more devastated than I. But our jobs continued. With newly wounded still arriving she needed additional medical supplies; so once again I was off. On this last run, I ran through bursting flames, choking smoke, and a hail of metal. It must have been about midnight, less than 24 hours after my last close encounter with Hitler. Mass groupings of Russian tanks had been reported, and we expected them to approach on Wilhelmstrasse and Hermann Goering Strasse. As a result, I reversed my route, went through the garden to the emergency entrance, and via the lower and upper bunkers, I continued underground to the air raid shelter below the new Chancellery where the *Notlazerett* was located.

None of the supplies Dr. Gertrud needed were on hand anymore. I left empty-handed and returned the same way I came. I checked at the anteroom to see if dispatches were to be picked up. Two officers whom I had never seen before were there. One of them yelled at me to leave and then asked the other officer "Who permitted this lad to enter?"

(The German word he used was "*Kerl*", a bad sort of a fellow.)

Volksturm Hitler Youth uniforms were not common in Hitler's bunker, and not even my decorations legitimized my presence, as far as this officer was concerned.

I left through the emergency exit, passing sentries for the last time. No nametags were worn, and I never knew any of these guards by their names. Whenever I had talked to one, I addressed him by his rank. For most of them I was the "*Junge.*" Nobody had ever called me a *Kerl* as this officer did. It had a derogatory connotation.

Frequent expressions were: "Boy, here again so soon?" and "Lucky boy, you made it once more!"

I was without military rank. Earlier I had been addressed as *Melder,* which I preferred above all. One of the steady guards, I learned after the war, was Master Sergeant Erich (sometimes identified as Harry) Mengershausen. He must have been on long 12 to 16 hour shifts. With my constant runs, we saw each other frequently, exchanging words. During the very last days and nights, we even shared bits of information, such as how close the Russians were, where sharpshooters had been sighted, who was among the casualties, etc.

I believe it was *Hptschfr.* Mengershausen who came up to the emergency exit door on this occasion while I was waiting for a break in the shelling. Now, I had an opportunity to make some inquiries. Dr. Gertrud wanted to know about how the Hitlers were buried and where their graves were.

"There I believe!" he answered without hesitation, pointing to a place in the garden that looked like a shell-crater.

"We didn't bury them!" he said. With "we" he must have meant the regular guards. I didn't think of it as important to know who did and didn't lay the Hitlers to rest. Later, upon my return, I told Dr. Gertrud that there was just one grave for both, a shell-crater, unmarked and still smoldering.

Once again, she seemed visibly shaken but continued to go about her work.

I didn't tell her that, through the rising smoke, I had seen what I thought was a bone, from an arm or a leg sticking out. Not having viewed it close-up, it could have been a metal pipe or for that matter anything that didn't burn down. It had looked as if the soil was steaming. Obviously dirt had been shoveled upon the burned corpses, but not enough to eliminate the smoldering.

The surroundings of this historic grave looked more like a junkyard than a garden. Clutter covered the area, fragments of explosions, debris, drabs of stone and metal, and several corpses yet to be buried. I also remember a cement mixer and a burned out car, both full of bullet holes. No actual man-to-man fighting had taken place in the *Reich* Chancellery garden. The dead soldiers and civilians must have been victims of bomb or grenade hits.

On the other side of Wilhelmstrasse in the air raid shelter, the one that was open to the public, a mood of *Weltuntergangsstimmung* (the-world-is-coming-to-an-end) had started to take hold and would increase greatly after Hitler's suicide. With alcohol on hand and available, the looming catastrophe turned rapidly into an orgy.

On one occasion, a young girl in the uniform of a *Nachrichtenhelferin* (signal auxiliary), approached me with open arms. She just hugged me, kissed me, and then babbled: "You sweet little one: from you I, too, want a baby..." She put her hand over my Iron Cross. When I felt her tongue and her hair in my face, I told her, "I am on duty," and slipped loose from her embrace in as courtly a fashion as possible.

"I don't want to be captured by the Russians." Now she sobbed.

How could I prevent it?

I felt sorry for her. I felt pain. I felt helpless and disturbed.

But the situation was entirely different now than the one I had experienced a year earlier with Trudel. Then I wasn't sure of myself. Later, with Anne-Maria I experienced a relationship. One of love and commitment.

Even with death approaching, I felt bound by a pledge. Anne-Maria might be pregnant with a child, our child.

The wellspring of renewal, of life's continuation, might survive where she was, in Hof. There, life might not end, as mine would parch and turn into ashes.

The power to reason failed me. Here I was in the middle of a crowd, of soldiers, of civilians, including an attractive young girl who had wanted to make love with a stranger.

CHAPTER 62

Preparing for the Breakout

After I had been issued a written permit to enter by Axmann's friend, Johann Rattenhuber, Chief of the *Reich* Security Service, I wasn't required to surrender my Walther 6.35 anymore. This clearance enabled me to use the emergency exit/entrance. This privilege most likely saved my life on several occasions.

My runner activities increased further. I believed they were strictly for military reasons. *Rjfr.* Axmann, at a feverish pace, wanted to know all about location, strength, munitions still at hand, and the degree of fighting spirit of all Hitler Youth units he thought could still be reached. I was the only runner left at his command post.

Dr. Gertrud had learned that the Goebbels intended to kill their children. It wasn't I who had told her. Most likely it was one of the nurses who rotated between the two hospitals below the *Reich* Chancellery and Party Chancellery.

Dr. Gertrud was visibly upset. She wanted to save these children and came up with a plan how it could be done.

Her idea was to use two girls from among her aides to take the children underground to a nearby clinic she was familiar with. I cannot be sure, but somehow I seem to remember that this clinic was located near the Weidendamm *Bruecke* (bridge) where Dr. Gertrud would perish during the breakout.

What I remember clearly is that Dr. Gertrud spoke at length to *Rjfr.* Axmann and persuaded him to let Dr. Goebbels know what she had in mind.

To my surprise, *Rjfr.* Axmann left to see Dr. Goebbels and

extended this offer. As he later reported back to Dr. Gertrud, Dr. Goebbels didn't even think about it or consult his wife but stood firm that the children would die together with their parents and their *Fuehrer*.

It might have been at this point that Dr. Gertrud, too, began to realize that dark forces were at work, and what we had to look forward to was *Untergang und Tod* (doom and death). Had she remained in her makeshift hospital, she would have lived.

I carried a *Meldung* (message) for *Rjfr*. Axmann that the Hitler Youth fighting group in Neukoelln had been wiped out by a Russian tank attack. Those still alive would be prisoners by now. Soon to be reduced to diseased skeletons. The *HJ-Kampfgruppen* defending Weissensee and Pankow were also engaged in fierce fighting. How were they faring?

On a delivery to the air raid shelter after Hitler's suicide, I noticed some children. Obviously alone, without anyone to look after them. I thought of the two boys on the hospital train and wondered about the one that survived, if he might still be alive.

I heard a young girl say: "We will get out of here. The *Fuehrer* won't leave us in the lurch!" She was maybe eight or nine years old and she looked younger than my sister Doerte.

"The *Fuehrer* is dead," her mother replied, whispering.

"Dead?"

"He left us to the Communists," the mother explained to her daughter. "The *Fuehrer* left us. The war is lost. The enemy will finish us off."

Couples, visibly engaged in more than embraces, were not able to understand their instinctive actions. Perhaps in fear of death. There were sweet sounds and curses, panting, wheezing, gasping. Yet, most of us, if not all, knew of the terror that surrounded us.

After Hitler's death, the Russians, or German communists, must have intimated that the man closest to Hitler, Martin Bormann, was in fact one of the Soviet Union's secret agents and that he was the so-called "leak" from which the Russians had obtained secrets. How could this have been? After Hitler's suicide,

M

Bormann expected Captain Baur to fly him to *Grossadmiral* Doenitz, the new Chancellor. Had he been a Soviet agent wouldn't he have wanted to make contacts with the Russians, whose advanced positions were already within walking distance?

Flugkapitaen (flight captain) Baur was without a plane ever since Field Marshal Ritter von Greim and Hanna Reitsch left.

But even had there been a *Fieseler Storch* or an *Arado* still at his disposal, he would have been without a take-off strip. The *Ost-West Axe* (east-west axis) was already in Russian hands.

Captain Hans Baur, also an *SS-Gruppenfuehrer*, prepared himself for the breakout on foot. So did his deputy, Hitler's second pilot, *SS-Standartenfuehrer* (Colonel) Georg Betz. Bauer survived. Betz died.

Thus, Bormann could not be flown out and would have to join the breakout forces on foot too. Probably a good reason, once more, for him to reach for the bottle. He was in a state of intoxication when he turned to *Rjfr.* Axmann.

Could Hitler Youth couriers channel him (I believe he used the word *durchschleusen*) to the Pichelsdorfer *Bruecken* (bridges) and transport him from there to Germany's new Chancellor? Immediately?

Bormann knew that Axmann had promised Hitler to get him out of Berlin by putting a human shield around him—a Hitler Youth *Kampfgruppe* that would crack the Russian encirclement and take him to the fortress in the Alps.

Hitler had declined.

His physical condition was beyond such a task.

Bormann must have concluded that he was in better shape and that his chances of survival would be better if he left in advance amidst a small group of Hitler Youth. Previously, they had successfully "channeled" staff officers through the Russian front to Dr. Schluender's *Kampfgruppe* at the Pichelsdorfer bridges.

It was Major Weltzin who discussed Bormann's request with *Rjfr.* Axmann when I was resting on the cot. Axmann seemed flabbergasted.

Not being asleep, I listened in.

With Hitler dead, Bormann had become *Parteichef* (party leader). As such, he wanted the offer Axmann had made to Hitler renewed and applied to him.

For a moment I wished that *Rjfr.* Axmann would oblige. If he went along with Bormann's request then I, for sure, would have been one of the boys assigned to this task.

With Hannes, I had been to the Havel bridges twice. Together with a few Berliners who knew the city above and below ground, we might have a better chance of getting through than during a massive breakout.

I got up and encouraged *Rjfr.* Axmann to approve of Bormann's plan. So did *Hauptbannfuehrer* Boldt and *Oberbannfuehrer* Dietrich. But Major Weltzin or Major Theilacker, perhaps even both, suggested that such an undertaking had to be authorized by General Mohnke and General Weidling. I doubt that General Weidling was contacted but remember *Rjfr.* Axmann sending Major Weltzin to Gen. Mohnke's command post in the New *Reich* Chancellery.

I, too, waited.

Weltzin returned. "Out of the question!"

The outcome was: "No!"

There was to be no separate breakout, not even for Martin Bormann. As party chief, he had no control over the military forces or military actions.

I think it was Axmann himself who went to tell Bormann and afterwards visited with Dr. Goebbels.

Bormann was a typical *Goldfasan* (gold pheasant, as party officials were called sarcastically). He was not a soldier-type. He acted like a bully probably to hide that he really was a coward. Axmann must have been of the same opinion but openly he only expressed *"er konnte viel vertragen,"* (he could hold his liquor.) After Hitler's suicide, Bormann seemed to lose confidence and go over the limits, possibly *um sich Mut anzutrinken* (to find courage in alcohol). His state of intoxication became an embarrassment.

With his request denied, he must have realized that he was without real power. The fact that Hitler, in his testament, had named him party chief amounted to nothing. I disliked Bormann but would have welcomed the chance to break out with him ahead of the pack.

Ready to die, what would I die for? Hitler was dead. The *Volk* (nation) was badly beaten and the Fatherland had lost this war. I wouldn't die for my mother, my sisters and brothers. They didn't want me to die. What about my father? Being a traditionalist, might he still see my demise as an act of honor?

A last sacrifice to glory in spite of defeat? A noble example for future generations?

I knew that Anne-Maria was waiting for me.

CHAPTER 63

The Breakout

As liaisons, Axmann's adjutants, Weltzin and Theilacker, were on a rotating schedule. I believe at this time Boldt was at Gen. Mohnke's command post in the *Reich* Chancellery and Dietrich was with Dr. Goebbels in the *Fuehrerbunker*. A whirlwind of activities followed involving me with runs back and forth, having to deal with officers and radio men, now several of them with short tempers.

When Dietrich returned we were told to prepare for a breakout.

Then Axmann was informed that the breakout would be postponed by at least 24 hours, so we could get some sleep. Soon my turn came to rest, but I was not apt to fall asleep. With Hitler dead, I was convinced that soon I would be dead too.

As would all of us be.

It just couldn't be any other way.

I knew how close the Russians were. The intensity of their non-stop artillery barrages still increased.

Thoughts of God and angels floated through my head.

Life must have a meaning.

Shouldn't life be preserved and not destroyed! Sudden and simple realizations advanced my *Gottglaeubigkeit* (belief in God).

Could there still be a chance to avoid the grim reaper, to survive and then to lead a meaningful life? To take off and try to reach the Russians with hands up was not an option I would have considered at that time.

I had to follow orders, participate in the breakout and hopefully survive.

M

I remembered my *Grossmuttel* (grandmother). As a little boy, when I prayed asking of God favors, she had urged me to thank him instead of begging.

I ended up praying most of this night, not asking for my life, but promising to do something with it should I survive.

Thoughts of dying generated flashbacks, flashbacks, and more flashbacks—many having to do with motorcycles. As a child in Waldgut Horka riding with a stranger. I remembered motorcycle rides with Kurt in Breslau and the daring *Meldefahrten* (courier trips) just days ago with Hannes. Where was Hannes now? I longed for his company more than ever.

And then Anne-Maria entered my mind, so vividly, crying as vehemently as Dr. Gertrud had, not over Hitler's death, but that I had left her, never to return. That I would die.

Her image seemed so real in my head. I heard her talk to me. She said: "You could have stayed here and become an instructor in the pre-military training camp. Why did you have to return to the front? Why didn't you stay with me? With your war injury, that would have been possible!" The girl I loved now haunted me.

It was too late to write parting words. The letter to her and the one to my mother, which I had given Hannes, didn't say all I wanted to say.

And now, it seemed that Hannes was dead and these letters would never be posted. Nothing I wrote now, I was convinced, could ever get mailed. The shock of disappointments, one after the other, was devastating. While I struggled with my disillusionment and mortification, the outside world changed drastically.

Hitler's suicide took place on April 30, around 4 p.m. (by the time Axmann returned to his command post it was about 6 p.m.) Our departure was postponed and then rescheduled for shortly after 10 p.m. on May 1, 1945.

I recall a nerve-shattering conversation with *Rjfr.* Axmann. I asked him why the breakout scheduled for earlier this night had been cancelled. He replied that not all of the troops could be informed. Also that peace negotiations were under way. (Not true, as we know now. The Russians were approached but insisted on unconditional surrender. Axmann realized later that he had received incomplete information about the attempt to negotiate a ceasefire.) Dr. Goebbels had left the negotiations up to the military leaders.

Still unable to grasp why Hitler had committed suicide, I now felt up to asking painful questions. "Why did the *Fuehrer* kill himself?"

Axmann's answer was: "We are near the end."

To my mind, he just confirmed that we would die. Interestingly enough, fifty years later, Axmann published his memoirs, titled: *This Can't be the End*,[161] It was. Of the Hitler era. Of the Third *Reich*. Of my upbringing!

I continued my questioning: "Where are the miracle weapons we are waiting for?"

He replied: "Not yet finished."

Axmann erred, knowingly or unknowingly then, because there was no V-3 or any other miracle weapon in production that could have changed the outcome of the war in Germany.

In the United States, the atomic bomb was near completion. At that time, I had never heard of an atomic bomb (only to become very active in the anti-nuclear movement decades later), and I doubt that Axmann knew anything about this catastrophic weapon on the last day of April.

"Now there will be no more heroes' death. Now God will just let us perish!" I dared to say, blaming God instead of the *Fuehrer*.

"We have to break out!" Axmann declared.

After conferring with all of his liaison officers, often described as his adjutants, Axmann seemed to work up some hope. A plan developed that we, together with *Kampfgruppe* Mohnke, break out and then on the way other Hitler Youth units would attempt to team up with us. He envisioned a combined force of over a thousand Hitler Youth, smashing through the Russians cauldron.

"What then?"

"Keep on fighting as ordered by the *Fuehrer!*"

"What about the wounded?" I wanted to know.

"They have to be left behind."

Dr. Gertrud, to my surprise, insisted that we take her along. At first, *Rjfr.* Axmann said that we couldn't.

"You will be needing me!"

Finally, Axmann gave in.

Dieter, wounded, would be left behind. I left my poems with him. One I have recreated:

> *From an*
> *unknown grave, my burning soul*
> *And the winter wind*
> *reach an*
> *endless sea,*
> *with wondrous*
> *waves*
> *of eternity.*

Whatever happened to Dieter Schroeder and to my poems, written under the most adverse of conditions, I still don't know.

That I had the urge to write is as much a mystery as life is. When I parted with my poems, I faced death but had hope that the wounded that remained behind, would survive!

***

On the night of May 1-2, the time had come for the breakout. It was Dr. Gertrud who inquired if the Goebbels' children were dead already. No one knew.[162] Bormann appeared still so inebriated that Major Weltzin turned to Axmann: "In this condition we won't take him along." Gen. Mohnke, whose group was the largest and first to leave, had ignored him. (I remember that Bormann had a bitter, loud-voiced argument with one of Mohnke's officers). *Rjfr.* Axmann was even less inclined to take him. It was Dr. Naumann, with personnel from the Propaganda Ministry, who took Martin Bormann along. He also took Dr. Stumpfegger, Hitler's last personal physician. Stumpfegger appeared to be sober and must have assisted Bormann to steady himself. Both, as we know now, were in possession of a *Blausaeure* (prussic acid) capsule.

To my mind, taking poison was an act of cowardice. According to Axmann, Hitler had committed suicide with a shot through the mouth. Axmann was wrong. Hitler apparently had a poison capsule in his mouth and bit it open when he shot himself through the temple. Martin Bormann and Dr. Stumpfegger poisoned themselves that night during the breakout, although decades would go by before this evidence emerged. Of our group, only a few survived, and Axmann was among them. When the garage with the Mohnke troops became overcrowded, we moved to a storage section below the Chancellery. I remember neatly stacked wood. If there were fireplaces in the Chancellery this might have been the remaining wood supply.

There were perhaps 20 groups scheduled to leave in short intervals. I remember that we were the fifth group, but Axmann, becoming impatient, decided to move us up to third position. We were supposed to meet other Hitler Youth units past the river Spree, as well as in the Havel River region. We would become a sizeable force, strong enough to smash through the Russian encirclement. United with as many as possible of the Hitler Youth fighting units, still in action in and around Berlin, there was belief that we could assemble a *gewaltige Streitmacht* (formidable fighting force), which would be able to break open the Russian cauldron and reach the Alpine fortress.

Not until the operation was underway, would Axmann give me an envelope for *Grossadmiral* Doenitz. Only then did I learn that we would not try to reach the Alps, but Flensburg. It was there where the Navy Chief, Hitler's successor, had his headquarters.

My last recollection of World War II is that *Rjfr.* Axmann, Major Weltzin, and I, ahead of our group, approached what appeared to be a tank barricade at the Weidendamm Bridge. Hell broke loose.

It seemed that we were fired at from every direction, even from

M

behind. Didn't some of our own troops realize that we were ahead of them?

Bullets hissed through the air, as did shrapnel pieces, and jagged metal hit the street. I saw sparks in front of me. A deadly rain of shards of metal.

This is it, I thought. This will be the end.

An explosion ahead of us caused spewing flames and a strong tremor.

All three of us were able to take partial cover, pressed against a wall. A few meters in front of us, there was an entrance, probably leading into a protective cellar. We crawled to there but then did not go down because emerging from the cellar shaft was thick, biting smoke. Although I was situated right next to *Rjfr.* Axmann, he had to yell so that I could hear him. He ordered me to bring up the end of our group.

"We won't be able to get across the bridge. We have to by-pass it."

"Assembly point?" I questioned him, shouting as loud as I could.

"Over there!" He pointed with his left arm to the building on the opposite side of the street. I think that it was the Admiral's Palace, but I am not sure. It wasn't filled with smoke as yet. "There in the cellar!" Axmann repeated. Weltzin now, too, pointed to the building across the street. Off I went.

Without being hit in this merciless hail of metal, I reached Dr. Gertrud. With her was Axmann's adjutant, Heinz Boldt, followed by some of the girls in single file. I yelled Axmann's order to Boldt, which he acknowledged. I noticed two of the *BDM*-girls had been wounded already with blood on their uniforms. As far as I could tell, Dr. Gertrud had not been injured as yet. Not until after the war would I learn that she advanced, but shortly after she was dead.

Meanwhile, I had to cross the street again to reach Schroeder and Grimm. Each carried a briefcase stuffed full with money— over half a million *Reichsmark* in cash. At the beginning of the breakout, I had been asked to carry one of these two briefcases. I did carry one from the Chancellery exit until we reached *Unter den Linden* (Fifth Avenue-like street in Berlin). There, Axmann halted and gave me the letter addressed to Doenitz. We heard shots nearby. I returned the briefcase. I was still Axmann's *Melder* and for a runner it was too cumbersome.

Now I had lost sight of Schroeder and Grimm. Small fragments hit the top of my steel helmet. I felt a knock and heard the jagged sound of metal thwacking metal. I threw myself on the pavement, ever more closely pushed against the wall for minimum exposure.

Since last night, my "night of thoughts," my mind kept scrutinizing what might come after death. I assured myself that, even should my body be *zerfetzt* (torn apart), my soul was bullet-proof and would remain whole.

CHAPTER 64

Paralysis

I never reached Grimm and Schroeder and the trailing group members behind them.

I remember bits and pieces of what happened next. I remember my shrieking.

I must have gone down.

I had no inkling that a piece of shrapnel hit my spine.

Did the outer wall of the building I had pressed my body against collapse to bury me under heaps of debris?

Following the screams, my memory went blank.

It reconnects after an undetermined stretch of time, when I see myself in a dream, looking from above at my very own body, mutilated but still alive.

As a young boy, I had visions of a twin brother. Now, in my apparition, I had become two.

I didn't realize at my first awakening whether I was dead or alive. I was paralyzed. Axmann believed that I had been killed. He told me six years later when he was surprised and visibly glad to see me alive.

I had been lucky despite my misfortune. Hit but not killed, I had been dug out before dying.

Whether by Germans or Russians, I don't know.

My first mental awareness, after an undetermined length of unconsciousness, was that of a Russian female officer. She must have been a physician. She spoke German and wanted to know my name and age. Then she asked me if I was a Fascist.

I answered: "No!" To my mind, it was the truth.

At that time, all I knew was that Facism was Italy's political and economic system during the time the Duce (Mussolini) was in power.

Had she asked me if I were a *Nationalsozialist* or Nazi, I would have answered "Yes." I still was a Nazi and I never lied to any of my interrogators.

Then she asked about my rank, unit, and where I fought.

My replies were: "*Volkssturmman*" and "Fortress Regiment Berlin."

"Who was your last commander?"

"Gen. Weidling," I answered.

Although, Axmann no longer reported to him (if he ever had), *General der Artillerie*, Helmuth Weidling had been Berlin's commandant. This I knew for sure.

Her assistant, after he had written down my name and birth, then asked "Company?"

I replied "*Kampfgruppe* Axmann." I thought that I had papers on me, signed by him.

But the name Axmann did not make him or her suspicious and, as it turned out, I was without identification whatsoever, even my dog tag had been removed. In all likelihood, I was dug out by Germans, perhaps by so-called "rubble women," who saw my young face and removed everything that would have identified me as a member of the armed forces especially with a *Waffen-SS* paybook, together with my *Volkssturm* paybook in my pocket. Had Russian soldiers, dug me out, they might have taken my decorations as souvenirs, but not my pay books and my dog tag so that I would be identified.

Panzernahkampfbrigade Artur Axmann was not a unit on record. Apparently none of the *Volkssturm* units were.

Nobody ever asked me if I had seen or come in contact with Hitler. Then, and during all subsequent interrogations, I answered all questions honestly, but I never offered information.

I slipped in and out of consciousness. The extent of my injuries was not at all clear.

M

I was only able to move my arms and my head but not my legs. I had no control over my bladder or bowels. I was helpless and soiled, lying on a stretcher. I wore a shirt and nothing else, covered by a blanket.

At the time I did not know that my condition was caused by a spine contusion, sufficient to produce temporary paralysis but not unremitting. It did not kill the nerve fibers. The Russian physician did not know that it was a compression that soon would disappear with me regaining control of my legs and intestines. If she had, she undoubtedly would have added me to the wounded that were shipped first to Frankfurt/Oder and from there into Russian POW-Labor camps. Of course, I, too, didn't think that I could recover.

I found myself in a helpless, horrible mess, believing that I was beyond recovery. My death wish became so intense that, days later, I would plead with an old man to please shoot me.

"Boy, are you crazy? We don't have weapons anymore," was his reply.

I asked for a razor knife. He did not have one he said.

It was a woman who interfered.

"I'll clean you up, you will be OK. Be brave!" It didn't make sense under these conditions—to be a helpless invalid for the rest of my life. I couldn't stand the thought.

At this time I still thought that my family would be able to return to Breslau, but I was also convinced that our house had been destroyed. I knew that it had been located in the southern battle zone of the fortress. (It did survive but, since Silesia was turned over to Poland, we couldn't have returned, regardless of what condition it was in.)

The woman, a refugee, undressed me, washed me, without soap and with an old rag. She dressed me in underwear and a uniform with all of the insignia removed.

"From a fallen comrade." She must have taken the cloth from a dead corpse, since mine was so soiled and had stunk so badly. Although, because of my head injuries, my ability to smell might have been impaired, the stench was so strong that it affected me nevertheless. Feeling nauseated all along, I had to vomit. The strange woman lifted my head and I can still hear her saying: "It will get better, don't despair, oh my boy, don't die on me."

But that was what I wanted—to die.

Instead I must have become unconscious again, because what I remember next were screams by a girl on a military truck. I can't be sure that she was being raped. It appeared to be that way. I also remember hearing a baby cry—but I couldn't see it. A Russian soldier had given me bread to eat and had handed me a cube of butter that was melting in my hand. Then he poured vodka in my mouth.

Intoxicated himself, he poured the vodka all over my face. The alcohol penetrated into my eyes, stinging like fire; for hours I couldn't see. My screaming infuriated him and another besotted soldier on the truck. They both kicked me and possibly threw me off the truck, because the next memory I have of myself is lying in the ditch of a road.

Taken from there to a farmhouse, cleaned again and fed, miraculously I gradually regained my sanity and my feeling below the waist. Oddly, I have a complete lapse of memory from the time I recovered until my arrival at the farm of my uncle and aunt.

My luck continued. Two or three weeks later, I left. On a foggy night, I crossed the Mulde River where the Americans had stopped when the war ended. As far as I can ascertain, it must have been the last night before the four powers retreated to their agreed-upon occupation zone. While wading through the river with a heavy backpack, the current knocked me down and my injured spine must have been bruised once more, because when I was pulled out, I was numb again.

Since many refugees from the Russian side crossed over to the American Occupation Zone, transports were waiting. I was driven in an ambulance to a reception camp, and I ended up in the encampment's medical facility. There, I was not only interrogated by an intelligence officer, but also was shown the documentaries that General Eisenhower had ordered to be made when the concentration camps (Buchenwald and Bergen-Belsen) were liberated.

I was so shocked. At first I couldn't believe what I saw. One of the older, apparently totally desensitized soldiers whispered: "Made in Hollywood." I could not see it that way. There were heaps of skeletons and some of the bodies still moved.

This couldn't have been staged, with so many bodies of skin and bone.

There were others, mostly older soldiers, who shrugged it off as propaganda.

"How could that be?" I kept asking myself, impacted by the images shown.

One of the wounded Germans knew and confided: "It's true! These are concentration camps."

The officer who had interrogated me had still-photos as well, horrendous portrayals of destruction and death.

This was before I was steady on my feet again. While paralyzed for the first time, I had wanted to die. Now I wanted to vanish because the way these documentaries were presented made me feel that I shared guilt in these heinous crimes committed by Hitler, the *Fuehrer* I had believed in and served.

It affected me physically. I could neither eat nor sleep the following night and day.

Once again, I snapped out of my embarrassing predicament and this time for good.

I found my mother, who was no longer at my grandfather's. He had been interned.

My father had also survived the war and stuck to his old beliefs. He saw what happened as events that are part of history; war itself, and the way it was expanded beyond battle fields by both sides, was to blame for all of the slaughter in concentration camps, as well as in cities turned into infernos by air raids.

His beliefs never changed.

CHAPTER 65

The Tribunal

For me, nothing would justify the cruelty and slaughter. The "Final Solution" which led to the extermination of Jewish people was abhorrent beyond belief.

Meanwhile, I had learned about the many additional concentration and extermination camps, especially Auschwitz.

I agonized physically and mentally. My whole belief system crashed and, only gradually, established itself anew. I became a pacifist in the true sense of the word while following the Nuremberg trials intensely.

I began, with the help of a Catholic university professor, Dr. Wuerth, to search for the truth of what had happened during Germany's immediate past.

The man who I would be touched by the most was Baldur von Schirach! The predecessor of Artur Axmann (whose whereabouts at the end of the war were not known to me) was the Youth Leader who was also a wordsmith and who had once written me a short note, encouraging me to continue writing poetry.

When had he come to realize what kind of a man his former leader was, our *Fuehrer?*

He stated in front of the tribunal on May 24, 1946 on the first day after I had reached adulthood:[163]

> *What happened in Auschwitz is the greatest, most satanic*
> *mass murder committed in world history. Hoess, the comman-*
> *dant of Auschwitz, was just the hangman; it was Hitler who*
> *had ordered the killings. He and Himmler committed these*

M

crimes jointly, which will forever disgrace us. The youth of Germany, however, is innocent of what Hitler has done (in the name of the German people) to the Jewish people. They (the youth of Germany) didn't know that the Jews were being exterminated and would never have wanted it to happen. I am guilty before God and this nation to have guided the youth to follow Hitler, whom I considered to be unimpeachable but who turned out to be a murderer of millions.

Thus, von Schirach stood up for Germany's youth, and I felt assured that the rest of the world would now know that the *Fuehrerkult* (leader worship) was something we had been conditioned for and that my generation never knew any other form of government. Nor did we know of the mass murders that had been committed.

In the *Neue Zeitung (New Press)*, the occupation newspaper, I read that the *Waffen-SS* had been declared a criminal organization because it was the military branch of the *SS*. It was originally Hitler's Security Corps that under Heinrich Himmler became the "Black Order" of the National Socialist movement. As the Nazi's "political police," it had been put in charge of administering the concentration and later the extermination camps.

The *Waffen-SS* was comprised of Hitler's most fanatical and enduring combat soldiers, including over 25,000 volunteers from various European nations (see Appendix B). It was strictly a military force for use in combat, often spearheading his assaults. Their fighting spirit had become legendary. The commandos charged with carrying out liquidations were called *SS* action groups, comprised of *SD* Security Service and the GESTAPO (Secret State Police) members. The concentration camp complements were *Totenkopfverbaende*[165] (Death Head Units). Before the Nuremberg trials, I had heard the term *Einsatzgruppen* but never knew that it was a terrorist organization. The *SS* and all of its branches, encompassing every single member, had also been put on trial at the International Military Tribunal.

The verdict: "Criminal!"[164]

I had obeyed and carried out what I had been taught was my duty. For how long I would have continued to do so, I will never know. I struggled for years with the concept of collective guilt and finally decided I can hold myself only responsible for my own actions. Nevertheless, I came to the conclusion that had Hitler won this war, I would have most likely, without realizing it, become a criminal. We had to be dutiful to our *Fuehrer*, blindly loyal!

In 1945, the Buchenwald/Bergen-Belsen documentaries (later the Auschwitz revelations as well) had forever put into my heart a mortal terror.

Because of my youth in 1945, I was exempt from having to face a court. I wasn't even called to appear before a *Spruchkammer* (literally: verdict chamber), an invention of the Joint Allied Forces to identify and, when warranted, to punish ex-Nazi functionaries.

My father withheld information. He maintained that it was the "smart" thing to do. I remember him telling me that the *SD* had been a secret organization. It had served the state, and its members were duty bound never to reveal their membership (He had a lawyer friend, Dr. Weidenkopf, who supported this position). To deny the truth was a lie.

With Axmann the situation was different. In matters he was willing to discuss, I always felt that he was truthful with me. Yet, his admiration for Hitler never ceased. In fact, he always prided himself for having remained loyal to his *Fuehrer*.

I am all for loyalty but loyalty must have its ethic too! Human life, on any scale, is worth more than the esteem accorded to an absolute ruler or for that matter to any leader.

It was Baldur von Schirach's admission of guilt and not Artur Axmann's demonstration of loyalty that propelled me to find non-aggressive solutions and to vanquish hate once and for all.

I wrote a fairy tale (I called it a peace story) about an invading army that expected to be shot at when crossing its neighbor's border. Instead, the conquered had decided to treat the soldiers like guests. Baffled by the unexpected hospitality, the invaders didn't kill anyone. Instead they made an effort to understand the behavior of those they had invaded. They came to the conclusion that most of the population in the area they had occupied wanted to live in peace. Thus, without any fighting having taken place, some of the occupiers remained, keeping the border open for all to settle where they preferred.

Obviously, no dictators were involved.

My "fairy tale" was dismissed as unrealistic.

Over 50 years later, a noted Sinologist gave my fantasy-story credit. He wrote: "The tale described by you has happened many times in China. More than once, conquerors had been subdued by the gentle, refined culture of the Chinese. After one generation, even the fiercest warriors became fat and fond…"

I wrote poems and more poems and many a short story. Of the ones submitted to what was then called the "licensed press," the only one published appeared in a Catholic paper periodical. The title, "The Brother from Home," reflected on the fate of refugees.

The denazification process came to an end. However I remained disturbed by my father's continued falsifications about his past. He, who once had beaten me mercilessly for having lied, never revealed that he had falsified his past. He seemed all right with having gotten away with it. Even though he was my father, in good conscience I could not sanction a lie—any lie.

Relatives and friends as well as I, remembered that on his black SS-uniform he had worn an SD diamond patch. In Breslau, he had openly and proudly shown that he was a member of Hitler's elite intelligence and security force.

Now we were in Eberspoint, Bavaria. No one knew him except the members of his family. Obviously we didn't turn him in, and fortunately, I was never questioned by any officials about his past. I believe that he was classified as an inactive party member.

I, in turn, benefited as a result of my youth. Had I been two years older, I most likely would have ended up in the *Waffen-SS* Hitler Youth Division, the one with the "Langemark Spirit."[166]

Axmann had reminded us from time to time of these young

gallant fighters. We had been conditioned to look upon them as great heroes. Now I see them as what they became in the eyes of critical military analysts: cannon-fodder! In Berlin we had been expected to set forth the same willingness to sacrifice ourselves. And to the war's end, many of my comrades had fulfilled this expectation.

Had I known what the Nazi's had on their conscience, I would not have wanted to belong. I had to prove this to myself.

Some of my friends have told me that it would not be in my best interest to emphasize my conviction that Hitler is responsible for more than one holocaust. But he is. In the end he had no concern for human life whatsoever.

None of the statistics of this catastrophic war estimate the end-of-the-slaughter casualties, and nowhere in the historical literature reviewed during my research did I find an estimate of the casualties suffered by the youngest soldiers, those of my age. Frequently it states that less than a hundred boys lost their lives at the Pichelsdorfer Bridges.

That might be true at this particular location, and Capt. Boldt might not have been correct when he stated that several thousand perished there.

However, if he included the boys stationed at the *Reichssportfeld*, and the casualties at the heavy fighting along Heerstrasse, the losses were substantial.

At least 12 additional Hitler Youth *Kampfgruppen* were engaged in fierce fighting at various locations in Berlin. And what about all of the Hitler Youth in *Volkssturm* units that fought in the Eastern provinces, in the fortress Breslau, and East of Berlin, starting with Koenigsberg?

The only known survivors of the *Kampfgruppe* Gutschke were Kurt Ruppelt and I.

After tragedy and disappointment caused dejection, I pulled myself out of the dilemma.

My adult life began. Soon in a newly established democracy, I could become a law-abiding and productive member of society, transform into a humane human being, and try to rid myself of all prejudices.

M

I believe I have become a principled person and have maintained high moral standards and defended some of my strong beliefs, outspokenly, but non-violently. For almost five years, I became an activist for the antinuclear movement. I will, to the end of my life, remain a strong advocate for the sanctity of life.

I see the new Millennium as a challenge for future generations to gradually transform our planet, non-violently, into one world for one humanity. Not to hate!

Not to cause unnecessary pain! Not to afflict cruelties! Not to kill! We have to start with the minds of our children and be willing to give up some of our freedoms whose effects can be too destructive and therefore endanger others.

We, the people of this world, have to examine our religions, our traditions, and our teaching to increase our efforts to replace the violent aspects of life with peaceful ones, through caring and sharing. Gentleness is not a weakness, it is a strength.

Once a dispatch rider on a motorbike, once a runner for a despot, after surviving the horrors of war, I was able to seize the opportunity for a spiritual transformation.

At the age of 16, I had stepped in and out of history.

It's still incomprehensible to me that I survived and that, as of this writing, I am still alive and able to influence the future—to perhaps help humanity not repeat the grim chapters of history. The challenge for the third millennium is co-existence and values based on truth. Sanctity of life is dependent upon our devotion to freedom.

POSTSCRIPT

James P, O'Donnell's *The Bunker*[167] ends with: "Epilogue—1945 and After." In this final chapter, O'Donnell reflects on the Hitler-Stalin relationship and of Stalin's morbid obsession to get hold of Hitler's body. It also mentions Hitler's double, supposedly a fellow countryman from Breslau. This old man, the one with the "darned socks," was thought to be in the bunker. It is possible that he was one of the Berlin civilians who were among the last casualties.

Did he require make-up to somewhat resemble Hitler? It's hard to tell based on the widely publicized Russian photograph. All I know is that I do not remember seeing him.

That the real Hitler was burned beyond recognition is no longer being challenged by acknowledged historians.

Although I had not been an eyewitness to the cremation, judging from the behavior and reactions by the guard personnel, I, too, believe that the *Fuehrer's* remains were buried near the emergency exit/entry. Most certainly the burial site was more than three meters away from the entrance and the bunker's heavy metal door. Once upon my return, the door was locked from the inside. I banged at it from the outside and feel sure that I stood on a hard surface, probably a two-meter cement slab.

O'Donnell quotes Red-Army Lieutenant Colonel Iwan Klimenko: "We started to dig and pulled from the crater the bodies of a man and a woman and two dogs." A week hence on or about May 10 (as reported later), the male remains were positively identified by a dental technician.[168] Thus, the charred skeletons of Hitler, his wife, and the dogs were indeed recovered from this shell crater closest to the steel-door. This distance couldn't have been three meters but was more than double—exceeding six meters for sure.

What about those who were watching? Not only would the onlookers have occupied one to two meters of linear space, but also if they were within three meters they all would have been caught by the flames when the gasoline that had been poured over the bodies was ignited.

O'Donnell never mentioned that the breakout, initially scheduled for late evening April 30, had been cancelled and that later, after Goebbels' suicide, Bormann wanted to get out ahead of the pack. I never was able to learn from Artur Axmann why he had failed to mention this in his book. (Although he had answered questions earlier, by the time I got to this line of questioning, his wife had sent me a fax that he was ill and unable to answer my questions).

O'Donnell finished his book, *The Bunker*, with comments from *Flugkapitaen* Hans Baur[169] and *Ruestungsminister* Albert Speer.[170] Then O'Donnell wrote—envisioning a peculiar image of Hitler: "On this truly giddy thought of the *Fuehrer*, Adolf Hitler, being rained out by clouds formed from his own hot air mixing with the beery sweat and throaty '*Sieg Heil!*' cheers of his frenzied followers, my last interview ended. In Berlin, the hourglass city, a city where it all could have happened."

I never saw a need for reading the German translation of *The Bunker*, thinking that the original English version would be the most authentic one. But then, when my wife and I visited Berlin in 1997, it was mentioned that *Die Katakombe* had a co-author (Uwe Bahnsen) and an entirely different ending.

Thereupon, I read the German version as well. It ends with the recollections of a male civilian, the only one employed in the *Fuehrerbunker* (lower bunker). He was *Elektromaschinenmeister* (Master Electrician/Chief Technician) Johannes Hentschel. Although Hentschel was very important and often talked about in the bunker, I don't recall ever having met him face-to-face. I remember having met Rochus Misch, but he doesn't. Thus, it is possible I met Hentschel and don't remember. I do remember having heard of him and was somewhat familiar with his name. I have my doubts about the story told by Hentschel of the six or seven soldiers dangling from lantern posts in Voss Strasse.

The ending of *Die Katakombe* states (my translation from German into English):

> *In the mixed company of POWs, Hentschel was thrust through the old, still impressive main gate of the new Reichskanzlei, built in 1938 by Albert Speer.*
>
> *It was 12 noon in Berlin, or shortly thereafter, and the sun was shining. Johannes Hentschel now saw the Voszstrasse and the city's ruins beside those of the Reichskanzlei for the first time after the fourteen seemingly endless days he spent underground.*
>
> *The uncommon brightness caused his eyes to blink. Suddenly he noticed, and with him the entire troop, the last, dreadful scene of this tragedy. Let him describe it in his own words: "We were at peace now, at least that's what I told myself, taking comfort from being alive. Now, as we were being led from the Reichskanzlei into Voszstrasse, where a truck waited to take us to an unknown destination, we looked up and what we saw was gruesome. Six or seven German soldiers, brought to the gallows, dangled from lantern posts. All of the slack corpses were covered with signs stating: Verraeter (traitor); Deserteur (deserter); Feigling (coward). These were the last victims of the fliegende SS-Standgerichte (Flying SS-Court Martials) of the crazy executioners.*
>
> *They were all so young. And so lifeless. The oldest might have been 20, the others a couple of years younger. Half of them were in Volkssturm or Hitler Youth uniforms. As we were loaded onto the truck, being rushed by unkind bayonets, I noticed my hand almost coming in touch with a boot of one of the hanged soldiers. He looked as if he was hardly sixteen years old. His expired blue eyes, bulging out, were gawking at us, expressionless. I shuddered and looked away. I felt ashamed in front of the Russian soldiers whose silence couldn't have been more reproachful. This executed German boy wasn't much older than the son I*

always wanted but never had. "Fuer Fuehrer, Volk und
Vaterland" (for leader, people and Fatherland)."
      That was the slogan then. Ironically, the story of Johannes
Hentschel's long watch in the bunker ended exactly there where
Lili Marleen's catching story began: 'Vor der Kaserne, vor dem
grossen Tor, stand eine Laterne…' (In front of the barracks, in
front of the big gate, stood a street lamp). Seven lampposts.
Around noon on May 2, 1945 in Berlin.

That's the ending of *Die Katakombe*. It makes for captivating
reading, a shocking, barbaric ending of a savage war fought by a
demonic leader. But was it true?

The last time I looked down Voss Strasse was during daylight
hours on May 1, 1945 and I recall no such sight. There were shell
holes in the street. There was battle-litter strewn about. There
were patches of smoke. There were some corpses, not hanged on
posts, but lying on the sidewalks. If still alive, they had a chance to
be rescued, because the wounded were still being picked up by
Gen. Mohnke's medics. Near the Hermann Goering Strasse inter-
section, I remember the shell of a burned out *Kuebelwagen* (jeep).
At the street corner there was some activity, but I had no reason for
going there to check it out. I could hear bullets whizzing by my
ears and sought cover as fast as possible. Thereafter I didn't use any
of the Voss Strasse entrances anymore but only the emergency
entry/exit in the Chancellery gardens.

I don't even think that there were seven lampposts on Voss
Strasse, at least not in close enough proximity to match Hentschel's
description.

(Jens Lemcke checked some old photographs of Voss Strasse
and did not detect any lampposts at all.)

Also, if there were six or seven last-minute hangings, could
they have been boys of the Hitler Youth? Absolutely not!

How can I be so sure? Because, of the two or three *HJ*-fighting
units within the *Zitadelle* complex, no one was left behind. All had
joined the Axmann *Ausbruchsgruppe* (breakout unit); even some of
the wounded that were able had joined our group.

No one who could later have tried to desert was left behind. The other *HJ-Kampfgruppen* still in action were not near enough. Plans had been made to join up with them beyond the Spree and Havel rivers.

At the Weidendamm bridge, after midnight, in the first hours of May 2, 1945, the fifth *Ausbruchsgruppe*, which had moved up to third place because Axmann had become impatient, was wiped out mercilessly.

Most were killed, many severely wounded, and some died there as well. How many ended up as prisoners is not known. Only a handful escaped, among them Axmann, Weltzin and Hartmann. I was on my last courier run, buried alive. I survived.

+++THE END+++

M

RECOMMENDED
RELEVANT READING

Books written about Hitler number nearly a hundred. I have not read all of them and I see no need to add a bibliography listing of all of Hitler's biographies and all of the books that address certain aspects of his life—of crafty deeds or horrendous crimes, of seemingly great accomplishments, and of his final failures. Scholars and historians have access to the wide range of titles covering the subjects of interest. For the average reader, I shall list books whose contents enhance and illustrate my story which, based strictly on personal memories, is consequently very limited in scope. Although Hitler was the *Fuehrer* while I grew up in Germany, I didn't come directly in contact with him until April 20, 1945 and, thereafter, indirectly served him as a courier for 10 days until April 30, 1945, the day he committed suicide.

A multitude of works describes, in full or in part, the war on the Eastern front that ended with the battle of Berlin. Many of those books are available in English as well as in German. Some, however, have not been (and might never be) translated from German into English. Those which are currently only available in German will be listed in bold.

The following describe wartime Berlin as realistically as possible:

Anthony Read and David Fisher, *The Fall of Berlin*, © 1992, W.W. Norton & Co. New York.

Tony Le Tissier, *The Battle of Berlin—1945*, © 1988, Jonathan Cape, London.

Tony Le Tissier, *Berlin—Then and Now* © 1992, After the Battle, London.

W. Venghaus (Hrsgb.),[171] *Berlin 1945*, © 1996, Venghaus Selbstverlag, Freudenberg.

Von zur Muehlen (Hrsgb.), *Der Todeskampf der Reichshauptstadt*, © 1994, Chronos, Berlin.

The immense superiority of the Red Army is especially well documented by:

David M. Glantz & Jonathan House, *When Titans Clashed*, (1995) University Press of Kansas, Lawrence

The literature about Hitler that I am familiar with, I found amazingly repetitious. When it comes to Hitler biographies—not being a historian—I am not in a position to judge which are the most authentic and comes closest to portraying Hitler the way he really was.

However, the one book that, to a great extent, critically reviews the Hitler biographies and portrays him strictly from the viewpoint of a historian is:

John Lukacs, *The Hitler of History*, © 1997, Alfred A. Knopf, New York

Books about Hitler covering specifically the time period, or parts thereof, from April 20 to April 30, 1945, include:

H.R. Trevor-Roper, *The Last Days of Hitler*, © 1947, The Macmillan Co., New York.

Gerhard Boldt, *Hitler—The Last Ten Days*, © 1947, Coward, McCann & Geoghegan, Inc., New York.

Anton Joachimsthaler, *The Last days of Hitler*, © 1996, Arms & Armour Press, London

Ulrich Voelklein (Hrsgb), *Hitlers Tod*, © 1998, Steidl Verlag, Goettingen

Ada Petrova & Peter Watson, *The Death of Hitler*, © 1955, W.W. Norton & Company New York.

During the 10-day period, I saw Hitler at close range several times and my impression was that he looked ill. The following two books throw light on his condition:

Fritz Redlich, M.D., *Diagnosis of a Destructive Prophet: Hitler*, © 1998 Oxford University Press, New York
Ernst Guenther Schenck, *Patient Hitler*, © 1989, Droste Verlag, Dueseldorf

The widely acclaimed bestseller *THE BUNKER* contains a few factual errors. It is important to note that the English and the German texts are not always consistent, since not just a translator, but a co-author took part in creating the German version.

Several corrections increased the credibility, although the fictional ending remains to be eliminated.

James P. O'Donnell, *The Bunker*, © 1978, Houghton Mifflin Company, Boston
James P. O'Donnell Uwe Bahnsen, *Die Katakombe*, © 1997, Bechtermuenz Verlag, Augsburg (Lizensausgabe.)

The most relevant works about the Hitler Youth consist of:

Artur Axmann, *Das kann doch nicht das Ende sein,* © 1995, S. Bublies Verlag, Koblenz
Dr. Jutta Ruediger (Hrsgb.), *Die Hitler-Jugend,* (1983) Askania Verlagsgesellschaft mbH, Lindhorst

Axmann was *Reich* Youth Leader and Dr. Ruediger headed the girls' branch. Both attempted to highlight social accomplishments and there were many. But within a totalitarian regime, these concepts could not, and did not, survive the defeat.

Axmann included some recollections of the occurrences during the time I had become his courier but in my opinion omitted many historically significant events he had witnessed or even participated in.

I was shocked to find that Dr. Ruediger, in her book, downplayed the enormous sacrifices of the HJ-*Volkssturm*. Thousands, if not tens of thousands, of those born in 1927, 1928, 1929, and some in 1930 were drafted into the *Volkssturm*.

Thousands were sacrificed and not just in Breslau, Koenigsberg, and Berlin. Thousands ended up in Russian prison camps and many did not return.

Reflecting contemporary perspectives are:

H.W. Koch, *The Hitler Youth*, © 1996, Barnes & Noble Books, New York

Arno Kloenne, *Jugend Im Dritten Reich*, © 1982 R. Piper GmbH Co. KG, Muenchen

Any book pointing to the dangers of racism (there is no master race!), of persecution and terror, of the insaneness of war, would be recommended reading by this author. Conflict resolution without bloodshed is the challenge of the future.

Finally, one book doesn't just relate to the last phase of WWII in Europe but encompasses its entire scope:

Olive Ponting, *Armageddon*, © 1995, Random House, New York

This book breaks down the statistics of the war fatalities and the war-related casualties worldwide. 85 million human beings were killed in the infernos and holocausts this war unleashed. Now with wars no longer restricted to battlefields, with nuclear power that could wipe out the entire world, only one solution prevails: Peace!

M

Every book that promotes peace and deals with the complex issues of multi-racial, multi-religious, and multi-cultural societies, this author recommends for reading.

APPENDIX—A

PEOPLE IN THE BUNKER

The British historical magazine, *After The Battle*,[172] published a compilation of 46 names of Zeitzeugen (contemporary witnesses), signified as "Dramatis Personae," who occupied in April of 1945, together with Hitler, the so-called *Fuehrerbunker*. What follows is my review of this list to point out those I recognized and those that I came in contact with.

AXMANN-*Reichsjugendfuehrer* (*Reich* Youth Leader) Artur Axmann. Leader of the Hitler *Jugend* (Hitler Youth) and at the end of the war, commander of the Hitler Youth Home Defense Force, which included *Panzernahkampfbrigade Artur Axmann*, a close-combat tank destruction brigade named after him. He was my commandant whom I served as courier from April 21, 1945 to May 2, 1945.

Axmann's command post was located in the cellars of the *Parteikanzlei* (Party Chancellery) on Wilhelmstrasse 64 (the building was still in existence when I visited the historical site in May 1997). In addition to attending the daily briefings, Axmann spent an increasing amount of time in the *Fuehrerbunker* during the last days of the battle.

He had been a soldier earlier in the war and lost one arm in Russia in 1941. He knew what went on in the streets of Berlin. Unlike Hitler and Bormann, he left the bunker several times and visited Hitler Youth units defending the *Reich* Chancellery.

Goering's telegram (where he stated that he would assume power if he did not hear from Hitler by a certain time) upset

Axmann visibly, and he agreed that he should be taken prisoner—
if not shot on the spot. Later Axmann changed his mind when he
became familiar with all the facts! Axmann learned of Himmler's
negotiations with Count Bernadotte, and Himmler's *Treuebruch*
(disloyalty) also had a devastating effect on him. "How disappointed
the *Fuehrer* must feel. What a blow!" Axmann expressed sorrow
and, at that time became even more determined to show Hitler
that he and members of the Hitler Youth would remain loyal to
the bitter end. After the war, I visited him and we had long
conversations. He made admissions: *"Fehler wurden gemacht"*
(Mistakes were made), but he never said anything bad about Hitler.

Axmann, after Hitler's suicide, and upon having inspected the
body, told me personally on April 30, 1945 that *"Der Fuehrer
erschoss sich durch den Mund,"* ("Hitler shot himself through the
mouth"). Few shared Axmann's opinion. Most maintained that
the bullet from Hitler's revolver had entered his head through the
right temple.

BAUR—*SS-Gruppenfuehrer* (Major-General) Hans Baur,
Hitler's Chief Pilot. I never met him. I may have seen him without
recognizing who he was. There were several high-ranking *SS*-offic-
ers in the bunker. I learned only after Hitler's suicide that Baur
was in the bunker, when, according to Axmann, *Reichsleiter* Bormann
wanted Baur to fly him to *Grossadmiral* (Grand Admiral) Karl
Doenitz.

I have no first-hand knowledge of this, but I was told that
Captain Baur, whom Hitler had given Anton Graff's painting of
Frederick the Great, didn't even bother to crate this valuable picture. Probably because no aircraft was available to put it on. Instead, he removed the canvas from the frame, rolled it up, and put
it in his rucksack, by now expecting to leave the bunker on foot.
And that is what happened.

BEERMANN—*SS Hauptsturmfuehrer* (Captain) Helmut
Beermann, member of *RSD (Reich* Security Service). I have no rec-
ollection of him. However, a guardsman of his, *SS-Unterscharfuehrer*
(Sergeant) Max Koelz, was one of the "inside" guards who always

seemed to be on duty at the stairway exit to the lower bunker (probably on 18-hour shifts). Due to my frequent appearances, he soon knew me as Axmann's *Melder* (courier).

BETZ (NOT: BEETZ)—Hitler's second pilot, Baur's deputy, *SS-Standartenfuehrer* (Colonel) Georg Betz was also in the bunker. I did not know him or know of him but must have been near him during the breakout on May 2nd, since he was one of the fatalities at the Weidendammer Bridge.

BELOW—*Oberst* (Colonel) Nicolaus von Below, Goering's *Luftwaffe Verbindungsoffizier,* (Air Force liaison officer). I have no recollection of him although he, too, participated in the May 1-2 breakout.

BOLDT—*Rittmeister* (cavalry captain) Gerhard Boldt, *ADC* (aide-de-camp). I remember him well. He was one of three officers *(Major* von Loringhoven and *Oberstleutnant* Weiss were the other two) with orders to break through the Russian lines and to hand-deliver Hitler's last, desperate orders personally to General Wenck. Axmann had offered Hitler my services to guide them to the Pichelsdorfer bridges held by Dr. Schluender's *Kampfgruppe* (fighting unit). My left hand was still in a cast. Boldt looked at it and said, "We don't need you, we know the way."

It is my recollection that another courier from Axmann guided them to the bridges. There they arrived but never reached Wenck. Boldt wrote in his book, *Die Letzten Tage*[173] *(The Last Days)* about it. Boldt claimed that *Obergebietsfuehrer* (third highest rank in the Hitler Youth) Dr. Schluender had told him that most of his 5,000 boys defending the bridges had perished.

I remember having been at Dr. Schluender's *Gefechtsstand* (command post) twice as a courier. There were never 5,000 boys positioned there to defend the two bridges. I estimate that the number ranged between 500 and 700—1,000 at the very most.

Stationed in the *Reichssportfeld* (stadium), however, were probably as many as 5,000 boys under the command of *HJ-Gebietsfuehrer* (Hitler Youth province leader), Otto Hamann. In addition, hundreds of girls (many of them trained in first aid),

M

ready to serve, had been assembled there waiting for their orders. The *BDM* girls' leader was Gisela Hermann. Later, Hamann fell and Hermann was wounded.

BORMANN—*Reichsleiter* (*Reich* party leader) Martin Bormann functioned as Hitler's "right hand man" (with more power than a private secretary). He looked "out of place" among all the military men. His breeches seemed too big, his boots too high. Overweight, he had this burly-beefy appearance, his eyes usually appeared to be just a bit too glossy. Often his facial expression was a smirk, as if he knew something you didn't. Most of the time he looked like a *Luestling* (debauchee) which I found appalling, especially in view of the situation we were in.

In Berlin, the *Reich* Chancellery was Hitler's and, across the street, the *Partei* Chancellery was Bormann's. Axmann and his staff were now stationed here as well. Since we had moved in, Bormann didn't come over once. There was no subterranean tunnel and to cross Wilhelmstrasse had become too dangerous.

We didn't actually occupy his office because bullets and shrapnel from constantly exploding Russian shells bombarded us with few intermissions. We dwelled in the safer air raid shelter below.

Since none of the living quarters in the lower bunker were Bormann's, he must have slept in one of the cellar rooms below the east wing of the *Reich* Chancellery, which was connected by underground passages to the bunker. This was where most of the bunker people (those who surrounded Hitler at the end) had been assigned sleeping quarters. (During the last nights, some, including one of the secretaries, didn't even bother going to their billets but slept on the floors in the bunker).

I sensed that Axmann disliked Bormann, perhaps even hated him (Axmann never expressed such sentiments to me), because in the past, the *Reichsleiter* had been able to block the *Reichsjugendfuehrer* from gaining access to Hitler. Only after Hitler's last birthday was Axmann able to by-pass Bormann to see Hitler.

Bormann also seemed to be eating a lot. In *Vorzimmer Lage* there was either a small table or teacart with open-faced sandwiches, which were replenished day and night. While I was sitting on the bench waiting for dispatches, I would frequently observe Bormann coming out again and again to grab a sandwich.

After Hitler's suicide, I no longer noticed Bormann in the lower bunker. Could he have realized that at least in the bunker he had become powerless? He apparently raided Kannenberg's galley for bottles of liquor still in storage there. Word was out that supplies, including cigarettes and alcohol were being made available to those in the bunker. Bormann, personally, it was said, had secured some of the finest spirits.

It was observed in the bunker during the last hours of his life that Dr. Goebbels openly distanced himself from Bormann. Of course, we didn't know at that time that Goebbels had the murder of his children on his mind as well as his and his wife's suicide.

The news that Captain Baur was unable to fly Bormann to Grand Admiral Doenitz circulated through the bunker and Bormann, supposedly, had remarked: "I wish that Hanna Reitsch were still here." Hanna Reitsch, a few days earlier, had flown out the new air-force chief, Field Marshall Ritter von Greim. Meanwhile, the Russians had advanced within 100 meters of the bunker. No small plane was stored in the subterranean *Reich* Chancellery garage and, had there been one, no strip for takeoff was available. Bormann's expectations were totally unrealistic. During the last week I doubt that he ever left the bunker.

I am not sure anymore if General Mohnke assigned Bormann to the first or second group of the breakout. Axmann's was to be the fifth to depart, but after Mohnke had left, Axmann changed his mind and we were the third batch to take off.

There must have been another conference with Mohnke, other than the one I attended, and at which Bormann was present. Prof. Schenck, in his book *Das Notlazarett der Reichskanzlei (The Emergency Hospital in the Reich Chancellery)*, describes a conference before the breakout during which Mohnke read Hitler's testament. It must have followed Mohnke's deliberations with Axmann that lasted less than 15 minutes. Then, only the escape routes were discussed and in what order to leave.

That's when I saw Bormann for the last time. He wore an oversized leather coat that made him look even bulkier than he was.

Bormann definitely took part in the breakout. Axmann later reported having seen his lifeless body and Dr. Stumpfegger's as well.

BRAUN—Eva Braun, the *Fuehrer's* mistress, who, one day before their suicides, became his wife. Close-up, I saw Eva Braun on three occasions, never with Hitler. Once she was talking to Hanna Reitsch, once she was with Traudl Junge (one of Hitler's secretaries). My memorable first meeting with Eva Braun is described in Chapter 58 in detail.

Looking for a toilet, I once ended up in the *Hundebunker* (dog shelter) where I saw two grown shepherd dogs. One must have been Hitler's "Blondi," who had had pups a month earlier. But there were no whelps in the *Hundebunker*, and I remember the caretaker telling me that Eva Braun had the puppies taken up to the Goebbels' children to play with.

BURGDORF—*Generalleutnant* (lieutenant general) Wilhelm Burgdorf, Chief Adjutant of the Army to Hitler. I have no recollections of him, although I must have seen him without recognizing who he was.

CHRISTIAN—Gerda Christian, one of Hitler's secretaries. I don't think that I ever saw her in the bunker. I believe she was one of the women, wearing a steel helmet, who, together with other women from the bunker, had assembled in Mohnkes' command post prior to the breakout.

FEGELEIN—*SS-Gruppenfuehrer* (Major General) Hermann Fegelein, Himmler's Liaison Officer at Hitler's Headquarters and Eva Braun's brother-in-law. I never met Hermann Fegelein face-to-face. However through Axmann I became involved in activities surrounding Fegelein, his escape attempt, his capture, and his execution.

Hitler had discovered that Fegelein was no longer in the bunker and had left without permission. He ordered a search party and Fegelein was captured and returned to the bunker.

Axmann had previously participated in the court martial that condemned a former *Leibarzt* (personal physician) of Hitler, Dr. Brandt, to death. His execution was prevented by the fast advancing Allies. One of the main defendants in the "Doctor's Trial," he was sentenced to death and hanged in 1948. Three years earlier, Fegelein was shot in the Chancellery garden by an *SS* execution squad.

Axmann never spoke about any of the proceedings. In the last (telephone) conversation I had with him (1996, shortly before his death), he didn't rule out O'Donnell's contention about the woman Fegelein was with when arrested. She might, indeed, have been a spy and the "leak" through which secret information got out of the bunker.

GOEBBELS—*Reichsminister fuer Propaganda und Volksaufklaerung (Reich* Minister for Propaganda and People's Enlightenment) and *Gauleiter* (party leader) of Berlin. Dr. Joseph Goebbels was in the bunker with his wife and children. I saw his wife more often than I saw him. Both spoke to me when I delivered a radio-telegram that had arrived from *Gauleiter* Karl Hanke in Breslau (my hometown).

I also saw the Goebbels' children frequently as they were out and about in the upper bunker. One girl resembled my sister Anje, another my sister Ute. The likenesses were striking—only their ages were reversed.

I saw Hitler's secretary, Traudl Junge, play with the girls.

GUENSCHE—*SS Sturmbannfuehrer* (Major) Otto Guensche was one of Hitler's two personal adjutants, Schaub was the other one. Schaub left for Berchtesgaden; Guensche remained. (Linge was not one of Hitler's adjutants but his personal valet.) Guensche, a tall, handsome officer was, at least toward me, always friendly, never arrogant. I seem to remember that, among his decorations, he wore the golden Hitler Youth badge, identifying him as one of the earliest members of the *HJ*. I now belonged to the last-ditch

HJ home defense force. As a soldier, I didn't even have a rank, but Guensche never ignored my presence. To the contrary, he acknowledged me as a young comrade. I don't think he knew my name, but he recognized me as one of the members of the birthday delegation and knew that I was Axmann's courier.

After I had received the Iron Cross First Class, he congratulated me and said, (using the informal "*Du*"): "*Wir sind alle stolz auf Dich!*" ("We are all proud of you!"). This was one day before Axmann received his *Goldenes Kreuz des Deutschen Ordens* (Golden Cross of the German Order), Germany's highest nonmilitary award—probably on April 26 or 27.

One distinct memory I have is that once (perhaps even twice) he had me deliver a personal or confidential communication to the *Reichsjugendfuehrer* (Axmann).

HAGEN—Stenographer Kurt Hagen. I never met him and I don't recall anybody ever mentioning him. I was, to the very last day, under the impression that, of Hitler's office staff, only two female secretaries remained in the bunker. (In my research I discovered, however, that one of Hitler's stenographers was Dr. Kurt Haagen—note the different spelling of the last name—but he is believed to have left the bunker when Hitler's first secretary Johanna Wolf departed on April 22.)

HENTSCHEL—*Elektromaschinenmeister* (electro-mechanical engineer) Johann Hentschel was, aside from Hitler, perhaps the most talked about person in the bunker. Although I never saw him in person, I believe his *Werkstatt* (engineer's room) was in front of the stairs where the guards were stationed, but I am not 100% sure. I was among the lucky few who had access to the lower toilets that weren't overflowing yet.

Hentschel was in charge of maintenance. The reason that I had heard his name so often was that both in the upper and lower bunkers, a great deal of repairs had to be made and the diesel generator and air filtration system needed constant attention. In fact, the lives of the people in the upper and lower bunkers depended on the proper functioning of these installations.

Hentschel must have been constantly "on the go!" I believe it was Rochus Misch who said: *"Hentschel und ich kommen auch nicht mehr zum Schlafen"* ("Hentschel and I get no sleep anymore"). Misch was in charge of the phone and the teletype equipment.

(Russian interrogation records place a Josef Henschel in the bunker at the time I was there. I suspect that Johann Hentschel and Josef Henschel are one and the same.)

HERRGESELL—Stenographer Gerhard Herrgesell. I never met him, nor have I ever heard of him. He, too, must have departed from the bunker before I was there. He probably left with Dr. Haagen on April 22, 1945, and with Dr. Buchholz as well. (There were supposedly four stenographers in the *Fuehrerbunker*, two each on duty in 12 hour shifts, supervised by Bormann, to report every word spoken by Hitler. So far, I have been unable to determine the name of the 4th member of this stenography team and his or her departure from Berlin.)

HEWEL—*Botschafter* (Ambassador) Walter Hewel. He was one of the few who once came to visit Axmann in his command post (instead of the other way around). The *Aussenministerium* (Foreign Ministry) where he came from was located just across the street. I left the room so that Axmann and Hewel could confer in complete privacy.

Rumors had been circulating that *Aussenminister* (Foreign Minister/Secretary of State) von Ribbentrop had established contact with the Swedish diplomat, Count Bernadotte, to find ways to end the war. Hewel had investigated and concluded that *"keine Friedensverhandlungen im Gange waren"* ("no peace negotiations were under way"). What apparently did not occur to Hewel was that someone besides the Commander of the Armed Forces or the Foreign Minister could have put out feelers to get in touch with the enemy. All that mattered to him was that von Ribbentrop had not turned against Hitler.

He and Axmann soon left together to ease the *Fuehrer's* mind. Before Axmann and Hewel could reach the *Fuehrer*, however, Bormann had reported proof that someone very close to Hitler had, indeed, "stabbed him in the back." Of all people, it was *Reichsfuehrer-SS*. Heinrich Himmler, *der treue* Heinrich (the loyal Heinrich)!

Hitler was outraged! Axmann told me later that Fegelein's life might have been spared had Hitler not learned of Himmler's *Hochverrat* (high treason).

I never saw Hewel again; I don't recall him being at the Mohnke briefing just prior to the breakout. Supposedly he left the bunker together with Bormann, Baur and Dr. Stumpfegger. All of them, except Baur, ended up committing suicide. Hewel was newlywed. His wife, many people in the bunker seemed to know, was Fegelein's former girlfriend.

HITLER—The *Fuehrer* (leader) Adolf Hitler, *Reichskanzler* (*Reich* Chancellor) of Germany, Commander-in-Chief of the Armed Forces and Leader of the *National Sozialistische Deutsche Arbeiter Partei* (National Socialist German Worker's Party), the NSDAP. I had seen Hitler in person—from a considerable distance—for the first time in 1938 at the height of his peace-time power. Greeted by an enthusiastic, cheering crowd (myself, a boy of 10, included), he spoke and the entire audience seemed mesmerized. He came across as a strong person with radiant qualities.

Now as I saw him in the bunker, he was a changed man. Physically ill and frail, clinging to foreign *Waffen-SS* volunteers and Hitler Youth to defend him.

HOEGL—*SS-Obersturmbannfuehrer* (Lieutenant-Colonel), also *Kriminaldirektor* (chief detective) Peter Hoegl. He was second in command (after Rattenhuber) of the *Reichssicherheitsdienst* (*Reich* Security Service known as *RSD*) and the leader of the *Fuehrerschutzkommando* (*Fuehrer* protection commando), Hitler's bodyguards. According to Axmann, (who called him Direktor Hoegl), it was Hoegl who took the place of Mueller at the Court Martial proceedings of Fegelein. Although I have no recollection of having been in contact with Hoegl, I might have seen him in the bunker without having recognized who he was. Axmann, however, had vivid recollections of him.

JOHANNMEYER—Army-Major Wilhelm (Willi) Johannmeier, Hitler's *Heeresadjutant* (army ADC) Of him I have a good memory since he was a *Ritterkreuztraeger* (bearer of the Knight's Cross), which impressed me. He also wore red stripes on his trousers, which identified him as a high-ranked ordinance officer. Sometimes it was he who took the dispatches I brought or handed me those to be delivered for transmission. He was always concerned that I survive crossing Wilhelmsstrasse. He knew of the intensity of the constant "Stalin Orgel" (Katyushas—BM-21) barrages.

While Boldt, von Loringhoven, and Weiss were sent off to penetrate through the Russian line to reach General Wenck, Johannmeier, single-handedly, was then dispatched to reach Field Marshall Schoerner south of Berlin. Was he successful? I still have not been able to determine if he became a POW before reaching Schoerner or after.

JUNGE—Gertraud (Traudl) Junge, one of two of Hitler's secretaries (the other was Gerda Christian) who had remained in the bunker. Junge, in fact, was the one to whom Hitler dictated his political and personal testaments.

I had never seen Junge at work in the bunker and don't know where her office was, but I saw her several times and even talked to her briefly in the upper bunker. I thought that she was the governess of the Goebbels' children. (I believe she was a young widow, had no children, but loved kids.)

She acted as if she was a tutoress or nursemaid, and I remember her playing with the girls on the floor of the upper bunker. I think that I told her that I was the oldest of six and she remarked about the Goebbels kids, *"Wie artig diese Kinder sind."* (How well behaved these children are).

KARNAU—*Oberwachtmeister* (a police rank comparable to the military rank of Master Sergeant) Hermann Karnau seemed continually on guard duty in the lower bunker. Because of my frequent appearances, he soon knew who I was. He was a skinny guy with wavy blond hair, about Axmann's age.

It was said that he was among those who burned and buried

Eva and Adolf Hitler's bodies in front of the emergency exit. He was one of the few guards who survived the breakout.

KEMPKA—*SS-Obersturmbannfuehrer* (Lieutenant Colonel) Erich Kempka. He was Hitler's personal chauffeur and in charge of all of Hitler's automobiles, those in Berlin, in Munich, and in Berchtesgaden/Obersalzberg.

I never met or saw Kempka in the bunker, only in his garage. Bormann and some other high officers ignored me most of the time, but Kempka and Reitsch actually bawled me out. Kempka must have had a residence in the Chancellery garden, because I remember the guards at the emergency exit occasionally referring to *"das Kempka Haus"* (the Kempka house). This alone indicated to me that he was among those who were closest to Hitler.

He was one who survived the breakout, but I don't remember him being at Mohnke's briefing or being part of our group.

KREBS—General (of the Army) Hans Krebs was Army Chief of Staff and one of the high officers with red stripes on their trousers. I must have seen him, but not knowing who he was and not having had any direct dealings with him, I paid no attention. As far as I can remember, in Axmann's circles, Krebs was only talked about after he had been sent as an emissary to negotiate with the Russians.

Krebs is listed among those who committed suicide after he was informed by the Russian generals that peace would not be negotiated; there would be only unconditional surrender.

KRUEGER—*Sekretaerin* (secretary) Else Krueger. She was Bormann's secretary. I thought at first that she was either Rochus Misch's secretary or a teletype operator. She looked athletic, like a *Sportslehrerin* (physical education teacher). After it had been brought to my attention who she was, I saw her several times, usually in the presence of Misch, not of Bormann.

She survived the breakout either in the first or second group. I also learned, after the war, that she and her British interrogation officer were married and that they lived in England.

LINGE–*SS-Sturmbannfuehrer* (Major) Heinz Linge. He was

Hitler's valet and thought to be constantly in attendance upon Hitler. However, I don't remember seeing (or recognizing) him. Linge was captured during the breakout attempt, and as was reported in the German press, he returned from Russia in the autumn of 1955.

LORENZ—*Reichspressechef* (Chief of the press in the *Reich*) and *Pressereferent* (press secretary) of the Propaganda Ministry and in the end, of the *Fuehrerbunker*. Heinz Lorenz, I remember, was much talked about. He and Axmann had personal conferences, but I was not present at any of them. I don't remember ever meeting or seeing him. Supposedly, it was Lorenz who supplied Bormann with the information about the "Himmler—Count Bernadotte negotiations." Whether Lorenz reported to Dr. Naumann or the other way around, I am still not sure. Both seemed to have access to foreign press and monitored newscasts from neutral and enemy countries.

I don't know if Lorenz participated in the breakout. As a civilian, he could have just left the bunker and mingled with the Berliners awaiting the Russian's arrival. Reportedly, he was not only among the survivors, but escaped to the West and worked for British Intelligence after the war.

LORINGHOVEN—Major Bernd Freytag von Loringhoven was a staff officer in the *Hitlerbunker* and one of the three (Boldt and Weiss were the others) who had been chosen to break through the Russian lines to deliver special orders (see Boldt). The only time I saw Major von Loringhoven was at the time a courier was selected to guide the three officers to the *Pichelsdorfer Bruecken*. Since I was not chosen, I had no further contact with him or the other two officers.

MANZIARLY—Hitler's Austrian dietician, Constanze Manziarly, was also his vegetarian cook. I saw her frequently in the upper bunker where she had her kitchen and where there was an eating area (mini-canteen). When I left Germany in 1953, reporters still speculated as to whether she had been killed during the breakout or survived and assumed a new identity. Meanwhile, historians suspect that she had been given a *Blausaeure Kapsel* (Prussic acid capsule) and used it, committing suicide shortly after leaving the bunker.

MENGERSHAUSEN—*SS-Hauptscharfuehrer* (sergeant-major) Harry Mengershausen became well known because of his testimony about Hitler's death. (In the literature his first name is often Erich instead of Harry. I don't know which one is correct.) I only knew him as the leader of the guard detachment at the emergency exit and the observation tower. (There were two observation towers but one had remained unfinished, and I don't think there was ever a guard in it.)

I have two distinct memories of Mengershausen. Once I arrived via the path along the Foreign Ministry under heavy fire only to find the door of the emergency exit locked from the inside. My banging could not be heard, and under the heavy barrage of fire, I had to race to Voss Strasse to get to the underground passages.

When I told this to Mengershausen, he replied dryly: "I can't give you a key." Of course there were no keys. It was an air raid shelter steel door. The other memory is that it was Mengershausen who, after I knew that Hitler was dead, pointed out to me: "*Dort sind sie begraben*" (There they are buried.)

Mengershausen participated in the breakout but was among those who were captured.

MISCH-*SS-Oberscharfuehrer* (Technical Sergeant) Rochus Misch was in charge of the *Telefon Zentrale* (Central Telephone Exchange). He and I sat once at the same table in the upper bunker eating together. He wanted to know all about where I had fought, how I had earned my Iron Cross (Misch, too, had been awarded the Iron Cross), why I ended up in the bunker, etc. But our conversation was interrupted when one of his men came to get him. A Russian hit had torn apart a major cable that needed to be repaired immediately. We never found time to get together again and finish our conversation.

I found Misch to be one of the friendliest members of Hitler's staff in the bunker. I don't think he participated in the breakout.

The emergency hospital could not be evacuated and others remained as well. Misch's switchboard apparently functioned up to the time when the first Russian soldiers arrived and took the bunker without resistance.

MOHNKE-*SS-Brigadefuehrer* (Brigadier General) Wilhelm Mohnke was commandant of the "Citadel," the area of the last holdout, the *Regierungsviertel* (government district). He had been awarded the Knight's Cross. Axmann, who had a very high opinion of him (a former *HJ* leader, I believe), readily accepted him as the *Ausbruchskommandant* (Breakout Commander). As mentioned already, I attended with Axmann and Weltzin one of Mohnke's last briefings. Bormann appeared and we all noted that he was drunk.

Mohnke survived the breakout and was captured by the Russians. He remained alive during his captivity and returned to Germany.

NAUMANN—*Staatssekretaer* (State Secretary) Dr. Werner Naumann was a main operator of Goebbels' huge, well organized, and highly effective indoctrination machine. He had become the Propaganda Minister's liaison officer and kept Hitler informed of foreign press and radio reports.

Axmann seemed to have had especially cordial relationships with Goebbels and his men. As he had with Lorenz, he met with Naumann two or three times at his Party Chancellery command post.

Naumann, (jokingly or cynically) said once to me: "*Ich gehoere jetzt auch zum Volkssturm*" (I am now a member of the *Volkssturm*, too).

It reminds me that the *Propaganda Ministerium* (propaganda ministry), located in the former *Leopold Palast* near us and across from the *Reich* Chancellery, was defended by a Hitler Youth *Kampfgruppe* (fighting group). They fought valiantly and tenaciously to the bitter end. There were many casualties. Most of the wounded ended up in our cellar in Dr. Huhn's improvised medical station. It is my recollection that Axmann and Naumann kept in steady contact during the last days of the battle. Naumann, too, survived the breakout.

OLDS—Unknown

RATTENHUBER—*SS-Gruppenfuehrer* (Major General) Johann Rattenhuber was in charge of the *Reichssicherheitsdienst (RSD—Reich* Security Service), which included the *Fuehrerbegleitkommando (FBK-Fuehrer's* Escort Detachment), Hitler's bodyguards.

I am quite sure that Major General Rattenhuber personally checked out Major Weltzin and me on the first time we entered the lower bunker where Hitler was. He had to verify that Axmann's adjutant and his *Melder* (who was a mere *Volkssturmman*—home defense unit member without rank) were permitted to enter the "inner sanctum" of Hitler's last temple, the bunker.

I remember that Rattenhuber was at the Mohnke briefing when Bormann appeared to be visibly intoxicated. Rattenhuber, assigned by Mohnke to lead the second group, exchanged words with Axmann. Both seemed appalled by Bormann's behavior.

In any case, they departed before we did. I learned from Axmann after the war that Rattenhuber, although badly wounded, survived the breakout. He spent 10 years as a POW in Russia and died two years after his release in 1957.

REYNITZ—Unknown.

SCHAEDLE—*SS-Hauptsturmfuehrer* (Captain) Franz Schaedle was in charge of Hitler's bodyguard unit (*RSD*). He was wounded and became one of Prof. Schenck's patients in the Chancellery's emergency hospital. Not able to participate in the breakout, he reportedly committed suicide.

I have no recollection of ever having met or seen him.

SCHAUB—*SS-Obergruppenfuehrer* (Lieutenant-General). Julius Schaub was Hitler's chief adjutant and manservant. I only saw him once—at the April 20th birthday reception. Days later he departed. It was no secret in the bunker that he, under the *Fuehrer's* orders, had left for Munich and the Alps to destroy personal and party records which were not to fall into enemy hands. A "mission-completed" *Funkmeldung* (radio message) was received before Hitler committed suicide. Somehow Schaub had also blown up Hitler's private train (in Berchtesgaden?).

SCHWAEGERMANN—*SS-Hauptsturmfuehrer* (Captain) Guenther Schwaegermann. Dr. Goebbels' adjutant who, according to Axmann, burned the corpses of Dr. Goebbels and his wife and then joined our (Axmann's) group. But I have no recollection of this. It could have been after I was wounded and covered by the rubble of the house that had been hit and had collapsed on me.

STUMPFEGGER—*SS-Standartenfuehrer* (Colonel) Dr. med. Ludwig Stumpfegger (Dr. med. is the same as M.D.) was Hitler's last personal physician. He was another of the *"Huehnen"* (tall ones) in the lower bunker (Guensche was one of the others). A few times I got a glimpse of him but never close up. I knew that Dr. Gertrud Huhn tried to establish contact with him. She needed guidance to perform some surgeries for which she had not been trained.

(Prof. Haase and Prof. Schenck were also in desperate situations, requiring another doctor if not two, because of the mounting casualties and Prof. Haase's impairment. He suffered from a lung disease and needed rests between operations.)

Stumpfegger, however, was not available to help out. He remained in the lower bunker in case Hitler needed him. He did have, for a few days, another patient I knew of, the newly appointed head of the German *Luftwaffe* (air force), Field Marshall Ritter von Greim. It was said that he also treated Mrs. Goebbels.

Today, it is believed that Dr. Stumpfegger and Bormann both committed suicide and died together during the breakout.

VOSS—*Vizeadmiral* (Vice Admiral) Hans Erich Voss, the Navy's liaison officer at Hitler's headquarters. I have no recollection of him. It seems strange, however, because he must have been in charge of the *Marine Funkstelle* (Navy radio station) for which I had become a runner. If Voss ever showed up at the radio room, I wasn't there then. But the danger crossing Wilhelmsstrasse was so great that Voss might have remained in the safety of the bunker and not visited his *Funkstelle* during the last weeks of the battle.

A final memory I have is of one of the Navy men in the radio dispatch station mentioning that American Forces already occupied Munich. The Americans reported that the population had greeted them with flowers when they marched in. Hitler's "Capital of the Movement" had welcomed the Americans with open arms, while we in Berlin kept on fighting.

WEIDLING—General Helmut Weidling, last Commander of *Festung* (fortress) Berlin. I remember overhearing frequent conversations Axmann had with his adjutants and aides about General Weidling. By orders of Hitler, he was to be shot for deserting his position and retreating to Doeberitz. He decided to appear before Hitler in person, with the result that Hitler reinstated him as the *Festungskommandant* (fortress commander) of Berlin.

Following this appointment, Axmann had a *Besprechung* (conference/deliberation) with Weidling from which Axmann returned visibly *veraergert* (unhappy). When it came to the deployment of Hitler Youth *Volkssturm* units, Axmann and Weidling didn't see eye-to-eye. As a result, I believe Axmann, with Hitler's blessing, assumed military command not only of the *Panzernahkampfbrigade Artur Axmann,* but of all of Hitler's Youth *Volkssturm* units assembled in and around Berlin.

I remember seeing General Weidling face-to-face only once, not in the bunker, but at his last command post on Bendlerstrasse.

WEISS—*Oberstleutnant* (Lieutenant Colonel) Rudolf Weiss, General Burgdorf's adjutant, one of the three officers ordered on April 29, 1945 to reach General Wenck's headquarters with urgent orders from Hitler to rescue us. I saw him with the other two briefly in the *Lageraum* just before they left.

WOLF—*SS-Standartenfuehrer* (Colonel) Karl Wolf, Hitler's chief secretary. I have no recollection of him.

ZANDER—*SS-Standartenfuehrer* (Colonel) Wilhelm Zander, Martin Bormann's adjutant. I have no recollection of ever having seen him.

APPENDIX—B

WAFFEN-SS UNITS, WHEN FOUNDED,

AND NATIONALITY OF MEMBERS

NAMES OF UNITS	YEAR FOUNDED	NATIONALITY OF MEMBERS (Non-Germans
SS-Panzerdivision-Leibstandarte Adolf Hitler	1933	Germans
SS-Panzerdivision-Das Reich	1939	Germans
SS-Panzerdivision-Totenkopf	1940	Germans
SS-Polizei-Panzergrenadierdivision-Polizei Division	1940	Germans
SS-Panzerdivision-Wiking	1940	Germans
SS-Gebirgsdivision-Nord	1940	Germans
SS-Freiwilligen-Gebirgsdivision-Prinz Eugen	1942	Ethnic Germans
SS-Kavalleriedivision-Florian Ge er	1942	Germans/Ethnic Germans
SS-Panzerdivision-Hohenstaufen	1943	German
SS-Panzerdivision-Frundsberg	1943	German
SS-Freiwilligen-Panzergrenadierdivision-Nordland	1942	Germans/ *Scandinavians*
SS-Panzerdivision-Hitler Jugend	1943	Germans
Waffen-Gebirgsdivision der SS-Handschar	1943	*Yugoslavs*
Waffen-Grenadierdivision der SS-Galizische No. 1	1943	*Ukrainians*
Waffen-Grenadierdivision der SS-Lettische No. 1	1943	*Latvians* /Germans
SS-Panzergrenadierdivision-Reichsfuehrer-SS	1943	German/Ethnic Germans
SS-Panzergrenadierdivision-G tz von Berlichingen	1943	Germans/Ethnic Germans
SS-Freiwilligen-Panzergrenadierdivision-Horst Wessel	1944	German/Ethnic Germans

M

Waffen-SS-Grenadierdivision der SS-Lettische No.2	1944	*Latvians*
Waffen-SS-Grenadierdivision der SS-Estnische No.1	1944	*Estonians*
Waffen-SS-Gebirgsdivision der SS-Albanische No.1-Skander Beg	1944	*Albanians*
SS-Freiwilligen-Kavalleriedivision-Maria Theresa	1944	Ethnic Germans/Germans
Waffen-Gebirgsdivision der SS-Kama	1944	*Yugoslavs*
SS-Freiwilligen-Panzerdivision-Nederland	1945	*Dutch*
Waffen-Gebirgsdivision der SS-Karstj ger	1944	*Italians*/Ethnic Germans
Waffen-Grenadierdivision der SS-Hun adi No.1	1944	*Hungarians*
Waffen-Grenadierdivision der SS-Hun adi No. 2	1944	*Hungarians*
SS-Freiwilligen-Grenadierdivision-Langemarck	1945	*Flemish/Belgians*
SS-Freiwilligen-Grenadierdivision-Wallonie	1945	*Walloons/Belgians*
Waffen-Grenadierdivision der SS-Russische No. 1	1944	*Russians*
Waffen-Grenadierdivision der SS-Italische No.1	1945	*Italians*
Waffen-Grenadierdivision der SS-Russische No. 2	1944	*Russians*
SS-Freiwilligen-Grenadierdivision	1945	Germans
SS-Freiwilligen-Panzerdivision-B hmen-Maehren	1945	Germans/Ethnic Germans
Waffen-Grenadierdivision der SS-Januar 30	1945	Germans
Waffen-Grenadierdivision der SS-Charlemagne	1945	*French*
SS-Freiwilligen-Grenadierdivision-Landstorm Nederland	1945	*Dutch*
SS-Polizei-Grenadierdivision der SS	1945	German Policeman
Waffen-Grenadierdivision-Dirlewanger	1945	Germans
SS-Freiwilligen-Kavalleriedivision-Lutzow	1945	Ethnic Germans
SS-Panzergrenadierdivision-Nibelungen	1945	SS Cadets

APPENDIX-C

RANK COMPARISON CHART AS OF APRIL

1945

WAFFEN-SS (MILITARY SS)	*HEER (GERMAN ARMY)*	*U.S.ARMY*
Reichsfuehrer-SS(1)	Generalfeldmarschall	General of Army
SS-Oberst-Gruppenfuehrer und Generaloberst der Waffen-SS	Generaloberst	General
SS-Obergruppenfuehrer und General der Waffen-SS	General (der…)	Lieutenant General
SS-Gruppenfuehrer und Generalleutnant der Waffen-SS	Generalleutnant	Major General
SS-Brigadefuehrer und Generalmajor der Waffen-SS	Generalmajor	Brigadier General
SS-Oberfuehrer (2)	—	Senior Colonel (3)
SS-Standartenfuehrer	Oberst	Colonel
SS-Obersturmbannfuehrer	Oberstleutnant	Lieutenant Colonel
SS-Sturmbannfuehrer	Major	Major

WAFFEN-SS	HEER	U.S.ARMY
SS-Hauptsturmfuehrer	Hauptman	Captain
SS-Obersturmfuehrer	Oberleutnant	First Lieutenant
SS-Untersturmfuehrer	Leutnant	Second Lieutenant
—	—	Chief Warrant Officer (4)
—	—	Warrant Officer —Junior Grade (4)
SS-Sturmscharfuehrer (a)	Stabsfeldwebel (a)	Sergeant Major (3)
SS-Stabsscharfuehrer (5)	Hauptfeldwebel(5)	First Sergeant (6)
SS-Standartenoberjunker	Oberfaehnrich	Senior Officer Candidate (3)
SS-Hauptscharfuehrer (b)	Oberfeldwebel (b)	Master Sergeant (f)
SS-Oberscharfuehrer (c)	Feldwebel (c)	Technical Sergeant
SS-Standartenjunker	Faehnrich	Officer Candidate (3)
SS-Scharfuehrer (d)	Unterfeldwebel (d)	Staff Sergeant
SS-Junker	Fahnenjunker-Unteroffizier	Appointed Officer Candidate— Senior Grade (3)
SS-Unterscharfuehrer (e)	Unteroffizier(e)	Sergeant
—	Stabsgefreiter (7)	Staff Corporal (3)

WAFFEN-SS	HEER	U.S.ARMY
SS-Rottenfuehrer (g)	Obergefreiter (8) (g)	Corporal
SS-Fuehrerbewerber	Fahnenjunker-Gefreiter	Appointed Officer Candidate— Junior Grade (3)
SS-Unterfuehreranwaerter (9)	Unteroffizieranwaerter (9)	NCO Candidate (3)
Unterfuehrerbewerber (9)	Unterfuehreranwaerter (9) (10)	NCO Applicant (3)
SS-Sturmmann (h)	Gefreiter	Acting Corporal (3)
SS-Oberschuetze	Oberschuetze	Private First Class
SS-Schuetze	Schuetze	Private

EXPLANATION OF REFERENCES

(1) A political rather than a military title (held by Heinrich Himmler) but which nevertheless applied to the *Waffen-SS* to the same extent as it did to the other branches of the *SS*.

(2) A rank in the *Waffen-SS* that had no equivalent in the German Army.

(3) These ranks did not exist in the U.S. Army and the English translations are therefore only shown for the purpose of establishing a comparison.

(4) These U.S. Army ranks had no equivalent in the *Waffen-SS* or in the German Army.

(5) An appointment (not a rank) usually held by the ranks which, in the above chart, are followed by (a) or (b) but which was also occasionally held by the ranks followed by (c), (d), or (e) in which case the holders were then called *"SS-Stabsscharfuehrerdiensttuer"* or *"Hauptfeldwebeldienstuer"* (the added *"diensttuer"* meaning "doing the service of" or in other words "acting as").

(6) An appointment held by the rank which, in the above chart, is followed by (f).

(7) A German Army rank which was dropped in 1942 and which had no equivalent in the *Waffen-SS.*

(8) In the German Army, a distinction was made between an *"Obergefreiter"* (Corporal) with less than 6 years of service and with more than 6 years of service.

(9) Although NCO Candidates and NCO Applicants were usually assigned the ranks, which in the above chart are followed by (g) or (h), they also occasionally held one of the two lower BM ranks.

(10) In the German Army, a distinction was made between the *"Kapitulanten-Unterfuehreranwaerter"* (Re-enlisted NCO Applicant) and the *"Ergaenzungs-Unterfuehreranwaerter"* (Recalled NCO Applicant), however, said distinction did not affect the actual rank held by these NCO Applicants.

NOTE: *Volkssturm* units were lead by NCOs and officers of the German Armed Forces, mostly Army and *Waffen-SS.*

APPENDIX D

REGIONAL ORGANIZATION

OF THE HITLER YOUTH

Jungvolk and *Jungmaedel* Included

There were a total of six *Obergebiete,* each containing a minimum of six *Gebiete* and a maximum of eight. Since 1940, a *Gebiet* corresponded with a NSDAP Gau. Each Gebiet, depending on size, contained several *HJ Banne, DJ Unterbanne, Jungmaedeluntergaue* and *Untergaue.* There were 42 *Gebiete* and 223 *Banne* (with corresponding *DJV, DJM and BDM* formations) as well as *RJF* command centers in Bohemia-Moravia (CSR), the General-Government (Poland), Ost (Baltic countries, Russia, Ukraine, Balkans) and the Netherlands.

One *Bann* had five *Unterbanne,* each *Unterbann* four *Gefolgschaften,* each *Gefolgschaft* three *Scharen* and each *Schar* three *Kameradschaften.* This applies equally to the equivalent *DJV, DJM* and *BDM* formations.

HITLER YOUTH
ORGANIZATIONAL STRUCTURE

(Figures comprise approximate number of Hitler Youths in area or unit respectively)

Obergebiet 375,000	Gauverband 375,000

Gebiet 75,000	Obergau 75,000

Oberbann 15,000	Gau 15,000

DJV Ages: 10-14	**HJ** Ages: 14-18	**DJM** Ages: 10-14	**BDM** Ages: 14-18
Jungbann 3000	Bann 3000	Jungmaedeluntergau 3000	Untergau 3000
Stamm 600	Unterbann 600	Jungmaedelring 600	Maedelring 600
Faehnlein 150	Gefolgschaft 150	Jungaedelgruppe 150	Maedelgruppe 150
Jungzug 50	Schar 50	Jungmaedelschar 50	Maedelschar 50
Jungenschaft 15	Kameradschaft 15	Jungmaedelschaft 15	Maedelschaft 15

APPENDIX D continued

In the course of the short history of the Hitler Youth, the ranks changed frequently. Those shown below were the greatly simplified ones in use in 1943.

Jugendfuehrer des Deutschen Reiches (Reich Youth Leader): Baldur v. Schirach, succeeded by Artur Axmann.

HJ- Hitler Jungen (Hitler Youth)	*DJV Deutsches Jungvolk* (Junior grade of Hitler Youth)
Stabsfuehrer	
Obergebietsfuehrer	
Gebietsfuehrer	
Oberbannfuehrer	
Bannfuehrer	*Jungbannfuehrer*
Stammfuehrer	*Unterbannfuehrer*
Gefolgschaftsfuehrer	*Fahnleinfuehrer*
Scharfuehrer	*Jungzugfuehrer*
Kameradschaftsfuehrer	*Jungenschaftsfuehrer*
Hitlerjunge	*Pimpf*

BDM Bund deutscher Maedel (Union of German Girls girl s division of Hitler Youth)	*DJM Deutsche Jungmaedel* (Young German girls junior grade of Hitler Youth)
Reichsreferentin	
Obergaufuehrerin	
Hauptmaedelfuehrerin	
Untergaufuehrerin	*JM-Untergaufuehrerin*
Maedelringfuehrerin	*JM-Ringfuehrerin*
Maedelgruppenfuehrerin	*JM-Gruppenfuehrerin*
Maedelscharfuehrerin	*JM-Scharfuehrerin*
Maedelschaftsfuehrerin	*Jungmaedelschaftsfuehrerin*
Maedel	*Jungmaedel (JM)*

M

ENDNOTES

1 Klaus came to visit me in the autumn of 1999 and died a few days after his return to Germany.

2 The last time I visited my mother in France, she was in her seventies. "We left the church, but I never lost my faith," she told me. By this time, she had returned to Christianity, through a branch of the followers of Rudolf Steiner.

3 *Sturm-Abteilung* members were Hitler's brownshirts, which numbered over half a million when Hitler became Chancellor in 1933. A year later, in June, shortly after my first visit to Rudi's house, the *Roehm Purge*, that became known as the "Night of the Long Knives," took place. The *SA* was disarmed, while the *SS, Schutz-Staffel*, of which my father became a member, took over the party's defense unit and other "security" functions.

4 Crystal Night 9/10 Nov. 1938. The night of the broken glass, a pogrom following the murder of Ernst von Rath by Herschel Gruenspan. Throughout Germany, nearly 200 synagogues were set on fire and over 800 Jewish-owned shops were destroyed.

5 SS – initials of *Schutz Staffel* (protection guard), originally Hitler's personal protection unit. It grew into a "state within a state."

6 SD – initials of *Sicherheitsdienst*, the intelligence and security service within the above.

7 The meaning of the German word "*Mut*" is courage, and one who is *mutig* is courageous.

8 Hitler had his "racialism" legalized with the Nuremberg Laws on citizenship and race, limiting German citizenship to only those of German or kindred blood and excluding Jews specifically.

9 Among my ancestors was a Lord Mayor of Dublin by the name
of Daniel Weybrandt. Born in Ireland on Dec. 5, 1599, he
died in Amsterdam on Sept. 6, 1657, after having been driven
from office by papal forces. His daughter, Christine Weybrandt,
married Christoph Schlaaf and their daughter married Samuel
Boccius in 1788.

10 Baron Justus von Liebig (1803-73), famous 19th century German chemist who pioneered the early advances of organic, biological and agricultural chemistry. His hands-on educational
methods, developed in his laboratory at the University of
Giessen, set new standards for effective academic teaching and
attracted some of the brightest students from all over the world.

11 A reference work on European royalty and nobility published
from 1764 to World War II.

12 Lyrics by Hoffman an Fallersleben (1798-1874) to the melody
composed by Joseph Hyden (1732-1809).

13 Horst Wessel (1907-30), one of Hitler's stormtroopers, killed
in Berlin in a street fight with communists. After his death,
his song was added to the German national anthem.

14 Since Hitler had assumed power, it was the swastika flag, with
the black rectilinear cross, its oblique arms turned clockwise
on a white circular background, in the middle of a blood-red
banner.

15 Erich von Ludendorff (1867-1937), Army general and World
War I hero, supported Hitler initially but then founded his
own political organization, the *Tannenbergbund.*

16 Frederick II became known as Frederick the Great (1712-86).
Although despised by his father as an effeminate aesthete, he
surprised everyone because of his great leadership abilities. A
benevolent monarch, he promoted, with great foresight, far-
reaching legal and social reforms.

17 Rococo palace at Potsdam with a magnificent park. Believed to
have been designed by Frederick the Great himself, who then
commissioned the famous architect, Georg von Knobelsdorff,
who built it.

18 Adolf Hitler *Schulen* were also Nazi elite schools, admitting boys selected at the age of 12.

19 *Gymnsaium* – High school with a college preparatory curriculum. It begins in what would be the 5th grade in the United States

20 Named after Field Marshal Albrecht Graf von Roon (1803-79), who succeeded Bismarck as president of the Prussian ministry.

21 Hans Sachs (1494-1576), famous shoemaker who became master of his guild, as well as an important poet and dramatist, historically known as a *Meistersinger* (master singer) of Nuremberg.

22 Later Zwinger Oberschule.

23 Founded in 1293, at the end of the Crusades, as *Pfarrschule zu St. Elisabeth* (parochial school of the church of St. Elisabeth), later known as *Gymnasium Elisabetanum*, it was one of the city's most renowned classical, college-preparatory, secondary schools. Maria Magdalena and Matthias *Gymnasium* claimed similar status.

24 *KZ*—the initials for *Konzentrations Lager*—concentration camp.

25 *Pennaeler—Slang word for high school student.*

26 *Pimpf*—Lowest level of a scout.

27 In 1933, the Hitler *Jugend* was formed as the official youth organization of the *NSDAP* (National Socialist German Worker's Party), incorporating all existing German Youth organizations, banning the International Boy Scout and Girl Scout movements. In 1936, a law organized all youth into the Hitler Youth. Accordingly, the entire German youth had to join the Hitler Youth to be "educated, physically, mentally and morally, in the spirit of National Socialism." A youth service law of March 25, 1939, expanded the mandatory services to be performed in the *Deutsche Jungvolk* and *Hitler Jugend* (*Bund Deutscher Maedel* for girls), paving the way for military-type training.

28 The Sudetenland, a region named after the Sudeten Moun-

M

tains between the Elbe and the Oder rivers separating Bohemia from Germany, was home to over two million *Sudetendeutsche* (Sudeten Germans).

29 Czechoslovakia didn't even exist prior to World War I. Formed in 1918 from provinces of the former Austro-Hungarian Empire and the predominantly German Sudeten mountain ranges, it encompassed the regions of Slovakia, Morevia, and Bohemia. After German (1938-45) and Russian (1948-89) domination, the country, in a peaceful separation, split into two, establishing, in 1993, the independent nations of Slovakia and the Czech Republic, demonstrating to the world it is possible for new nations to emerge without bloodshed.

30 The German-Soviet Non-aggression Pact was signed in Moscow on August 23/24, 1939.

31 Verbatim in German: "Das kann nicht gut gehen!"

32 Danzig was named a free city, and the Polish Corridor was created by ceding most of West Prussia to Poland in the 1919 Treaty of Versailles.

33 *Blitzkrieg*—the strategy of "lightning war," utilizing the ability of fast armored units to create surprise raids, advancing rapidly through swift tactical attacks. Hitler first used the term in a speech given in 1935 at a Nuremberg party rally.

34 *OKW—Oberkommando der Wehrmacht* (High Command of the Armed Force) retained by Hitler as his own planning staff.

35 Kopernikus, Nikolaus—Copernicus, Nicholas (1473-1543). Polish astronomer, who developed the Copernican system, proving the earth revolves around the sun, thus establishing the foundation for modern astronomy.

36 Sklodowska, Marie—(1867-1934). Noted Polish chemist and physicist, married French chemist Pierre Curie. In joint research, they discovered polonium and radium and shared in the 1903 Nobel Prize for Physics. In 1911, Marie Sklodowska Curie was awarded the Nobel Prize for the isolation of metallic radium.

37 Chopin, Frederic (1810-49). Composer and pianist. His sets

of polonaises and mazurkas reflect strong Polish nationalism.

38 Pulaski, Casimir (1748-1779). Polish folk hero who as cavalry commander participated in the American Revolution. While leading his troops, he was mortally wounded in an attack on Savannah.

39 German-Soviet Friendship Treaty and Boundary Agreement. Signed 8/23/39 by Foreign Ministers v. Ribbentrop and Molotov. The terms of the settlement created the "Baltic Situation."

40 Mannerheim, Carl (1867-1951). Finland's President and Commander in Chief during World War II. Mannerheim Line-Finnish Defense Fortifications.

41 Leningrad is now St. Petersburg.

42 *Warthegau* (Warthe Region) annexed to Germany in 1939.

43 *Stuka* (Sturzkampflugzeuge). German dive-bomber that had sirens attached to their fixed landing gears.

44 Prien, Guenther (1908-1941), joined the merchant marine at the age of 15, advancing to the rank of officer on the Hamburg-America Line. After being laid off during the Great Depression, he joined the Navy.

45 Kretschmer, Otto (1912-) Until his capture, one of the *Kriegsmarine's* leading U-boat aces.

46 *The Second World War*, A Complete History by Martin Gilbert, published by Henry Holt & Company, New York —First Owl Book, Revised Edition—1991, page 162.

47 Moelders, Werner (1913-41), Major, last rank Major General, with 115 combat victories to his credit. Ironically, he died in 1941 in a plane crash caused by bad weather while en route to attend the funeral of the World War I fighter ace, Ernst Udet. At the time of his death, Moelders was the most highly decorated hero of the war. He had been awarded the Knight's Cross of the Iron Cross with Oak Leaves, Swords, and Diamonds.

48 Galland, Adolf (1911-), Rapidly promoted, Galland became in 1942, at the age of 31, the youngest officer to be promoted to the rank of General in the German Armed Forces, Due to

his outstanding record as fighter pilot and top scorer during the Battle of Britain, he was also awarded the Knight's Cross of the Iron Cross in all stages, culminating with the highest, that of Oak Leaves, Swords, and Diamonds. After becoming Inspector General in command of all fighter aircraft, he had major disputes with *Reichsmarschall* Goering who removed him from High Command. Galland returned to action taking command of the new jet fighter (ME-262) crack squadron until grounded for lack of fuel.

49 Goethe, Johann Wolfgang von (1749-1832), dramatist, novelist, poet, scientist, lawyer and chief-minister at the court of Saxe-Weimar.

50 Berlichingen, Goetz von (1480-1562), Captain. Became famous as the leader of the Franconian peasants during the Peasant Wars

51 Schiller, Friedrich von (1859-1905), dramatist, poet, philosopher. A literary giant, second only to Goethe, known for his idealism and hatred of tyranny.

52 Rousseau, Jean Jacque (1712-78), French philosopher who contended man is good by nature but is corrupted by civilization. Laws were instituted, he believed, to maintain the inequality of oppressors and oppressed.

53 *Sturm und Drang* (storm and rush, or storm and stress), a period of German literature (1765-90) during which Lessing, Klinger and lesser known writers protested against questionable moral standards (as did Rousseau in France before he was forced to seek asylum in Switzerland.)

54 Hauptmann, Gerhart (1862-1946), Prolific German (Silesian) dramatist and novelist who devoted his entire life to writing. He received the Nobel Prize for Literature in 1912.

55 Marx, Karl (1818-83) German social philosopher who emerged as the chief theorist of modern forms of Socialism and Communism. Founder of the economic-political system named after him.

56 See Appendix D

57 Frank, Hans (1900-1946), early storm trooper who had taken part in the 1923 Beer Hall Putsch. He became Hitler's lawyer and drafted the *Gleichschaltung* of the legal system that outlawed opposition in any form of organized activities.

58 Frank kept extensive diaries and confessed his guilt before the Nuremberg tribunal. He was hanged. Frank's own son, Niklas, typified him in his book, *In the Shadow of the Reich* (Alfred A. Knopf – 1991) as a "bloody footnote to the history of our times."

59 Dietl, Eduard (1890-1944), Commanding General of the *Gebirgskorps Norwegen* (Mountain Corps Norway), he was Germany's most prolific and successful leader of mountain troops until he lost his life in a plane crash.

60 *Waffen-SS*, the military arm of the *Schutzstaffel* (defense unit) formed in 1939 from the Death's Head and VT-military units, built up to a strength of 39 divisions. Scandinavian volunteers fought in the Nordland and French volunteers in the Charlemagne divisions. See Appendix B "Nationality of *Waffen-SS* units."

61 Goering, Hermann (1893-1946) *Reich* Marshal, Commander-in-Chief of the German Air Force. A fighter ace in WWI and first commander of the *SA* (storm troopers), he was, next to Hitler, Germany's most prominent war leader. Found guilty by the Nuremberg Tribunal, he committed suicide one day prior to his scheduled death by hanging.

62 Petain, Henri Philippe (1856-1951) Marshal. French military hero of the battle of Verdun (1916), became commander of the French Army after WWI. After the defeat of France by Hitler, he was influenced by the *Fuehrer's* scheme of creating a new Europe. He acted as head of Vichy France from 1940-44 until General de Gaulle liberated France, whereupon he was convicted of collaboration. His death sentence was commuted to life imprisonment

63 BBC – British Broadcasting Corporation, state-owned, but an independent authority.

64 Antonescu, Ion (1880-1946), served as Defense Minister and Chief of the General Staff under King Carol. Later aligned himself with the right-wing Iron Guard and was imprisoned. Restored to favor after the collapse of France, he was named Prime Minister and sided with Hitler. Rumanian forces joined the German Army in the war against the Soviet Union. As a collaborator, he was sentenced to death and executed in 1946.

65 Lettow-Vorbeck, Paul von, (1870-1964), Lt. Col. Served on the expedition that put down the Herero and Hottentot rebellion. In WWI, his force of 3,000 Germans and 11,000 native Africans held in check a force of over 200,000 British, Belgian, and Portuguese troops. Returned to Germany in 1919 as a hero, Lettow-Vorbeck served as a deputy to the parliament in 1929-30 and tried, unsuccessfully, to organize a conservative opposition to Hitler.

66 Pavelic, Ante (1889-1959) Lawyer. Turned revolutionist, he became leader of the Croation fascists and headed the Croation state, established by Germany and Italy during WWII. He escaped to Argentina and from there returned to Europe. Died in Spain.

67 Gram=15.4 grains (troy)

68 Jungmaedel, girls' (10-14 yrs) branch of the Hitler Youth, known as *BDM Bund Deutscher Maedel* (Union of German Girls)

69 Original German text: *Wir marschieren fuer Hitler/durch Nacht und durch Not/mit der Fahne fuer Freiheit und Brot!* (Baldur von Schirach).

70 Its official German name was *Akademie Fuer Jugendfuehrung.* It was the top training facility for future Hitler Youth leaders.

71 J.F. Lehmann Verlag, Muenchen, publishers of race-related literature and texts used for lectures based on party doctrine.

72 Hinderburg, Paul von (und Beneckendorff) (1847-1934). German field marshal and WWI hero who became Germany's president (1925-34). In 1933, he appointed Hitler as Chancellor.

73 Bismarck, Otto, Fuerst von (1815-98), Premier of Prussia

(1862-90) and Chancellor of Germany (1871-90). Known as the "Iron Chancellor," he was the creator of the Second German Reich. Premier of Prussia (1862-1890) as well as Chancellor of Germany from 1871 to 1890.

74 Painting of a farmer. Whoever served as a model had facial and body features (characteristics) which resembled mine.

75 The following statement precedes the German film: *Die im Film geschilderten Erlebnisse beruhen auf geschichtlichen Tatsachen.* (The events shown in this film are based on historical facts.)

76 Wuerttemberg emerged from the former duchies of Swabia and Franconia. After WWII, it was partitioned between Wuertttemberg-Baden (capital, Stuttgart) and Wuerttemberg-Hohenzollern (capital, Tuebingen). Known worldwide as the "Black Forest" region.

77 Feuchtwanger, Lion (1884-1958), noted novelist and playwright. Exiled from Germany in 1933. Lived and worked in France. After the German invasion, he escaped from a concentration camp to the United States. Made a living in Hollywood as writer and translator.

78 Arthur Ditner, a German writer with a legitimate doctorate (Dr. phil. nat, Latin abbreviation for Doctor philosophiae naturalis) had written a book *Die Suende wider das Blut* (literally: *The Sin against the Blood)* in which he advanced a hypothesis that Aryan women who had sexual relations with Jews were destined to bear thereafter, no matter who their current mate was, only Hebroid (Jewish) children.

79 ORPO *(Ordnungpolizei)* Reserve Police Battalion 101.

80 Pushkin, Alexander, Sergeyevich (1799-1837). Russian dramatist, novelist and poet. Died in a duel at age 38.

81 The name of the restaurant was *Zum gruenen Pollack.* The Schauermann family acquired it in 1936 and they located records that indicated it had been established as a roadhouse in the year 1263.

82 Walther Troeger, born 1929. Chairman of the German Olympic Committee.

83 Dogs suitable for police and military usage were officially drafted in 1943. However, Seeing Eye dogs, and especially those serving Jewish people, were apparently taken from their owners earlier than 1943.

84 Rust, Bernhard (1883-1945). A teacher by profession and one of Hitler's early followers. He was named *Reich* Minister of Science and Education in 1934. He dismissed leading scientists from Germany's educational institutions (including Albert Einstein) because they were Jews, Social Democrats, or unwanted by the Nazis. He attempted to educate Germany's youth in the spirit of militarism and paganism and established the NAPOLAS to assure leadership for the new "Aryan generation." He committed suicide at the end of the war.

85 Ley, Robert, Dr. (1890-1945). He was head of the *Deutsche Arbeitsfront* (German Labor Front). He substituted collective bargaining with *Kraft durch Freude* (Strength through Joy), offering German workers access to cultural events, sport and recreational activities, including mass vacations into mountain regions as well as cruises and even visits to foreign lands. Although a practicing alcoholic, he, nevertheless, remained one of Hitler's favorites. With huge funds at his disposal, and in his capacity as *Reichsorganisationsleiter* (Reich Organization Leader), he was given the task to establish the *Ordensburgen* and to help with the financing of the Adolf Hitler Schools from which *Ordensburg* candidates were to be selected. He committed suicide in his prison cell in Nuremberg.

86 Baldur von Schirach (1907-1974) first Reich Youth Leader, son of a German father and an American mother.

87 *Luftwaffenhelfer* (Flak helper) continued part of their schooling and underwent a mixture of service life and school life. In the outskirts of Breslau, where my classmates were stationed, this continued until the city became a fortress and fighting ended schooling.

88 *KLV Lagermannschaftsfuehrer* were youth camp leaders in schools where the students had been evacuated from cities that were

frequent targets of heavy bombing raids. Teachers provided ongoing education while the youth camp leader was in charge of free-time activities.

89 Although this method of beheading was common during the French revolution, it was used in other countries as well.

90 Roland Freisler (1893-1945), studied law in Jena after returning to Germany from a WWI POW camp. In 1942, he participated in the Wannsee Conference that initiated the extermination of European Jews and became head of the *Volksgericht* (court of the people). Known as the "hanging judge," he was ruthless and heaped abuse on his victims, vilifying judicial procedures and desecrating his court. He was killed during an air raid by an Allied bomb.

91 Heydrich, Reinhard (1904-1942), Chief of the Reich Security Office, had been named "*Protector*" (governor) of Bohemia and Moravia. He was assassinated by Czech partisans who had been trained in Britain.

92 Lidice, a Czechoslovakian coal-miners' village whose entire male population was executed as reprisal to Heydrich's assassination.

93 The common nickname for Getrud is Trude in most of Germany. Trudel, however, was typical for Silesia, where *Mutter* became *Muttel* (mother) and *Vatel* was more common than *Vater* (father).

94 As in most European countries, prostitution was a legalized profession in Germany, even under National Socialist rule. Government control in many countries had followed an epidemic of venereal disease affecting in great numbers soldiers of various armies. Napoleon is said to have decreed in 1785 that all prostitutes must be registered and undergo periodic checkups, not to safeguard them, but to protect his soldiers.

95 Hitler's *Tausendjaehriges Reich* (thousand year nation) lasted 12 years, four months, and eight days to be exact.

96 *SS-Totenkopfverbaende (SS* death head squads) assigned to concentration camps as guards and to undertake the extermina-

M

tion of Jews, gypsies, and communists. They were drawn from overage Order Police units supplemented by thousands of auxiliary policemen recruited mainly from the Baltic nations and from the Ukraine. This caused the Allies to treat all members of the *Waffen-SS* as criminals. Throughout the war, I had believed that the *Waffen-SS* consisted of exemplary, military units only, similar to those of the United States Marine Corps, maintaining the highest degrees of discipline and courage.

97 12th *SS-Panzer Division*

98 Prior to joining the Armed Forces, all able-bodied young men had to serve in the *RAD*, the State Labor Service for six months. Before carrying guns, German youth shouldered shovels.

99 Allied Forces successfully landed at Anzio on Jan 22, 1944. It was a remarkable accomplishment with 36,000 soldiers coming ashore, suffering only 13 casualties and capturing the harbor facilities without major destruction.

100 Muenchhausen, Karl Friedrich Hyronimus, Freiherr von (1720-97) whose fables of incredible adventures *Die wunderbaren Reisen und Abenteuer des Freihern von Muenchhausen (The Wonderful Travels and Adventures of Baron von Muenchausen)* became a folk classic in Germany and was eventually translated into major languages worldwide.

101 Vlassov, Andrei (1900-1946) Lt. General. A Russian captured by Germans in 1942. He turned anti-Stalinist and became head of the Russian Liberation Army under German command. U.S. forces captured him. When returned to the Russians, he was hanged as a traitor.

102 Wunsiedel, the birthplace of Friedrich Richter, the writer and poet who become known as Jean Paul.

103 Hitler Youth provincial headquarters

104 The *HJ* unit also known as *Regiment Hirsch,* consisted of two Battalions, #55 (Seifert) and # 56 (Lindenschmidt).

105 *Kampfgrupee Gutschke* saw action ahead of the forces inside the fortress.

106 Ilya Ehrenburg(1891-1967, one of Stalin's war correspon-

dents who told Russian soldiers to practice revenge – to be merciless with the Germans and not just the soldiers. He received the Stalin Prize in 1942.

107 *Reichsarbeitsdienst*—National Labor Service, mandatory six-month duty in public works or agriculture that preceded military service. Waived at end of war for *Volkssturm* draftees.

108 Clausewitz, Karl von (1970-1831) Prussian general, became director of the German Military Academy in Berlin. In his book, *On War*, he distinguishes between judicious and injudicious warfare.

109 Scharnhorst, Gerhard von (1755-1813) assumed fame as General Bluecher's chief of staff. Later, as head of the War Ministry, he circumvented the treaty limitations on Prussia's armed strength, initiated compulsory military service, and reorganized the Prussian Army, replacing autocratic rule with more democratic principles.

110 *Muckefuck*, German slang expression for *Ersatzkaffee*, substitute coffee.

111 *Kommissbrot*, course rye bread, baked in rectangular loafs.

112 Rilke, Rainer Maria (1875-1926), popular poet who blended impressionism and mysticism

113 NSV – *Nationalsozialistische Volkswohlfahrt*, National Socialist People's Welfare

114 Herder, Johann Gottfried von, (1744-1803). German theologian, philosopher, educator and noted poet

115 Winger, a sculpture and flower garden in Dresden of rococo style. It was built in 1711-22 by architect, Poeppelmann. It was adorned by sculptor Permoser's statues of Michelangelo, Raphael, Dante, Goethe and others.

116 Canaris, Wilhelm Franz (1887-1945) Admiral, appointed 1934 as head of the German Armed Forces High Command Intelligence Department. As head of *Abwehr* (counter espionage), he provided protection to members of the resistance. Tried on charges of treachery, he was found guilty and hanged in the Flossenbuerg concentration camp on April 9, 1945.

117 *Machtergreifung* (seizure of power) anniversary
118 Published in *Schlesische Tageszeitung* (16. Jhrg. Nr. 27) Archive: GLEISS, Rosenheim.
119 Duerer, Albrecht (1471-1528), German artist famous for paintings and engravings, rich in detail and filled with symbolism.
120 Kaergel, Hans-Christoph (1880–1946), teacher and writer, died at the age of 56 in a Polish prison camp.
121 Hirsch, Herbert (1907-1979), Hitler Youth *Gebietsfuehrer* (province leader) of Silesia, served in the German Army during the French Campaign. Became Hitler Youth Fortress Commander of the home defense regiment named after him.
122 Hitler had ordered, in October 1944, the establishment of the *Vokssturm*, calling all men from the ages of 16 to 60 to serve in the *Volkssturm* (people's storm) the nation' s home defense force. In February 1945, he decreed that all boys born in 1928 be removed from the *Vokssturm* and inducted into a branch of the regular Armed Forces.
123 *Werwolf* (Werewolves), an underground army (partisans) trained in 1945 for guerrilla warfare against the invading Allies. Few saw action and had little success in delaying advancing troops on any front.
124 Langemarck, World War I battlefield, northeast of Ypern, where young German cadets stormed enemy lines, singing the *"Deutschlandlied"* (German national anthem). The majority of them perished with *"Deutschland, Deutschland ueber alles..."* *(Germany, Germany above all)* on their lips.
125 *"Panzermeyer"* nickname of *SS-Brigadefuehrer* (Brigadier-General) Kurt Meyer (1910-1961), heroic commander of the 12th *Waffen-SS Panzer Division Hitlerjugend,* awarded the Knight's Cross of the Iron Cross, with Oak leaves and Swords.
126 This was indeed the "12th *SS-Panzerdivision HJ"* or, as referred to in some literature, the "12th *SS-Panzergrenadier Division HJ."*
127 Noted historian A. Le Tissier places *Waffen-SS* Pz. Abt. 502 in

woods near Komturei Lietzen. From there, on April 17—the day in question—a company was sent in support of the "Kumark" at Schoenfliess.

128 *Katyushas,* called by the Germans "*Stalin Orgeln*" (Stalin's pipe organs), multi-barreled, lorry-mounted rocket launchers, officially BM-13 & BM-21.

129 *Fall Barbarossa* (Case Barbarossa), code-name for Germany's surprise attack on the Soviet Union (June 22, 1941). The term referred to emperor Frederick I, known as "Red Beard" (1122-1190). Legend has him forever asleep at a marble table inside the Kyffhaeuser Mountain, surrounded by knights. They will protect him until he awakes to unite the German people and lead them victoriously against her enemies into a future of great glory.

130 Artur Axmann: *Das kann doch nicht das Ende sein,* published in 1995 by S. Bublies Verlag, Koblenz, Germany.

131 Ehrenburg, Ilja (1891-1967) Russian journalist and war correspondent, awarded the Stalin Prize.

132 Fichte, Johann Gottlieb (1762-1814) German philosopher. Participated in the great effort of Germany for national independence, stating: "It depends on you, if you want to be the ending of an unworthy age or if you want to be the starting point of a new, beyond expectation, wonderful time, with those following you counting the years of splendor!"

133 Volunteers were also sought for the *Freikorps* Mohnke. As far as I could determine, *Kampfgruppe* Mohnke and *Freikorps* Mohnke were the same.

134 The *Waffen-SS* division "*Frundsberg*" was named after Georg von Frundsberg (1473-1528), chivalrous officer and devoted servant of the Hapsburgs who became famous as leader of the mercenaries known as *Landsknechte* established by Maxmillian I

135 Kurland (Courland Peninsula) occupied by Army Group North, of which 26 divisions were cut off and left in Latvian and Estonian territory, north of East Prussia. Although Hitler's generals wanted these forces withdrawn by sea so that they could be

    used for the defense of Berlin. Hitler refused and took pride in the fact that Army Group Courland never surrendered.

136 In Bad Toelz, a small spa in Bavaria, one of the *Waffen-SS Junkerschulen* (cadet schools) was located. Others had been established in Braunschweig (Brunswick—by then already in enemy's hands), Posen-Treskau, and Prague. The latter two were for non-German *Waffen-SS* cadets, to fill the need for leaders of units from other European countries whose volunteers exceeded 400,000 in all.

137 I did not know Himmler's adjutant or aide. He did not wear a Knight's Cross. This rules out Lieutenant-General Hermann Fegelein, Himmler's liaison officer to Hitler, bearer of the Knight's Cross with Oak Leaves.

138 In the German language, the terms girlfriend and boyfriend are not used, it is *Freund* (friend/male) and *Freundin* (friend/ female) and unless specified as *Geliebte* (beloved/sweetheart) a *Freundin* could be either, a friend or a girlfriend.

139 *Landser*— Derived from *Landsknecht*, German slang for foot soldier.

140 Valhalla—In Nordic mythology, home of the fallen heroes, attended to by Odin's daughter (Valkyries).

141 Ivan (German: *Iwan*)—As the British soldier was called "Tommy" and the American "Ami," Germans called the Russian soldier, *"Iwan."*

142 One of Koeck's NCOs who survived the war was *Uffz.* Guenter Joost. He remembers a novel defense task that had been assigned to him and his boys. They covered a hundred yard stretch of the *Autobahn* with incendiary slabs, pressed flat straw pieces soaked in flame thrower oil, that looked like tar tiles. *Uffz.* Joost, hiding with his boys, awaited the approaching Russians. After the T-34 tanks came close enough, the boys pulled the trigger and the *Autobahn* surface flamed. Self-igniting bazookas exploded causing bedlam and generating a huge cloud of smoke, which enabled *Uffz.* Joost and his boys to retreat to a *Waffen-SS* unit in the rear. Guenter Joost believes

that the date of the above occurrence was April 22, 1945, the day Hannes and I, reunited, set out to return to Berlin. So this was probably the huge cloud of black smoke we saw.

143 After the war, he and I both believed, on the basis of information obtained from the German Red Cross that the *Kampfgruppe Gutschke* had been wiped out in the Petersdorf/Jacobsdorf area. I would learn 50 years later from Kurt Ruppelt, whom I located, and was perhaps the only survivor, Gutschke's unit fought valiantly and suffered great casualties but in the aftermath, the survivors were thrown into the cauldron of Halbe and for the most part, perished there.

144 By Hans Muencheberg, and published by Morgenbuch Verlag © 1991.

145 *Das Notlazarett Under der Reichskanzlei* (c) 1995 by Ars Una Verlagsgesellschaft

146 *Fliegen mein Leben* © 1979; F.A. Herbig Verlagsbuchhandlung, Muenchen (Munich).

147 Testimony by Dr. Kuntz that he injected morphium (telling the children that they were being vaccinated) and that Mrs. Goebbels inserted the capsules in their mouths, while they were asleep already, remains in dispute.

148 *Hitler's Helpers*—Taeter und Vollstrecker von Guido Knopp © 1998 by C. Bertelsmann Verlag GmbH Muenchen Munich)

149 A plausible explanation could be that he turned away the newsreel cameramen, preventing them from filming Hitler who was shaking so visibly.

150 *Gestapo*—Abbreviation for *Geheime Staats Polizei* (Secret State Police).

151 Krueger, Else, Martin Bormann's secretary. Born 1915. Survived the breakout, married Col. James, her British interrogator, and lives in England.

152 Located in the cellar of the chancellery was also a *Telefonzentrale* (phone exchange) with one of the operators (*'Blitzmaedchen'*) believed to have been one of Bormann's girlfriends. Another one, a young actress, was not present in the bunker.

153 *Bendlerblock*, a military building complex that was Gen. Weidling's last command post.

154 *Gestapo Chief,* Gregory Douglas, R. James Bender Publisher, San Jose © 1995.

155 My research attempts to find information about Erich Baerenfaenger's previous Hitler Youth activities remain unsuccessful. Axmann maintained that Baerenfaenger had been an *HJ-Obergebietsfuehrer* (the same rank held by Dr. Schluender) and had been in charge of *Wehrertuechtigung* (pre-military training). I was unable to obtain documentation that this was the case. I learned, however, that Axmann was best man at his wedding. The young couple, following the end of the war, committed suicide.

156 Petrova, Ada, and Watson, Peter, *The Death of Hitler,* W.W. Norton & Co., London.

157 Keitel, Wilhelm—Field Marshal, Chief of Staff of the High Command (OKW).

158 Jodl, Alfred—General, Chief of Armed Forces Operations (OKW).

159 Speer, Alhert—*Reich* Minister for Armament & Productions, Hitler's favorite architect.

160 Manziarly, Constanze (1920-1945) Prepared Hitler's vegetarian meals.

161 *Das kann doch nicht das Ende Sein* © 1995 Bublies Veriag.

162 The children were killed late in the afternoon, and at the time the breakout started, Dr. and Mrs. Goebbels committed suicide.

163 On May 23, 1946, I celebrated my 18th birthday. We didn't have a radio then and it was a day or two later that I read von Schirach's statement in the *Neue Zeitung* (the newspaper published by the occupation forces for the German population).

164 Not to be confused with the *SS-Ponzerdivision Totenkopf* (SS Tank Division Death)—one of the *Waffen-SS* original field units.

165 Not before 1968 did I become aware of exceptions that were made on account of Francis Biddle (1886-1968), U.S. Attorney General under President Franklin D. Roosevelt (so stated in an Associated Press newspaper obituary). Biddle, who had outspokenly opposed the detention of Japanese-Americans, nevertheless (under President Truman) was appointed a member of the International Military Tribunal in Nuremberg. It was he who protested the blanket guilty verdict, insisting that those be exempted who were drafted into membership, as well as those who had no knowledge of any criminal activities by the organization joined.

166 Langemark, battlefield in Flandres in World War I. There young Germans were mowed down by enemy fire with the *Deutschlandlied* (Germany's national anthem) on their lips.

167 Published © 1978 by Houghton Mifflin Co., Boston

168 Heusermann, Kaethe, former employee of Dr. Hugo Blaschke, Hitler's dentist.

169 Baur, Hans (1897-1993), Hitler's private pilot.

170 Speer, Albert (1905-1981) Hitler's favorite architect and from February 1942 to April 1945, *Reich* Minister for Armaments and Production.

171 Hrsgb.—Herausgeber (editor) A self-published compilation of reports by eye-witnesses including Dr. Naumann, Dr. Schenck, Gen. Weidling, Col von Dufving and many more.

172 *After the Battle*—Volume 16, No. 61, published 1989 by After The Battle Publications, Church House, Church Street, London E15 3JA, England.

173 Published by ROWOHLT, Hamburg, 1947